Constant Fouard, George F. X. Griffith

Saint Peter and the First Years of Christianity

Constant Fouard, George F. X. Griffith

Saint Peter and the First Years of Christianity

ISBN/EAN: 9783337340292

Printed in Europe, USA, Canada, Australia, Japan

Cover: Foto ©Lupo / pixelio.de

More available books at **www.hansebooks.com**

SAINT PETER

AND THE

FIRST YEARS OF CHRISTIANITY

By THE ABBÉ CONSTANT FOUARD

Translated from the Second Edition with the Author's sanction

By GEORGE F. X. GRIFFITH

With an Introduction

By CARDINAL GIBBONS

NEW YORK AND LONDON
LONGMANS, GREEN, AND CO.
1893

INTRODUCTION.

I HAVE been requested to introduce the present volume to the English-speaking public, and I gladly do so, in the persuasion that it will be welcomed on all sides as a valuable addition to our religious literature.

In a previous work the gifted author gave us a most happy presentation of the "Life of Our Lord." In this book he undertakes to describe the first beginnings of the (Christian) Church.

No subject, after the Gospel narrative, could be more grateful to the Christian reader. There is none which the thoughtful student approaches with a keener interest, for it is the opening of the great era of human history, and of that higher form of life which the whole civilized world gradually came to accept as its ideal, and to which it has never since ceased to pay homage.

Unhappily, our sources of information regarding the early days of Christianity are very imperfect, being almost entirely confined to the Acts of the Apostles. But under the intelligent guidance of Abbé Fouard, how much may be gathered even from so short and fragmentary a narrative! With all the varied information and cultivated tact of an historian, he adds to the clearness and consecutiveness of what we knew before, while giving distinctness and life to numberless details hitherto obscure or unnoticed.

With him we follow the Jews of the Dispersion as they come back at stated intervals from all parts of the world to the Holy City, and carry away with them the first knowledge of the Gospel. Jerusalem, Rome, Antioch, are no longer to us mere names recalling only faint images of ancient cities. We see them; we walk their streets; we catch the voices and the thoughts of the crowds that throng them; we watch with wonder the divine seed as it springs to life and spreads and flourishes amid the worst forms of moral decay.

In the earlier chapters of the Acts, Saint Peter takes the leading part, thus exercising from the beginning the privilege to which he had been called when Christ Himself made him the foundation of His Church, and later on committed to him His lambs and His sheep, that is, the care of His whole flock. It was only proper, therefore, that the name of Saint Peter should be found in the very title of the present volume. But it should not convey the impression that the work is written in a polemical spirit. Controversy is entirely absent from it. It is only at the very close that the writer sets forth the reasons which have led almost all impartial historians, Protestant as well as Catholic, to admit the fact that Saint Peter was the first Bishop of Rome, and that he suffered martyrdom in the imperial city.

It is a pleasure to know that the learned author has been engaged for several years on another work, having for its object the life and writings of Saint Paul. Books thus written with a thorough knowledge of the subject, and leading the mind back without effort to the very fountain-head of the faith, are an incalculable benefit to the public at large, and to none will they prove more welcome than to Catholic readers.

We have every reason to believe that the present translation is a faithful transcript of the original, expressed in idiomatic English; and we hope that the volume now presented to us in its new dress, by the talented translator, will be as eagerly sought as were those that preceded it.

J. CARD. GIBBONS.

NOTE

ON THE SYMBOLICAL DEVICE, SAINT PETER STRIKING THE ROCK.

". . . the primacy of Saint Peter is distinctly attested . . . by another symbol which can hardly be misunderstood. We mean that in which he appears under the type of Moses striking the rock. The rock, of course, at once suggests the passage of Saint Paul: 'They drank of that spiritual rock that followed them, and that rock was Christ;' but we should hardly have ventured to affirm that the figure striking the rock was Saint Peter, if his name had not, in two instances, at least, been unmistakably given at his side. . . . They show us that Saint Peter was considered to be the Moses of 'the new Israel of God,' as Prudentius speaks, and they explain why the rod, the emblem of Divine power, is never found except in three hands, — those of Moses, Christ, and Peter. It belongs primarily, and by inherent right, to Christ, the eternal Son of God. By Him it was of old delegated to Moses, of whom God testified, 'He is most faithful in all My house.' For a few years the rod of power was visibly wielded by the Incarnate Word; and when He withdrew His own visible presence from the earth, 'afterwards,' to use the words of Saint Macarius of Egypt, 'Moses was succeeded by Peter, to whom is committed the new Church of Christ and the new priesthood.'" — NORTHCOTE AND BROWNLOW: *Roma Sotterranea,* vol. ii. pp. 313-315.

PREFACE.

> Ubi Petrus, ibi Ecclesia.
> *Saint Ambrose,* in *Ps.* xl. 30.

THE title of this book is not the one I had intended to give it. According to my first plan, the name of Saint Paul was to have been predominant throughout this story of the beginnings of Christianity; I expected to demonstrate thereby that in the makings of this new institution the great Apostle had exerted so preponderating an influence that the history of the new-born Church was the history of his life and labors. But by degrees, and as the work advanced, another countenance in place of the one I had set myself to sketch, stood forth, so to say, developing itself from the features of my first subject. Thus the position destined for the Apostle of the Gentiles was taken by the Leader and Head of the Twelve.

And assuredly Peter does play a preëminent part during the first scenes in the Church's life. He presides in the College of the Apostles, he acts, decides, organizes. Servant of the Divine Spirit, he goes whither the breath from on High impels him, often blindly, sometimes resisting instinctively, as upon the housetop in Joppa,[1] but always in the end yielding to his Master's orders and submitting his own will to that of Grace. Thus it came about that through Peter's ministrations, and within about fifteen years after Pentecost, Jesus completed the constitution of the Church in her essential parts. The body already possesses all its organs, which need only to develop themselves thereafter: the Gospel preached by the Apostles; the Hierarchy founded; Deacons ordained; the Priesthood established in very various communities; a separate Episcopate at Jerusalem, — even in

[1] Acts x. 14.

Rome itself;[1] the Breaking of the Bread,[2] around which all her liturgy was to be concentrated; sacraments, baptism, holy orders:[3] in fine, the Church has detached herself from the Synagogue.[4] This, the ground-plan of the Work, appears, to our thinking, as finished before ever Paul begins his labors. Indeed, far from being the organizer, Saul of Tarsus is, at this date, a simple layman,[5] meditating upon the Lord's revelations to him;[6] if he speaks before the synagogues of Damascus and of Jerusalem, it is only as occasion demands, and as a subordinate.[7] He remains in this attitude of an inferior during the seven or eight years which follow upon his conversion (from 37 to 45), until the day when the elders of Antioch, with the laying-on of hands, confided him to the promptings of Grace. It is Peter, therefore, who has done everything since the birth of Christianity, and his name must, of right, be written over the head of any study of the Beginnings of the Church.

The Acts are our principal source of knowledge, whence to draw a history of these first years. Still, we need not confine ourselves to this single document, for as to many facts which the sacred text passes over with but a word, there are the Talmudists, Josephus, Philo, the historians of Greece and Rome, who add many a confirming circumstance, many a precious detail, to the general outline given us by Saint Luke: to them we shall very often have recourse.

For what properly concerns the Prince of the Apostles, it

---

[1] This early institution of the Hierarchy appears so plainly indicated in the Acts that M. Renan considers it as one of the theories which Saint Luke was most anxious to establish by his narrative. "One feels that the principles of the Roman Church have had their weight with the author. This Church, from the first centuries, had the political and hierarchical character which has always been its distinguishing note. Our good Luke may have imbibed this spirit. His ideas respecting ecclesiastical authority are very advanced; in him we note the first movements of the germs of episcopacy" (Renan, *Les Apôtres*, Introduction, xxiii).

[2] Acts ii. 42, 46.

[3] Acts ii. 41; vi. 6; viii. 12, 14–17, 36–38; x. 47, 48.

[4] Acts x. 9–18, 34–43.

[5] The common opinion is that S. Paul did not receive the sacerdotal consecration until about the year 45, when the Elders of Antioch made him a priest of God by the laying on of hands: "Consecratricem fuisse eam manuum impositionem docent SS. Chrysostomus et Leo Magnus, estque hæc communior in hac quæstione sententia et omnino tenenda" (Beelen, *Commentarius in Acta Apostolorum*, in loco).

[6] Gal. i. 15–24; Acts xi. 25.   [7] Acts ix. 20, 28; xi. 26.

must be acknowledged that after his miraculous deliverance from the prison in Jerusalem, little is known about his ministry. Saint Luke shows that he was present at the Council of Jerusalem;[1] Saint Paul relates the discussion he had with him at Antioch:[2] there ends the testimony of inspired writers. Quite uncertain as the traditions may be, on whose authority the sequel of his life-story is based, we have not failed to gather them together here, because, among details of less-assured historical value, two conclusions seem to us to stand out as worthy of full faith, — one, that Saint Peter made Rome the principal seat of his Apostolate; the other, that his coming to that city was coincident with the reign of Claudius.

So far as concerns the last-named point at issue, modern criticism is exceedingly disdainful. That speedy journeying of the Apostle, mentioned by Eusebius and Saint Jerome, has been regarded by certain authors as "an unfortunate hypothesis, for which no reasonable defence can be constructed."[3] In answer to these dogmatic decisions, we may be permitted to call in evidence the twenty-five years of Saint Peter's Pontificate inscribed at the close of the second century upon the pontifical catalogues of the Roman Church;[4] the memorials of the Apostle's two comings to Rome, preserved from this same date, both in her liturgy and by the archæological monuments, together with the entire mass of traditions,[5] which our adversaries are unable to explain away by any theory as to their origin, confirming, as they do, the chronology adopted by the historians of the fourth and fifth centuries. To throw aside these arguments because, taken separately, they are not of sufficient weight to overbalance all possible doubt, is to sin against the rules of criticism. Mere hints, testimony which is either vague or confused with much that is false, yet, when all bearing in support of

[1] Acts xv. 7-11. [2] Gal ii. 11-14.
[3] Renan, *L'Antechrist*, Appendice, p. 553.
[4] "Just as the Philocalian Chronicle relies, so far as concerns the catalogue of the Popes, on the authority of the Chronicle of S. Hippolytus, compiled at Rome in 235, so the Chronicle of S. Hippolytus itself is based on that of older pontifical lists, and thus we are led to infer that the twenty-five years of Peter's sojourn figured in the Episcopal Catalogues of Rome as early as the close of the second century" (Duchesne, *Les Origines chrétiennes*, p. 78).
[5] See Appendix IV. and chapter xviii.

the same point, these may give us new light, may correct each other, may even confirm us as to the fact, when we look at them thus taken together. As scattered hints, they are glimmering sparks; once bound together, they shed forth a steady light upon the student's path. The essential rule, however, is not to regard any induction, however well authorized it may seem to be, with the same certitude wherewith we accept the account of events attested by contemporary writers; nor have we failed to observe this rule.

Whatever opinion one holds as to the beginnings of the Roman Pontificate, the traditions referred to above indicate this much at least, — that Peter had two principal centres of action: Jerusalem before the dispersion of the Apostles, Rome in the years which came after. This conclusion, which no moderate critic will deny us, makes it possible not to abandon our study of the Apostle's ministry, so summarily ended after his imprisonment, but to go farther, and show whither the Spirit of God led Peter's steps, and what new lands thereafter were opened to receive him. We have confined ourselves to these general views, deferring to their time the few incidents of his Apostolate which are known, and of which the details are intimately connected with the life of Saint Paul.

The Church at Jerusalem under the Apostles; the establishment of Peter's seat in Rome, — such is the twofold theme of this book. In the latter half of the volume the necessity I was under of setting forth impartially what was the real religious and moral state of the Roman Empire, forced me into undertaking a study which belongs to the apologist rather than to the historian. The task was far easier for the earlier period, for of the Church of Jerusalem Saint Luke has left us a picture with outline and coloring still clear and vivid to-day. Rationalists, it is true, assume that it must be treated as a composite of separate pieces without historical value; but it is enough for the scholar to study the origin and structure of the work, and he will understand that their suspicions are born of foregone conclusions, not the results of severe and serious examination.

The Author of the Acts recalls in his proem that he had written "a former treatise of all that Jesus had done and taught." [1] There is no doubt that the work thus designated

---

[1] Acts i. 1.

PREFACE. xiii

is our Third Gospel; for the two works, alike dedicated to Theophilus,[1] show such a conformity of style and ways of thinking that the most guarded critics do not hesitate to recognize the same handiwork in both.[2] The writer of the Acts does not claim to be an Evangelist merely; in the course of his narrative he ranks himself among the companions of Saint Paul,[3] and by constantly using the word "we" after the sixteenth chapter, declares that he was a witness of the facts he is relating. As for his name, if not written in the Acts, we know it from tradition[4] and from the title given to the third Evangelist by all the manuscripts.[5] That name is *Lucanus*, or *Lucas*, and it designates a well-known Christian whose devoted zeal is thrice praised by Saint Paul in his letters. "Luke, the physician, our dearest brother" (Coloss. iv. 14). "Luke alone is with me" (2 Tim. iv. 11). "Epaphras . . . salutes you with Mark, Aristarchus, Demas, and Luke, who are my fellow-laborers and companions" (Philem. 23, 24). Even our adversaries recognize the legitimate foundation of these deductions; for them as for us, "the Author of the Third Gospel is certainly Luke, Paul's disciple."[6]

Thus, then, historians of the beginnings of the Church possess the testimony of a contemporary, a trustworthy man, well instructed, who has taken part in the events he narrates, and is acquainted with the persons whose words and deeds he recites. Our faith could not desire firmer foundation; hence no efforts have been spared to shake it, and at the same time to ruin the authority of his narrative. Writers have been especially anxious to retard to the latest possible date the year he wrote this book, — thankless toil, for to the eyes of every man not swayed by preconceived

---

[1] Luke i. 3; Acts i. 1.
[2] "One thing stands beyond a doubt, and that is that the Acts were compiled by the same author who wrote the Third Gospel, and are but a continuation of that Gospel. We need not stop to prove this proposition, which has never been seriously called in question. The prefaces with which both documents begin, the dedication of each to Theophilus, and their perfect resemblance in style and ways of thinking, furnish us with abundant demonstrations of that fact" (Renan, *Les Apôtres*, Introduction, x.).
[3] M. Renan has a long and masterly proof of this second proposition in the Introduction to his work on the Apostles (x–xviii).
[4] Fragment of Muratori (170); S. Irenæus (180); Tertullian (207), etc.
[5] Εὐαγγέλιον κατὰ Λουκᾶν (Λ. C. D.). Κατὰ Λουκᾶν (ℵ. B. F.), etc.
[6] Renan, *Les Apôtres*, Introduction, xviii.

opinions, the Acts also do in like manner bear their own date. After having brought Saint Paul a prisoner to Rome, they end with these words: "Thereafter Paul remained two whole years in lodgings which he had hired, where he received all that came to see him, preaching the Kingdom of God, and teaching the things which concern the Lord Jesus Christ with all freedom, without prohibition."[1] The two years which the Apostle passed thus, in comparative liberty under the surveillance of a Roman soldier, take us from 62 to 64. It was then that Saint Luke finished writing his Acts; for in no other way can we explain why he has said nothing of the incidents which followed, and, in particular, of the death of the Apostle, — that great event, occurring as it did only four years later.

Nothing shows the force of this argument better than the pitiful reasons brought forward to explain the brusque ending of the Acts. Some fancy that as Theophilus was living in Rome, it would have been superfluous to write down for him what was then occurring in that city under his own eyes. According to some exegetical scholars, the narrative ends with the Apostle's arrival in the capital of the world, because thereupon was fulfilled the prediction that the Gospel should be preached "unto the ends of the earth;"[2] or again that saying of the Lord, "Paul, be of good courage, for even as you have given testimony of Me in Jerusalem, so must you bear witness unto Me in Rome."[3] The better-advised critics renounce such puerilities. Starting with their principle that all prophecy is impossible, and finding the ruin of Jerusalem foretold in Saint Luke's Gospel, they draw their conclusion that that book did not appear until after the year 70, and the Acts at the earliest about 72. But here again our historian is too near the events he is detailing to make it easy for them to rob his evidence of all its value, which is their real end in view. They must needs defer the composition of the Acts until 80, in order to put a half century between the first years of the Church and the period when Saint Luke was writing; to the thinking of these critics, the birth and growth of a legend requires only this length of time. The only arguments vouchsafed us in support of their choice of

---

[1] Acts xxviii. 30-31.   [2] Acts i. 8.
[3] Acts xxiii. 11. The student will find these hypotheses ably set forth in the commentaries of Meyer and De Wette.

this date are notes of correspondence, — the spirit of the book reminding us of the reign of the Flavians, the peaceful life of those days reflected so well in a narrative which is so gentle, placid, and forbearing to all. I must be forgiven if I attach scanty importance to these essays in comparative criticism. Arguments from correspondence: who does not know what wonderful opinions an inventive mind can draw from such sources?

The attacks of our adversaries are not pushed with the same zeal against every portion of the book; their special point in view is the acts of Peter (chapters first to twelfth), which they reject, although they keep those of Paul, the work appearing to them more credible as it nears its end. To justify so arbitrary a distinction, it is assumed that Saint Luke knew little of Palestine and the Jewish world; that he speaks of it without exact knowledge; rather, to speak plainly, jumbling history with legends in an inextricable confusion. Here they overlook the fact that the writer when accompanying Paul during his last journey to Jerusalem remained near him at Cæsarea during the two years of captivity which the Apostle passed there,[1] and that during that time, according to all appearances, he collected the facts contained in the twelve first chapters of the Acts. However young we may suppose Saint Luke to have been at this time, he was not, as is often insinuated, of another generation than that of the founders of Christianity, for at Jerusalem he had seen James, the "brother of the Lord,"[2] at Cæsarea the Deacon Philip,[3] and at Rome Saint Peter. What he had not seen with his own eyes, his master, Paul, knew from the beginning. Furthermore, he himself could have learned all his facts from the actors who played the principal parts in the scenes which he is describing. Peter undoubtedly told him of the beginnings of the Church in Jerusalem, his preaching to the Jews, the conversion of Cornelius. "Entertained at Cæsarea in the dwelling of Philip the Evangelist, one of the seven, . . . abiding many days with him,"[4] the Author of the Acts had heard from his lips the story of his missions in Samaria, and of the baptism of the Ethiopian eunuch. From Saint Paul he takes the rest of the events which fill the first part of his book, — the trial and martyrdom of Stephen, where-

[1] From 59 to 61. Acts xxiv. 27. [2] Gal. i. 19.
[3] Acts xxi. 8-10. [4] Acts xxi. 8.

in Saul had taken part, together with the conversion of the Apostle, so often recounted by himself.[1] So then, if Luke, with these sources of information, was unable to separate the truth from the fables which obscured it, we might well despair of all certitude in the history of those times.

It is true that he has been suspected of accommodating his history to his own views, thereby making it a plea for his own party. According to this supposition, the Church was then divided into two factions: on one side were Peter and the Judaizers, stubbornly fighting for the legal Observances; on the other the adherents of Paul, just as zealous to throw off the yoke. Luke, so they say, set about conciliating his brethren, trying to persuade them that under apparent disagreements they had but one heart and one soul; every incident which does not exactly support this notion they either suppress or disfigure. The sequel of our narrative will show what weight is to be accorded to these fantasies; but in a word, it is easy to reply here that the Author of the Acts, far from concealing the dissensions in the Church, does, on the contrary, depict very strikingly their numerous features. It is he who best exhibits these divisions of sentiment, who details their origin and their developments.

From his earliest chapters, the causes of disagreement are to be noted in the attachment of the Christians of Jerusalem for the Mosaic Observances. All, being Israelites, continue to consider the keeping of the Law an essential condition of salvation. All in vain did Stephen utter the cry of the new freedom in their ears; in vain did Peter himself proclaim, in God's Name, that Gentiles and Jews have equal rights in the Kingdom of Heaven, — always their aversion for the uncircumcised lingered deep down in their hearts. The dominant spirit in the Church of Jerusalem was ever striving, not only to preserve all the externals of Israel's ancient religion, but to bind the new believers thereto. Of this the Acts give proof after proof: the Christians of the Holy City keeping jealous watch of Antioch and those Pagan converts who were becoming so numerous there;[2] while later on, fanatics from Jerusalem, coming into that same town, "trouble them all with their talk, subverting souls,"[3] insomuch that Paul and Barnabas are forced "to contest strenuously against them,"[4]

---

[1] Acts xxii. 4-21; xxvi. 12-19.   [2] Acts x. 19-24.
[3] Acts xv. 24.   [4] Acts xv. 2.

and finally succeed in obtaining from the Apostolic College a condemnation of the Judaizer's pet doctrine, — "No Salvation without Circumcision."[1] Disavowed by the leaders of the Church,[2] the Judaizing members retain, at least for themselves, what they could not impose upon their brethren among the Gentiles. "They multiplied by thousands, and all continued zealots for the Law,"[3] says the Bishop of Jerusalem, speaking of his flock. It is easily seen, how aside from certain new practices and the faith in Jesus, everything there remained Jewish in appearance and in feeling. So, when about 59 Paul came to the Holy City, Saint James conjured him to be careful of the scruples of the faithful. Surrounded by his priests, he warned him that he had been accused of "renouncing Moses, of striving against the circumcision and received customs,"[4] and he obtained a promise that the Apostle of the Gentiles would purify himself solemnly in the Temple.[5] By these last-named incidents Saint Luke marks how far the division between the Zealots of Jerusalem and the great body of Christians had been carried; yet not among the Apostles is this variance to be seen: rising above these discussions, they intervene only to conciliate, to settle and decide.

Such is the portrayal of these differences in the Acts. To go farther and show us the whole Church, shepherds and flocks alike, split up into hostile factions, one must distort the facts, or twist certain strong words of Saint Paul, easily explained by the stress of controversy; we should have to forget that in the height of these discussions the Apostle, far from breaking with his brethren at Jerusalem, gathers alms in every place for that very Church;[6] in fine, we must regard Saint Luke as only another of those prejudiced minds who distort their facts unscrupulously, in order to adapt them to their theories. Certainly he might have wrought his history after this fashion, minimizing the dissensions in the Church, or even coloring them cleverly, so as to blind our eyes: yet there is nothing of the kind in his narrative, as we all know. Indeed, on the contrary, the simplicity

---

[1] "Now some who were come down from Judea taught this doctrine to the brethren : If you be not circumcised according to the practice of Moses, you cannot be saved " (Acts xv. 1).
[2] Acts xv. 2-31.   [3] Acts xxi. 20.
[4] Acts xxi. 21.   [5] Acts xxi. 23-26.
[6] 1 Cor. xv. 8-10 ; 2 Cor. xi. 5 ; xii. 11 ; Gal. i. 11-16, 19 ; ii. 1-14, etc.

with which he announces his intention to be precise in all things may well be taken as a guarantee of good faith; for to make claims of exactness, when relating important and public facts to one's contemporaries, is the sharpest spur to awaken their attention and to arouse the severest criticism. Saint Luke, had he been intending to deceive, and gifted with sufficient subtlety to succeed in his designs, would not have committed this imprudence. Was it, indeed, a time for such artifices of language as those we excel in to-day? Throughout the whole New Testament, Paul, James, Jude, John, speak without circumlocutions or concealments. It is the same with Saint Luke: the tone of the Acts [1] discloses a man of sincere soul, honest rather than clever.

Our adversaries are so well aware of the impossibility of refusing for this reason all credibility to the sacred text that they have made the twofold division alluded to above; and even they consent to treat certain of these latter chapters as "the only really historical pages which we possess, telling of the origins of Christianity." [2] The only motive for this preference, although none of them openly avows it, is that miracles abound in the beginning of the book, and that modern criticism rejects them on principle. But such a preconceived notion not only shakes the authority of the first chapters, it ruins the whole work; for the narrative of Saint Paul's missions is no less filled with prodigies. Nay, we may ask, with this canon of criticism, what would become of the Apostle's epistles, which some compare with Saint Luke's narrative as documents of superior worth and less questionable sincerity. In them Saint Paul tells the Galatians of his revelations; [3] to the Romans he mentions the miracles he has worked in every land, from Jerusalem as far as Illyria; [4] to the Corinthians he enumerates those divine signs which were day after day appearing in every Christian community, — prophecies, healings, the gift of tongues. [5] Equally with the Author of the Acts, the Apostle is a witness to the marvels of the new-born Church. If this his faith is no bar to his recognition as a writer of historical veracity (and this they concede), why should we refuse to the disciple what is granted to his master?

---

[1] Luke i. 3–4.
[2] Renan, *Les Apôtres*, Introduction, xxvii.
[3] Gal. i. 12; ii. 2.
[4] Rom. xv. 19.
[5] 1 Cor. xii. 8–11, 28–30.

And indeed Saint Paul has taken pains to authorize the work of his Evangelist.[1] During the time when the latter was finishing the Acts, the Apostle was writing his letter to Philemon; in it he speaks of Luke by name, as working by his side, under his eyes.[2] He must, then, have read this record of the origin of Christianity and approved it. Taking his initiative, every tradition has accepted the work as an utterance of the truth, nay, as the very words of the Apostle of the Gentiles. "What Paul gives us to understand concerning the Twelve," says Saint Irenæus, "and Luke's witness thereto, agree at all points, and, so to speak, form but one and the same testimony."[3]

It would be easy to carry this demonstration farther; but the arguments enumerated will suffice for any one who, with an unbiassed mind and in simplicity and uprightness of soul, considers them as a whole. Nor need we be surprised that they do not so strike certain thinkers, occupied solely with matters of detail, eager to raise a cloud of dust in order to obscure the real points at issue. In the realms of history there are prejudices which blind men as completely as passions. "Obscuratum est insipiens cor eorum,"[4] says the Apostle. To such men, rather preoccupied in denying the supernatural than in discussing the authenticity of the Acts, we must content ourselves with recalling the words of the sole Witness they are willing to listen to, when there is question of the beginnings of Christianity, — the only one who, in their eyes, speaks with authority. Paul had foreseen that men would make misuse of his preachings, as to-day do our "doubters of miracles,"[5] and that they would transform it into the seed of death. With unselfish compassion, he besought forgiveness for these strivers against the truth; but at the same time he foretold to them the victory of that Faith which they were to attack in vain: "Now thanks be to the God Who maketh us to triumph in Jesus Christ, Who

---

[1] In primitive times the Third Gospel was always regarded as nothing more than the preaching of S. Paul as compiled by S. Luke, his disciple and fellow-laborer (S. Irenæus, *Adversus Hæreses*, iii. 1 ; Tertullian, *Contra Marc.*, iv. 5).
[2] Philem. 24. "Is Lucas inseparabilis a Paulo, et cooperarius ejus in Evangelio" (S. Irenæus, *Adversus Hæreses*, iii. 14, 1).
[3] "Est consonans et velut eadem, tam Pauli annuntiatio, quam et Lucæ de Apostolis testificatio" (S. Irenæus, *Adversus Hæreses*, iii. 13, 3).
[4] Rom. i. 21.   [5] Pascal, *Pensées*, art. xxv. 61, éd. Havet.

by us in every place doth shed forth the knowledge of His Name as a sweet savor, . . . an odor of death unto some, unto others of life unto life. . . . For we are not as many who corrupt the word of God, but in all sincerity as from God, before God, in Christ do we preach."[1]

[1] 2 Cor. ii. 16, 17.

TABLE OF CONTENTS.

PAGE

INTRODUCTION BY CARDINAL GIBBONS v

AUTHOR'S PREFACE ix

CHAPTER I.

PENTECOST.

The Apostles in the Supper Room. — Election of Mathias. — Descent of the Holy Spirit. — Gift of Tongues. — Peter's First Discourse. — Community of Goods. — Daily Life of the Disciples at Jerusalem   1

CHAPTER II.

THE APOSTLES BEFORE THE SANHEDRIN.

The Cripple at the Beautiful Gate. — Peter's Second Discourse. — Peter and John before the Sanhedrin. — Unity of the Faithful. — Barnabas. — Ananias and Saphira. — Imprisonment and Release of the Twelve. — Gamaliel undertakes their Defence. — They are scourged and dismissed 19

CHAPTER III.

THE JEWS OF THE DISPERSION.

The Babylonian Captivity. — Jewish Colonies scattered over the World. — Their Privileges. — Popular Prejudices aroused by their Arrogance and Prosperity. — The Attractions and Power of the Synagogues. — Jewish Literature of Alexandria. — Proselytes of Israel   38

CHAPTER IV.

SAINT STEPHEN.

The Seven Deacons. — Stephen's Manner of Preaching. — His Discourse before the Sanhedrin. — His Martyrdom 58

CHAPTER V.

THE MISSIONS OF THE DEACON PHILIP.

I. SIMON THE MAGICIAN.
Philip at Samaria. — Baptism of the Magician. — He is repulsed by Peter and John. — His Doctrines 77

II. ST. PHILIP AND THE EUNUCH FROM ETHIOPIA.
The Kingdom of Ethiopia. — The Eunuch in Jerusalem. — His Baptism on the Road to Gaza. — Philip's Mission-work in the Country of the Philistines and in Sharon 90

CHAPTER VI.

SAUL OF TARSUS.

Saul's Family. — Tarsus. — Corrupt Morals of that City. — Celebrated Schools. — Saul goes up to Jerusalem. — School of Gamaliel. — Saul the Persecutor of the Church 100

CHAPTER VII.

THE CONVERSION OF SAINT PAUL.

Damascus. — Paul struck down at the City Gates. — He secludes himself in Arabia. — Appearance and Character of Saul. — Returns to Damascus, but is constrained to flee. — Paul and the Twelve in Jerusalem. — Paul returns to Tarsus 117

CHAPTER VIII.

THE PEACE OF THE CHURCH

The Jews and Caligula. — Peter visits the Churches of Sharon. — Eneas. — Tabitha. — The Vision at Joppa. — Conversion of Cornelius . . 136

TABLE OF CONTENTS. xxiii

CHAPTER IX.

ANTIOCH.

Peter at Antioch. — Description of the City. — Depravity of Morals. — Jews of Antioch. — The Gospel proclaimed to the Gentiles. — Barnabas and Saul preach at Antioch. — Believers called Christians . . 157

CHAPTER X.

THE PERSECUTIONS UNDER HEROD AGRIPPA.

Prophecy of Agabus. — Herod Agrippa in Jerusalem. — Martyrdom of Saint James. — Peter delivered by the Angel of the Lord. — Death of Agrippa. — The Great Famine. — The Princes of Adiabene . . 171

CHAPTER XI.

THE DISPERSION OF THE APOSTLES.

College of the Twelve. — Saint James of Jerusalem. — Apostolate of the Hierarchy. — Ministry of the Apostles 188

CHAPTER XII.

SAINT MATTHEW'S GOSPEL.

I. THE EVANGELICAL PREACHING.
Oral Tradition the only Form of Teaching among the Jews. — The Halaka and Hagada. — The Spoken Gospel 206

II. THE GOSPEL OF SAINT MATTHEW.
Origin of this Gospel. — Written in Aramean, it was composed for the Benefit of Jerusalem Jews. — Greek Translation of his Work. — Gospel of the Nazarenes 216

CHAPTER XIII.

THE TEACHING OF THE CHURCH OF JERUSALEM

Gradual Progress of Revelation. — The Apostles' Creed. — The primitive *Credo* of Rome. — Origin of the Formulary of Faith 227

CHAPTER XIV.

SAINT PETER AND THE JEWS OF ROME.

Saint Peter in Asia Minor. — His Arrival at Rome. — The Roman Jews. — Hatred and Calumnies suffered by them. — Their Influence. — Parts of Rome inhabited by Jews. — The Roman Synagogues . . 246

CHAPTER XV.

THE RELIGION OF ROME.

Character of Roman Religion, — The Gods numbered in the *Indigitamenta*. — Importance of Worship and Ceremonies. — Decline of Belief among the Upper Classes. — Lively Religious Sentiments extant in the People. — Attraction felt for Oriental Rites and Mysteries . . 272

CHAPTER XVI.

THE CONDUCT OF LIFE IN THE TIME OF AUGUSTUS.

Decadence of Moral Ideas in the Family, among Women, and in Public Life. — The Client's mean Condition under the Empire. — The Pursuit of Heritages. — Scanty Number of Virtuous and Noble Characters 291

CHAPTER XVII.

THE STOICS OF THE EMPIRE.

Zeno's Philosophy. — Stoics of Rome less enlightened than the Sages of Greece as to God, Providence, Immortality. — Their Propagation of Ideas of Humanity and Social Equality. — Sterility of their Doctrines 315

CHAPTER XVIII.

SAINT PETER'S MINISTRY IN ROME.

The Gospel spread through Rome by Slaves, the Lower Orders, and Women. — Pomponia Græcina. — Various Places where Peter abode, — on the Aventine, in the Residence of Pudens, at the Ostrian Cemetery. — Peter and Simon the Magician 335

TABLE OF CONTENTS. xxv

CHAPTER XIX.
THE LEGAL STATUS OF THE CHRISTIANS.

PAGE

Roman Respect for Foreign Religions. — Customary Tolerance of the Magistrates. — Christians of the First Century enjoy the Franchises decreed for the Jews. — Early Conversions of Certain Patricians contribute to strengthen their Position. — Submissiveness of the Church to the Laws of the State 351

CHAPTER XX.
THE GOSPEL OF SAINT MARK.

Saint Mark's Gospel is only Saint Peter's Preaching to the Pagans at Rome. — Peculiarities of this Gospel. — Date of its Composition. — Saint Peter and the Church of Alexandria 367

EPILOGUE.

Providential Resources ordered for the Speedier Diffusion of the Gospel. — Obstacles which hindered the Success of the Apostles' Ministry . 382

Appendix.

I. CHRONOLOGY OF THE FIRST YEARS OF THE CHURCH . . 391
II. DATE OF THE MARTYRDOM OF SAINT JAMES 393
III. TESTIMONY OF SAINT IRENÆUS AS TO THE DATE OF THE COMPOSITION OF SAINT MATTHEW'S GOSPEL . 395
IV. SAINT PETER IN ROME 398
V. SIMON THE MAGICIAN 411

MAP OF THE APOSTOLIC MISSIONS . . . . *Frontispiece*
NOTE ON THE SYMBOLICAL DESIGN FOR COVER . viii
MAP OF ANTIOCH IN THE TIME OF THE APOSTLES 157
MAP OF ROME IN THE TIME OF THE APOSTLES . 246
INDEX 417

SAINT PETER

AND THE

FIRST YEARS OF CHRISTIANITY.

CHAPTER I.

PENTECOST.

JESUS was gone away from earth. The Apostles, obedient to His commands, descended the Mount of Olives and re-entered the city. Great was their emotion, for the Master had foretold "that they should not depart from Jerusalem until His promises should be fulfilled;"[1] and the Angels had said, "This Jesus whom you have seen ascending into the skies shall return in like manner as you have seen Him going up thither."

The Eleven, with meagre conceptions of what was to come, waited in expectation. What did He mean by that "gift of the Father, that Holy Spirit, the Comforter"[2] so many times promised them; and "those cups, the banquets, the twelve thrones, and that kingdom,"[3] which were reserved for them, — what did it all portend? Still too earth-bound in their ways of thinking to glimpse the truth underlying such figures, the Apostles could do no more than by devout longings hasten the time when these mysteries should be unveiled. It was a season of watching and of prayer.

[1] Acts i. 4. [2] John xiv. 16, 26 ; xv. 26 ; xvi. 7, 13, etc.
[3] Luke xii. 32 ; xxii. 29-30 ; Matt. xx. 20-23.

And accordingly from that hour "they were seen every day in the Temple praising and blessing God."[1] They quitted it only to return to the Supper Room; there, gathered in that upper chamber[2] where the Lord had instituted the Eucharist, they persevered in prayer, having with them both Mary, the Mother of Jesus, and His cousins.[3] The latter, for so long time incredulous, had yielded faith in presence of the wonders of His Resurrection; thereafter they remained with their kinsmen, James and Jude. Other disciples joined the company, and very shortly one hundred and twenty believers were assembled in the Supper Room, all so intimately united that they greeted each other as brethren.

Thus reassembled, the lowly flock gathered about that one to whom it had been said: "Feed My lambs, feed My sheep."[4] But the consciousness of his fall still burned so deep in Simon's heart that he durst do nothing; like all the rest, and as one of them, he gazed Heavenwards. God accepted this self-distrust, this inactivity of the humble soul; so then during those days He inspired Peter's mind with only the one design, that of filling the place left vacant in the College of the Twelve.

This mystic number was for a figure of the Twelve Tribes of Israel, and of that union which had once made them invincible; it reminded them that no defection had reared its head among them during the forty years in the wilderness; that upon their entering into the promised land, Reuben, Gad, and Manasseh, although already in possession of their pasture-lands, had crossed over the Jordan

---

[1] Luke xxiv. 53.
[2] 'Υπερῷον, which the Vulgate translates "cœnaculum," is meant to designate the upper chamber which the Jews built upon the terrace of their dwellings and used for gatherings of every description. The Supper Room became naturally the first church at Jerusalem. S. Epiphanius (*De Ponderibus*, xiv.) relates that Adrian, on his entrance into the ruined city, found this Sanctuary standing alone, like a hut in the midst of a devastated vineyard.
[3] Acts i. 14. Four of His cousins, "James, Joses, Jude, and Simon," are mentioned by S. Mark (vi. 3). Their father was Alpheus, and their mother Mary, sister of the Blessed Virgin.
[4] John xxi. 15–17.

and done battle side by side with the rest as sons of the one same Father. So likewise on the eve of the combats foretold by the Lord it was fitting that the Apostles should be present as a body ready to enter into the Kingdom of Heaven. Therefore Peter rose up in the midst of their gathering.

"My brethren," he said,[1] "it must needs be that what the Holy Spirit has prophesied in the Scripture by the mouth of David touching Judas, the leader of those that apprehended Jesus, should be accomplished. He was of the same number with us, and had been called to the functions of the same ministry. Now he has taken possession of the field, the price of his iniquity; there he hanged himself, and falling headlong to the ground, his belly burst asunder in the midst, and all his bowels gushed forth."[2] (This was become known to all the inhabitants of Jerusalem, so that this same field was called in their tongue Hakeldama, — that is to say, The Field of Blood.[3])

This death of the traitor disowned of God Peter had seen predicted in the psalms, for ever since the Resurrection the Apostles had had a clearer comprehension of these prophetical songs, finding their Master's Passion all detailed therein, — His Soul snatched from the deep pit, His Ascension to the right hand of Jehovah; doubtless during their prayers, in an ecstasy of longing hope, they had often uttered those invocations in David's solemn hymn, —

"The throngs of the wicked have besieged Me;
They have pierced My feet and My hands;
All My bones I can number.

[1] Acts i. 16-19.
[2] We have noted elsewhere (*The Christ, the Son of God*, vol. ii. p. 290, note 4) the sense in which we are to understand that verse in the Acts, "Judas hath possessed the field, the price of his iniquity." S. Peter does not thereby contradict the testimony of S. Matthew, according to which it was the High Priests who purchased Hakeldama; he simply makes use of a figurative expression, "The corpse of Judas hath taken possession of the field in recompense for his crime."
[3] The explanation of the word "Hakeldama," and probably the whole of verse 19, is an addition of S. Luke's.

> They have parted My garments amongst them,
> Upon My robe they have cast lots.
> Do not thou, then, Jehovah, remove far from Me;
> Thou art My strength, make haste to aid Me.
> Save my life from the sword,
> Deliver My Soul from devouring dogs." [1]

But the Psalmist's malediction attracted the Apostles' attention even more strongly than these Oracles of God; for in the former they read with terror and awe of the fate of one of their own number, Judas: —

> "Let his dwelling be made desolate,
> And his tent stand alone; [2] . . .
> He hath loved cursing: let him be accursed!
> Let it envelop him even as a garment!
> Let it penetrate like water into his bowels,
> Like oil to the marrow of his bones!
> May it be like the mantle which covers him,
> Like the girdle which encircleth his loins!"

From among these imprecations Peter had noted particularly the following prophecy, —

> "May his days be shortened,
> And let another possess his charge!" [3]

"Brethren," he continued, "from among those who have been in our company all the time that the Lord Jesus dwelt in our midst, beginning from the baptism of John until the day when He left us to return to Heaven, one must needs be chosen who may be with us a Witness of His Resurrection."

Indeed, had not the Master said, "You shall bear testimony of Me, you who have been with Me since the beginning"? [4] But few of the disciples had followed Jesus since the beginning of His public life; the little gathering contained only two, Mathias and Joseph, son of Sabas (Bar-Sabas), surnamed The Just, on account of his holiness of life. The virtue of Mathias, of no less lofty a

---

[1] Ps. xxii. 16-20, according to the Hebrew Bible
[2] Acts i. 20; Ps. lxix. 26, according to the Hebrew.
[3] Ps. cix. according to the Hebrew.
[4] John xv. 27.

character, rendered a choice between them difficult; the Apostle had recourse to an ancient usage in Israel, and left it for the lots to decide this election.

The Supper Room was hushed in prayer. "Lord,"[1] they cried, "Thou Who knowest the hearts of men, show unto us whether of these two Thou hast chosen, that so he may enter into this Ministry and into this Apostleship,[2] from which Judas hath fallen by his crime, that he might go unto his own place."[3]

Then in the folds of a mantle the two names, written upon tablets, were shaken together. The first to fall out was that of Mathias, and he was made an associate of the Eleven Apostles.[4]

This manner of election shows how completely the Apostles confided in the divine assistance.[5] They knew that the Lord would manifest Himself shortly, and in this trust they abandoned themselves to Him. These were the feelings which animated the holy women as well, they who had been first at the Sepulchre and the Resurrection. The Apostles left them their place in the midst, which they had occupied during the Saviour's life, without any pretence of keeping them in a place apart,

---

[1] Σὺ, Κύριε. This prayer is probably addressed, not to the Heavenly Father, but to Jesus, who had Himself chosen His Apostles: "Ego elegi vos," John xv. 16 Indeed, after the Resurrection we find that the Apostles worshipped Him and implored His aid (Luke xxiv. 52).

[2] Διακονίας is used to designate the active work of the ministry; ἀποστολῆς, the dignity of the Apostolate.

[3] Τὸν τόπον τὸν ἴδιον. Judas deserted the post which was assigned him among us to go into his place, the place of torments. Lightfoot (*Horæ Hebraicæ*, in loco) cites this passage from the Baal Turim on Numbers: "Balaam ivit in locum suum, id est Gehennam."

[4] Like S. Mathias, Joseph Barsabas was probably one of the seventy disciples (Eusebius, *Historia Ecclesiastica*, i. 12). Far from feeling wounded because he was not chosen, his humble virtue attained that state of innocence predicted by S. Mark (xvi. 18), wherein no evil could harm him. According to a tale recorded by Papias, after drinking poison on one occasion, he received no injury (*Patrologie grecque*, t. V. p. 1255) The Martyrologies of Usuard and Addon set down his feast-day for the 20th of July, and add that while busied in the ministry of preaching, he suffered many things from the Jews and had a victorious end; that is to say, he died a Martyr.

[5] "Electi sunt duo judicio humano, et electus de duobus unus judicio divino" (S. Augustine, *Enarratio in Psalm. XXX.*, Serm. ii. 13).

as the Jews were wont to do in the Temple and the synagogues. They prayed with them in common, and "in union with Mary, the Mother of Jesus."[1] From the early dawn of Christianity the Virgin's prayer was what it is for us to-day, — a mother's help, the pure incense of Love which penetrates our hearts and sweetly disposes them for the coming of the Holy Ghost.

Lively as were their holy hopes, nothing of all this had become known in the world outside. The little band gathered in the Supper-room was of too obscure a character to attract attention; as for the Galilean, the rumors of His Resurrection were gradually dying away. With good reason the Sanhedrin people could congratulate themselves on having immolated this teacher of new doctrines. With Him so satisfactorily disposed of, there was no cause for any anxiety lest their Pentecost should be disturbed as the Pasch had been.

The fifty days which separate these two feasts make the time of harvesting for Judæa. It begins with April in the warmer valleys; thence came the sheaves of barley offered as first-fruits on the second day of the Pasch.[2] Two months later, the sickle is put to the last ears of wheat; this end of their labors was consecrated by the Feast of the Fiftieth Day, — the Pentecost. The ritual proper of the solemnity consisted in presenting to the Lord two loaves from the fruits of the new harvest,[3] to which was added a holocaust and burnt offerings of peace and of expiation.[4] At sunrise the victims and the loaves of bread were scattered by the priests towards the four winds of heaven; then above and below, in order so to consecrate them to the Eternal who directs the winds, and has created the heavens and the earth. During this

---

[1] Acts i. 14.
[2] This second day of the Passover was the sixteenth of the moon. Starting from this point, forty-nine days must needs elapse, and the fiftieth was the great solemnity called by Moses "The Feast of the Weeks" (Exod. xxxiv. 22; Deut. xvi. 10, 16), and later on designated by the Greek name Πεντηκοστή, "Fiftieth": Pentecost.
[3] Lev. xxiii. 16; Num. xxviii. 26; Deut. xvi. 10.
[4] Lev. xxiii. 18-20; Num. xxviii. 27.

oblation the Levites chanted the Great Hallel, the people mingling their voices with the harmony of the musicians. Originally this thanksgiving after the harvest home was the only object the Jews recognized as proposed by this festival; later on, however, they made it also a time for thanking God for the Law which had been given to Moses on this very day, according to a tradition common in the time of the Christ.[1] This second meaning of the feast recommended it to the Saviour's choice as a fitting season for the fulfilment of His promises and the promulgation of the New Law.

In accordance with custom, the disciples shut themselves up in the Supper Room, and there kept the holy watching which has remained down to our day in the traditions of Jewry. "When God wished to reveal the Law," so say the Rabbins, "He was obliged to wake His people from sleep; that we may escape this sinful torpidity, we keep watch the whole night."[2] Gathering in the synagogues or private houses, the sons of Israel chanted the holy books which their descendants still recite to-day, — the Song of Songs, wherein is sung Jehovah's love for His people; the Law, sweeter than honey on the lips of the spouse; and the Story of Ruth, which describes the toils of the harvest. These present goods were not allowed to efface from memory the terrors of Sinaï; for besides the Canticles and Ruth, they repeated at the same time Habakuk's prayer:[3] —

"Eloah cometh from Theman, and The Holy from Mount Paran.[4] . . . He halteth and maketh the earth to quake; at His glance the peoples tremble, the eternal

---

[1] Schoettgen, *Horæ Hebraicæ*, on Acts ii. 1; S. Jerome, *Epistola ad Fabiam*, mansio xii.; S. Augustine, *Contra Faustum*, xxxii. 12.
[2] Kitto's *Cyclopædia*: PENTECOST, 3, c.
[3] Such is still the order of reading in the synagogues.
[4] Theman, the southerly region of the land of Edom, here designates the whole of Idumea; Paran, the mountains of Arabia Petræa, whose central point is Sinaï. Habakuk has drawn his inspiration from a passage in Deuteronomy, where Moses refers to Idumea, not as Theman, but Seir: "The Eternal hath come from Sinai and risen for their sake from Seir; He hath shone on high from the Mountain of Paran. . . . From His right hand hath come forth for them a Law of fire" (Deut. xxxiii. 2).

hills are nought. . . . The deep lifteth its voice; it lifteth its hands towards heaven. The sun, the moon, flee away at the glare of Thy darts, at the dazzling gleam of Thy sword. In Thy anger Thou tramplest the earth; in Thy fury Thou tramplest on the nations; Thou comest forth to save Thy people and to save Thy Christ."[1]

What was this coming of the Lord, a subject so fraught with fear and hope? Another seer, Joel, had announced it, and whether it was Jewish usage to connect his prophecy with that of Habakuk, or whether the Apostles were inspired by Heaven so to do, these were the oracles recited by them during their night-watch; for with the morning we see how Peter's mind is still charged with the prophet's thought.[2] These words especially remained graven upon his memory: "I will pour forth My Spirit upon all flesh. Your sons and your daughters shall prophesy; your old men shall dream dreams, and your young men shall see visions; and upon your slaves also, and upon your handmaidens, will I pour out My Spirit in that day. I will cause wonders to appear in the heavens and upon the earth beneath, blood and fire, and clouds of smoke. The sun shall be turned into darkness, and the moon into blood, before the Day of Jehovah is made manifest, — the great and terrible day. What time whosoever shall call upon the Name of Jehovah shall be saved."[3] The two advents of the Christ were blended together in this prophecy, — one most terrible, to come at the end of time; the other, full of mercy and of grace, whereof the hour was fast approaching.

The morning light was upon them, and while the offerings of the first-fruits of the harvest were already begun upon the Mount of the Temple, the disciples and the holy women still waited in the Supper Room rapt in prayer. "Of a sudden there was heard a great noise, as of a mighty wind which came from heaven and filled the whole house where they were sitting; and they saw at the same time, as it were, tongues of fire which parted

---

[1] Habak. iii. 3-13.   [2] Acts ii. 16-21.   [3] Joël ii. 28-32.

and rested over above each one of them."[1] More suddenly than these flaming orbs, the Holy Spirit filled the Apostles and transformed them. Ignorant hitherto, all absorbed in their earth-bound longings, incapable of grasping higher truths, and so carnal-minded that Jesus, when about to go away from them into Heaven, once more rebuked them for the hardness of their hearts, in an instant these common men were seen to be lifted above their old selves, remembering and understanding the teachings of their Master. The Descent of the Holy Spirit was indeed what John the Baptist had foretold, — "a Baptism of Fire,"[2] consuming in them all that was impure, enkindling their hearts with such zeal that they were ready from that moment to dare all things for Him Whom they had so miserably abandoned. And for that hour, thus invested with the rays of the Godhead, penetrated and thrilling with His presence, one and all felt as if lost in a glorious flood of light and love; flowing over them and sweeping into the inmost recesses of their souls, God's Spirit took possession of their faculties, even making them His mouthpiece, insomuch that each one there "began to utter speech in divers tongues according as the Holy Spirit put words into their mouths."

Transports of feeling so mighty as theirs, the sound of women's voices lifted high in an ecstasy of joy, were enough to arouse the attention of the Jews, who were passing in either direction outside the Supper Room. They were not less numerous at Pentecost than upon the day of the Pasch, for besides the inhabitants of Palestine who came up again to Jerusalem for this time, great numbers of strangers made it a religious duty not to take their departure until after having celebrated the second feast-day of Israel. The city was therefore full "of pious and God-fearing Jews from every nation under heaven."[3] These sons of Abraham had no bond of union besides a community of faith and hopes; the majority, indeed, not knowing Hebrew, spoke only the language of the land

[1] Acts ii. 2-3.   [2] Matt. iii. 1; Acts i. 5.   [3] Acts ii. 5.

they lived in. Now, among those who were encamped in the neighborhood of the Supper Room, or who were passing by at this time, there were people from all parts of the world, — "Parthians, Medes, Elamites, dwellers in Mesopotamia, from the distant provinces of Judæa, from Cappadocia, Pontus, Asia, from Phrygia and Pamphylia, from Egypt, and from the parts of Lybia about Cyrene; many were from Rome, Jews by race and proselytes as well; others were from Crete or from Arabia."[1]

These strangers, attracted by the sounds which they heard, climbed the outside staircase which led to the upper chamber; there they beheld the Apostles possessed by the power of God, burning with the fiery breath of His Spirit, in an ecstasy exalting the wonders of the Lord. With the Hymns of Israel, chanted in all the majesty of the Hebrew tongue, were mingled, according to the divine inspiration, words borrowed from various idioms; and yet, however obscure in themselves these overflowings of supernal rapture may have been, every one who entered there understood clearly what was said, each in his own tongue. Affrighted by this prodigy, they whispered among themselves: "Are not all these people who are speaking, Galileans? Then how is it we hear them speaking the language of our own land?"

Others followed in their turn; and as the miracle was equally manifest to them, they too were filled with wonder and delight.

"What does this mean?"[2] they exclaimed to each other.

The audience, growing larger every moment, did not at first interrupt the disciples in their thanksgiving. But very soon their number was increased by other Jews who were not in sympathy with the simple and respectful piety of the first comers; at sight of these men beside themselves with holy emotions, they soon began to laugh and sneer.

"These people are drunk," they said; "they 're full of sweet wine."[3]

---

[1] Acts ii. 9, 11.   [2] Acts ii. 12.
[3] Γλεύκους: sweet wine, not new; perhaps the wine made from the

This slur startled Peter from his ecstasy; it was his place to act now in the name of the brethren, and to avenge God's Spirit insulted in their person. He rose up, surrounded by the Twelve, and stood forth upon the threshold of the Supper Room.

"Oh, Jews," he began, "and all you who dwell in Jerusalem, pay heed to what I am about to say, and attend well to my words. These men are not drunk, as you think, seeing it is but the third hour of the day.[1] But this is that which was spoken of by the Prophet Joel: 'In the last days I will pour forth My Spirit upon all flesh: your sons and your daughters shall prophesy; your young men shall see visions, and your old men shall dream dreams.'"

Peter went on to recall the sequel of this prediction: the Messiah's coming to be marked by a new overflow of the Holy Spirit; His return in the hour of Judgment accompanied by awful wonders, the heavens tottering, the sun wrapped in darkness, the moon changed to blood. In the eyes of the Apostles, as in the Prophet's thought, these two events so eclipse all the rest of the history of man that the interval between is lost sight of; the Christ made flesh, Christ judging all flesh: of what importance are the evolutions of earthly empires when considered in the light of these great doings of God?

"Ye Israelites," he continued, "hear these words. Jesus of Nazareth was a Man approved of God by the wonders, the prodigies, and the miracles which God hath given Him to do in the midst of you. This you know, and nevertheless, when, by a determinate counsel and foreknowledge from on High, He was delivered into your hands, taking Him, you crucified Him and put Him to death by the hands of wicked men. But Him God hath

---

small sweet grape called by Jewish interpreters שָׂרֵק. Gen. xlix. 11; Is. v. 2; Jer. ii. 21. According to Suidas, it is the first juice which comes from the press before it is trampled.

[1] "Ὥρα τρίτη: the first hour of prayer (nine o'clock in the morning), before which no Jew ate or drank: "Non licet homini gustare quidquam antequam oraverit orationem suam" (*Berachoth*, f. 28, 2).

raised up, snatching Him from the travailings[1] of Death which could have no power over Him."

This is what David had prophesied when he said to the Lord: "Thou wilt not leave My Soul in the tomb, neither wilt Thou suffer Thy Holy One to see corruption."[2]

This tomb of their great king, which still stands to-day upon Mount Sion, close beside the Supper Room,[3] was in sight of all, and Peter could by a gesture call the Jews' attention to it, as he went on, —

"My brethren, let me speak boldly to you of the Patriarch David, that he died, that he is buried, and that his sepulchre is with us to this present day. But whereas he was a Prophet, and knew that God had promised him with an oath to bring forth from his seed a Son Who should sit upon his throne, — in this knowledge of the future he has spoken of the Resurrection of the Christ, saying that He has not been left in the tomb, and that His flesh has not suffered corruption. This is that Jesus Whom God hath raised up, whereof we all are witnesses. Raised up by the power of God, having received the fulfilment of the promise which the Father had made Him, that He would send forth the Holy Ghost, He hath here poured it forth, as you now see and hear. Now, David is not ascended into heaven, for he says himself, —

> "Jehovah said unto my Lord,
> Sit Thou at My right hand
> Until I subdue Mine enemies
> Even as a footstool unto Thy feet.[4]

---

[1] Λύσας τὰς ὠδῖνας τοῦ θανάτου. S. Peter undoubtedly made use of the Hebrew word חֶבְלֵי (Ps. xvii. 5): "the bonds" wherewith Death held the Lord captive; in rendering this passage, S. Luke has adopted the version of the Septuagint, which here translates חֶבְלֵי by ὠδῖνας, "the pangs of childbirth." [2] Ps. xv. 10.

[3] We read in the Third Book of the Kings (ii. 10), that David was interred in the fortress of Sion. This tomb had been opened by the High Priest Hyrcanus, and later on by Herod, who seized the treasures it contained (Josephus, *Antiquitates*, vi. 15, 3). It had fallen into ruins at the time of Adrian (Dion Cassius, lxix. 14); but S. Jerome found it restored (*Ep.* xlvi. [xvii.] *ad Marcellam*, 12). [4] Ps. cix. 1.

Let all the House of Israel know most certainly that God hath made Lord and Messiah this same Jesus Whom you have crucified."

These words touched his hearers, who for the most part had seen Jesus, while very many among them did in secret detest the crime of the Sanhedrin party.

"Men, brethren," they said to Peter and to the rest, "what must we do?"

"Do penance," Peter replied, "and be baptized, each one of you, in the Name of the Christ Jesus, to obtain remission of your sins; and you shall receive the gift of the Holy Ghost." Then he explained how the Lord, before going up into the skies, had promised that they should receive the power of the Spirit from the Father; this promise had just been accomplished in the person of the disciples gathered there in the Supper Room, but it belonged likewise both to the Jews now present and to "all that are far off, as many as the Lord our God shall call." By this the Apostle alluded, not to the sons of Israel scattered afar, but the Gentiles who, according to Judaic prepossessions, were destined eventually to become sons of Abraham, and thus find their chance of salvation in the Law. From this point of view, Peter's teaching contained nothing which could shock his hearers, for, like them, he still believed that every Pagan, if he would become a disciple of the Master, must first of all practise the external forms of Judaism.

Brilliant as was the light which had encircled the Supper Room, it had not as yet illumined all the mysteries of Faith; the mists lingered here and there, though soon to be cleared away, little by little, by the breath of the Divine Spirit. But these last shadows in no way obscured the preaching of the Apostle; simple, burning with great faith, it was enough to set their hearts aflame, recalling the loving-kindnesses and the wondrous deeds of the Master. In this spirit he ended his exhortation to the Jews who stood before him. "Save yourselves from this perverse generation," he said; thus branding the hypocritical righteousness of Israel, demanding of all a change of heart and the reception by baptism of that new life which Jesus had come to proffer to the world. The majority of his listeners received Peter's words; about three thousand persons were baptized upon the spot, and joined the number of these disciples of the Christ. Among them were included many strangers, who, on their return home after the Feast, carried afar the seeds of Christianity; but a saintly company still remained in Jerusalem, all the closer bound together because they were so few in numbers.

Day by day the Apostles continued to instruct them, ever repeating the divine teaching thus kindled anew in their memories by the coming of the Holy Ghost.

"Blessed are the poor, for theirs is the Kingdom of Heaven! . . . You cannot serve God and riches; be not troubled, therefore, as to what you shall eat or what you shall drink, for they are Pagans who seek such things, and your Father knows that you have need of them. And for this reason seek first the Kingdom of God and His righteousness, and all the rest shall be given unto you, added to them." [1] But even more than this trustfulness in our heavenly Father, the duty of brotherly charity was inculcated by their preaching; for this indeed was their Master's own commandment, the oftenest repeated, the one of which He had said: "By this shall all men know that you are my disciples, if you have love one for another." [2] In the exaltation of new-born faith, all worldly prudence was despised, all examination of the past, all considerations for the future, discarded; these ardent souls dreamed of nothing less than to lose their own identity in that unity of the brethren which the Saviour had demanded of them before His death. "May they all be one, as Thou, Father, in Me, and I in Thee, that they may be likewise one in Us, in order that the world may believe that Thou hast sent Me." [3]

This holy enthusiasm did not continue without practical consequences. "All those that believed lived together,

---

[1] Matt. v. 3; vi. 24–34; Luke xii. 29–31.
[2] John xiii. 35. [3] John xvii. 21.

and everything they possessed was common among them. They sold their lands and their goods,[1] and distributed among them all according as each one had need."[2] Strange as it may seem, in contrast with our customs, there was nothing about this community of goods which would be apt to amaze Jerusalem, for the priests who came from a distance to perform their offices in the Temple were accustomed to live in common, after much the same fashion; taking example from them, the Pharisee-scribes had established societies in which the members gathered together every day for repasts sanctified by religious rites: there were the numerous ablutions, dishes scrupulously preserved from any uncleanness; the table was blessed, while sweet spices burned in the presence of the guests, to remind them of the incense of their altars. The Essenes went still farther; among them there was no distinction in property,—the same dwelling, the same table where they sat in silence, the same wardrobe furnishing to each the white habit by which this sect was known. Hence the common life of the disciples had nothing singular about it for the multitude, and attracted no more attention than the opening of some new synagogue in the town.

So far as concerns their outward conduct of life, there was nothing to distinguish them from other devout Israelites. We find in the Talmud and contemporary authors an account of what were then the customs of Jews commended for their virtuous life. These differ so widely from the practices which go to make up the duties of a Christian's day in this age that we must try to form some notion of them, in order to conceive any correct notions of the early manners of the Church.

[1] Acts ii. 44, 45. Κτήματα, lands; ὑπάρξεις, other sources of wealth.
[2] This community of goods was never made obligatory as a law (Acts v. 4), and it existed in Jerusalem alone; in the other Churches, on the contrary, from the time of the Apostles we find both rich and poor (1 Tim. vi. 17; 1 Cor. xvi. 2). It may have been owing to the strictness with which they accomplished this act of renunciation that we find that state of poverty which always prevailed among the Christians of the Holy City, and which obliged S. Paul to solicit charity from the other Churches on their behalf (Rom. xv. 25, 26; 1 Cor. xvi. 13; 2 Cor. viii., ix., etc.).

Upon awakening, the first duty of every Israelite was to praise God, and then wash his face and hands; for sleep, the image of death, defiled a man as much as does the tomb. The dawn found him in the Temple waiting the moment when the watchmen stationed upon the roofs of the Sanctuary should catch the white light flushing the hills of Hebron, whereupon their cry resounded over all, —

"Priests, begin your ministry! Levites, fulfil your functions! Israelites, to your places!"

Crowded in the Jews' Porches, all united in the morning sacrifice, following its every detail: first the lamb slain, its blood sprinkled upon the corners of the altar; then incense burned in the Holy Place; afterwards the victim was consumed, amid various offerings and libations. It was just as the sun was rising: nine times the trumpets pealed forth over the terraces of the Temple, and the priests repeated that ancient benediction given to Israel, —

"May the Lord bless and keep you! May the Lord show His countenance unto you and have pity on you! May the Lord incline Himself unto you and give you peace!"

With these first hours of the day hallowed by religion, the public life commenced, — a serious and laborious life, its features visible to all, since it was carried on in the open doorways of houses and in the public streets, just as we find it still among the bazaars in the East. Narrow, winding streets lined with open shops; in these dark recesses the workman squats, with the wares he has for sale displayed about him, — here, a heap of fruit or grain; there, precious cloths, brilliant garments, handiwork in iron or in bronze; farther on, there are glittering jewels, costly perfumes and oils. In that network of tortuous streets an hundred various arts were exercised before the eyes of every passer-by: such has always been the general aspect of Oriental cities, such was Jerusalem in those days. The different trades, then as now, were collected in bodies, each in its own locality; indeed, Jeremy mentions the street of the bakers, Josephus speaks of the clothing market, another for linen goods, and one for metal ware.[1]

In the shops of these artisans we should have found the first Christians, and that without any preference for any particular kind of work; for while the Rabbis of Israel shunned trades which were liable to contact with what was legally impure,[2] the Holy Spirit recognized no such distinctions: breathing where it listed, its call was heard by the great and the humble ones of the city, and the latter were more highly favored. But with all its workings were so efficacious that it transformed the lowliest members of the new-born Church; their virtue, their brotherly love, and notably their devotion to their religion, were strikingly manifest to all.

The time had passed when Israel regarded the Temple as the only place for prayer; the four hundred and eighty synagogues[3] erected in Jerusalem gathered together in one place the congregations of Cyreneans, in another the Alexandrians, elsewhere the Jews from Cilicia, the first idea of each being to collect friends of common origin, having the same education, language, and customs. But this was not the case with the community of Jesus' disciples; more faithful to the spirit of the Law than these others, "they persevered daily in the Temple, united among themselves in heart and mind."[4] At the third hour, at the sixth, and at the ninth,[5] they were seen laying aside their work to ascend to the Porches of the Jews, and there mingled their voices with those who besought the aid of the God of Abraham, Isaac, and Jacob.[6] But though in this

---

[1] Jer. xxxvii. 21; Josephus, *Bellum Judaicum*, v. 8, 1.
[2] See article under TANNER, Smith's *Dictionary of the Bible*.
[3] *Megilla*, iii. 1.   [4] Acts ii. 46.
[5] Nine o'clock in the morning, noon, and three in the afternoon, according to our manner of counting the hours of the day.
[6] "The God of Abraham, of Isaac, and of Jacob." This title of the Almighty is used much oftener in the Acts than in the other books of the New Testament; thereby the Apostles avoided the appearance of introducing new dogmas, and thus linked their faith in Jesus with the testimony of the Patriarchs, David, and all the Prophets.

way they had everything in common with Israel,—the Sabbath, their prayers, libations, offerings, bloody sacrifices,—there was one rite, nevertheless, which distinguished them, containing in itself the new worship: that rite was the Breaking of the Bread, whereby the Master had bade them renew the memory of Himself.

Obedient to this behest, they gathered together every evening; and as the Supper Room could no longer contain the growing throng of disciples, they made use of private houses [1] to conceal the holy mysteries from the gaze of the profane. These gatherings, as representations of the Last Supper, were opened by a frugal meal, where "each one, with thanks to God, partook of his food in gladness and simplicity of heart;" at the close, one of the Apostles, breaking the bread and blessing the cup, consecrated them as the Saviour [2] had done: each one ate and drank, and their union with Jesus, prepared all day long by prayer, was consummated by this their communion. Hence arose that close concord of heart and soul, with their virtue, which was of so lovable and attractive a character to all who knew them, insomuch that "every day the Lord increased the number of such as should be saved in the unity of the one same body." [3] Even those whom Grace had not attracted, could not suppress emotions of amazement and fear; for "many wonders and signs were done by the Apostles, and all were filled with great awe." [4]

---

[1] Acts ii. 46. Κατ' οἶκον, "circa domos" (Vulgate), is used in contrast to τῷ ἱερῷ.
[2] In Christian sanctuaries, when none of the Twelve was at hand, everything leads us to infer that the Holy Eucharist was reserved, and distributed to the disciples every evening.
[3] Acts ii. 47.
[4] Acts ii. 43.

CHAPTER II.

THE APOSTLES BEFORE THE SANHEDRIN.

REASSURED by the fifty days which followed the Passion, the Sanhedrin party believed that they had buried the Christ forever; their vexation was therefore the more intense upon learning that great rumors were rising about His disciples, whose number was increasing daily. Though at first they did not employ against them the same rigorous measures they had used against the Nazarene, this was only because they did not find among the Apostles what they had so much dreaded in Jesus, — the words of the Master which captured the people's heart, and branded the hypocritical masters of Israel for what they were; most of all, His more than human superiority, to which all men were forced to yield. The first Christians, timid and simple, men of the people, had nothing illustrious about them except their great virtue, no other eloquence save such as was inspired by the faith with which they repeated the precepts of the Master. Indeed, it would seem that among the Lord's instructions which they gave the people, those which shocked the Jewish doctors by condemning their sabbatical superstitions and puerile ablutions were not mentioned at the first. From earliest childhood bending under the yoke of the synagogue, the disciples did not dream as yet of casting it off; they continued to live as strict Pharisees, — austere in manners, exact in their observances, as pious as they were charitable.

This exterior life, in perfect conformity with the doctrines of the Scribes, both edified and reassured them;

but this was not the case with the Sadducees. These sectaries, for the most part priests, and drawing their revenues from the Temple, looked with an evil eye upon anything which was likely to derange the established order. What might not be expected of this association, so suddenly formed, animated by a common spirit, and rapidly increasing? Besides such fears, there was another reason for their aversion which was peculiar to the Sadducees: no dogma was more hateful to them than the Resurrection of the dead and faith in a future life; yet this was what the Apostles never ceased to preach, affirming that their risen Master was living in Heaven Accordingly, the Sadducees, who to the last had shown themselves quite indifferent concerning Jesus, were now the first to declare themselves against His disciples. Their animosity, held in check during the Sanhedrin's meetings by the opposite opinions of the Pharisees, could not at once look for revenge; but it brooded in secret, and at the first opportunity broke forth.

At the top of the steps which led from the Gentiles' Porches to those of the Jews stood a door of Corinthian bronze, called, because of its splendid design, the Beautiful. Although nine other entrances gave access to the first terrace of the Sanctuary, this one, opening right opposite the Holy Place, grander and more ornate than all the rest, was also the most frequented by all. Hence, very many beggars were seated here. Among them was a man, lame from his mother's womb, who was carried in and set down on this spot, in order to ask alms of those who entered into the Temple. Now, as Peter and John were going up to the Porches about the ninth hour (three in the afternoon) to take part in the public prayers, they heard the cripple repeating the plaint of the poor, —

"Help me, good sirs, and God will bless you."

The unselfishness of the Apostles went so far as to wish to keep nothing for themselves from the goods given into the common treasury by the faithful; they kept neither purse nor money. Peter, and John with him, stopped, and, resting his eyes upon the poor man, the former said, —

"Look at us."

The lame man fixed his gaze upon the Apostles, hoping to receive something. Then Peter said to him, —

"I have neither gold nor silver; but what I have I give thee. In the Name of Jesus Christ of Nazareth, arise and walk." Taking him by the hand, he lifted him up. Immediately the soles and ankles of his feet were strengthened; the lame man bounded up, stood upright, walked, and then entered with them into the Temple, leaping with joy and praising God.

Once their prayer was ended, the Apostles found themselves encircled by a great crowd; for every one recognized this man as the same they had seen seated at the Beautiful Gate asking alms, and all thronged about, full of admiration for his benefactors. Notwithstanding, Peter and John descended the broad steps and made their way towards Solomon's Portico, the man they had healed holding them by the hand. The people, amazed at this wonderful happening, followed after them under the colonnade. Here Peter raised his voice.

"Israelites," he said, "why do you marvel at this? Why fix your eyes upon us, as if by our power or our piety we had made this lame man walk? The God of Abraham, Isaac, and of Jacob, the God of our fathers, hath glorified His Servant, Jesus, Whom you delivered up and denied before Pilate, even when that man had judged He should be released. You have denied the Holy One and the Just, and, demanding the pardon of a murderer, you have put to death the Prince of Life; but Him God hath raised from the dead, of which we are witnesses. It is faith in His Name which gave strength to this man you see here, whom you know; it is faith in His Name which has given him perfect soundness in the sight of you all."

After these reproaches, which awakened repentance in their souls, Peter spoke words of pardon and forgiveness, as the Master had done upon the Cross.

"My brethren,[1] I know that in this you have acted through ignorance, as also did your princes; but in this wise hath God accomplished what He had predicted by the mouth of all His Prophets,[2] that it was necessary that the Christ should suffer. Do penance, then, . . . that so your sins may be washed away." And as the outcome of this conversion he told them of "the days of refreshment"[3] so often and so passionately desired, repeating the words of Isaiah: —

"O heavens, shed down your dew,
And let the earth bud forth her Saviour."[4]

This salvation, so ardently longed for, was none other than Jesus; in Him they had beheld the Christ, of Whom Moses had said: "The Lord your God shall raise up unto you from among your brethren a Prophet like unto me. Hearken unto Him whatsoever He shall say to you, for every soul that shall not accept Him shall be exterminated from the midst of the people."[5] And now, in truth, the Prophet, thus announced to His people, had been slain at their Passover, and no longer appeared in the habitations of Israel; and yet had not this too been foretold since the beginnings of the world?[6] "It must needs be that Heaven should receive Him until what time He shall come to restore all things."[7] Peter continued his discourse, as he had begun it, by referring to the Holy Books, as no other argument would be better understood by the Jews.

"You are the children of the Prophets," he went on, — "the children of the Covenant which God hath estab-

---

[1] Ἀδελφοί. At this point the Apostle tempers the severity of his language; he reminds the Jews that they are of the same blood and the same Covenant as he, and he imputes their crime to blindness. All have crucified Jesus while they knew not what He was; even the Sanhedrin did not condemn Him with a full knowledge of what they were doing.

[2] "Omnes prophetæ in universum non prophetaverunt nisi de diebus Messiæ" (*Sanhedrin*, 99, 1). Here the Prophets are regarded as a body animated by one and the same spirit, and thus the whole of their testimony goes to forecast the sufferings of the Messiah.

[3] "Cum venerint tempora refrigerii" (Acts iii. 20).

[4] Is. xlv. 8.   [5] Acts iii. 22, 23.   [6] Acts iii. 21.   [7] Acts iii. 21.

lished with our fathers, saying unto Abraham: 'In thy seed shall all nations of the earth be blessed.' It was for you that God raised up His Servant; to you, first of all, He sent Him, that He might bless and turn you from your wickedness."

Peter and John were still speaking when an armed band forced its way under Solomon's Porch; at the head marched the captain of the Temple-guards;[1] then came the priests and the Sadducees. The last-named had listened to the preaching of the Apostles, and angered at hearing them announce that the resurrection of the dead was made manifest in Jesus, they had hurried to the Pontiffs, and obtained an order of arrest for these innovators whose speech was exciting the people. It was too late to bring the Apostles before the judges on that day; they were content for the present to see them flung into prison. But, far from intimidating the crowds, this deed of violence only heightened their faith; many of those who had heard Peter's discourse yielded to Grace, and the number of the new believers grew until it reached five thousand.

The night did not still the storm gathering in the Temple. The princes of the priesthood, now openly arrayed against the Apostles, were bent upon stifling their voices at any cost; they assembled on the morrow, with Annas, the High-priest, presiding. Saint Luke designates him by that title, although in fact the office belonged to Caïphas; and thereby he shows us here, as in his Gospel, that Annas always remained, in the eyes of the Jews, the real head of the sacerdotal body. Caïphas, John, Alexander,[2] with all who were of the Levitical race, shared

---

[1] As to this Captain, see Josephus (*Bellum Judaicum*, ii. 12, 6; vi. 5, 3; *Antiquitates*, xx. 6, 2); 2 Mac. iii. 4.

[2] Acts iv. 6. We know nothing about these last named pontiffs. Lightfoot supposes that John is the same personage as Jochanan ben Zaccha, spoken of in the Talmud (*Yoma*, 39, 2). According to another hypothesis, Alexander was the brother of Philo (Josephus, *Antiquitates*, xviii. 8, 1); but this opinion is hardly probable, for the Alexander mentioned by Josephus dwelt in Alexandria, where he was Alabarch of the Jews.

the Sadducees' animosity. Their example carried with them the great body of Pharisees, up to this time tolerant towards the new community. So, too, the three classes of the Sanhedrin, — "priests, ancients of the people, and the scribes,"[1] — equally zealous, hastened to make common cause with them. Their meeting was held "in Jerusalem,"[2] says the sacred Historian, — probably in the place where Jesus was condemned, — in that Pontifical Palace where Annas and his successors believed themselves all-powerful. Thither Peter and John were brought, the lame man they had healed, still following them. Faithful to his benefactors, he pushed his way to the foremost ranks of those who surrounded them; thus it came about that every one there was pointing him out as the man on whom a miracle had been wrought.

The examination was begun.

"By what power," they were asked, "and in what name have you done this deed?"

Filled with the Holy Ghost, Peter replied, —

"Chiefs of the people and Ancients of Israel, since we are to be judged this day for having done good to an infirm man, and you would hear in whose name he has been healed, know this, all you and all the people of Israel, that it is in the Name of Jesus Christ of Nazareth, Whom you have crucified, Whom God hath raised from among the dead, even by Him this man stands here healed, as you see him before you. This Jesus is the Stone which was rejected by you who are the builders, and which is become the head of the corner. Neither is there salvation by any other, and no other Name under heaven hath been given to men, whereby we must be saved."

The Sanhedrin was astonished at such language as this; for the outward bearing and rough speech of these men, everything about them, showed what they were, — "ignorant men, and of the common herd."[3] Most of the judges, moreover, remembered having seen them in the company of Jesus, and were not ignorant of

---

[1] Acts iv. 5.   [2] Acts iv. 5.
[3] Ἀγράμματοι καὶ ἰδιῶται. Acts iv. 13.

the fact that the one who was speaking in the others' name had fled from this very house, weeping and denying His Master. How had this great change come about? Whence this hardihood to brave all things with such firmness? And what were they to say in presence of this cripple, now cured and standing before the whole court, close beside the men who had saved him? Giving orders that the Apostles should be taken outside the hall, they held a secret deliberation among themselves.

"What shall we do with these men?" was the question they asked each other; "the miracle they have performed is known to every one in Jerusalem, — so much is certain, and we cannot deny it."

But after this unanimous avowal, no one of them felt moved to confess the truth; their only anxiety was concerned about the best means to prevent it from spreading among the people.

"Let us forbid them," they said, "to speak in His Name for the future, to any one whatsoever."

And forthwith, summoning them again before the court, they charged them to preach no more, at any time or place; neither were they to teach in the Name of Jesus. At once Peter and John made answer, —

"Judge for yourselves before God whether it is just that we should obey you rather than God. For our part, we cannot conceal what we have seen and heard."[1]

Thus, in a word, they laid down the principle of the Christian's liberty of speech.

Their constancy confounded the Sanhedrin, now utterly at a loss how to proceed. To have the Apostles whipped would be likely to arouse popular feeling, for the people were glorifying God over the miracle worked by their means: to silence the reports of this marvel, or to seek to explain it away, was equally impossible, for "the man healed" in this extraordinary fashion "was above forty years old." The judges confined themselves, therefore, to uttering threats of severe punishment, and sent them away without venturing to do anything against them.

[1] Acts iv. 19-20.

Peter and John betook themselves speedily to their brethren,[1] whom they found waiting and watching; for their distress was all the deeper as they saw that the first blow had struck straight at the very heart of the Church, — Simon Peter, the Head of the Twelve, and John, the beloved disciple of the Master. The two disciples related all that the Princes of the priesthood and the Ancients[2] had said to them; whereupon, as with one voice, in the Supper Room, this prayer was heard, — the first prayer of the Church which has come down to us: —

" Lord, Thou art the God[3] Who didst make heaven and earth, and all things that are in them; Thou art He Who hath said by the Holy Ghost, by the mouth of Thy servant, our father, David, ' Why do the nations rage, and the people meditate vain things? The kings of the earth have arrayed themselves, and the princes have met together against the Lord and His Christ.' Yea, of a truth, Herod and Pontius Pilate, with the Gentiles and the people of Israel, have gathered together in this City against Thy Holy Servant,[4] Jesus, Whom Thou hast consecrated by Thine anointment: yet have they accomplished nought save what Thy power and Thy counsels had decreed should be done. And now, Lord, pay heed to their threatenings, and grant unto Thy servants that

---

[1] Τοὺς ἰδίους comprises the Apostles, and very likely a number of the faithful who were in company with them.

[2] Οἱ ἀρχιερεῖς καὶ οἱ πρεσβύτεροι. S. Luke does not mention the scribes who, Pharisees for the most part, left the duties of acting and speaking to the other two classes of the Sanhedrin, without mingling in their violent disputes.

[3] Ὁ Θεός, though omitted in the manuscripts of the Vatican, Sinaï, and Alexandria, is found in Beza's Codex.

[4] Παῖδά σου Ἰησοῦν (Acts iv. 27). The Saviour was not invoked by name as a general thing, for the Apostles and baptized Jews who surrounded them could not at once cast aside the custom prevalent in their race of invoking none but the Lord. Nevertheless, no one doubted the truth that Jesus and the Lord are one. When Peter preached his first sermon on the threshold of the Supper Room, his concluding words were, " Let all Israel know that God hath made Lord [Adonaï] and Christ this Jesus Whom you have crucified " (Acts ii. 36). And very soon we shall hear the dying Stephen commit his soul to Him: Κύριε Ἰησοῦ, δέξαι τὸ πνεῦμά μου (Acts vii. 59).

they may tell forth Thy Word with all boldness, by stretching out Thy hand to heal, to work wonders and signs, through the Name of Thy Holy Servant, Jesus."

Hardly had they finished their prayer when Heaven answered it by a Miracle: the place where they were assembled shook; all were filled with the Holy Spirit, and with intrepid souls they spoke to all the Holy Word of God.

So far, then, from crushing the new-born Church, this storm had but hardened and helped its growth. And yet the community, though fast developing, lost nothing of its unitedness; the more formidable the threats breathed against them, the closer the little flock pressed about the Apostles. Shepherds of their souls, at first the latter limited their Ministry to spiritual cares; "with great power they bore witness to the Resurrection of the Saviour."[1] But Grace was then so mighty in believing hearts, and their detachment from the world so absolute, that soon the care of their bodies as well as of their souls devolved upon the Twelve. The abandonment of all earthly goods, counselled by Jesus, and practised, as we have seen, by the first disciples, speedily became, although not a law, at least a custom.[2] "Every one who possessed property in land or houses sold these, and brought the price of them, laying it at the feet of the Apostles; and thereupon it was distributed to each one according as he had need, so that there was not any poor among them." Thus "the multitude of those who believed had but one heart and one soul, and no one looked upon what he possessed as belonging to himself individually, but all things were held in common among them."

[1] Acts iv. 33.
[2] In fact, though at first the Acts allude to this division of goods as a spontaneous movement on the part of all believers (Acts ii. 44-45), it is afterwards described as coming under the authority of the Apostles. Three times it mentions that their riches were deposited "at their feet" (Acts iv. 35, 37; v. 2). Apparently they chose some hour for making this offering when the Twelve, gathered together in the Supper Room, occupied the platform reserved for the leaders and pastors in the synagogues. Consequently the expression, "they laid it at their feet," is meant to be understood literally.

As it seems quite evident that these sales and this community of goods excited no troublesome demonstrations in Jerusalem, we are led to believe that, for the most part, the new converts were not persons of great wealth. Held in common, the few possessions of these poor folk so blessed by God were sufficient for the maintenance of their confraternity, austere and laborious as was the life they led. Nevertheless, among their number were reckoned some of the Princes of Israel: such were Nicodemus, Joseph of Arimathea, and Lazarus, whose riches were at their disposal in case of any greater need.

Only one of these renunciations of personal property is recorded in the Acts as having attracted considerable notice: this was that of a Levite, whose name was Joseph, a Cyprian born. Distinguished either for his birth or his fortune, he showed no more hesitation than his needier brethren in sacrificing all; he sold his lands, and brought the price to the Apostles. This generosity won for him the grace of Apostleship; a little later we see him, with Paul, admitted to the ranks of the Twelve. Like them, he had followed the Master from the first days of His Ministry;[1] and over and above this great advantage he possessed a still more precious gift in the vivacity and charm of his eloquent speech. Often in the Christian synagogues he was intrusted with the instruction which followed the reading of the Law and the Prophets, — what they called "the Word of Consolation." Hence he got the name of Barnabas, given him by the Apostles, which means "the son" of Prophecy, of inspired exhortation, "of Consolation."[2]

---

[1] According to Clement of Alexandria (*Stromata*, ii. 20), Eusebius (*Historia Ecclesiastica*, i. 21), and S. Epiphanius (*Adversus Hæreses*, xx. 4), he was one of the seventy-two disciples.

[2] בַּר נְבוּאָה: literally "Son of Prophecy." The title of Nabi, נָבִיא, "Prophet," is not reserved exclusively to one who predicts future things, but to any man beloved and inspired of God. In Genesis (xx. 7), Abraham is called Nabi; in Exodus (vii. 1), Jehovah says to Moses, "Aaron, thy brother, shall be thy Nabi," in other words, as it is translated in the Targum of Onkelos, "thy interpreter." So, too, in the New Testament; the word προφητεία refers not only to the gift of prophesying, but also that of admonishing, preaching, and exhorting in God's name. Thus it is

Under such leaders, so pious and unselfish, overflowing with thoughts of God's Kingdom, whither they were rapt by the memory and love of Jesus, the little community enjoyed a heavenly existence, — days of such peace and happiness as the Church has never known since, such as even our monasteries have never tasted, save, perhaps, in the seasons of first celestial fervor. Mutual love was warm at their hearts; living together, they collected, it would seem, as near as possible in the same quarter of the town, close to the Supper Room, now hallowed by the institution of the Eucharist and the descent of the Holy Ghost. No strifes, no ambition, no scandals, no cares, save for things divine; truly the Church was already like that luxuriant harvest which the Master had pointed out upon the banks of Genesareth, bearing some thirty, some sixty, some an hundred fold. But for this Field of God the calm was more to be dreaded than tempest-blasts. In the hour when all slept, the enemy came to sow the seeds of sin.

It was just at this time that a man named Ananias, with Saphira his wife, together sold a piece of land and kept back a part of the price they had received. Thus they fancied they could satisfy their avarice and obtain the same great renown for saintliness which their brethren had merited; they hoped at the same time to serve God and Mammon. In this the husband and wife had acted in common; Ananias, however, was the first to go through with the hypocritical scene. Coming forward in the room where the Apostles were assembled, he laid the money at their feet, to indicate that he thereby abandoned all his goods.

"Ananias," Peter said to him, "how hath Satan so filled[1] thy heart as to make thee lie to the Holy Ghost,

---

said of Silas and Judas that, "being Prophets, they *exhorted* (παρεκάλεσαν) their brethren" (Acts xv. 32). We know from the Acts that these exhortations, which had a fixed place in the rubric of the Synagogue, — after the reading of the Holy Books, — were called "The Word of Consolation," λόγος παρακλήσεως (Acts xiii. 15). Hence we have Barnabas' name, which S. Luke translates as υἱὸς παρακλήσεως.

[1] The lection ἐπείρασεν, which the Vulgate translates by "tentavit," is

and keep back by fraud part of the price of this land? While it remained in thy hands, was it not thine? And even after having sold it, did not the price belong to thee? Why then hast thou conceived this design in thy heart? Thou hast not lied to men, but to God."

Ananias, hearing these words, fell down and gave up the ghost. God struck this blow to testify His horror of hypocrisy. Doubtless the sinner was struck down in merciful compassion, thereby sacrificing the body to save the soul;[1] but the faithful could only see the outward effects of his punishment. All were seized with terror, and yielding to the horror all Jews felt for death, they besought Peter to have the corpse carried out forthwith. The younger men in the congregation[2] started up, caught up the body in great haste, and bearing it away, they buried him.

About three hours later, the wife of Ananias entered, without knowing what had taken place. Surprised at the emotion of the disciples and the strained manner of their salutations, she began to question them and talk of the gift her husband had made to the Church.

"Tell me," Peter answered,[3] "didst thou sell the field for so much?"

found in only a few rare Codices. The common reading, given by almost all the manuscripts, in the Italic and Syriac Versions, and in very many Fathers, is ἐπλήρωσεν.

[1] "Notat Origenes (*Tract.* viii. in Matt.), S. Augustinus (lib. iii. *contra Parm.* i.), Cassianus (*Coll.* vi. cap. i.), Isidorus Pelusiota (lib. i. ep. 181), hanc mortis pœnam Ananiæ divinitus inflictam ad terrorem novellæ Ecclesiæ, . . . neque tamen Ananiam in æternum damnatum, sed potius per carnis interitum consultum fuisse ejus et uxoris saluti spirituali et æternæ" (Cornelius a Lapide, *Comment. in Acta Apostol.*, v. 4).

[2] Did these "young men" compose a special order in the Church, and perform functions analogous to those which, later on, were confided to the inferior ministers of the Hierarchy? Such a supposition is not at all unlikely, for we shall see shortly (Acts xi. 30) certain "Priests," οἱ πρεσβύτεροι, set over the congregations; a name which recalls that of the "Elders" of the Synagogue. It is quite probable that the Apostles, when modelling the Church after the religious assemblies of Israel, put next in rank to the πρεσβύτεροι a lower order called οἱ νεώτεροι, whose ministry corresponded to that of the Chazzan, the servant or usher in Jewish meetings.

[3] Ἀπεκρίθη. This wording of the Sacred Text infers that Saphira was the first to speak.

"Yes," she said, "for so much."

"Why have you agreed together," Peter replied, "to tempt the Spirit of God? See, the feet of them that have buried thy husband are at the door, and they shall carry thee out also."

On the very moment she fell down at his feet and gave up the ghost. The young men, coming in, found her dead; they bore her without, and buried her beside her husband. This double blow, striking one after the other so suddenly, like pitiless thunderbolts, filled with great fear all who heard the tale. God's hand had appeared in the Kingdom of His Son, always as mighty to revenge as it was overflowing with grace. Such manifestations of severity are rare in the history of the Church; but there was special need of them in those early days, when their first duty was to preserve in its purity that seed which the Master was soon to scatter over the face of the earth.

The faith of the little flock was still firmer thereafter, their zeal more lively for the spreading of the Good News; "all together, united in the one same spirit, assembled in Solomon's Porch."[1] In this vast and lofty gallery there was less disturbance from the noise of traffic; for the preparations for the sacrifices, the tumult of the crowds, rose even to the Sanctuary,—hence the Doctors always preferred to meet here. Around them there thronged Jews of every sect and all lands,—Pharisees, Sadducees, Essenes, with foreigners imbued with the doctrines of Alexandria, Greece, and Rome. Mingling with this multitude, the disciples of Jesus taught the lessons of the Gospel, not by solemn sermons, but by means of those long conversations, in which the Oriental is wont to open his soul and confess his personal beliefs.

However, the Apostles did not confine themselves to preaching; every day the miracles performed by them were more numerous. The renown of these wonders was

[1] Acts v. 12.

so great "that none of the other Jews dared to join company with them. Nevertheless, the people gave them great praise, and the number of those who believed in the Lord increased largely; they brought their sick folk into the streets, they laid them on beds and litters, in order that, when Peter passed by, his shadow at least might fall upon some one of them, and that they might be delivered from their infirmities.[1] Great throngs also hastened up from the towns round about Jerusalem; thither they brought their sick, and those who were troubled with unclean spirits, and all were healed."[2]

These rapid strides of the Church re-awakened all the hatred aroused by its Founder. As always, the first ones to bestir themselves were "the High Priest and his company, and the whole body of Sadducees."[3] Furious at seeing their commands and threats set at nought, they resolved to put an end to the matter by laying hold of the leaders of this sect. The Twelve were therefore seized, thrown into the public prison,[4] and, as it was too late to hold trials that day, guards were posted at the doors.

But lo, during the night an Angel of the Lord opened the prison doors, and leading them without, said, —

"Go into the Temple, and there preach all the words of this Life."

The order from Heaven was formal and explicit; it was that new Life[5] which was so detestable to the Sadducees, but manifest to all men in the risen Jesus, — it was this Eternal Life which the Apostles must needs publish in the very presence of their persecutors. They obeyed without delay, ascended to the Temple, and

---

[1] This incidental phrase, preserved by the Vulgate, is found also in Beza's Manuscript and the Codex Laudianus (sixth century).
[2] Acts v. 13-16. [3] Acts v. 17.
[4] After the constitution of the monarchy, the King's palaces and fortresses were generally used for prisons (3 Kings xxii. 27; Jer. xxxii. 2 xxxviii. 21; Neh. iii. 25). The residence of the High Priests, the real Princes of Israel under the Roman domination, always contained some place of detention. There they kept their prisoners.
[5] Τὰ ῥήματα τῆς ζωῆς ταύτης (Acts v. 20).

when "at dawn"[1] the gates were opened for the morning sacrifice, they entered the Porches and began to preach.

Meanwhile, though the sight of the Apostles upon the heights of Mount Moriah was a surprise to the people, upon the opposite hill of Sion the excitement was still more marked. At daybreak, Annas and his household had already convoked the Sanhedrin-Council; as soon as they were assembled, word was sent to the prison to have the Apostles brought before them. The officers returned alone.

"We found the prison carefully closed," was their report, "and the keepers before the doors; but, upon opening it, we found no one within."[2]

This news caused a great commotion in the Council: the High Priests shuddered at the thought of how weak and ridiculous their authority would be made to appear; the captain of the watch was trembling for his life, since his head was the penalty for any escape of his prisoners. Every one began to ask what would happen next. Their apprehensions were soon confirmed; almost at the same time, this report reached them, —

"The men you put in prison are now in the Temple, teaching the people."[3]

The captain, taking the guards with him, did indeed find the Twelve preaching and conversing beneath the porticos. The throngs were surging about them, growing more excited as the story of their imprisonment passed from lip to lip; all were amazed to see them free again, as calm as if nothing had happened. To arrest these men once more was an undertaking not without peril, for they could hear the mutterings of anger now stirring up the people: some had already picked up stones to pelt the soldiers.[4] Their head officer was afraid of this multitude; so, avoiding any show of violence, he conducted the Apostles rapidly and quietly away.

[1] Acts v. 21. 'Υπὸ τὸν ὄρθρον.
[2] Acts v. 23.　　　　[3] Acts v. 25.
[4] Acts v. 26. "Timebant enim populum, ne lapidarentur."

The submissiveness of their captives rendered their task an easy one; for they had not to do with leaders of a sedition, but with men whose only crime was their intrepid declaration of their Faith. This the High Priest himself recognized; in beginning his examination, the only rebuke he uttered was couched in these terms, —

"Have we not expressly forbidden you to teach in this name? And, notwithstanding, you have filled Jerusalem with your doctrine, and have a mind to charge us with the blood of this man."

These words, big with threats, were powerless to shake the constancy of the Twelve! In reply, they repeated the words with which the Church has always answered her persecutors, —

"We must obey God rather than men."

And not content with this avowal, Peter boldly preached before his judges the Resurrection of this Jesus "Whom they had put to death, hanging Him upon the tree, but Whom the God of their fathers had raised up and exalted with His right hand to be Prince and Saviour, to give repentance to Israel and forgiveness of sins. We ourselves are the Witnesses of what we tell you," Peter concluded, " and the Holy Ghost, Whom God hath given to them that obey Him, is likewise Witness with us."[1]

The attitude of the Apostles and their steadfast gaze showed that these were no empty words, but that these men, once so timid as to run from a woman's questioning, now stood before them ready to sacrifice their lives. Seeing how the Apostles braved their authority, the Sanhedrin Council was consumed with thirst for vengeance; upon the spot, in the very presence of the accused, they decided to put them to death. Their peril was very great, for the Sadducean pontiffs, who predominated in the Council, knew neither scruple nor pity. The fear that Pilate might not ratify their sentence no longer deterred them for an instant: the death of the Christ had taught them what his resistance was worth.

A Scribe named Gamaliel saved the Apostles. Grand-

[1] Acts v. 29–32.

son of Hillel and son of the aged Simeon, who first saluted the child Jesus in the Temple, this doctor of the Law felt a secret sympathy for the new sect; his uprightness, which made him so revered by the people, would not let him prove false to his conscience. He rose up in the Council; ordered that the Apostles should be withdrawn; then he addressed the assembly.

"Israelites," he said, "take heed what you are about to do to these men. Some time ago a certain Theudas [1] rose up and pretended to be something very great. About four hundred men gathered about him; but he was slain, and all who had believed in him were dispersed and brought to nothing. After him rose up Judas of Galilee,[2] at the time of the enrolment, and attracted many

---

[1] Theudas, Θευδᾶς, Theodas in the Vulgate; in the Hebrew probably תודה. The leader of the sedition alluded to here is not the man of whose revolt Josephus gives an account as happening during the reign of Claudius, in 44, about twelve years after the date of Gamaliel's discourse. Throughout his work, S. Luke shows such faithfulness as an historian that we cannot charge him with so gross a mistake. We prefer to believe that two Jews, both named Theudas, stirred up the people at an interval of some years. The insurrection spoken of in the Acts (v. 36) preceded that of Judas the Gaulonite (Acts v. 37); this was one of the numerous acts of bloodshed which disturbed Judea at the death of Herod the Great. A slave of the late monarch, named Simon, profited by the troubles which followed that event to make an attempt upon the throne (Josephus, *Antiquitates*, xvii. 10, 6; *Bellum Judaicum*, ii. 4, 2). It has been suggested that Gamaliel had this conspirator in mind. Indeed Josephus attributes the same haughty ambitions to him which the Acts ascribe to Theudas: Εἶναι ἄξιος ἐλπίσας παρροντινοῦν (Josephus); Λέγων εἶναί τινα ἑαυτόν (Acts). Both suffer a violent death, and neither seems to have attracted any great following to espouse his cause. This supposition, it will be seen, is not without some foundation. To make the people forget the obscurity of his birth, the rebellious slave may have changed his name from Theudas for that of Simon, as sounding more aristocratic according to popular tastes. When addressing the Sanhedrin, Gamaliel would naturally make use of the original appellation as better known to the Jews; while Josephus, who is writing for the benefit of Greek and Roman readers, employs the second appellation which the impostor assumed when he attempted to seize the crown, and by which, consequently, he was better known outside of Jewry.

[2] From the report in Josephus (*Antiquitates*, xviii. 1, 1), we learn that this Judas was a Gaulonite, from the city of Gamala. His title of Galilean, doubtless, was due to the fact that his insurrection had its rise in Galilee. The census of Quirinius was the occasion of the uprising. Writhing under this new badge of servitude, the people let themselves be carried away by that sectary, whose cry was a watchword of revolt: "We have no Lord and Master but God alone."

people after him; but he too perished, and every one of his party scattered. Listen, then, to the advice I give you: Do not concern yourselves about those men yonder, but let them alone. For if this counsel, or this work, be of men, it will destroy itself; if it be of God, you cannot thwart it, and you will be in danger of fighting against God Himself."[1]

Strange as this advice may have sounded to the Jews, who admitted no work as divine except their Law, no other religion save that of Jehovah, they nevertheless accepted it; for Gamaliel's authority was great, his speech persuasive, and he made the councillors understand that although manifest errors merit no tolerance, the truth, even if obscured by clouds of errors, has a right to our respect. None dared contradict the most illustrious Scribe in Israel, and the Sadducees abandoned their demand for the Apostles' death. Their hatred, however, insisting upon some satisfaction, they decided that the Twelve should be whipped, in the presence of the Council, for having rebelled against the orders given them.

Though often inflicted, and that for trifling offences, the scourging of the Synagogue was a cruel torture. Deuteronomy limited the number of blows to forty.[2] The prisoner, stripped to the waist, was tied by the hands alongside the stone on which stood a servant of the Synagogue; thus, bending before this officer, he received thirteen blows on the breast, thirteen on the right shoulder, and as many upon the left. The number was thus reduced to thirty-nine, in order not to exceed the forty blows prescribed by law. Every detail in the punishment was the object of a like minute care.[3] The

---

[1] Acts v. 35–39.   [2] Deut. xxv. 3.
[3] See in the *Mischna* the treatise on *Punishments: Maccoth*. The accompaniments of the scourging described in the Talmud agree with all we know of the formalism of the Pharisees; it would certainly seem that they were in use in the time of the Christ, for S. Paul, who suffered this chastisement five times, received only thirty-nine blows from the whip. 2 Cor. xi. 24. In early days the method of procedure was simpler. The Judge ordered the prisoner to be stretched out on the ground, and he was lashed under the official's very eyes (Deut. xxv. 2).

whip was made up of two leather straps, — one of calf-skin, divided into four lashes; the other of ass's skin, divided in two.[1] One of the judges gave the signal for each blow, crying aloud, "Strike!" another counted them, and all the while a presiding judge read in a loud voice these three passages from the Holy Books: —

"If you neither keep nor fulfil all the words of the Law written in this Book, and if you fear not that glorious and terrible Name of the Lord your God, then will the Lord make your wounds and the wounds of your children to be both great and stubborn."[2] Wherefore keep the words "of this Law and fulfil them, that you may prosper in all your deeds."[3] "Yet He, full of compassion, hath pardoned their iniquity, neither hath He destroyed them; more than once hath He turned aside His anger, and hath not kindled all His wrath against them."[4]

The Twelve, brought back before the Sanhedrin, endured this torture, one after the other, and so for the first time gave testimony to Jesus in their blood. The Law, which ordained that the executioner should use only one hand in striking, also enjoined upon him to use his full strength. But nothing could touch the serene souls of the martyrs; when the Sanhedrin judges let them go, after having forbidden them anew to speak in the Name of Jesus, "they went forth filled with joy, because they had been accounted worthy to suffer this outrage for the Name of Jesus; and every day, both in the Temple and in their own houses, they ceased not to teach and to proclaim Jesus Christ."[5]

[1] A leathern lash fastened on a wooden handle is the instrument still used in the East for striking criminals on the soles of their feet. As the Rabbis interpreted it, the skin of an ass and an ox, which composed the scourge used by the Synagogue, was an implied allusion to that passage in Isaiah, "The ox knoweth his master, and the ass the crib of his lord; but Israel hath not known Me, and My people have been without understanding" (Is. i. 3). Thus it seemed just that those beasts who do recognize their master should furnish the instruments to punish them who know him not.
[2] Deut. xxviii. 58, 59.   [3] Deut. xxix. 9.   [4] Ps. lxxvii. 38.
[5] Acts v. 41-42.

CHAPTER III.

THE JEWS OF THE DISPERSION.

ALTHOUGH up to this time the faithful were all Jews by religion, and as united in heart as they were in belief, they were made up, nevertheless, of two very different classes. Those of the class called in the Acts "Hebrews"[1] lived in Palestine, spoke Aramaic, and read their Bible in the original text; those of the other class belonged to the body of Jews known as Hellenists, scattered over the world, and speaking generally the Greek tongue, even in their public prayers making use of the Septuagint Version.[2] The latter had synagogues at Jerusalem, in which they assembled when on a visit or sojourning in the Holy City. They are destined to play a notable part in the Church, and from the very first we find their number increasing so rapidly that, before continuing our narrative, it will be well to understand

---

[1] Acts vi. 1.
[2] The word "Ελληνες, "the Greeks," in the New Testament, is used to distinguish them, sometimes from the Barbarians, at other times from the Jews. In the former case it means all peoples who speak the Greek tongue (Rom. i. 14); in the latter it is equivalent to the word Gentiles (Rom. i. 16; ii. 19; iii. 9; 1 Cor. i 22-23; x. 32, etc). The meaning of the term 'Ελληνισταί is quite different. By it we are to understand the Jews scattered through Greece and the Roman Empire, "where they forgot not only their ancient language, which was Hebrew, but also the Chaldean, which they had learned during the Captivity. They developed a Greek dialect of their own mingled with Hebraisms, which got the name of the Hellenistic language; the Septuagint and all of the New Testament is written in this tongue" (Bossuet, *Discours sur l'Histoire universelle*, i. 8) This term is used to distinguish them, not from the Jews, since the Hellenists were Israelites by birth, but from the "Hebrews" who read the Bible in the original text. The word 'Ελληνισταί is employed only twice in the New Testament, and always to indicate the Jews of the Dispersion (Acts vi. 1; ix. 29).

by what peculiar features we can distinguish them from the Jews of Judea.

It was in the days of the Babylonian Captivity that the stem of Jesse was thus divided into two branches. Transplanted by violence into Mesopotamia, at first the Israelites felt all the bitterness of captivity. The Kings of Egypt and Assyria continued to show themselves merciless to the vanquished; their earlier policy, prompted entirely by revenge, was to rivet the yoke upon all such as they had not massacred; employing them as beasts of burden, as mere human machines; and by their labors they accomplished gigantic feats. What a story of suffering the Nile and the Euphrates could tell! Only fancy what the monuments which cover their banks once cost in sweat and blood! But these furies of persecution lasted only for a time; it was but rarely that a whole generation succumbed beneath the whip of its taskmasters. As pliant under suffering as they were arrogant in seasons of good fortune, the children of Israel knew very well how to appease their conquerors, how to insinuate themselves into their confidence, and transform servitude into a bearable subjection, sometimes even to their advantage. Even in the first years of the captivity at Babylon, we see Daniel brought before Nabuchodonosor [1] and put at the head of the Magi; later on, Mardochai becomes the Minister of Xerxes, [2] Esther is a King's wife, [3] Tobias and his nephew, Anchialus, [4] are officers of the Palace, and Nehemiah is a cup-bearer. [5]

Without aspiring to such high fortune, the common people, little by little, lifted themselves out of their servile state; prudently guided by their Prophets and resigned to their lot, they were laying the foundation of better days by toil and the fruitfulness of their race: "Build for yourselves houses and dwell therein," Jeremy had said; "plant gardens and eat their fruits, marry and

---

[1] Dan. v. 11.   [2] Esther viii. 2, 8, 9, 15.   [3] Esther ii. 17.
[4] Tobias, Greek text, in the Septuagint Bible, i. 13-22.
[5] Nehem. ii. 1.

bear children; give wives to your sons, and husbands to your daughters; multiply in the regions where you abide, and let not your numbers diminish." [1] The Prophet went still further. In Jehovah's Name he charged the Jews, dwelling in infidel cities, to draw down the divine blessings thereon. "Strive, by your toil, to make prosperous the city into which you have been taken, and pray unto the Lord for it, because your peace is concerned therewith." [2]

Such wise counsels bore their fruit; by their unity and their industry the Jews soon rose from this wretched condition: many even became wealthy. At Ecbatana, Raguel possessed great riches.[3] Among the many Jews established at Rhages, upon the eastern frontiers of Media, there was only one poor man, Gabael;[4] and even he succeeded in repairing his fortunes, so that he was able to pay back a considerable sum, — ten talents of silver,[5] — which Tobias had lent him.

It was to commerce that the Jews owed this sudden prosperity: it belonged to them by instinct; they had a genius for it; and this aptitude, restrained up to this time by the prescriptions of the Law, has ever since been the distinctive trait of the sons of Israel. So powerful, even, became this new attraction that it lessened their sighs after their lost country. We notice this when Cyrus grants leave to the captives to return to Jerusalem. Only a small number make use of the permission;[6] by far the greater part of the nation remain on the unhallowed soil; they multiply, and extending little by little over the whole inhabited world, they come to form a body of people as vast as they are various, — the Jews of the Dispersion.[7]

But as the riches of these exiles increased, their destiny became ever more uncertain. As they were forbidden by

---

[1] Jer. xxix. 5, 6.   [2] Jer. xxix. 7.
[3] Tob. (Greek text, in the Septuagint Bible) i. 14, 16, 20.
[4] Tob. (Vulg.) i. 17.   [5] Tob. (Vulg.), iv. 21–22; v. 3; ix. 6.
[6] Esdr. i. 5; ii. The exiles who took advantage of Cyrus' Edict to return to Judea belonged, for the most part, to the tribes of Juda and Benjamin; they did not number over 50,000 all told.

[7] This expression, commonly used to designate such Jews as settled in Pagan territory, is to be found in many passages of Scripture (2 Mac. i. 27; James i. 1; 1 Pet. i. 1; John vii. 35).

the Law to mingle with Gentiles, they remained a distinct nation, and by that very fact made more conspicuous to other men, marked out for envy and persecution. The monarchs of the Orient alone were so far superior to popular passions as to be able to estimate the industrial genius of the Hebrews at its real value; they alone had power enough to protect the children of Israel; and they were wise enough to attach this people to their own persons by making the fortune of the Jews depend upon the power which protected them.

The colonies afforded the richest field for the business enterprise of the Jews, and from them the Assyrian kings reaped the greatest advantages. After extending their empire till it included very many nations not hitherto submissive to their rule, these princes were in continual expectation of new uprisings. To avert this danger in a measure, as soon as any country came under their dominion, they transported its inhabitants to some far-off region, and gave their lands to foreigners in their stead. But in these transfers of whole peoples the iron chain was never strong enough to keep some from escaping its hold. These remnants of the former population, dearly attached to the soil, were only intent upon recovering what had been wrested from them by force; consequently it was to the interest of the new-comers to be on their guard against treachery, to foresee and to denounce the plottings of their neighbors,—in a word, to fulfil the duties of a wary police-force in every land; for any revolt which threatened the supreme power was a menace to their own security as well. By this far-seeing policy the kings of Nineveh and Babylon managed to assure peace along their borders by making the foreign communities which they founded there the bulwarks of established government.

The Jews, more than any other people, were successful in this office. The pliancy of their character fitted them for the hardest trials; their thirst for wealth and their indefatigable activity in acquiring it made them forget the miseries of exile: far from discouraging them, these struggles only increased their vigorous life. The Assyrian monarchs, and the Persians after them, were not likely to neglect such valuable auxiliaries; everywhere they intrusted their colonial enterprises to them, at first banishing them to these distant parts by force, but very soon only adding to attractions already sufficient in themselves to tempt these traders any distance in search of gain.[1] Upon soil thus delivered into their possession, whole tribes, transported in a body, could multiply and enrich themselves unhindered. Doubtless, it was not the fatherland; but neither was it any longer exile in the midst of haughty conquerors, like that they had known of old; for the colony thus formed, remained Jewish in manners and religion, and always was governed according to the Law of Moses. The Israelites, in their happiness at recovering thus much of their independence, became deeply attached to these territories, which they found at first both untenanted and insecure, and they defended them from attacks from without by a system of military outposts courageously maintained.

The successful results of the policy adopted by the kings of Assyria were not lost upon Alexander. Hardly had he become master of the East when the Jewish race was marked out for favor, with ample recognition of the unhoped-for aid it offered to him. The Jews, hastening to answer the first summons, fairly thronged Alexandria, where the conqueror accorded them the same privileges he gave the Macedonians.[2] After his reign they continued to reach out over the land of the Pharaohs, just as in the days of Joseph and Moses. Two of the five districts of Alexandria were peopled by them, and throughout all Egypt, from the Delta to the farthest

[1] The proposals made by Sennacherib to the citizens of Jerusalem prove that the deportation of the inhabitants, as accepted by the conquered and arranged in concert with the Conqueror, was carried out in a spirit as humane as it was politic: " Do you make an alliance with me and come over to my side ; then shall each one of you eat the fruit of his own vine and fig-tree and drink the water of his own well, until I come to carry you away to a land like unto your own, a land of corn and wine, a land abounding in bread and vines " (4 Kings xviii. 31-32).

[2] Josephus, *Contra Apionem*, ii. 4 ; *Bellum Judaicum*, ii. 18, 7 ; Quintus Curtius, iv. 8.

recesses of the Thebaïs, the traveller would find Jewish synagogues with their girdles of palm-trees. During the first century after Jesus Christ their number touched a million, which is to say an eighth part of the population which then dwelt along the Nile.[1] Like the Ptolemies in Egypt, the successors of Alexander in Syria followed the same policy. Antiochus the Great transported two thousand Jewish families from Mesopotamia into Asia Minor, and thereby transformed Lycia and Phrygia into a region entirely devoted to the Seleucides.[2] In Antioch, whither Seleucus Nicator did his best to attract them, Israelites composed the principal body of the nation.[3]

This Dispersion of Israel never ceased for more than five centuries to send forth new branches from the parent stock, always moving forward to take possession of the most distant lands, — and this in such numbers that in Strabo's time there was no city nor harbor in which the Jews had not established themselves, no corner where this tenacious people had not managed to get a foothold.[4] They were equally prosperous in the empires of Rome and of Parthia. In the territory of the latter, who were then supreme in India as far as the Euphrates, the Jews, accustomed of old to the Persian yoke, soon ingratiated themselves with the new victors. But it was the Roman Empire, after all, which offered the greatest advantages to them: their "ghettos" and their synagogues were to be seen in every land, — along the shores washed by the Mediterranean; in the Crimea, where frequent tumulary stones still mark the sites of former Jewish communities;[5] in Arabia;[6] and even in the heart of Africa.[7]

[1] Philo, *In Flaccum*, vi. [2] Josephus, *Antiquitates*, xii. 3, 4.
[3] Josephus, *Antiquitates*, xii. 3, 1; *Bellum Judaicum*, ii. 18, 15; vii. 3, 2–4.
[4] Strabo, quoted by Josephus (*Antiquitates*, xiv. 7, 2).
[5] Stephani, in the *Bulletin de l'Académie de Saint-Pétersbourg*, 1860, vol. i. pp. 244–246; *Corpus Inscriptionum Græcarum*, vol. ii. add., p. 1005, No. 2114; p. 1006, No. 2126; p. 1008, No. 2131; Chwolson, *Pierres tumulaires hébraïques de la Crimée*, in the Memoirs of the Academy of Sciences of St. Petersburg, viii. series, ix. (1886). No. 7.
[6] Mishna, Shabb. 6, 6. [7] Acts viii. 27.

Herod Agrippa, in a letter to Caligula,[1] and Saint Luke in the Acts,[2] both enumerate the lands where Jewish colonists had settled; we find them among the Parthians, Medes, and Elamites; in Mesopotamia, Cappadocia, and Pontus; all through Asia Minor, Syria, Phœnicia, Egypt, Cyrene; along the African coast; in the provinces of Greece; from Thessaly to the Peloponnesus; among the islands in Eubœa, Cyprus, and Crete. So spread abroad and bound together by strong commercial ties, the Jews encircled the world without restrictions, and wellnigh without fear of the future, for no power could attack the whole race. If one town, even if a province, slaughtered its Jewish inhabitants, others soon came to replace them, more numerous than their persecutors; they comforted themselves in their sorrows by repeating the words of their Sibyl, —

"All lands, all seas, are filled with thee:
If all men are thy foes, 't is because thou excellest them all." [3]

Furthermore, these violent attacks were never long continued. Adroit enough to foresee them, and wary in avoiding them, the Jews did not then lead the precarious existence to which they have often been subjected in Christian or Mohammedan lands. The rights given them were generally respected. Alexander, as we have seen, granted them the same privileges as the Greeks. Their successors confirmed, even enlarged, the favors bestowed on them by their capital city. In the countries which for a time made up the Macedonian Empire, — in Greece, Egypt, Syria; indeed, in all Asia, from the Indies to the Archipelago, — the Israelites as a general rule obtained the rights of citizenship, with the right of governing themselves by their own laws. They had courts of their own, independent of the ordinary magistrates; they had their presiding officials, called variously, according to the locality, Alabarchs, Archontes, Genarchs, or Ethnarchs, who

---

[1] Philo, *Legat. ad Caium*, p. 587.
[2] Acts ii. 5–11.
[3] *Oracula Sibyllina*, iii. 271, 272.

directed the affairs of the community and acted in its name.[1]

If any town denied them these prerogatives, they assumed the air of a persecuted people, lamented their unhappy lot, all the time intriguing, buying up powerful patrons, and never abandoning their importunities until they had succeeded in at least obtaining perfect liberty for their religious rites. This simple concession sufficed to make them a privileged class; for it exempted them from military service and the taxes which were incompatible with the Mosaic prescriptions.[2] It was forbidden to summon them before the court during their festival seasons.[3] When any distribution of food was ordered by the city government, they were allowed the right of refusing wheat, wine, and oil, contaminated by the touch of Pagan hands, and could claim an equivalent sum of money as their compensation; they even got permission to have this price paid them on some other day besides the Sabbath.[4]

These franchises were in full vigor throughout the whole Roman Empire, and attracted thither Jews from all parts. Their fortunes and their business enterprise assumed such political importance under Julius Cæsar that the Dictator thought it the wisest plan to follow the same policy which Alexander had adopted in governing them. By four successive edicts he assured to them, not only their entire independence, but other privileges as well. The sons of Israel were permitted to live openly according to their laws and customs, might hold assemblies, and collect taxes for the Temple at Jerusalem, or for the support of the synagogue.[5] His tolerance went so far as to exempt them from the tax-levies every seventh year, so that they might be free to observe the rest of the Sabbatic Year, and not be forced to gather any of the fruit

---

[1] Cicero, *Ad Atticum*, ii. 17; Juvenal, *Satiræ*, i. 130; Josephus, *Bellum Judaicum*, vii. 3, 3; *Antiquitates*, xiii. 6, 7; xiv. 7, 2; 10, 17; xvii. 12, 4; xix. 5, 2; xx. 5, 2, 3.
[2] Josephus, *Antiquitates*, xiv. 10, 12.
[3] Id. xvi. 6, 4.   [4] Id. xii. 6, 4.   [5] Id. xiv. 10, 8.

of their lands.[1] The High Priest of Jerusalem was recognized as patron of the dispersed Israelites, and had the right of setting forth his clients' complaints before the Emperor's or the Proconsul's tribunal, always finding free access thereto.[2]

These ordinances of Cæsar were confirmed by Augustus, and decreed anew by Claudius, after the persecutions of Tiberius and Caligula. All this resulted in constituting the Jews as a real national body existing throughout all the empire, for even in the cities, which had kept their own autonomy, the magistrates conformed their conduct towards this people with that of Rome, in so far that the intervention of the High Priest was sufficient to put a stop to any undertaking against the liberties of Israel. This was the case at Ephesus and Delos; when they tried to subject the Jews to their common laws they were compelled by the Consul Dolabella to dispense them from military service, in order that they might observe that law which forbade them to touch unclean meats, or to march on the Sabbath day.[3] Everywhere, in fact, the Roman governors evidenced the greatest care to consult the wishes of Judaism, so powerful did they feel it to be! If but one of them attempted to meddle with their property, or with the rights of some synagogue, the Israelites of all lands, particularly those of the capital, stirred up their countrymen to combine against the aggressor; thereupon followed nothing but tumults, deputations, suppliant letters, and apologies; once the agitation had become general, it was prolonged with an obstinacy which overthrew all obstacles.

Formidable as the Jewish influence appeared to magistrates in the provinces, their power was no less dreaded by the merchants of the cities where they did business. In every branch of traffic the close union between members of their race, and their connections, bringing them into touch, commercially, with the whole world, gave them a notable advantage over their rivals. As soon as

---

[1] Josephus, *Antiquitates*, xiv. 10, 6.   [2] Id. xiv. 10, 2, 3.
[3] Id. xiv. 10, 12–14.

they appeared in any place they first managed to get the small tradesmen's business into their hands; after that they would begin quietly and by degrees to get control of the more considerable business interests; finally, they even took charge of the farming of taxes; for although in principle, the receipt of public moneys was reserved to the Romans, oftentimes the wealth and ability of the Jews made it necessary to ask their aid. In the region about the Euphrates they exercised such predominance that diplomacy made use of them as intermediaries.[1]

The important position they occupied in finance and trade deepened their disdain for all not of their blood. They forgot their Prophets' counsellings, that they should not separate their fortune from that of the cities where they dwelt, but love them and pray for them. With no longer any higher motive than their individual interests in view, they regarded discretion as superfluous, and hurried to Rome whenever any difficulty arose between them and the Gentiles. The favor they found with the imperial officials was enough to win them popular hatred; every ingenuity was exercised in blackening their character, depicting them as infamous alike in the conduct of life and from their origin. In Egypt, where we have seen how powerful they were, the story went that in olden times this whole race, when infected by leprosy and every loathsome disease, took refuge in the temples, and lived there as beggars. Heaven, angered by this profanation, scourged the land with epidemics and sterility, whereupon Bocchoris, who was then reigning, sent to consult Ammon; the oracle made answer that they must purify the sanctuaries, drive this impious people into the desert, and drown those who were contaminated, since the sight of them was unendurable to the Sun: only by this means could the soil recover its fertility.[2] Elsewhere other calumnies, not less odious,

---

[1] Josephus, *Bellum Judaicum*, i. 13, 5; *Antiquitates*, xiv. 13, 5; xv. 2, 3. At Alexandria the grain trade and, consequently, all bread stuffs destined for Rome were intrusted to them.

[2] Josephus, *Contra Apionem*, i. 34.

were repeated. Their synagogues, without idols or sacrifices, offered occasion to accuse them of atheism; the life they led apart from the general people was sufficient proof, men said, of their savage and inhospitable manners, and their hatred for humankind.[1]

But if the Jews of the Dispersion excited the aversion of the peoples among whom they lived, the latter were exercising a great influence upon the race. While their brethren of Jerusalem were multiplying Observances about their Law, those outside the City, far removed from the Temple, mingling daily with Orientals, Greeks, and Romans, subject in part to their laws, dealing with them through commerce, little by little dispensed themselves from rites which had become impracticable in their new surroundings. In Palestine, a land very little travelled, without great marts or harbors, separated from other regions by mountains and deserts, it was possible to avoid contact with the foreigner, as if one was contaminated by his touch; if traffic was regarded as incompatible with the strict observance of the Law, such rigorous views were bearable there; but it was not the same in Pagan countries, where the Rabbis themselves forbore any preaching of the "Pharisaic Separation." Far from treating merchants as Canaanites, they undervalued the pastoral life of their ancestors, and reserved all their praise for trade. "There is no meaner calling than agriculture," said Rabbi Eleazar, as he was looking at a field ripe for the sickle; and Rabbi Rabh added: "All the harvests of the world are not to be compared with commerce."[2] With these novel sentiments, the Jews began to adopt the language of the lands they lived in; Hebrew sounded so strange to their ears that the service of the synagogue came to be conducted in Greek, and the Holy Books read only in the Septuagint Version. As sacrifices could not be performed outside the Temple, they retained only a spiritual worship, in which Jehovah, the one God, was adored in prayer and song.

[1] Josephus, *Contra Apionem*, ii. 14; Diodorus of Sicily, *Bibl.*, xl. 3.
[2] *Jebhamoth*, f. 63, 1.

THE JEWS OF THE DISPERSION. 49

But these changes in no way encroached upon either doctrine or religion. Disengaged from practices which were inconvenient outside of Jerusalem, belief in the Eternal, the Law, and the Holy Word to these scattered Jews still remained the object of a worship from which nothing could ever detach them. In the money-lenders' shops, as in the homes of wealthy tradesmen, there was the same love of country, the same hopes. The abundance of offerings which the synagogues collected for the Temple shows how rich in fruits their faith continued to be; but they were not content with sending this tribute to the Holy City:[1] every year the deputation which carried it up to Jerusalem was accompanied by numbers of pilgrims, every son of Israel going at least once in his life to sacrifice in the only spot on earth where victims were acceptable to God.

This piety of the Jews manifested itself at every opportunity. Their first care was to establish a church in the cities where they were settled. If they lacked means to build a sanctuary, they set aside at least some meeting-place, some enclosure near a fountain, or on the heights, where they could go through with their ablutions and pray undisturbed. In the wealthy cities, in Alexandria and in Antioch, it was regarded as a point of honour that their synagogues should rival the Pagans' temples in the point of richness.[2] Their zeal was no less striking in the fidelity with which they observed such legal prescriptions as appeared compatible with exile. A life in which religion was so predominant resulted in giving the Jews a great ascendency over the Pagans. The loftiness of their dogmas, their pure system of morality, their brotherly helpfulness and austere worship,— all these were powerful attractions to souls wearied of Paganism, and hungering for some new thing. Probably Josephus has not over-

---

[1] These contributions were looked upon as sacred by the magistrates of the Empire; accordingly, the robber who, after stealing any sum belonging thereto, sought refuge in the temples, could be seized as a sacrilegious offender and handed over to the Jews (Josephus, *Antiquitates*, xvi. 6, 4).
[2] Philo, *In Flaccum*, ii. 528.

drawn the picture he has left us of the influence of Judaism: " For now a long time it has been the fashion, even among the people, to imitate our piety. There is no town, whether Greek or Barbarian, nor any nation, whither the custom of keeping the Sabbath has not penetrated, — not one where our fasts, our lighted torches, our abstinence from forbidden meats, is not a received custom. Others strive to imitate our unitedness of soul, our generosity, our activity in the arts, our courage in suffering everything for the Law. What is most admirable is that, with no intrinsic charm of its own, the Law has been so powerful, has been spread abroad among all men, even as is God in the world." [1]

The only point in which Josephus exaggerates is in denying any attractions to the Law. For the senses, certainly it offers little that is seductive; but to numberless souls despairing of light from Paganism, it was the morning sun dispelling the gloomy night. The One and Only God, terrible in His Majesty,[2] but overflowing with loving-kindnesses,[3] "His word, sweet as honey to the lips," [4] "the Law without spot," [5] mirror of His eternal justice, the ceremonies as holy as they were imposing, — everything in Israel's Faith astonished and attracted them. The sanctuaries of the Jews of the Dispersion impressed the idea of an altogether spiritual religion; for here there was no altar to be seen as in Jerusalem, no bloody sacrifices, but only a Book treated as worthy of all homage and piously interpreted to the people, only prayers with the sweet, touching music of their Psalms. The Mosaic worship showed itself in its most favorable light, freed from the coarse shell which Jesus Christ had disowned. Even more than the majestic austerity of their worship, more than their dogmas and their virtues, their certitude that they possessed the Truth gave the Jews an irresistible sway. The hardier minds

---

[1] Josephus, *Contra Apionem*, ii. 39.
[2] Deut. x. 17; Ps. xlvi. 3; xxviii. 3, etc.
[3] Num. xiv. 18; Ps. lxxxv. 5, 15, etc.   [4] Ps. xviii. 11; cxviii. 103.
[5] Ps. xviii. 8.

of Paganism might jeer at their credulity, if they pleased; but in misfortune, or at the approach of danger, all eyes turned towards the synagogue; many hastened to its doors, and once entering, left it no more.

Jewish society, gloomy as it appeared outwardly, captivated the Pagans by the peculiar charm of its life and its incessant novelty. Israelitish gatherings were to the outsider, scenes of vivid interest; nowhere else was the latest news known so soon, and nowhere were ideas and passionate dreams as ardent and effective as here. It was a rare thing not to meet some foreign guest on his journeys, the magnates of finance going from one city to another, missionaries whom zeal for the Law impelled "to traverse lands and seas."[1] On being invited to speak before them, the new-comers would recount what they had seen by the way, and rehearse the doctrine of celebrated masters. Still oftener, the head man of the community would appear in the chair to publish some message from the great Sanhedrin or from neighboring colonies of Jews. By these daily communications, each "ghetto" kept in contact with the whole world; for as Judaism extended like roots from one stem, the slightest movement was transmitted through the entire body, from India to the Atlantic coasts, from Africa to the regions of the North.

Another attraction of the synagogue lay in the fact that its members still enjoyed a certain independence, a life of their own. While all through the Empire, prying laws determined upon just what conditions a society should be tolerated, — the number of its members, the frequency of its meetings, and the largest sum to be allowed in its treasury, — Jewish associations were made an exception; regarded as purely religious assemblies, they were formed and governed openly, with perfect freedom from these restraints.[2]

Such privileges as these, added to the superiority of the Law, explain the favor with which Mosaic law was regarded. In the large cities there were as many friends

---

[1] Matt. xxiii. 15.   [2] Philo, *Legat. ad Caium*, M. 592.

of the Jews as the Jews themselves. The women especially were attracted by the mystery of the synagogue, its peaceful atmosphere, and the kindly brotherliness they found there, as well as by the songs which fell so gratefully upon their ears. There was no trouble about obtaining some knowledge of Jehovah's Law from the daughters of Israel; and finding that woman's condition was freer and more honorable under its dispensations, they embraced the new faith in great numbers. At Damascus, almost all the women were proselytes;[1] and in Thyatira and Thessalonica,[2] Saint Paul, on entering the Jews' place of prayer, found women to be in the majority; in Rome the number of converts among the patrician ladies was so well known that Ovid advises his readers, if they wish to see the renowned beauties of the capital, to stand guard at the doors of the synagogues.[3]

The masters of Israel encouraged this movement among the Pagan ladies; for the conversions of women, always sincere, and exciting no great attention from outsiders, gave rise to no embarrassing or troublesome consequences. But among the men they had learned by experience to expect self-interested motives: some came to Judaism with the view of gaining the privileges we have been speaking of, — exemption from taxes, public duties, and military service; others in the hope of making rich marriages.[4] There were "the Proselytes of the Royal Table," who became Jews the better to pay court to the princes of Israel;[5] "the Lions' Proselytes," whom reverse of fortune or some affliction had impelled to seek Jehovah, like those Assyrian colonists who had been converted in order to escape the lions of Samaria;[6] "Proselytes of Fear," as, for instance, the tribune Metilius, who followed the Mosaic system in order to save his life.[7]

These nicknames which the Rabbis were ever invent-

---

[1] Josephus, *Bellum Judaicum*, ii. 20, 2.
[2] Acts xvi. 14; xvii. 4.   [3] Ovid, *Ars Amat.*, i. 76.
[4] Josephus, *Antiquitates*, xvi. 7, 6; xx. 7, 2, 3.
[5] *Kiddouschin*, iv. 1.   [6] 4 Kings xvii. 26.
[7] Josephus, *Bellum Judaicum*, ii. 17, 25.

ing for them, show with what distrust they welcomed Pagan men. In their thinking it was not enough to be attracted by the pure doctrine of one only God,— for many sects taught the same dogma, and might win away the new converts. Such were the schools of Alexandria, which were filled with deserters. From the annoyance caused them by these apostasies, the Rabbis of Palestine came to detest the proselytes; they called them the leprosy of Israel,[1] accused them of delaying the appearance of the Messiah,[2] and affirmed that their descendants were to be regarded with suspicion down to the fortieth generation.[3] Even in Jerusalem, however, these prejudices did not blind the minds of all. Hillel and Gamaliel, on the contrary, displayed great zeal in the matter of conversions, and Simon, Gamaliel's son, was fond of repeating: "If a Pagan come forward to enter the Covenant, give him your hand and draw him under the wings of the Divinity."[4] In the Dispersion, far from repulsing the Proselytes, very many Rabbis were only seeking how to smooth the way for them; with this view, they declared that circumcision and the observance of all the legal precepts[5] were not indispensable conditions for participating in the salvation of Israel. Many went so far as to dissuade

[1] *Jebam*, 47, 4; *Kiddouschin*, 70, 6.
[2] Lightfoot, *Horæ Hebraicæ*, in Matt. xxiii. 5.
[3] *Jalkuth Ruth*, f. 163, a.
[4] Jo-t, *Judenthum*, i. 447.
[5] The extent of the obligations imposed on proselytes varied with the times. According to the Law, a foreigner might be admitted to fellowship with Israelites if he promised to keep the Sabbath (Exod. xx. 10), never to blaspheme the Name of Jehovah, and not to partake of blood or of a suffocated beast (Lev. xxvii. 12; xxiv. 16). After the destruction of Jerusalem the Rabbis taught that the Law obliged Jews alone. God had revealed to Noë the only commandments which could be made binding on all nations. This special code for the Gentiles comprised seven interdictions, — against blasphemy, idolatry, homicides, sins against nature, blood taken as food, robbery, and sedition. In the epoch of the Apostles there is good reason to believe that the proselytes' obligations were limited to the precepts determined by the assembly of Jerusalem: "It hath seemed good to the Holy Ghost and to us to lay no further burden upon you than these things which are necessary, to wit, that you abstain from things sacrificed to idols, from blood, from strangled creatures, and from fornication" (Acts xv. 28-29).

them from undergoing the bloody incision;[1] the only important thing, in their eyes, was to acknowledge Jehovah as the only true God, to worship Him, and meditate upon His Law, without adopting Jewish rites: this was what was meant by a person's remaining "a Proselyte of the Gate."[2] Those who were urged by the more rigid and zealous doctors to undergo circumcision, to take part in the numerous ablutions and in the offering of sacrifices, became "Proselytes of Justice,"[3] and were in no way distinguishable from pure Israelites.

Whatever part these newly initiated may have taken in the Observances, they were all deeply affected by the religion and morality of the Mosaic law; for it was this loftiest side of Revelation which the dispersed Jews were most eager to spread abroad. As skilful in their preaching as in their commercial dealings, they adapted their teaching to the dispositions of the Pagans about them, and painted the Jewish doctrine so happily as to make it acceptable and quite natural to very opposite minds.

The progress of this movement is most easily followed at Alexandria. There the Jews had recognized the fact that, in order to convince minds, it was not enough to speak the same language as those they were addressing; for three centuries their Sacred Books, translated into Greek, had been accessible to all, but without results: the holy text, though known to a few of the learned, was still a dead letter to average men of all ranks. The masters of Israel were clever enough to conceive that they could reach this multitude by calling the authority of Greek genius in support of Revelation, and confirmed their dogmas by explaining them in the words of Pagan poets and philosophers. Thus, by the use of supposititious works, Linus, Pythagoras, Hesiod, Homer, and Plato were made to preach faith in the supreme God, and a Messiah who should bring glory and happiness to the world.

[1] Josephus, *Antiquitates*, xx. 2, 5.
[2] This name was in allusion to that verse of Exodus (xx. 10): "The seventh day thou shalt do no work, neither thou nor thy son . . . nor the stranger that is within thy gates."
[3] They were also known by the name of "Sons of the Covenant."

It was through a preference which was due at once to the mistiness of his history and his marvellous deeds that Orpheus became, so to say, the principal patron of this kind of preaching. A collection of sentences had circulated for some time in the Schools, under the name of "Orphic Wisdom," furnishing many a text for the orators; from it they extracted their lofty thoughts concerning Jupiter, — who embraces all power in his person, — and on the perpetuity and recompenses of the future life. An hundred and sixty years before Jesus Christ, the Jewish Aristobulus, philosopher and courtier under the Ptolemies, inserted among these poems a few lines in praise of Moses' Law, and retouched the ancient verses with phrases of Jewish coloring. Thereupon, pursuing his plan, he made shift to show that the Old Testament was the single source whence the poets and sages of Paganism had drawn their inspiration. A fragment of these Orphic Songs which has come down to us, gives us an opportunity of studying this forger of antiquities at work.

"God in Himself I know not, for a cloud envelopeth Him;
But His Ten Commandments declare Him to Men;
Mortal man hath never beheld Him;
One alone hath been so favored, — he who was born of the waters [Moses],
He hath received from Heaven its knowledge on a twofold Table." [1].

But Orpheus himself was to yield place to the ancient Sibyl. Throughout the entire world, at Babylon, in Libya, at Delphi, Samos, Troy, and in Italy, [2] this voice which laid bare future things, was listened to religiously. The Jews were not slow to make use of prophecies so revered; they constrained even these to testify in their favor. In the Third Book of the Sibylline Oracles we find traces of this work, done by a Jew of Egypt in the

[1] Eusebius, *Præparatio Evangelica*, xiii. 12; cf. S. Justin, *De Monarchia*, 2; *Cohortatio ad Græcos*, 15.
[2] Plato knew of but one Sibyl (*Phædrus*, p. 244). Others name two, others four, and others ten, — those of Babylon, Libya, Delphi, Cimmerium, Erythræ, Samos, Cumæ, Troy, Phrygia, and Tibur (Pauly, *Real Encyclopädie:* SIBYLLÆ).

reign of Ptolemy Philometor (about the year 150 before Christ). The Sibyl here makes Noë's daughter-in-law relate the whole history of the world after the Tower of Babel. Stories from the Old Testament are jumbled with Pagan theogonies; the sons of Abraham mingle with the Titans and the gods of Hesiod; the predictions of Pagan oracles are put side by side with those of the Seers of Judea. All these prophecies agree in foretelling misfortunes nigh at hand, whose sole cause is the idolatry of the people; no other hope is held out to humanity save in a return to the true God, to the God of the Hebrews.[1]

If we read through the Jewish literature of Alexandria, which was so rich at this epoch and in the following period, we find the same method, — the same eagerness to show that all truth springs from Israel, the same address in making the different aspects of their respective doctrines either stand out in bolder relief, or sink out of sight, according as their purpose demanded. "Since our laws," says Josephus, "embody the perfectest justice, we ought, thanks to them, to become friends of all men and well-wishers towards all."[2]

This influence, which was so active at Alexandria, made itself felt, under various forms, in every place where Judaism flourished. Everywhere a throng of proselytes crowded the "ghetto," frequented the synagogue, and thus insensibly drinking in the faith of Israel, partook of the pure truth. In the ranks of these new believers the Gospel received the warmest welcome. Like the sons of Abraham, they too awaited the Messiah, and with Him salvation; but they were not obstinate in the belief that His Kingdom must be at Jerusalem, nor did they dream night and day of a restoration of the throne of David and the Maccabees. They accepted the universal predominance of the Jewish race as foretold by the Rabbis, but without longing for the realization of these prophecies. When from synagogue to synagogue the rumor spread

---

[1] *Oracula Sibyllina*, iii. 97–807.   [2] Josephus, *Antiquitates*, xvi. 6, 8.

that the Christ had appeared, telling men of God in terms higher than those of the Law, calling Him Father, and claiming, for Him and in His Name, a worship of spirit and of truth, — when it was known that He rejected the fleshly wrappings of Mosaic teaching, thus retaining nought but its pure morality,— the proselytes thronged to embrace the New Faith as one man. Josephus alludes to this fact with considerable sorrow: "Many Greeks have embraced our Law; some have remained faithful, others have been unable to bear its austerities, and have fallen away."[1] And so, all over the earth, the Jewish communities were as vast fields open to the workmen of the Gospel; according to the Master's words, "the harvest was already white,"[2] only waiting for the Lord's servants to gather it into the heavenly storehouses.

[1] Josephus, *Contra Apionem*, ii. 10. [2] John iv. 35.

CHAPTER IV.

SAINT STEPHEN.

To prepare the way for Christianity was the mission of the Jews of the Dispersion all over the Pagan world. In Jerusalem, too, they had quite as important a part to play. Known in the Holy City by the name of Hellenists, and marked off from the Hebrews by their different language, it was natural that they should wish to have synagogues of their own. Many of them had believed in the Gospel from the very first;[1] every Passover, pilgrims coming "from the Dispersion," listened to the Apostles' preaching and entered the fold of Jesus. These Jews, half Greek in character, equalled and even surpassed in numbers the Galileans and Hebraïsts, among the first generation of Christians.

Love for the Saviour kept these members united in one body, however divided from other points of view, and, according to the expression in the Acts, there was only one heart, one soul, in the Church.[2] But though Grace was then so mighty, it did not destroy those prepossessions which sway the wisest among us. Now, none of these prejudices was more firmly rooted in Israel than the mutual distrust which separated the Hebrew Jews from the Hellenists. The latter, as we have seen, although invincibly attached to their dogmas, had lost their scruples about observing the Pharisaic laws, owing to their intercourse with Pagans; they cultivated the profane arts,[3] and strove to reconcile the austerity of the Law

---

[1] Acts ii. 5, 9, 10, 11, 41.   [2] Acts iv. 32.
[3] Especially at Alexandria the Jews applied themselves thus to Greek literature. There we see Hellenists composing tragedies on the life of Moses and the abduction of Dinah; another writes an epic poem on Jeru-

with the more amiable manners of Greece. Indeed, there were some few exceptions to the general body which was so faithful; these went so far as to appear to have apostatized, leading a Pagan life and trying to efface the sign of the Covenant imprinted on their flesh. These fallings-off aroused the liveliest resentment among their brethren of Palestine, and kept alive an antipathy for them which broke forth on more than one occasion. Even in the bosom of the Church, this feeling of opposition, long restrained by Christian charity, finally made itself manifest. "The number of the disciples increasing, there arose a murmuring of the Greeks against the Hebrews, for that their widows were neglected in the distribution of what was given out each day."[1]

The Law had not left the widows uncared for; one portion was set aside for them out of every harvest reaped, from the tithes collected every three years, out of the feast-day banquets and the spoils taken from the enemy.[2] After the Captivity, the Sanhedrin pushed these charitable practices still farther, and consecrated a share in the treasures of the Temple to the succor and support of widows: each family and every community had its own to sustain. The Church followed the same usage; but it came about that the head men, who were all Palestine Hebrews, found it much easier to discover poor people dwelling in their own parts and speaking the same tongue as themselves; hence they appeared to be less assiduous in their care for foreign women. The neglect was only apparent, but it was keenly felt, and complaints were soon heard from the converted Greeks.

On learning it, the Twelve resolved to pacify their minds by proving their own disinterestedness. To this end they gathered the disciples together.

"It is not fitting," they said, "that we should abandon

salem; Demetrius and Eupolemos are authors of profane histories. The most illustrious and at the same time the most prolific of all was the Alexandrian Philo.

[1] Acts vi. 1.
[2] Deut. xxiv. 19-21; xiv. 29; xxvi. 11, 12; xvi. 11, 14; 2 Mac. viii. 28-30.

the word of God to serve tables.¹ Therefore, brethren, choose from your number seven men of well-known uprightness, full of the Holy Ghost and of wisdom, to whom we may commit this ministry. For our part, we will give ourselves wholly to prayer and the ministry of the word." ²

The congregation was pleased with this discourse, and Stephen, a man full of faith, was forthwith elected, and with him six others, — Philip, Prochorus, Nicanor, Timon, Parmenas, and Nicholas, a proselyte of Antioch. As they are Greeks by name, these faithful men were apparently all Hellenists; that they were chosen to the exclusion of Hebrews, not only goes to show how the number of Jews of the Dispersion had multiplied in the Church, it also testifies to the charity of their brethren of Judea, who made no demands for their share in this new office. Together, they presented the newly elect to the Apostles, and the latter laid their hands upon them in prayer.

The development of the Hierarchy, which we shall see gradually growing in the Church, was begun by this sacramental act. Hitherto the Apostles, in common and without distinction, had exercised the various orders which they had received from him in whom resides the fulness of the Priesthood. Now, obliged to share their powers, they took good heed that no innovations should arise which might wound the converted Hebrews; and this is the reason why, while they remained united at the head of the community, like the elders of the synagogues, they instituted below them seven Deacons, whose title recalls the servers at Jewish gatherings. The charge of

---

[1] As τράπεζα meant not only tables for eating, but those also on which the money-changers set out their coin, διακονεῖν τραπέζαις, may signify "to administer the property of the community;" but it is more probable that this expression is to be taken in the sense of "to serve at the tables where the faithful sat at meat." Doubtless the Apostles obeyed the Master's injunction literally: "Whoso would be the first, let him be the servant of all; for the Son of Man is not come to be served, but to serve, and to give His life for the redemption of many." The word καθημερινή, in the first verse of the chapter, seems to indicate that it alludes to material daily cares.

[2] Acts vi. 2-4.

SAINT STEPHEN. 61

the Christian ministers, however, was far loftier, since besides the care of the poor and the temporal affairs of the Church, other altogether spiritual functions were intrusted to them. This was the season of first fervor, when believers partook of their daily bread and of the Body of Jesus at the very same table. The first Deacons, consequently, were the dispensers of the Eucharist; with this office they had also that of preaching, for we shall see shortly one of the most illustrious of their number, Stephen, a martyr of the holy word, and another, Philip, evangelizing Samaria.

The seven, though subordinate to the Apostles so far as their powers were concerned, showed not a whit less zeal in publishing far and wide the new Reign of Jesus. " Thus the word of the Lord spread farther and farther, and the number of disciples was greatly increased in Jerusalem. There were many priests among those who obeyed the faith." The conversion of the latter is enough to give us a notion of what was then the mighty power of Grace, for among all the children of Israel there was no class more attached than the Levites to the worship whence they drew the wealth and esteem of their tribe. Though the leaders of the priesthood, and Annas' family in particular, were engrossed in politics more than in religion, the great majority of the sacrificers had not lost their zeal for the Law. The Christians' fidelity to the Mosaical rites, their steadfastness in visiting the Temple, the fervor with which they prayed thrice a day, with faces turned towards the Sanctuary, — all this could not fail to attract the attention of the priests. Furthermore, the City was ringing with their renown; the people stood in reverence of them; Gamaliel had taken up their defence: all these rays of truth were to enlighten the sons of Levi; without longer delay, many of them yielded to Grace and entered into the Kingdom of Heaven.[1]

---

[1] Critics have resorted to the strangest hypotheses to elude this testimony of S. Luke. Casaubon, with Beza and Valckenaer, proposes the reading, " A numerous throng and certain priests," πολύς τε ὄχλος καὶ τῶν ἱερέων (τινὲς) ὑπήκουον, but nothing supports this conjecture. Heinsius,

The record of these conversions marks the highest point in the favor which the Church attained in Jerusalem. Immediately thereafter, the Acts proceed to show how the opinions of the populace turned in an opposite course. The disciples, regarded hitherto as the best of people, incapable of injuring any one, are now become objects of suspicion; their doings and their words are spied upon, until soon they undergo a bloody persecution. The causes of such a sudden change are clearly seen in the sequel of the narrative in the Holy Book. The peace which the Church had enjoyed for six years was due to the fact that outwardly nothing distinguished it from Judaism; the Apostles were brought up in the Law, submitting always to its observances; and accordingly they preserved it as the natural form of their religion, at the same time imposing its precepts upon all proselytes whom they baptized. Such conduct as this gained them the good will of the people, who looked upon them as only new zealots for the Mosaical system, — Pharisees only a degree more perfect than others. But their hatred sprang into life on the day when they suspected the disciples of the Christ of harboring the intention of freeing the new Faith from the yoke of the Synagogue. The first inkling of this design did not come from any one of the Apostles; rather we may say that at that time not one of them dreamed of severing the Church from the trunk on which Jesus had engrafted it. It was but natural that this idea should arise first in the minds of Hellenists, already freed, by their foreign customs, from the galling shackles of Pharisaic Observances. Living at a distance from the Holy City, worshipping the God of Israel without bloody sacrifices, they were better prepared than were the Hebraïsts for the teachings of Jesus, which announced the separation of the two Testaments. It is not surprising

Wolf, Kuinoel, and Elsner try to make a distinction between ὄχλος τῶν ἱερέων, "the priests of the people, — the commoner sort," and the educated priests; a distinction with as little foundation as the foregoing. Others again, relying on an unfounded lection, found in a few manuscripts in cursive letters and the Syriac Version of Philoxenus, read Ἰουδαίων instead of ἱερέων.

that they should have had a presentiment of that which God's Spirit must needs enjoin upon Peter a little later on the housetop at Joppa, nor that they should have been the first to understand certain words of the Master which still remained veiled to the Apostles, — how that it was folly to put a patch of new cloth on an old garment, or new wine in old bottles,[1] and that destruction of the Temple,[2] the worship of God in spirit and in truth,[3] with an hundred other lessons of the Gospel which all carry the same moral.

But the scandal burst forth when Stephen undertook to spread these novel ideas. The hardihood of the saintly Deacon seems all the more remarkable from the fact that Peter and the Twelve kept silence. Who then gave Stephen the authority to speak and act before the Apostles? Where did he come from? Was he one of those Hellenists whose language he knew so well, and whose mind he represented? Scripture tells us nothing of his origin, and the tradition which makes him one of the seventy-two disciples[4] is founded upon testimony of too recent a date to merit our confidence. Nevertheless, it would seem that Stephen had seen and been a follower of the Lord, for he recognized Him at once when, as he was about to die, he beheld " the glory of God and Jesus standing at the right hand of His Father."[5] Properly speaking, the history of this Deacon begins with his election; thereafter his zeal was so noteworthy that he is named at the head of the seven as " a man full of Faith and of the Holy Ghost."[6] The laying on of hands so far developed this saintliness that soon the humble servant of the Church was venerated as highly as were the Apostles. Like them, " he worked great wonders and great miracles among the people."[7] Besides these supernatural gifts, Stephen possessed very advantageous resources for a preacher at that time. As he was well versed in Greek literature, he could enter into controversy with foreign

---

[1] Matt. ix. 16–17.   [2] Matt. xxiv. 1–2.   [3] John iv. 24.
[4] S. Epiphanius, *Adversus Hæreses*, xl. 50.
[5] Acts vi. 55.   [6] Acts vi. 5.   [7] Acts vi. 8.

Jews and preach before their meetings. Thus it is that the Acts [1] show him bearing the burden of the battle in the Synagogue belonging to the Roman freedmen,[2] in that of the Cyreneans,[3] and in the Alexandrians'; again we find him in the Cilicians' Synagogue, which, probably, Saul of Tarsus was wont to attend; and finally in the Synagogue of Asia,[4] head-centre for the turbulent Zealots.[5]

Religious discussions, though always ardent at Jerusalem, burned most fiercely among the Jews come from Egypt, Asia, and Greece, who were more accessible to new ideas than their brethren of Palestine. There, as everywhere else where Jews and Christians encountered each other, the dispute was continually renewed as to the belief in Jesus, that Object of the latter's adoration, but in whom the former could not acknowledge the promised Saviour, since the Law declared that a criminal dying upon the gibbet was condemned by God.[6] In answer, Stephen had only to unroll the Scriptures, contrasting

---

[1] "Certain of the synagogue, which is called that of the Freedmen, and of the Cyrenians, and of the Alexandrians, and of them that were of Cilicia and Asia, rose up against Stephen" (Acts vi. 9). This text leaves us in uncertainty as to whether S. Luke is speaking of only one synagogue frequented by Jews of these various nations, or whether each one had a separate meeting-place of its own. The latter interpretation would seem preferable in view of the fact that Jerusalem then contained 460 or 480 synagogues supported by foreign Jews (Vitringa, *Synag.*, p. 256).

[2] Since the word Λιβερτίνων is joined to Κυρηναίων and Ἀλεξανδρέων, some expositors think it refers to a city near Cyrene and Alexandria, and would have us understand thereby the Jews of Libertum, a city of Proconsular Africa, which later on sent a Bishop to take part in the Synod of Carthage in 411 (for, according to them, the expression τῆς λεγομένης Λιβερτίνων implies that this little town was not well known); but this hypothesis is gratuitous. Later on we shall see that the Jewish community of Rome, made up in great part of Freedmen, was usually designated by that name.

[3] At Cyrene one fourth of the population (Josephus, *Antiquitates*, xiv. 7, 2; xvi. 6, 1), and at Alexandria two fifths, were Jews (Philo, *Legat. in Flaccum*, 8; Josephus, *Antiquitates*, xiv. 7, 2).

[4] Proconsular Asia, an important province of the Empire, comprised Mysia, Lydia, Caria, and Phrygia; it was spoken of ordinarily as *Asia cis Taurum*.

[5] The Acts (xxi. 27) describe these Jews of Asia as prone to sedition and acts of violence.

[6] Deut. xxi. 23.

the triumphs of the long-waited-for Messiah with His sufferings, also foretold therein. Did not the Rabbis themselves recognize Jehovah's Anointed in the Man acquainted with grief announced before by Isaiah ?[1] And not only was the death of the Nazarene pictured in Scripture, His whole Life was there traced out in advance, His Ministry along the banks of Genesareth, the ungratefulness of His fellow-citizens, His ignominious death, and the glory of His tomb. It is true, this continual reference to the Prophecies made the basework of all the Apostolic discourses; but Stephen did not limit his teachings to this point. Setting the Christ far above Moses, he declared that His doctrine was independent of the rites and prescriptions of the Law; thus he even went so far as to publish openly that the Temple would cease to be the sole spot where Jehovah was willing to be worshipped.[2] The feelings of irritation in the synagogues which first listened to this preaching, were very strong. Stephen's Messiah was no longer the risen Nazarene Whom the Twelve announced, but the destroyer of the Law, of the Holy of Holies, of everything which the Lord had done for Israel.

The language of the young Deacon was all the more shocking to them because he was not content to speak as the Apostles were wont to do, — simply setting forth his doctrine; on the contrary, he defended it, conducting the discussion according to rule, and pushing the attack as well as parrying their blows. In doing this, he was the first to use the weapons of controversy in the Church's behalf, — weapons which Paul was to wield victoriously, — and more vigorously than the ordinary teaching of her pastors, more to be dreaded by the adversaries of the Faith, but at the same time, more likely to excite their bitter hatred. Stephen was to be its first victim. " Cer-

---

[1] Wunsche's *Die Leiden des Messias*, iii.
[2] Acts vi. 13-14. "This man ceaseth not to utter words against the Holy Place and against the Law; we have heard him say that Jesus the Nazarene shall destroy this place and shall change the customs which Moses hath taught us."

tain ones of the synagogue, which was called the Synagogue of the Freedmen, with others of the Cyreneans, the Alexandrians, and those from Cilicia and Asia, rose up and disputed with him, yet without being able to resist the wisdom and the Spirit that spoke in him."[1] But after all arguments were ended, the fanatics had the power of crushing this importunate truth by doing away with the man who overpowered them with its puissance; this resolution was the easier of execution because the political circumstances were all in favor of his opponents.

Tiberius was still on the throne of the Empire, growing ever more implacable as his years drew to a close. Rome's only knowledge of him was gathered from the decrees of death and confiscation which were issued from his distant retreat. Capri alone had fleeting glimpses of this old man, "his tall form bent over, his limbs worn with disease, with bald pate and a countenance pitted with ulcers, often almost covered with plasters."[2] But if those about him were trembling at the feet of Cæsar, the far-off provinces still continued to experience the effects of the moderate and intelligent policy he had adopted in governing them. We have seen that the Jews always obtained speedy justice from him; and at the time we are treating of, the Samaritans met with the same good fortune. Pilate had just repressed a religious uprising in that nation, showing great cruelty towards the people; hardly had their leaders made complaint of these massacres, when Vitellius,[3] the Legate for Syria, at once took their cause in hand: the Procurator was sent to Rome to justify himself if he could, and the government of Judea intrusted to the Legate's friend Marcellus. As the latter had only a provisional[4] title and limited powers, he could not maintain the authority of Rome with as much rigor as his predecessor. The Sanhedrin took advantage of this event to regain possession of the rights which the

---

[1] Acts vi. 9–10.   [2] Tacitus, *Annales*, iv. 57.
[3] Josephus, *Antiquitates*, xviii. 4, 2.
[4] He was only curator of the province: ἐπιμελητής (Josephus, *Antiquitates*, xviii. 4, 2).

Procurators had denied them. Taking this initiative, the Jews of Jerusalem showed themselves more fanatical than ever, more prompt to cut off from their number any one who attacked the Law. Under such circumstances, these Hellenists, whom Stephen had humiliated, now had it in their power to prepare a speedy revenge.

They restrained their ardor, however, during the sojourn of Vitellius, who had received orders to march against Aretas, king of Petra, and consequently made his quarters in the Holy City till Pentecost. On the fourth day of the Feast the Legate learned that Tiberius was no more. Forthwith he sent the army back to camp and betook himself to Antioch.[1] Relieved of his troublesome presence, with no fears of annoyance from Roman quarters, Stephen's enemies were quick to see that at the beginning of a new reign they might venture to do anything. Their first care was to excite the multitude. Men whom they had suborned went about Jerusalem telling everywhere how Stephen had uttered blasphemies against Moses and against God. This was all that was needed to arouse everybody, — people, scribes, and magistrates alike. In the height of this popular agitation the Hellenists threw themselves upon Stephen and dragged him before the Sanhedrin, which had now resumed its sittings in the Hall of Gazith. Formerly the Procurators had interdicted their meetings in this huge building, opening out on the Holy Place, since they could not station Roman guards there without violating the Porches reserved for Jews alone ; but in these days their orders were no longer observed. And so it happened that upon this spot, facing the very Holy of Holies, the first Martyr was heard and condemned.[2]

According to the Rules, the witnesses came forward one after the other, took the oath, and deposed as follows:

[1] Josephus, *Antiquitates*, xviii. 5, 3.
[2] The words of the witnesses against Stephen make us infer that they had the Temple before their eyes : " This man," they say, " ceaseth not to speak against this Holy Place." Κατὰ τοῦ τόπου τοῦ ἁγίου τούτου, is the reading authorized by the manuscripts of the Vatican and Ephrem. In the following verse we find the same expression : τὸν τόπον τοῦτον.

"This man never ceases to speak against this Holy Place and the Law; for we have heard him say that Jesus of Nazareth shall destroy this place and shall change the traditions which Moses left us."

In the trial of Jesus, the witnesses could not agree, — in this case there was no conflicting evidence; all had heard the Deacon reiterating what had been most offensive to the Pharisees in the Saviour's preaching: like his Master, he had said openly that God must be worshipped in spirit and in truth, that the time was coming when they should no longer adore Him upon this holy mountain, but in all places, wheresoever the pure of heart abide; and again, with even more freedom, following the example of Christ, he had reproached them for those Pharisaic customs which disfigured the Law, and which, the better to impose them on the people, the scribes had attributed to Moses.

Intrepidly facing his accusers, Stephen had no thought of either denying or evading these charges; but to the question of the High Priest, "Is this true?" he made no reply, for he knew they only waited a confession from him to throw themselves upon him. Now, he wished, this one last time, to make his judges listen to the words of the Christ. Accordingly, as his sole defence, he began to preach as he was wont to speak in the synagogues.

This long discourse, as preserved in the Acts, astonishes the modern reader, used to a methodical order, with clear and close arguments. At first it seems as if the Deacon lost himself in his many digressions; he appears to talk of everything except his own case. But we should not forget that all this is in the East, in the land of interminable conversations, where the principal theme is often drowned in a flood of contributing circumstances, leaving the fact to prove itself from episodes without end. Only let the speaker recall dear or glorious memories, only let him touch the soul or charm the ear, and he would be listened to without impatience as long as he chose to speak. Now and then some word, made more striking by voice or glance, sufficed to show what the orator wished to convey, and the point at which he was aiming.

Confused as Stephen's discourse appears to be, this mass of historical details, his quotations, which seem outside the question at issue, even the obscurity of his wording, all have their value; for they testify plainly that no changes have been made in the Deacon's speech. Elsewhere in the Acts, Saint Luke sums up in a few words the conversations he reports, — take Saint Peter's case in particular, where he gives only the substance of his preaching. But here the unusual length of the apology, and the digressions it is filled with, make it impossible to believe that the historian should have used the same liberties with it. A mind so methodical as Saint Luke's was, could not have helped making the matter which bore upon the accusation stand out in bolder relief than in Stephen's lengthy exposition. We may feel sure, therefore, that he has not contributed any part of this discourse. In every trial at law, the secretaries of the Sanhedrin took down the words of the accused very exactly: everything goes to show that it is their work we have before our eyes.[1] Thus this document — probably transmitted to Saint Luke by Saul, who was one of the judges [2] — makes the first page in our Acts of the Martyrs; and for the centuries that follow, we need only add to it

[1] Perhaps this is the best way to account for the mistake contained in this speech (Acts vii. 15, 16). Here Stephen is made to say that Abraham bought from the sons of Hemor, at Sichem, the field and the tomb wherein Joseph and his brethren were buried. Now, from the Books of the Old Testament (Gen. l. 26; Exod. xiii. 19; Josh. xxiv. 32), we know that it was Jacob who acquired this property, and, on the other hand, that Abraham purchased a double cave at Hebron for a resting-place for himself and his family after death. The Secretary, when taking down this part of Stephen's discourse, probably substituted, in a moment of abstraction, the name of Abraham for that of Jacob, and S. Luke in copying the text reproduced this error. Bede, Raban Maur, and after them Melchior Cano (*De Loc. Theol.*, ii.), think that the slip is to be charged to S. Stephen, who, all absorbed in his subject, confounds the two purchases, and names Abraham instead of Jacob. But as the Deacon was speaking before the most renowned doctors of Israel, it is scarcely credible that such a blunder would have been permitted to pass without protest.

[2] Acts xxii. 20.

those Proconsular Acts in which the examinations of the first Confessors of the Faith are all reported.

Yet there was something the Sanhedrin Archives say nothing of, but which the sacred Historian relates, and that is the splendor of that trial-scene, the wondrous signs made manifest to men. Traditions testify that the Deacon was then young and beautiful; but it was a supernatural beauty, for the Holy Spirit abode in him, enkindling his heart, his face, and his glance.[1] And so, when the members of the Council turned their eyes upon the accused, "his countenance appeared to them like that of an Angel." The feeling among the Sadducees was strong indeed, incredulous as they were by nature, and Stephen's words were far from weakening this impression.

"My brethren and my fathers," he began, "hear![2] The God of glory[3] appeared to our father Abraham when he was in Mesopotamia,[4] before he dwelt in Charan; and He said to him, 'Go forth out of thy country and from thy kindred, and come into the land which I shall show thee.' Thereupon, going forth from the land of the Chaldeans, he dwelt at Charan. And after that his father was dead, God made him pass over into this land where you abide to-day, wherein He gave him no heritage, no, not so much as a foothold; but he promised to give the possession thereof to him and to his posterity after him, even then when he had as yet no child. . . . Thereupon He made the covenant of the Circumcision with him, and so Abraham, when he had begot Isaac, circumcised him the

---

[1] See Cornelius a Lapide, *in loco*.

[2] There is every reason to believe that, in this speech, Stephen used the Greek tongue, for the turn of the thoughts is in no way Hebraic, and all the quotations are made from the Septuagint Version. Greek was in common use at Jerusalem, and easily understood by the members of the Sanhedrin. Replying to the Hellenists who were his accusers, it would be only natural for the Deacon to employ their language.

[3] That is to say, God, manifesting Himself in the cloud of glory which overshadowed the Tabernacle.

[4] This appearance of God in Chaldea is not mentioned in Genesis; it was a Jewish tradition known to Philo (*De Abrah.*, 15). The Scripture simply says that Abraham quitted Ur, in Chaldea, on the express command of the Lord (Gen. xv. 7; 2 Esdr. ix. 7).

eighth day. Isaac circumcised Jacob, and Jacob the twelve Patriarchs."[1]

One can easily fancy the surprise of the Sanhedrin as its members listened to this speech. They were expecting to hear Stephen try to clear himself by denying the accusations and pleading for his life, since it was now at stake; but they beheld him speaking before them just as he was wont to do in the synagogues, without a glance at the witnesses who surrounded him. They listened, nevertheless, for they were flattered by this discourse, which reminded them of the God whose Glory once overshadowed the Tabernacle, — He Who had appeared of old to Abraham their father, the God of the promises, Liberator of Israel in the land of Egypt, and God of the circumcision. One point escaped their notice; howbeit it was the only one which the Deacon had in view, — to wit, that the Lord had chosen His people in Chaldæa, before any such thing as circumcision was known, considering only the faith of Abraham; the carnal sign in which they gloried was therefore but the seal of their covenant with Jehovah, not the source of their merit nor of the Heavenly favor.[2]

Stephen was as little understood when, pursuing the history of God's people, he came to Joseph and insinuated that his judges had rejected a Saviour far greater than this son of Jacob. As for Moses, the Deacon exalted his memory all the more, because he was accused of wishing to destroy the Law. He recalled his beauty, perfect even in the eyes of God.[3] Adopted child of a daughter of the Pharaohs, learned in all the science of Egypt,[4] powerful in word and deed, the savior of his people,[5] what was wanting to make him listened to by

---

[1] Acts vii. 2-8.
[2] It was all the more important to bring this truth out so strongly, because the Rabbis attributed to Circumcision all the favors lavished on Abraham, and the promise of inheriting the Holy Land.
[3] "Beautiful before God" (Acts vii. 20), that is, "in the judgment of God;" a very common Hebraïsm (Gen. x. 9; Winer, *Grammatik*, S. 232). This expression is probably borrowed from the Jewish traditions.
[4] Philo, *Vita Mosis*, v. 84.   [5] Acts vii. 21-22.

them   And nevertheless, this was the very man they once disowned, saying, "Who hath appointed thee prince and judge over us?"[1] This Moses had himself prophesied that his Law should pass away; he had said to the children of Israel, "A Prophet shall God raise up to you of your own brethren, as myself. Him shall you hear."[2] Vain and useless teachings! For while Moses was in converse with the Angel of the Lord, and was receiving the words of Life, that he might bear them to his people, he was forsaken by them; and this nation, turning to Aaron, said, "Make us gods to go before us, for we know not what has become of this Moses who has led us out of the land of Egypt."[3] Faithless to their Prophet, they had been no less so to Jehovah; in the very hour when the Levitical sacrifices were instituted, they had abandoned them to sacrifice to the Golden Calf which Egypt adored,[4] abasing themselves before the unclean deities of Chanaan, before the Tent of Moloch[5] and the Star of Rephan.[6] And as for this Temple, the theme of so much pride, were they, too, ignorant that "the Most High

---

[1] Acts vii. 27, 35.   [2] Acts vii. 37.   [3] Acts vii. 38–40.

[4] Acts vii. 41. The bull or cow is one of the commonest of Oriental idols. Wilkinson (*Second Series*, ii. 97) thinks that the Golden Calf of Israel was an imitation of Mnevis, the bull which was kept in the temple of Heliopolis as a living symbol of the Sun. Diodorus of Sicily, ii. 21; Strabo, xvii. 803.

[5] Acts vii. 43. That is to say, the tent which enclosed the image of that god. Diodorus of Sicily relates (xx. 65) that these sacred tabernacles were to be seen in the camp of the Carthaginians. — Here S. Stephen appeals to a passage in Amos (v. 25) and quotes it from the Septuagint translation, where we read Μολόκ in place of מַלְכְּכֶם : "of your king," as it stands in the Hebrew. The statue of Moloch, god of the blazing sun, was a brazen bull, hollow withinside, having a man's arms stretched out as if to receive a burden. Therein young children were deposited, and were immediately consumed by the monster heated to a white glow. Moses had interdicted this abominable cult (Lev. xviii. 21; xx. 2–5); but his prohibition was constantly infringed upon, not only by the schismatic tribes of Israel (4 Kings xvii. 17; Ezech. xxiii. 37), but even by the Kings of Juda (4 Kings xvi. 3; xxi. 6; xxiii. 10; Jer. vii. 31; xxxii. 35).

[6] Acts vii. 43. Rephan, 'Ραιφάν in the Septuagint, Chioun, כיון in the Hebrew. We are ignorant of the meaning of these two words. According to Kircher, 'Ρεφάν ('Ρηφάν) is a Coptic word, which designates the planet Saturn. Hengstenberg supposes that 'Ρηφάν is a mistake of the Seventy, who read ריון in the Hebrew, instead of כיון.

dwelleth not in sanctuaries made by hands?"[1] Had they not heard the Prophet's words, "Heaven is My throne, and the earth My footstool? What house will you build Me, saith the Lord, and what spot can be My resting-place? Hath not My hand made all things?"[2] Far from blaspheming God and Moses, Stephen was but interpreting their words when he foretold that the Temple should not last alway.

The Sanhedrin judges scarcely comprehended him; they listened to the accused with disdainful curiosity, while around him the crowds, urged on by the Hellenists, murmured louder and louder. Saul of Tarsus was there, hatred burning in his heart and gleaming from his eyes. To touch their stubborn minds, Stephen could not appeal further to the annals of God's people; for after Solomon's time there was only a series of backslidings, worshipping of idols, with Prophets rejected or massacred, crime after crime, up to the very death of the Just One, condemned by this same Council, which was about to judge the speaker. The thought set his heart on fire.

"Stubborn-minded men!" he cried, "uncircumcised are you in heart and ears! always you resist the Holy Ghost. As your fathers did, so do you also. Which of the Prophets have they not persecuted? They have slain them who foretold the coming of the Just Whom you have but now betrayed and put to death, you who have received the Law by the ministry of Angels,[3] and you have not kept it."[4]

At these words a yell of fury rose up in the Sanhedrin. They were no longer judges that Stephen saw before him, but a raging throng of fanatics, grinding their teeth and screaming.[5] Stephen knew full well that he was about to die. The Holy Ghost filled his heart to

---

[1] Acts vii. 48; Amos v. 25.
[2] Acts vii. 49, 50; Is. lxvi. 1-2.
[3] All through the Old Testament Jehovah appears in the form of some mysterious Being, — the Angel of the Lord, or His Word, as we have explained in *The Christ, the Son of God* (vol. i. p. 369). This is the Angel referred to here.
[4] Acts vii. 51-53.   [5] Acts vii. 54.

overflowing; he lifted his eyes Heavenward, there he beheld the Glory of God and Jesus at the right hand of the Father, rising up to receive him.[1] Ravished in his ecstasy, he cried with a very loud voice, " Behold, I see the heavens opened, and the Son of Man standing at the right hand of God!"

They were the very words whereby Jesus had forewarned these same judges of His coming triumph[2]; but they looked upon them as only another blasphemy. Uttering loud cries and stopping their ears, they fell upon Stephen and dragged him outside the town to stone him.[3]

The traditions, though not precise as to the scene of his martyrdom, lead us to infer that Stephen traversed the Way of Sorrows, and went out by one of the gates which were open in the northern part of the town.[4] There he died, say some; while others tell that he was carried to Kedron Valley, below the Golden Gate, and facing Gethsemani, where Jesus strove in His Agony.

The trial, though regular at the outset, had ended in an execution by the mob; the witnesses, however, re-

[1] S. John Chrysostom, in Cramer's *Catena* on the Acts.
[2] " You shall see the Son of Man standing on the right hand of the power of God and coming on the clouds of heaven" (Matt. xxvi. 64).
[3] Acts vii. 57; Lev. xxiv. 14; 3 Kings xxi. 13.
[4] The first document in which there is a mention of the spot where S. Stephen died, is an account of the Finding of the Deacon's body, a document composed in the beginning of the fifth century. The Priest Lucian, author of this description, declares that the Holy Deacon was stoned " foris portam quæ est ad aquilonem, quæ ducit ad Cedar" (*S. Augustine's Works*, ed. Gaume, t. vii., Appendix, p. 1127). By this northern gate we are to understand the Damascus Gate, according to Robinson (*Biblical Researches*, i. 321), Herod's Gate, if we follow Schulz (*Jerusalem* (1845), p. 51). The basilica erected by the Empress Eudoxia in the year 450 marks the traditional site of his martyrdom with more precision. This sanctuary, destroyed in the time of the Crusades, had completely disappeared; but there is reason to believe that the Dominican Fathers of Jerusalem have discovered it in a piece of land lately bought by them, hard by Jeremy's Cave. (See the articles by Father Germer Durand in *Le Cosmos*, for March, 1888, and by the Baron de Vaux in the *Revue Archéologique*, June, 1886; April, 1888.) Another tradition asserts that it took place to the east of the town, in Kedron Valley, under the gate which nowadays bears the name of S. Stephen; but we cannot accord this the same credence due to Lucian's testimony, for we can find no traces of this second tradition earlier than the fourteenth century. Tobler, *Topographie von Jerusalem*, t. ii. p. 188.

mained faithful to the Law, which bade them cast the first stones.[1] "They laid down their garments at the feet of a young man named Saul,"[2] and then the scene of torture began. Stephen fell shattered and bleeding; but, rapt with the heavenly Vision opening before him, he cried upon Jesus and said, —

"Lord Jesus, receive my spirit!"

When dying, the Master had forgiven His executioners; Stephen remembered this, and drawing himself upon his knees, he cried with a loud voice, " Lord, lay not this sin to their charge!"

It was the Martyr's dying breath. He fell back and slept[3] in the Lord. One of those for whom the Deacon had prayed was Saul of Tarsus, "who had consented to his death."[4] The prayer of Stephen was heard; and to that prayer we owe the conversion of Saint Paul.[5]

According to an account which in ancient times was regarded as authentic, his body, left exposed to the beasts, remained a whole day on the spot where he was stoned. But on the morrow Gamaliel, touched by Stephen's virtue, encouraged the Christians to gather up his remains in the night, in order to carry them secretly to a piece of ground which he owned, about eight leagues from Jerusalem, at a place called Kaphar Gamala (the Village of Gamaliel).[6] There, "certain men who feared God took

[1] Deut. xvii. 5–7. [2] Acts vii. 58.
[3] Ἐκοιμήθη (Acts vii. 60). Sleep is a metaphor often used to signify death in Greek and Latin literature. Every one knows that beautiful epigram in the *Anthology*: Ἱερὸν ὕπνον κοιμᾶται· θνήσκειν μὴ λέγε τοὺς ἀγαθούς. But what with the Pagans was but a figure of speech, had come to be the expression of a dogma to the Christians : " In Christianis mors non est mors, sed dormitio, et somnus appellatur " (S. Jerome, *Epist.* xxix.).
[4] Acts xxii. 20.
[5] "Si Stephanus non orasset, Ecclesia Paulum non habuisset" (S. Augustine, *Serm.* 315).
[6] *Epistola Luciani de Revelatione corporis Stephani martyris primi*. The Benedictine Fathers, who give this letter as an Appendix to the *City of God* (S. Augustine's *Works*, t. vii.), think that that Father alludes to it in the text where he speaks of the Finding of S. Stephen's body. Tillemont does not hesitate to assert that the account given by Lucian, a man justly celebrated in the Church, has always been regarded as a very faithful and trustworthy relation. The Finding of the body of S. Stephen was a notable event in the fifth century, and caused great excitement; it is recorded

care to bury the Deacon, and performed the funeral rites with great mourning."[1] The Apostles were of their number, as Saint Jerome recounts;[2] in this secluded spot, free from their persecutors, they all, beating their breasts, and with mournful cries,[3] bewailed the first Martyr of the Church.

Stephen once done away with, the work which he preached, and which cost him his life, ceased for a time to be the ruling thought among the Christians. The converted Hellenists, who, with the sainted Deacon, had foreseen the progress of the Church, had not however received any mission to hasten its coming; and they kept silence now. As for the great number of believers, dispersed by the ensuing persecutions, it was enough if they could manage to survive their sufferings. The necessity for breaking with the synagogue was not to occupy their minds again until the day when Peter himself, enlightened by the Vision at Joppa, should tear away the veil.

in the most ancient Martyrologies, and celebrated in the Roman Church by a special feast on the third of August. For some curious details concerning the discovery, see *Mémoires pour servir à l'Histoire Ecclésiastique*, t. ii. p. 10-24.

[1] Acts viii. 2.   [2] S. Jerome, *Epist.* cix. 3.
[3] Ἐποίησαν κοπετὸν μέγαν. Acts viii. 2.

CHAPTER V.

THE MISSIONS OF THE DEACON PHILIP.

I. — SIMON THE MAGICIAN.

THE death of Stephen showed the Jews how far they could go now under the Roman rule. Such license added fuel to their audacity, and impelled the leaders of the people, rejoicing at being once more sovereign arbiters in matters of doctrine, to let loose all their terrors upon the associates of the Martyr. "A great persecution was raised against the Church of Jerusalem, and all the faithful were scattered through various regions of Judea and Samaria, except the Apostles."[1] They alone remained in the Holy City, in order to strengthen the courage of their flock. Perhaps, too, they were obeying the Master's orders, for, according to certain ancient traditions, Jesus had commanded them to stay in Jerusalem for twelve years,[2] and so make it the centre of their preaching.[3] This resolution to face every danger exposed the Twelve to the first blows of their enemies; but whether it was that their renown for virtue overawed the persecutors, or whether their quiet life excited less attention, they underwent no serious injury during this tempest which racked the Church.

[1] Acts viii. 1.
[2] Clement of Alexandria, *Stromata*, vi. 5; Eusebius, *Historia Ecclesiastica*, v. 18.
[3] It is in this wide sense that we must construe the tradition alluded to here, for we shall soon see SS. Peter and John journeying through Samaria, the coast towns, Lydda, Joppa, and the whole plain of Sharon. They visited these Christian communities to confirm them in the faith, but always returned to Jerusalem, the only seat of the Episcopate.

The storm-winds of trial swept over them only that it might thereby scatter afar the good seed. Into every place which offered a refuge to the believers hunted from Jerusalem, they carried with them the word of God, gained other hearts for Jesus, and left behind them new brethren, bound together by the most ardent charity. We shall soon meet with these Christian communities springing up all through the land of Juda. But nowhere did the preaching of the Gospel bear more splendid fruits than in Samaria. Of all the Pagan nations, this was the only one which had received Jehovah's Law, and shared in Israel's faith in the Messiah; it was likewise the only one in which Jesus had published the Glad Tidings. Had the grain falling from the Master's hand taken root outside Sichem, and was the great multitude of Samaritans still in expectation of the hour "when true worshippers should worship the Father in spirit and in truth?"[1] We are apt to believe as much, seeing the eagerness with which they welcomed the Deacon Philip.

Everything goes to indicate that it was not Sichem, the ancient city of Ephraim, whither the messenger of Jesus carried the Gospel, but Samaria,[2] once the Capital of the kings of Israel. And though this portion of the text of the Acts is variously understood, Samaria seems to be very plainly designated; furthermore, everything must have attracted the preachers of the Good News to that city. Far superior to Sichem, owing to the beauty of its site, and now crowned with temples and palaces, it quite effaced its rival, and had but recently received new and magnificent embellishments at the hands of Herod. Not

[1] John iv. 23.
[2] Some commentators translate εἰς πόλιν τῆς Σαμαρείας by "a city of Samaria," and suppose that by this S. Luke refers to Sichem; but the better founded opinion is that Σαμάρεια signifies, not the land of Samaria, but a town of that name. Indeed, the article may be dropped before πόλιν, without giving it the indefinite meaning "of a city" (Winer, *Grammatik*, § 19, 1). Furthermore, in the fourteenth verse, the word Samaria, Σαμάρεια, is repeated, and in this place it certainly means the city of that name, for all the incidents related in the fifth and fourteenth verses occurred not simply in the province, but in the city mentioned in the first of these verses: εἰς πόλιν τῆς Σαμαρείας.

content with rechristening it Sebaste (the City of Augustus), in memory of his protector, the Idumean prince had first restored it, then ornamented it with theatres, galleries, and sumptuous works of art, while over all rose the temple of the all-powerful Cæsar. But, more than such splendid buildings, there was one precious monument in particular which drew the hearts of the disciples of Jesus towards Samaria,— the tomb of John the Baptist. From the shores of the Dead Sea, where he met his death, his disciples bore the relics of the Forerunner to these regions, that they might lie beside those of Eliseus, so that the same sepulchre should hold the two Prophets who had inherited the spirit of Elias.[1] The crypt which enclosed these venerable remains is still to be seen beneath the ruins of a Gothic church.[2] As for Herod's city, nought remains but the bases of the colonnade which once stretched across the whole town, as majestic in size as the Porticos of Gerasa and Damascus. These ruins attest the important position of Sebaste at a time when Herod summoned thither six thousand veterans

---

[1] The Gospel merely informs us that the disciples of John "carried away the body for burial" (Mark vi. 29; Matt. xiv. 12). They fled from the territory subject to their master's murderer; and tradition asserts that they stopped at Sebaste, attracted thither, doubtless, by the tomb of Eliseus; for this monument, "whence the corpse of the Seer had prophesied" (Eccli. xlviii. 14), was celebrated throughout Israel. The Book of the Kings records the prodigy. Certain robber bands, come up from Moab, were scouring the country that year. Some of the citizens of Samaria who had followed a funeral train outside the city suddenly perceived their foes. Terrified, and not knowing where to seek safety, they cast their burden into the Sepulchre of Eliseus. Hardly had the dead man touched the remains of the Saint than he came to life and stood on his feet (4 Kings xiii. 20-21). To be laid to rest beside a man so mighty even in the grave was an envied privilege, which the disciples of the Baptist claimed for their master.

[2] "This crypt . . . contains a sepulchral chamber divided into three arched and connecting vaults. According to a very old tradition, one of these compartments formerly held the body of S. John the Baptist, and the two others those of the Prophets Abdias and Eliseus. When telling us of the pilgrimages of S. Paula, S. Jerome informs us that this pious Roman lady visited Sebaste, 'where,' he says, 'are interred the Prophets Eliseus and Abdias, as well as S. John the Baptist, the greatest of the children of men'" (S. Jerome, *Patrologia Latina*, t. xxii. p. 889).— Guérin, *Description de la Samarie*, t. ii. p. 189.

of the Roman legions, and when these colonists united with the former inhabitants of Samaria in restoring the capital of their country.[1]

So, then, the town to which the Holy Spirit conducted Philip was a flourishing one, peopled by Romans, Samaritans, and Orientals. In this picturesque throng, where so many different religions contended for the mastery, there were many minds wearied of doubtful teachings, and many seekers after truth who would lend an attentive ear to any one promising them relief; thus the magicians played upon many credulous minds to their own profit. We know how, in this period, false prophets were multiplying throughout the Roman world, imposing on the great as well as the common people; even those who banished and suppressed them often had recourse to their arts. Pompey, Crassus, Cæsar, gladly received assurance of prosperous fortunes from their lips. Before declaring himself Emperor, Augustus consulted the physician Theogenes,[2] and Tiberius, who caused such impostors to be thrown from the Tarpeian Rock, or ordered them to be whipped and beheaded "according to ancient usage,"[3] — even Tiberius kept soothsayers at his court.[4]

But though this race of men, "dreaded by the powerful, and deceiving all who put any trust in them,"[5] were numerous enough in Rome, it was after all in the Eastern countries that they multiplied most rapidly. The valley of the Euphrates was filled with schools of astrologers, and was really their birthplace; from this point they spread first to the neighboring cities, finally invading the whole Empire. Samaria, which always remained an Oriental town despite its Roman colonists, afforded them many opportunities of gain, with all the encouragement proffered by a more than ordinary credulity. However, the coarser sort of witchcraft would not have been enough to establish their fame if these swindlers had not been sharp enough to see that in the very

---

[1] Josephus, *Antiquitates*, xv. 7, 3; 8, 5.
[2] Suetonius, *Augustus*, xciv.   [3] Tacitus, *Annales*, ii. 32.
[4] Suetonius, *Tiberius*, lxix.   [5] Tacitus, *Historiæ*, i. 22.

THE MISSIONS OF THE DEACON PHILIP. 81

bent of this people's character there was a longing for the supernatural. Samaritans both by breeding and in belief, they hoped to obtain by Theurgy, not signs and wonders only, but also the fulfilment of those promises so dear to the whole race, — the Kingdom of the Messiah, with its joys and glories.
At this date the most noted magician was a dreamer, with high aspirations, who re-inforced his chimerical teachings by means of clever artifices. His name was Simon, and he came from Gitta[1] (to-day called Jit), a village in the neighborhood of Sichem and Samaria. Concerning his earlier career, we possess only the suspicious narratives of the pseudo-Clementine Homilies;[2] the only detail therein which seems worthy of belief is that Simon had studied at Alexandria, and belonged to the company of a Samaritan impostor named Dositheus.[3] Both apparently had been attracted by the preaching of John the Baptist.[4] Dositheus' mind was stirred at sight of the wonders which were then so frequent along the Jordan's banks, and he longed to pass himself off as the expected

---

[1] S. Justin, *Apologia*, i. 26; *Recognitiones*, ii. 7; *Clementinæ Homiliæ*, ii. 22.
[2] This is the term used to designate the legendary stories which give an account of the first years spent by S. Clement in Rome, his conversion, whereby he became the disciple and companion of S. Peter, and finally of the warfare which the Apostle waged against Simon the Magician while he journeyed through the borders of Syria. These writings have come down to us under a threefold form: 1st, the *Recognitions*, so called because they relate how the scattered members of Clement's family met and recognized one another in Syria; 2d, the *Homilies*, which is nothing more than the foregoing work, rearranged, augmented, and divided into short fragments, whence the title Homilies; 3d, the *Epitome*, an abridgment of the Homilies. The pseudo-Clementine writings are the work of Essenian Ebionites. The most ancient of these collections, the *Recognitions*, quoted by Origen (230), existed before this Father's day, for we find therein a passage from the Dialogues of Bardesanes, who, according to Eusebius, wrote in 173. However, as we find from the Syriac translation of these Dialogues that they were written not by Bardesanes, but by his disciple Philip, we must put down the date of the composition of the *Recognitions* at about the year 200. The *Homilies* are later, and the *Epitome* of a still later date.
[3] *Clementinæ Homiliæ*, ii. 220; *Epitome*, xxv.; *Constitutiones Apostolicæ*, vi. 8.
[4] *Clementinæ Homiliæ*, ii. 23, 24; *Recognitiones*, ii. 8; *Epitome*, xxv.

Messiah. Seeing that his pretensions were repelled in Judea, he renewed them among the Samaritans, and appeared before them surrounded by thirty disciples, among whom there was a woman called Helen (*Selene*, the Moon.)[1] What was the significance of this name, and the number of his disciples, corresponding to the thirty days of the lunar month? Did Dositheus, "the Stable, the Immutable One," as he called himself,[2] pretend to be the first cause and principle of the days, the months, the moon, the heavens, and the universe? The supposition is plausible, at least: for we know to what extremes the sectary went in the delirium of pride, how he even altered the books of the Law to make them accord with his visions.[3] The Samaritans' High Priest took alarm at these liberties, and adopted such vigorous measures against the innovator that the latter was forced to flee to the mountains, where he perished miserably.[4]

The pseudo-Clementine writings recount that, towards the end of his life, Dositheus, annoyed by the haughty airs of Simon, went so far as to strike him, but that by a miracle his staff passed through the disciple's body like a wreath of smoke.[5] This fable is evidently meant to represent the ambitious strife waged by the Magician against his master, and the adroit subterfuges by means of which he supplanted him. So complete was Simon's victory that the Acts speak of him as dominating over the whole people. "He had seduced the multitude, giving out that he was some great thing, in such wise that every

---

[1] *Recognitiones*, ii. 8. [2] Id., ii. 11. [3] *Philosophumena*, vi. 9.
[4] The pseudo-Clementine books are not the only ones which speak of Dositheus. Hippolytus, in the shorter of his two works on heresies, the Σύνταγμα (Photius, *Bibliotheca*, 121), made some mention of this sectary. The treatise is lost, but we have still other accounts of the heresiarch by S. Epiphanius (*Adversus Hæreses*, xxi.), Tertullian (*De Anima*, 34) and Origen (*Patrologie grecque*, t. xi. p. 1307; t. xiii. pp. 1643, 1865; t. xiv. p. 446). Beside the details given by these Fathers, the reader may refer to the two Arabian chronicles of the Samaritans, the *Book of Joshua*, and the *Chronicle of Aboulfatah*. After comparing and rectifying these various bits of evidence, it is quite possible to obtain a fair idea of Dositheus and his teaching.
[5] *Recognitiones*, ii. 11; *Clementinæ Homiliæ*, ii. 24.

one, from the very aged down to the littlest children, followed him, saying, 'This one is the Great Power of God.'[1] What induced them to follow him was that for a long time he had undermined their wits with his enchantments."[2]

Thus in Samaria everybody was yielding to these wiles when Philip reached there, escaping from his persecutors at Jerusalem. In those days of fervor, when Grace, like youthful blood, warmed their hearts, the thought of Jesus, and talking of Him, made the very life of His disciples; accordingly, as soon as he arrived, Philip began to preach without delay. The custom among Eastern nations of living out of doors — working and chatting in the doorways of their houses, in the streets and public squares, and at the gates of the town — furnished the Deacon with willing and eager hearers. The moment a stranger appeared in search of opportunities for trade, their first thought was to inquire whence he came, what was his object in leaving his native land, and what news he had to tell.

To such questionings Philip had but one answer, — Christ. And as he spoke so warmly of his Faith in the Messiah, he was listened to by a mingled company of Pagans and Schismatics, who were less hostile to the children of Israel than the native Samaritans.[3] "All were attentive to what he was saying," and very soon a goodly throng surrounded him. Noticing the many possessed folk, paralytics, and cripples among them, the Deacon called these to him. Forthwith the unclean Spirits, uttering loud cries, went out of their demonished bodies, paralytics and cripples were healed, and the whole city filled with such joy that they believed what this

---

[1] By this title the Samaritans probably understood the chief of the celestial spirits, he who in their theology was called the Great Angel (*Chron. Samaritan.* 10), for they gave Angels the title of "The Powers of God" (Gesenius, *Theologia Samaritano*, 21).

[2] Acts viii. 9-11.

[3] We have explained in several passages of *The Christ, the Son of God,* and especially in Appendix vi. of vol. i., in what relations the Jews and Samaritans stood to one another.

Jew told them of the Kingdom of God. "Men and women received baptism in the Name of Jesus Christ."[1]

Now, it so happened that Simon was a witness of these wondrous doings, and comprehended how wretched were his arts in the presence of such powers as these; he seemed touched, confessed his belief in the Saviour, and was baptized. Thereafter he joined company with Philip; but his faith, though strong in appearance, sprang from selfish motives: what had attracted the Magician was not so much the saintly life of the Deacon as the miracles worked by him; they filled him with envious admiration. Other signs still more astonishing soon gave him an opportunity to reveal his real feelings.

The Apostles while in residence at Jerusalem learned that the inhabitants of Samaria had received the word of God; they recalled the Lord's promise, "You shall bear witness unto Me at Jerusalem, through all Judea, and in Samaria,"[2] and in order to fortify the converts in their faith, the Twelve deputed Peter and John[3] to go to them. The latter, although mentioned equally with the Prince of the Apostles, really took only a secondary part, for in this mission to Samaria, just as at the Beautiful Gate and before the Sanhedrin, the Acts represent Peter as leader both in word and action. The Keys of the Kingdom of Heaven had been intrusted to him; to him it belonged to open its doors, — for the Jews first, as he had done heretofore; for the Samaritans now; and very soon for the whole Gentile world.

Philip had baptized the neophytes in the Name of the

---

[1] Acts viii. 12. We should be glad to discover some of the pools wherein a whole people were plunged and born anew as Christians, but no traces of any are to be found in the neighborhood of the devastated slopes of Sebaste. More fortunate than we in his investigations, Benjamin de Tudèle, in the twelfth century, saw huge reservoirs and many streams still watering the orchards and gardens (Benjamin de Tudèle, vol. i. p. 65).

[2] Acts i. 8.

[3] Here the Beloved Disciple figures in the Acts for the last time. Until the death of S. Peter he is seen no more in the holy books, and is only once named, as being present at Jerusalem when S. Paul went thither with Titus and Barnabas (Gal. ii. 9).

Saviour; but Faith and Baptism are not enough to complete the Christian's character: to perfect the likeness of Jesus in their souls there must be the Holy Spirit also descending upon them, and confirming them in God's light and holiness. From that day this administering of the sacrament of Confirmation was established in the Church; and then, as now, the power of communicating this fulness of the Christian life was reserved to the supreme shepherds of the flock. Accordingly, the Apostles prayed for the new believers; whereupon they laid their hands upon them,[1] and the Holy Ghost filled their souls. The supernatural gifts which, in the first years of the Church, were wont to accompany the descent of the Paraclete, here in Samaria were of such splendor that Simon was dazzled thereby. Greedy of this power, which surpassed all his magic, he approached the Apostles, holding his money in his hand, and said, —

"Grant me too this power, that those on whom I shall lay my hands may receive the Holy Ghost."

To Peter this offer was nothing short of revolting: to debase his Master's grace so far as to traffic with it was so sacrilegious a notion that the fervor of the first Christians felt the very mention of it insupportable. The Apostle answered him with the words which have condemned every simoniacal undertaking forevermore.

---

[1] Acts viii. 15-17. In these earliest days was the outward sign of the Sacrament only this laying on of hands spoken of in the sacred text, or was holy oil used even then to consecrate the baptized as priests and kings of the New Law? We can draw no conclusions from the silence of the Acts, since the historian does not go into the details of the facts he is relating; but as there is no mention of holy chrism until the time when the Spirit ceased to declare its advent by miraculous effects, it may be that the Apostles waited till then to give to the matter of Confirmation its twofold sensible sign. For the wonders which no longer attested the coming of the Comforter, they substituted the oil mixed with balm for a symbol of sweetness and light, and to figure forth the Paraclete shed down upon the soul like an odor from Heaven! " Alii melius respondent Christum, cum hoc sacramentum instituit, in Apostolorum et Ecclesiæ potestate reliquisse pro materia, prout res postulare videretur, adhibere vel solam manuum impositionem, vel unctionem, vel utramque simul. Ita inter alios Estius et Concilium Moguntinum, anno 1549, cap. xviii." (Liebermann, *Instituttones Theologicæ*, t. ii p 453).

"Thy money perish with thee, because thou hast thought of buying the gift of God with money. Thou hast neither part nor heritage in all this, for thy heart is not right before God. Repent, then, of this wickedness, and pray God that, if it be possible, the thought of thy heart may be forgiven thee, for I see thou art in the gall of bitterness and in the bonds of iniquity."

This reprobation caused such terror in Simon's soul that he conjured the Apostles to spare him.

"Pray the Lord for me," he besought them, "that none of these things which you have spoken may come upon me."

Without taking him with their company, however, Peter and John continued to preach the Gospel in many parts of this land, and did not return to Jerusalem until after having given testimony to the Saviour and published forth His words.[1]

The Acts do not tell what became of Simon after the Apostles' departure; but there is reason to believe that neither fear nor faith restrained him very long, for some years later we meet him again, still noted for his trickeries. A book entitled "The Great Revelation"[2] is attributed to his pen, and in it we find, along with many things borrowed from Platonism, the germs of the Gnostics' dreams. He became, in the eyes of the Church, at least, the father and leader of all heresy; his renown, extending beyond the Orient, reached Rome itself. The wonders he worked gave him such celebrity that a legend has grown up about his name, while in the apochryphal stories of the third century his historical deeds are quite disfigured by the popular imagination. It is easy to convince oneself of this by glancing over the documents of that period attributed by mistake to Saint Clement; in them Simon is made to teach the strangest doctrines, and we are told a number of his adventures as ridiculous as they are manifestly false. But putting aside these fables, we can find more reliable testimony

---

[1] Acts viii. 18-25. [2] *Philosophumena*, vi. 11.

anent the men in the writings of the first Fathers of the Church.[1] Saint Justin, Saint Irenæus, the author of the "Philosophumena,"[2] have all mentioned Simon, only giving a few incidents of his life, it is true, but going into his teaching more in detail. As they are so reliable in their accounts of the other sects, these worthy writers cannot well be accused of error when they treat of the Magician. Thanks to them, therefore, we can study the workings of the first heresy which afflicted the Church; the only difficulty rises when we try to distinguish between the theories peculiar to Simon and the additions to them made by his disciples.

At the bottom of this system, too, we find the central dogma of the Jews,— one only God, changeless, ruling over an undulating and fugitive creation. In "The Great Revelation" this primordial principle retains the sublime Name given to God in the Scriptures: it is the Eternal Being, Jehovah, the Jahveh of the Samaritans, "He Who is, Who hath been, and Who shall be."[3] Simon, like his fellow-countrymen, recognized no books but the Pentateuch as sacred, and hence in treating of the supreme God he could not appeal to the traditions of the Jews, their Prophets, and other inspired testimony. When he studied the Books of Moses to discover the inmost nature of that Infinite Being, he read that no man can behold Him face to face and live.[4] Here he learned that "The Lord thy God is a devouring Fire."[5] Simon had been taught by his Alexandrian masters that he must look to Greek philosophy for an interpretation of any obscure passages in the Bible. So, remembering that in the system of Heraclitus[6] and the School of the Porches, God is an Intelligent Flame, he imagined the

---

[1] It is worthy of note that none of these Fathers borrowed from the pseudo-Clementine books, which were never regarded as of great authority.
[2] S. Justin, *Apologia*, i. 26, 56; ii. 15; *Dialog. cum Tryphone*, 120; S. Irenæus, *Adversus Hæreses*, i. 33, 2-5; xxvii. 4; II. Præf; III Præf.; *Philosophumena*, iv. 7; vi. 1; x. 4.
[3] *Philosophumena*, vi. 18.   [4] Exod. xxiii. 20.   [5] Deut. iv. 24.
[6] "He was not satisfied with having falsely interpreted the Law of Moses, he even compiled that obscure Heraclitus" (*Philosophumena*, vi. 9).

Divinity as a centre of infinite light, which manifests itself outwardly through a concept emanating from God, — the *Ennoia*, "the Great Thought."[1] This Divine idea, the invisible power of an invisible Being, is creator and mother of all things; out of the void it has brought forth the hosts of spirits, angels, and archangels, which in turn produce matter and direct its action.

The opinion Simon formed of this government, and his manner of explaining the part played by vice and injustice, are the most original features of his doctrine. The angels, charged with the rule of the universe, become jealous of the superiority of *Ennoia*; they lay violent hands upon it, and immure it in a human body. Thus cut off from the upper world, bereft of the holy influence which permeated it, the lower world is left at the mercy of sin and suffering. But the Supreme Being cannot behold His Great Thought so debased without sending some one to be its liberator. Simon has been chosen by God for this work of redemption. Angel of Jahveh, and a power emanating from Him, after the same manner as the *Ennoia*, his coming had been foretold by those words in Deuteronomy, "The Lord shall raise up a Prophet like unto me from your nation and from among your brethren; Him you shall hear."[2] Hence he took the name of *Hestos*, "the one raised up"[3] for the salvation of the Divine Thought.

Such must have been the earliest doctrine of Simon, and the one he was preaching when Philip appeared in Samaria;[4] for even at this date the Acts tell how all men were running after him and crying, "This is the great Power of God." After the Apostles went away, Simon regarded the religion of the Christ as only another means of imposing on simple souls, and for corroborating his own pretensions. Far from denying the coming of a Messiah, he declared that the Christ and he were

---

[1] S. Irenæus speaks only of this one Emanation.
[2] Deut. xviii. 15.   [3] 'Ο 'Εστώς.
[4] Thereafter, indeed, the Acts describe the people as running after him and crying out, "This is the Great Power of God." Acts viii. 10.

one and the same person. Simon was He Who had appeared to the Samaritans as Father, to the Jews as Son in the crucified Jesus, and to the Gentiles in the Holy Ghost descending upon them.[1]

According to all appearances, these fables were not credited for any great length of time in Samaria; for Simon left that country to begin his wanderings over the world. At Tyre he became compromised in an adventure not very creditable to a divine personage. Meeting with a courtesan named Helen,[2] he fell into her toils, purchased her, and made her his companion. The scandal caused by this union was so great that the impostor had all he could do to maintain his authority over his mortified disciples. That he succeeded was due to his impudence in asserting that his weaknesses were really the fulfilment of a mission from on High. According to him, Helen was none other than the Great Thought of Jahveh, *Ennoia*, — banished by the angels and by them cast into a place of ignominy. In delivering her, Simon manifested himself as the Supreme Might and "The Great Power of God."[3]

We are not of the opinion that this incident ought to be relegated to the rank of those legends which, in the sequel, have distorted the history of Simon; for all the Fathers who speak of the Magician relate this fact. The book of the "Philosophumena"[4] makes mention of

---

[1] S. Irenæus, i. 23, 3; *Philosophumena*, vi. 19. Simon could not have added this feature to his teaching till after his departure from Samaria, when he travelled through the Gentile world.

[2] Helen is perhaps the woman of that name whom Dositheus counted among his adepts. Chap. v. p. 82.

[3] *Philosophumena*, vi. 19.

[4] Id. vi. 19. I put this work first, because the rationalist school sets so high store by it as an authority (see Renan, *Les Apôtres*, p. 267, note 3; p. 275, note 2), without seeing for myself, however, why the unknown author of this book should be considered as more trustworthy than SS. Irenæus and Justin, especially since, as a general thing, his testimony agrees with that of these holy Doctors. It is true that in the *Philosophumena* long quotations are given from a work attributed to Simon, entitled "*The Great Revelation*," while SS. Irenæus and Justin only give us an abridgment of its doctrine; but this fact by itself is not enough to weaken the testimony of the two Fathers.

them, as also do Saints Irenæus and Justin;[1] and, furthermore, it is very difficult, if we reject this last episode, to explain the important place Helen occupies in Simon's teaching. Later on we shall encounter this heretic again, and shall have to sift truth from fable in the accounts of his famous strifes with Saint Peter, his sojourn at Rome, and his death, which is so diversely recounted. Here our first duty was to restore to his place in History a personage who is ranked in the number of myths by some writers,[2] to set forth the mixture of mysticism and immorality in the man, so common among Gnostics, and thereby demonstrate that his doctrine contains the germ of certain fancies of the last-named sectaries. Simon is the first man who appears as an enemy in the field of the Father of the household; as we shall see, the cockle has been sown, and it will grow secretly until the day when, mixed with the ripened harvest, it will threaten the ruin of the good grain.

II. Saint Philip and the Eunuch from Ethiopia.

More and more in those days did the Holy Spirit of God blow where it listed. From Samaria, that land abhorred by the Jews, it wafted the Good News to the heart of Africa, by winning over to Jesus a powerful prince of those parts. Ethiopia, which had so often turned the balance in the fortunes of the Pharaohs, lay on the equatorial frontier of the known world. To reach this far-off country, the road passed through tropical regions to the south of Egypt and Syenë. Here, hemmed in by mountains, the Nile is no longer the peaceful stream which fertilizes the Delta. Five times the granite crags run athwart its bed and precipitate its waters in mighty cataracts; between the third and fourth falls, the river describes a huge circle, and encloses the ruined temples of

---

[1] S. Irenæus, i. 23, 2; S. Justin, *Apol.* i. 26.
[2] Baur, *Gnosis*, S. 310; Hilgenfeld, *Die Clement. Recognitionen*, S. 317.

THE MISSIONS OF THE DEACON PHILIP.   91

Napata, the ancient capital of Ethiopia. Lower down, the great Nile and its two tributaries, the Blue Nile and the Atbara, make a long peninsula to the east, where Meroë[1] once rose, becoming the principal city of the kingdom after the destruction of Napata by the Roman Petronius[2] (23 or 24 B. C.).

In the time of Jesus the supreme power there was wielded by women, who bore the title of Candace, just as the sovereigns of Egypt adopted that of Pharaoh, and afterwards that of Ptolemy. The pyramids of Meroë still show the figures of these queens, their diadems ornamented with plumes, and bearing the *uræus;* [3] over their breasts falls a necklace of large beads, a long robe envelops them, and the royal mantle rests on their shoulders. Like the many Rameses of Ipsamboul and Thebes, sometimes seated on a throne with lions' heads, they receive offerings of incense; sometimes, standing, they brandish their lance and slay the prisoners chained at their feet. It is one of these heroines who is referred to in the Acts, as having a Treasurer who had gone up to Jerusalem to worship the Lord.

Though the kingdom of the Candaces was so distant from Palestine, the Jews were well acquainted with the regions of the upper Nile. Isaiah pictures their papyrus boats dotting the stream, swift as a flight of birds, shaking out their sails with a noise like great wings.[4] The

[1] M. Cailliaud has discovered the ruins of this city round about the village of Assour; a considerable number of pyramids are still standing in the midst of crumbling and ruined sanctuaries. Napata lay further north, at the foot of Djebel-Barkal. There six temples have been discovered, and two of the number are in a fair state of preservation. To the west of Mount Barkal thirteen pyramids rise above the surface of the desert.

[2] Strabo, *Geographica,* xvii. 1, 54; Pliny, vi. 35, 8. In face of such formal evidence it is hard to understand why M. Renan (*Les Apôtres,* p. 158) would make Napata, at the period we are studying, the capital of Ethiopia.

[3] The serpent so named is none other than the asp. "Its habit of starting up almost erect at the approach of man gave rise to the belief among the Egyptians that it guarded the fields, and therefore they adopted it as the emblem of authority" (C. Vienot, *Les Bords du Nil,* p. 105).

[4] Is. xviii. 1, 2. These barks, as they are so very light, are invaluable on a stream whose course is broken up by rapids; they can easily be car-

Israelites trafficked with "this nation of lofty stature, savage eyes, and barbarous tongue."[1] They got ebony from them, with ivory, gold, incense, and precious stones.[2] Though always dreading this people — "from the first moment of its existence and forevermore, terrible to man, this people which tramples everything under its feet,"[3] — nevertheless the Jews were not slow to tell the rich merchants of Napata and Meroë of the hour predicted by Isaiah, when Ethiopia should come to Jerusalem and there, falling down, say, "There is no God save among you, and there is no other God but yours. Thou art of a truth the Hidden God, O God of Israel — Thou art the Saviour!"[4]

Are these promises, rehearsed so many a time during the centuries, sufficient to explain the Ethiopians' inclination towards the worship of Jehovah? or is it not likely that, since the Jews did business here, as everywhere else, their synagogues may have become centres for preaching the word of God? The latter hypothesis strikes us as all the more plausible from the fact that no country shows a deeper impress of Judaic thought. Even to-day, upon the tablelands of Abyssinia, whither the descendants of the Ethiopians have found their way, a whole people, — the *Falâshas*, — practise the religious rites of Israel, call themselves by Hebrew names, and claim to be originally from Palestine.[5] As for the other Abyssinians, though of a Christian sect, their beliefs and practices present a curious blending of the Mosaic rites. Circumcision, the Sabbath, distinctions between clean and unclean meats, and the law of the Levirate continue to be observed by this folk.

---

ried around the cataracts on men's backs, and replaced in the water when the smoother current permits.

[1] Is. xviii. 1, 2.
[2] Herodotus, iii. 97, 114; Job xxviii. 19; Josephus, *Antiquitates*, viii. 6, 5.
[3] Is. xviii. 2-7.   [4] Is. xlv. 14-15.
[5] The claim is doubtful, for the peculiar dialect of these Jews is not derived, like the ancient tongue of the Ethiopians (the Ghez), from the Semitic languages, and their version of the Bible has been made from the text of the Septuagint (Vater, *Mithridates*, t. iii.; Renan, *Histoire des langues sémitiques*, pp. 326–333).

In the time of Jesus, the Ethiopian Jews and their proselytes were so powerful that one of their number held a prominent position at the court of the Candace. He had the overseeing of the treasuries, — an important duty in those days when Meroë, a free and flourishing town, served as storehouse for the caravans of Africa, and distributed through the Roman world the rich products of its gold, iron, and copper mines. Following a custom common in all Eastern courts, and of still stricter obligation in the case of female royalty, the officials about the Candace were eunuchs; but in the maimed body of this man the soul was still as virile as ever, eager and athirst for righteousness and truth. This noble Ethiopian, not content with following the Law of Moses, wished to worship in that one spot on earth where Jehovah made His Presence to be felt more nearly; and with this design he went up to Jerusalem, following the route taken every year by the pilgrims from Abyssinia, — first the course of the Nile, then the sea-shore from Egypt as far as Gaza.

After leaving this town most travellers cross the Plain of the Philistines obliquely, thus reaching Ramleh and Jerusalem. However, there are two other roads connecting Gaza with the Holy City: one, shorter but very toilsome and rugged, passes by Beit-Djibrin (the ancient Eleutheropolis); the other ascends in a westerly direction as far as Hebron, and from there turns to the north. This route, which still preserves some vestiges of its old pavement, had been flagged over in the time of Solomon, so that the King's chariots might pass more easily from Hebron to the Capital. Though much preferable to the other roads for carriages, it was not much frequented by the inhabitants of those countries, who at all times have been wont to make their journeys in the saddle, — this is why Saint Luke calls it a deserted way.[1] And it was

---

[1] Αὔτη ἐστὶν ἔρημος. Acts viii. 26. The epithet ἔρημος cannot refer to Gaza, for though that city had been destroyed by the Jewish King Alexander Janneus (96 B. C.; Josephus, *Antiquitates*, xiii. 13, 3), it was rebuilt by the Roman General Gabinius (Josephus, *Antiquitates*, xiv. 5, 3), and, in Claudius' time, Pomponius Mela speaks of it as a great and strong city: "Ingens urbs et munita admodum" (*De Situ Orbis*, lib. i. cap. xi.).

on this road that the grace of our Saviour Jesus Christ
awaited the officer of the Ethiopian Candace.

Mighty man though he was, the Ethiopian was an
eunuch, and for that reason not allowed to enter the great
gatherings of Israel.[1] But albeit the severity of the old
laws obliged him to withdraw in the hours for common
prayers,[2] he might go alone into the Temple and there
offer his sacrifice; while, to comfort him in his loneliness,
he had those words of Isaiah, "Let not the eunuch say,
'Lo, I am but a withered trunk!' for hearken to what
Jehovah saith unto the eunuchs: 'To them that keep my
Sabbaths, performing what is pleasing in My sight and
remaining steadfast in My Covenant, to them I will give
a name in My house and upon My walls, better than that
of sons or daughters, — an eternal name will I give unto
them, a name which shall never perish. . . . I will make
them come up into Mine holy Mountain, and in My
house of Prayer will I fill them with great joy; their
holocausts and burnt offerings shall be acceptable upon
Mine altar, for My house shall be called a House of
Prayer unto all peoples.'"[3]

No other religion held forth such promises; and hence
the Ethiopian went away from Jerusalem more than ever
attached to the Law of Jehovah. Thereupon the Angel
of the Lord appeared to Philip and spoke to him.

"Arise," he said, "and go towards the south, to the deserted road which descends from Jerusalem to Gaza."

The Deacon obeyed. On his way he caught sight of the
eunuch seated in his chariot, reading that very Prophet
from whom he had gathered so much consolation and
hope.

"Go nigher," the Spirit prompted Philip, "and approach
this chariot."

He hastened his steps, walked along beside the pilgrim; and because the latter read aloud, as was customary

---

[1] Deut. xxiii. 1.
[2] We are not told whether the exclusion prescribed in Deuteronomy
was still observed.
[3] Is. lvi. 3–7.

among the ancients, Philip overheard the passage from Isaiah on which he was meditating.

"Do you believe," he asked him, "that you understand what you are reading?"

"How should I," replied the Treasurer, "unless some man enlighten me?" whereupon he begged Philip to get up and seat himself by his side.

Now, the passage of Scripture was this: —

"He was led as a sheep to the slaughter; like a lamb dumb before his shearers, He opened not His mouth. In His lowliness they have wrested His condemnation; yet of all them that surrounded Him,[1] who will be able to tell wherefore His life was cut off from earth?"[2]

Then the eunuch said to Philip: "I pray you explain to me of whom does the Prophet mean to speak? Of himself, or of some other man?"

Line for line, the Passion of Jesus is forecast in this Prophecy; it was easy for the Deacon to begin with these lines of Scripture and preach Jesus.[3] "The Man of Sorrows, contemned as a leper, . . . afflicted of God, beaten for our iniquities,"[4] was not this the Nazarene whom Jerusalem had beheld in His hour of torture, so meek, so patient, "not so much as opening His mouth?" "The Lord was pleased to crush Him beneath the winepress; like a Lamb, they have led Him to the slaughter."[5]

But the disciples of the Crucified had forgotten neither His miracles nor the Glad Tidings He had brought to the

---

[1] Τὴν δὲ γενεὰν αὐτοῦ (Acts. viii. 33) is to be construed as an accusative absolute: "As for his contemporaries, — those of his own generation." . . .

[2] Acts viii. 32-33. This passage of Scripture has been variously interpreted. The Acts quote it from the text of the Septuagint, the only one in use among the Jews of Egypt and Ethiopia. In the Vulgate, S. Jerome gives a rather obscure translation of it: "In humilitate judicium ejus sublatum est. Generationem ejus quis enarrabit? Quoniam tolletur de terra vita ejus." The interpretation we have adopted is the one proposed by Mgr. Beelen, and approaches more nearly to the meaning commonly given the Hebrew text by modern scholars: "By violence and by an iniquitous judgment He hath been reft away. Howbeit, what man of his generation will believe that He hath been cut off from the land of the living because of the sins of My people; yea, that He hath been smitten for them?"

[3] Acts viii. 35.   [4] Is. liii. 3-4.   [5] Is. liii. 7, 10.

world; growing every day more numerous, the faithful were filling Jerusalem and the Holy Land, — even Samaria had but now hearkened to the words of salvation. Surely this too was what Isaiah had foretold. "To Him will I give many peoples to be His heritage; He shall divide the spoils of the mighty, because He hath delivered up His Soul to death, because He hath let Himself be numbered among the wicked, bearing the sins of many, and making intercession for the sinful."[1] For how long a time had not Israel awaited this Victim of unblemished devotion? Consequently, what must have been the eunuch's emotion when Philip showed him how every line in the Prophecy had been fulfilled in Jesus, how baptism in His Name washes away all stains of sin, making man to be born again into the fulness of life.

Beside the road the great official spied a fountain.

"See, here is water," he said : "can I not be baptized?"

"You can," replied Philip, "if you believe with your whole heart?"

"I believe," he answered, "that Jesus is the Son of God,"[2] and instantly he bade them stop his chariot. Both men stepped down into the water, and Philip, immersing the eunuch, baptized him.

The stream where this ablution was performed still runs along the road from Hebron to Jerusalem, at the foot of a hill covered with the ruins of Bethsour.[3] A reservoir built of evenly hewn blocks receives its waters; a terrace just below it is strewn with the ruins of a Christian basilica. This is the spot where Eusebius and Saint Jerome venerated the fountain hallowed by the baptism of the Ethiopian.[4] Hardly were the two men come up out of

---

[1] Is. liii. 12.
[2] Verse 37 is wanting in the manuscripts of Sinaï, the Vatican, Ephrem, and Alexandria, also in the Coptic, Sahidic, and Ethiopian versions, and in the copy commented by S. John Chrysostom; consequently it has seemed of doubtful authenticity to many critics. It is retained here, nevertheless, because we find it in two important versions, the Italic and the Vulgate, in the Codex Laudianus, and the oldest Fathers, SS Irenæus, Cyprian, and Pacian.
[3] The modern name is Aïn ed-Diroueh.
[4] S. Jerome, *Liber de Situ et Nominibus: Patrologie latine*, t. xxiii. p. 882.

the water when the Spirit of the Lord caught away Philip, and the eunuch saw him no more, but proceeded on his way filled with great joy.

With him Faith in Christ was carried into the farthest parts of Africa, even in these earliest days. Did some one of the Apostles come, later on, to propagate the seeds brought thither by the Candace's Treasurer"?[1] We do not think it likely, for in the fourth century, when Frumentius and Ædesius founded the Church of Abyssinia, they discovered there, it is said, some lingering vestiges of Christianity,[2] but without a Hierarchy or any constituted Church. This is, indeed, a proof that the Apostles never evangelized these regions, for everywhere, in fact, they were most careful to insure a lasting fruitfulness to their work by establishing the Episcopate. Without mission or authority, the eunuch could do no more than preach his new creed; after he was gone, the good seed withered under the tempests of trial, only to revive some three centuries later.

"As for Philip, he was found in Azotus, and he proclaimed the Gospel everywhere he went, till he came to Cæsarea."[3] The land of the Philistines and the rich fields of Sharon, which the Deacon traversed, were then the busiest parts of Judea. Azotus, so powerful in the times of Psammeticus that it required a siege of twenty-nine years to subdue it,[4] — Azotus, more than a century

---

Epistola, cviii., *Epitaphium Paulæ.* Arguing from these evidences and that of the Pilgrim of Bordeaux (333), M. Guérin has proved that the modern traditions are at fault in locating the spot where the Eunuch was baptized at Aïn el-Hanieh, near Aïn Karim. See his *Description de la Judée*, t. iii. p. 291.

[1] The author of the *Life of the Apostles* gives S. Andrew (S. Jerome, *Patrologie latine*, t. xxiii. p. 722), Rufinus and Socrates designate S. Matthew (Socrates, *Historia Ecclesiastica*, i. 19; *Patrologie grecque*, t. lxvii. p. 125; Rufinus, *Historia Ecclesiastica*, i. 9; *Patrologie latine*, t. xxi. p. 478), as the preacher who evangelized this far-away region. But their testimony does not settle the question, for in these writers Ethiopia means not merely the banks of the Upper Nile, but Arabia, and even the Indies, as well.

[2] The Codex Auxumensis says that these two young Tyrians were astonished to see the sign of the Cross in use among a people which had never been evangelized by the Apostles.

[3] Acts viii. 40.   [4] Herodotus, ii. 157.

before Philip's day, had rebuilt her ruins and recovered her olden splendors, under the rule of Herod the Great. Willed by this prince to Salomë,[1] one of his sisters, it was afterwards made part of the imperial domain, and by this means was divorced from the Sanhedrin's rule and governed by Roman agents. In this half-Pagan city Philip could find as many facilities for preaching the Saviour's message as in Samaria. Later on, passing from town to town, he evangelized the whole country-side as far as Cæsarea; and hearing his voice, Lydda and Joppa forthwith are filled with communities of such fervid faith that Peter will shortly leave Jerusalem to visit them.[2]

But though Philip spread abroad the Good News through all Sharon[3] after this manner, still, Cæsarea was to become the spot where he preferred to dwell, and the centre of his Apostolate. Some fifty years earlier, in this very region where the Deacon found a flourishing city, eager for new light and every sort of novelty, there had stood only a hamlet of Greek fishermen, called the Tower of Strato.[4] Ten years were all Herod needed to make it the principal port of Palestine; immense blocks of stone were plunged into the sea at the depth of an hundred feet, forming a gigantic dike around a basin larger than that of the Piræus. This haven was exposed to the north wind alone, — the mildest breeze that blows in the Syrian sea; there were moles to protect it against the west and south winds, whose gusts heretofore had made its shores inaccessible.[5] To offer ships a shelter on this dangerous coast was enough to attract thither the commerce of the Mediterranean. In a short time, Cæsarea assumed such importance that there the Roman governors set up the seat of their administration, and made it the second capital of Judea.

[1] Josephus, *Antiquitates*, xvii. 8, 11; 11, 5; xviii. 2, 2.
[2] Acts ix. 32-43.
[3] This Hebrew name, meaning "a plain," is used to designate especially the rich pasture lands which stretch along the shores of the sea, between Carmel and Jaffa.
[4] Pliny, *Historia Naturalis*, v. 14.
[5] Josephus, *Bellum Judaicum*, i. 21, 5-7; *Antiquitates*, xv. 9, 6.

So flourishing a town, more Greek than Jewish,[1] where travellers of every race were to be met, was quite attractive enough to determine Philip's choice. He settled at Cæsarea with "his four daughters, virgins and prophetesses,"[2] and lived there for many long years, wandering about the harbor-docks, and mingling with the foreigners in order to publish the New Faith far and wide. Also his hospitable home became one of the centres of Christianity;[3] therein were gathered together, besides the disciples of the city, such Jews as had come from distant lands to go up to the Festivals at Jerusalem, as well as those who were returning thence, their minds filled with the words they had heard from the Apostles. The burning breath of Philip's speech kindled the flame anew, and they quitted Cæsarea all the more eager to spread abroad the Name and the love of Jesus. These never-ceasing pilgrimages account for the astonishing swiftness with which the Faith was borne into Greece and Rome, along the coasts of Asia, — everywhere where their passion for trade carried the sons of Israel.

[1] Only Greek was spoken there, and in the services at the Synagogue the Israelites read the text of the Septuagint (*Sota*, 21 b).
[2] Acts xxi. 9. [3] Acts. xxi. 8.

CHAPTER VI.

SAUL OF TARSUS.

WHILE these first rays of truth were glimmering over the Gentile world, God was raising up an Apostle who was to bring them the fulness of light. In the year 37,[1] by heavenly Grace, the persecutor of Saint Stephen fell at the feet of Christ, and rose up a defender of the New Faith.

Saul was born, at the opening of the Christian era,[2] at Tarsus, in Cilicia. Although residing in a Pagan land, his parents were Jews, and had not tainted the pure blood of their lineage by any unhallowed unions. "A Hebrew, born of Hebrew parents, circumcised the eighth day, and a descendant of Benjamin,"[3] doubtless it was due to this fact that he got the name of Saul, given him in memory of the first king of Israel, — one of the chiefest glories of that Tribe. But more truly than

---

[1] As to this date, see Appendix I.
[2] Neither in the New Testament nor in the first Fathers do we find any references which help us to exactly determine the date of his birth. S. Luke says that at the time of Stephen's martyrdom (37), S. Paul was still young: νεανίου (Acts vii. 58). In his epistle to Philemon (9), written about the year 63, the Apostle speaks of himself as an old man; but in the Greek language the two terms, νεανίας and πρεσβύτης, have the vaguest sort of meaning. Youth embraces the period between adolescence and maturity; accordingly every man is young between the ages of twenty and forty years. Old age begins about sixty, and extends to the end of life. Terms so indefinite as these cannot serve to fix the date we wish to ascertain. One tradition alone, unfortunately too late to be decisive, uses more precise terms. In a sermon erroneously attributed to S. John Chrysostom we read that S. Paul was martyred when in his sixty-eighth year. In default of more certain documents, we take this to be an indication of the common opinion in ancient times. Now as S. Paul, as we shall see hereafter, died in 67, his birth is coincident with that of the Christian era.
[3] Philip. iii. 5.

that monarch, this Jew of Tarsus was to make his race illustrious among the nations by fulfilling the prophecy of Jacob: "Benjamin is a prowling wolf; in the morning he devours the prey, in the evening he shares his booty."[1] The pillager of the Church in the first years of his life, Saul was to become one of her most glorious pastors.

We do not know for what reasons a family so closely knit to Judaic traditions became resigned to leaving the mountains of Benjamin and the neighborhood of the Holy City. Saint Jerome tells us that they first settled in Galilee, at Giskala,[2] but afterwards were driven from that village by an invasion of the Romans, and emigrated to Cilicia. The tradition which the holy Doctor refers to here, supposes that Saul first saw the light in Giskala; but on this last point it is certainly mistaken, for on two occasions the Apostle declares that he is a native of Tarsus.[3]

The child's parents followed the custom of the Hellenist Jews, and gave him a double name,—one in the Hebrew, Saul; the other a Greek one, Paul. He did not make use of the latter, which he is always known by, until the period when he began to evangelize the Gentiles.[4] From his forefathers, Paul possessed likewise the privileges of a Roman citizen.[5] Had some one of them acquired this rank in recompense for services rendered the govern-

---

[1] Gen. xlix. 27.
[2] S. Jerome, *De Viris Illustribus*, 5: "De tribu Benjamin et oppido Judææ Giscalis fuit, quo a Romanis capto, cum parentibus suis Tarsum Ciliciæ commigravit." Giskala, called nowadays El Jish, two hours' walk to the north of Safed, is the last town in Galilee which resisted the Romans (in the year 67 of our era). S. Jerome is not speaking of that invasion, but of another which preceded it, whereof history makes no mention. After Pompey (63 B. C.) the Romans were masters of Palestine; but more than once they were obliged to rivet the yoke laid upon these cities of Galilee, always prone to sedition. Luke xiii. 1.
[3] Acts xxi. 39; xxii. 3.   [4] Id. xiii. 9.
[5] Id. xxii. 28. It was not as a native-born citizen of Tarsus that he possessed this title, for that town had no claim to this privilege, being neither a municipium nor a colony (Pauly, *Real Encyclopädie:* COLONIA, MUNICEPS). Antony only saw fit to declare it a free town (Pliny, *Historia Naturalis*, v. 22), that is to say, exempt from certain charges, notably the expense of supporting a Roman garrison; it was governed by its own magistrates.

ment; or, again, may it not have been the result of
emancipation from slavery ? We know what misfortunes
befell Tarsus in the struggles occasioned by the death of
Cæsar. To punish the people for having taken Antony's
part, Cassius laid so heavy a tribute upon them that the
only way they could raise the requisite sum was by selling
a certain number of the inhabitants.[1] In this urgent
necessity, the Jews living in these Pagan cities were the
first victims. It is quite possible that Paul's parents, after
being reduced to slavery in this way, may have received
that solemn enfranchisement[2] from their master, whereby
the rights of Roman citizenship were conferred.[3]

Whatever the origin of this title, it was in their possession at Paul's birth, and was the most effectual guarantee
of safety to the family, though not so necessary to them,
at this time, it is true, as in the years which were to follow; for Tarsus, after its long season of troubles, enjoyed
at last a period of assured peace and prosperity. They
had to thank one of their fellow-citizens, Athenodorus
the Stoic,[4] for these days of rest. The tutor of Augustus,
over whom he retained a happy influence for a long time,
this philosopher was not content with having obtained
many privileges for his fatherland; he returned thither to
settle down, and by his prudent firmness calmed the
rival factions into which it was split.[5] With peace re-es-

---

[1] Appius, *Bell. Civ.*, iv. 64.

[2] *Lex Valeria de Libertate Vindicii.* Livy, *Historiæ*, ii. 5, 2; Pauly, *Real Encyclopädie:* LIBERTINI, MANUMISSIO.

[3] It is hardly likely that S. Paul's parents should have bought this title, since the first Emperors only granted it under exceptional circum-stances. Dion, lvi. 33; Suetonius, *Octavius*, 40; *Caligula*, 38.

[4] Athenodorus was not born at Tarsus itself, but at Cana, a hamlet in the neighborhood of that city. For an account of this Philosopher, see the Abbé Sevin's learned essay in the twelfth volume of the *Mémoires de l'Académie des Inscriptions et Belles-Lettres*, first series.

[5] Tarsus was governed by a sovereign Assembly representing the various classes of citizens (Pauly, *Real Encyclopädie:* TARSUS). A wretched poet, named Boëthus, had obtained a political power which he disgraced by his infamous acts (Strabo, xiv. 5). In order to rescue his country from the grasp of this demagogue, Athenodorus, although sustained by his powerful pupil, had to engage in a long and laborious struggle. His fellow-citizens evinced their great gratitude to him, for, after his death, they erected altars to him and honored him as a hero. Lucian, *Longævi*, 21.

tablished, the town found means to reap the advantages of its unique situation. Standing in a vast plain of Asia Minor, Tarsus is not more than four hours' journey from the Mediterranean, and about the same distance from the peaks of Taurus. To the north, crossing these mountains, there was a pass called the Cilician Gates, open to caravans coming to traffic with the Roman world; to the east were wide roads connecting them with the markets of Syria, while a navigable river, the Cydnus, carried the wood, felled in the Taurus, down to the sea, together with the wealth of the East, now accumulating in the store-houses of the city.[1]

But Tarsus was no less noted for its schools than for its commerce. In learning, it had only two rivals,— Athens and Alexandria; and according to Strabo's testimony, it excelled both of them. It is astonishing to scan the list of distinguished masters then in the town,[2] almost all of them natives of the city, and with such a reputation abroad that the emperors and noble families of Rome summoned them to instruct their high-born sons.[3] In this city of great tradesmen and great scholars alike, the philosophers, professors, and grammarians were more noisily active than the traffickers. Philostratus tells us how they used to sit in bands along the docks of the Cydnus, chattering like a flock of magpies.[4] Disrespectful as the moralist's comparison may appear, it must be a truthful picture, for the grave Strabo agrees with him in decrying these Rhetoricians.

Very vile passions disgraced their learning; caring little enough for morality, egoists, scoffers, and always ready with an insult, they revelled in coarseness;[5] from

[1] Strabo, xiv. 5, 10.   [2] Pauly, *Real Encyclopädie*: TARSUS.
[3] Strabo, xiv. 5, 14, 15. Besides being the tutor of Augustus, Athenodorus had charge of Claudius' education (Suetonius, *Claudius*, iv.). Nestor the Academician was the preceptor of Marcellus, Augustus' nephew (Strabo, xiv. 5). Another professor from Tarsus, Nestor the Stoic, was appointed to instruct Tiberius (Lucian, *Longævi*, 21).
[4] Philostratus, *Vita Apolonii*, i. 7.
[5] Witness the lines which Boëthus launched at the head of Athenodorus, and which he ordered to be graven on the walls: —
   'Έργα νέων, βουλαὶ δὲ μέσων, πορδαὶ δὲ γερόντων.

words they passed to acts, going so far as to befoul the doorways of their opponents;[1] sometimes they would even engage in pitched battle under arms, and ended their wordy wars in blood. How often the young lad whom we think of as Saint Paul, coming out of the "ghetto" at Tarsus, must have drawn near one of these knots of philosophers, and marvelled at their trivial discussions, — that wisdom of the world which one day he would brand as foolishness in God's sight.[2]

But even more than the emptiness of human learning, the corrupt life, which Saul saw all about him, disgusted his youthful soul. Even in Cilicia, a country noted as one of the most dissolute in the world,[3] Tarsus was famous for its unbridled license in the conduct of life;[4] its tutelary god was the infamous Sardanapalus, whom the legends confound with Hercules of Lydia, Baal of the Phœnicians, the Asiatic Sando; and, like all these, honored by voluptuous orgies under their sacred tents.[5] By the gates of Tarsus, at Anchialus, Paul beheld the idol of this shameless religion. There a marble statue represented Sardanapalus as a woman clad in the robe of a Lydian girl, with arms outstretched, and snapping his fingers with all a reveller's abandonment to debauchery. Underneath, an inscription in the Assyrian tongue expressed the whole moral of this cult, —

"Drink, eat, and enjoy; all else is nought."[6]

When, sixty years later, Saint Paul branded the shameful crimes of Paganism, Corinth was the city he had before his eyes, doubtless; but Tarsus too was in his mind, — Tarsus, stained with the foulness which had made his soul revolt even in childhood. "God hath de-

For his sole response, the Stoic inscribed this menacing variation of the last three words, just below the original: Βροντᾷ δὲ γερόντων. The reader must pardon me for not attempting to translate such a play on words.

[1] Strabo, xiv. 5, 14. [2] 1 Cor. iii. 19.
[3] Crete and Cappadocia shared with Cilicia the unenviable reputation of surpassing all other peoples in corruption. Whence the Greek proverb: Τρία κάππα κάκιστα. See Étienne's *Thesaurus Græcæ Linguæ:* K.
[4] Dion Chrysostomus, *Orationes*, i. et ii.; Philostratus, vi. 34.
[5] Pauly, *Real Encyclopädie:* SARDANAPALUS.
[6] Strabo, xiv. 5, 9; Arrianus, *Expeditio Alexandri*, ii. 5.

livered them over to shameful passions. . . . They wished not to know God; therefore hath God given them over to a depraved sense."[1]

The Israelites could have no intercourse with such schools. In Tarsus more than elsewhere they lived a life apart, shielding their children from contact with the teachers of perdition. Each father instructed his own son, and taught him, so soon as he could stammer its words, that most Jewish of all prayers, the *Shema*; " Hearken, O Israel, the Lord our God is one ! Thou shalt love the Lord thy God with thy whole heart, with all thy soul, and with all thy strength." With even-fall, in the family circle, the child heard his kinsfolk sing the beautiful psalms of the Hallel, and little by little learned to mingle his voice in those songs, from which our daily prayers are taken still. At the age of six he was ushered into what the Rabbis called the " Sacred Grove,"[2] " the Vineyard ; "[3] that is to say, the school so highly esteemed by the Jews that without it they believed a city destined to destruction. " The world," they said, " cannot be saved but by the breath of children gathered in their studious retreats."[4]

There Saul passed his earlier years,[5] reading the sacred texts from parchment scrolls, hearing from his master's lips the interpretation and the traditions which, from being a commentary on the Law, had come to be a repetition of it (the *Mischna*). Besides this study, each Jewish child learned some manual art, whatever his rank or fortune might be. Thereby the Jews sought to ennoble labor,[6] and at the same time provide a resource

---

[1] Rom. i. 26–31. " Nam fœminæ eorum immutaverunt naturalem usum in eum usum qui est contra naturam. Similiter et masculi, relicto naturali usu fœminæ, exarserunt in desideriis suis in invicem, masculi in masculos turpitudinem operantes, et mercedem, quam opportuit, erroris sui in semetipsis recipientes."

[2] *Midrash Coheleth*, 91. [3] *Rashi Yebamoth*, 42 b. [4] *Sabbath*, 119, 6.

[5] Tarsus was too important a town not to have a school of its own. The Jews were accustomed to maintain one master for every twenty-five children; when a community of Israelites had forty children, the professor was allowed an assistant. *Babha Bathra*, 21 a.

[6] *Nedarim*, 49 b.

against the evil days. Saul chose a branch of industry very common in Tarsus : he applied himself to braiding goats' wool, obtained from the flocks of Taurus ; thereafter plaiting it into the coarse coverings used for tents.[1] When he allowed his son to take up with this apprenticeship, how could the Apostle's father foresee that, for thirty toilsome years, the boy he was bringing up to noble studies would earn his daily bread from this low trade ?

As his family had decided that he was to be a Rabbi, Saul could not obtain at Tarsus the course of study required for an interpreter of the sacred books, an administrator of justice, and a pleader before the courts of Israel. When he reached his twelfth year,[2] the age at which a child became a "son of the Law," or, in other words, was initiated into the numberless traditions of his ancestors,[3] he was sent up to Jerusalem to attend the higher schools of Jewry. One of Paul's sisters was married, and lived in the Holy City ; probably he went to live with her, — at any rate, he won the strongest affections of one of his nephews, for we shall soon see this young man putting himself in very great danger, to save his uncle's life.[4] Whether guided by family counsels or consulting his own tastes, he betook himself to Gamaliel's company to pursue his studies. This master, one of the seven whom the Jews honored with the title of Rabban,[5] stood at the head of a school noted at this time for the high character of its doctrines. But it was

[1] Σκηνοποιός, Acts xviii. 3. These coarse stuffs were called "cilicium" (whence the modern word "cilicious"), and they were then as now in common use for tents. Vegetius, *Instit. Rei. Mil.*, iv. 6. They were also made into mats, cloaks, sacks, and rugs. See Forcellini, *Lexicon:* CILICIUM. "Capra pilos ministrat ad usum nauticum et ad bellica tormenta et fabrilia vasa. Sed quod primum ea tonsura (caprarum) in Cilicia sit instituta, nomen ad Cilicas adjecisse dicunt" (Varro, *Res Rustica*, ii. 11).

[2] Later on, he declared before Agrippa that he went to Jerusalem in his early youth. Acts xxvi. 4.

[3] *Aboth*, i. 1.   [4] Acts xxiii. 16.

[5] This name, which comes from רָבַב (to multiply, grow great, distinguished), in the Hebrew Bible signifies a man remarkable on account of his position or ability. Job xxxii. 9 ; Dan. i. 3 ; Prov. xxvi. 10. With the pronominal suffix of the first person plural, it takes the form רַבָּן ; "Rabban," "our master." This was the superlative title of honor.

just this lofty tone which repelled the Pontiffs and great personages. The majority, Sadducean for the most part, disdained the speculations of this Doctor, and looked to Schammaï, his rival, to provide them with a more easily acquired system and a stricter interpretation of the Law, which was all they asked for in the management of the political and religious affairs of Judea. The Pharisees, whose opinions were shared by Paul's family, held the teaching of Gamaliel in juster esteem. They recognized the fact that his zeal for the religion of their fathers was as pure as it was earnest, and in consideration of his lively faith they were not so much piqued at this master's innovations. Indeed, Gamaliel had separated himself rather boldly from the common run of doctors. Setting aside their subtle discussions concerning the Observances, he never treated these matters save in the hope of lightening the burden laid upon the people. Worthy son of Hillel, his only thought, even as his ancestor's had been, was "to reconcile mankind unto the Law;"[1] he brought them to love it by making the Sacred Text the theme, not of fruitless disputes, but of an eloquent exhortation. His most cherished study was to explain the Songs of Israel and the Oracles of the Prophets.

To young Jews coming thither from all parts of the world and grieving over the yoke Jerusalem was under, he recalled the future glories foretold for their race, and the unfailing theme of their hopes. If at this time it behoved them to repeat Jeremy's Lamentations, was it not also fitting that by word and deed they should hasten that great renewal of spirit concerning which Isaiah, Ezekiel, and all the Seers had forewarned them? Now that Judea was permanently united to the Roman Empire, what was the use of keeping up that bristling hedge which hemmed in the Holy Nation? To make their triumph certain, they had but to extend the spiritual kingdom of Jehovah over all the earth. With this

[1] *Aboth*, i. 11.

thought Gamaliel introduced those humane rules of his, — that every poor man, the Pagan as well as the Jew, had a right to glean his little portion from the fields; that when sick, the Gentiles were entitled to aid; that they ought to be greeted with the salutation of peace, and in death were entitled to the funeral rites.[1] Hence, too, his tolerance for the first Christians, and that hardihood with which we have seen him defending the Apostles, thereby rescuing them from the hatred of the Sanhedrin.[2] In fine, this is the reason of Gamaliel's aversion for the Rabbinical Schools, the earnestness he showed in the study of Greek philosophy,[3] his longing to find, what Jesus had already given the world, — an infallible Authority, which should cut short all profitless disputes.[4] Far superior to the rest, from the loftiness of his views and the generosity of his feelings, charitable, conciliating, so meet for the kingdom of Jesus that the traditions will have it that he was a Christian, this master of Israel was worthy to form the mind of Saul. According to the custom of Jewish scholars, the future Apostle came thither to seat himself on the ground beside the platform of Gamaliel, and so, during many a long year, "stationed in the dust at the feet of the wise man, he drank eagerly of his word."[5]

This teaching left an impression upon the disciple which we shall notice in after days; but it did not change the character he had inherited from nature, or from the prejudices of childhood and blood. Saul, as we have said, came up from Tarsus penetrated with the spirit of pure Judaïsm, "a Pharisee's son, and a Pharisee himself,"[6] — as scrupulous as any one for the legal Observances. Although brought up among Greeks, he did not know their language well; what he learned of it was gained at the School of Gamaliel. Five hundred of the scholars there,

---

[1] *Gittin*, 696, 61.   [2] Acts v. 34–39.
[3] *Babha Kama*, 83, 1.
[4] "Get for thyself some authority, that thus thou mayest be relieved from doubt." *Aboth*, i. 15.
[5] *Pirke Aboth*, i. 4.
[6] Gal. i. 14; Acts xxiii. 6; Philip. iii. 5.

it is said, were studying the Law, another five hundred Greek learning.¹ Saul was not of the latter number. He continued to speak the Aramæan tongue, to which his babyhood and boyhood had been wonted at home, and which was used generally by the Jews; he spoke it in Jerusalem, along the road to Damascus, and during his whole life continued to use it as the natural vehicle for his thoughts. Accordingly, when, even after he had become the Apostle of the Gentiles, he talked, preached, or wrote in their language, his Greek was never anything but a borrowed dialect. As for his Epistles, with so little that is Hellenic in their form, incorrect in their style, obscure even to his contemporaries, a speech "which betrays the foreigner,"² oftentimes the surest way of getting at his meaning is by going back to the Aramæan term which he is translating.

Nor had Greek literature any attractions for him; he had taken no interest in it when at school in Tarsus, and at Jerusalem he disdained to study it. In his writings we find no reminiscences of its orators, historians, and poets; there are only three³ quoted in as many various places, merely going to show that he was not ignorant of those masterpieces of human genius.

His principal study, therefore, was the Law of Jehovah. "In Judaism," he tells us, "I made greater progress than all my companions of the same age, and I gave signs of an unmeasured zeal for our Traditions."⁴ Gamaliel had so broad a mind that he could adapt himself to very different characters; by him Saul "was instructed in the exactest manner of observing the Law of his fathers,"⁵ and Paul continued for very long to be that model scribe whose duties Jesus the son of Sirach has defined : " He who giveth his soul to the law of the Most High, searcheth the wisdom of the ancients, and meditateth upon the Prophecies. Revolving in his mind

---

¹ *Babha Kama*, 83, 1.
² Bossuet, *Panégyrique de Saint Paul*, premier point.
³ Tit. i. 12; Acts xvii. 28; 1 Cor. xv. 33.
⁴ Gal. i. 14.   ⁵ Acts xxii. 3.

the words of noted men, he delveth into the winding paths of allegories, scrutinizeth the meaning hidden in proverbs, and meditateth upon the enigmas of parables."[1] The Judaic education was like a mould from which the Apostle's thought received from the outset that form which it kept ever after, and is especially to be noted in his Epistles. It would be vain to look to them for the clever arts of the Rhetoricians, or for the Peripaticians' deductions, with their orderly reasonings, which illumine one's path from beginning to end of the way. The light Paul gives us is like that of the thunderbolt. Little he cares whether his style be rude, his transitions abrupt, his figures incoherent, or his periods broken; all his thought is how to make his idea stand out, impressing and engraving itself upon the soul. So, too, David, Solomon, and all the Seers and Prophets of Israel had spoken. His method is the same which the Talmud has preserved for us,— the method of Jewish Schools, where the lesson consisted in a long conversation between the master and his disciples. The interrogative and colloquial forms, so frequent in the Apostle's letters, his persevering endeavors to base his argument upon the Jewish Traditions or the mystical meaning of Scripture, — what is all this but the vestiges of an earlier education, a reminiscence of Gamaliel?

In fact this Doctor had collected and commented on the Seven Rules of Interpretation[2] compiled by his grandfather, Hillel. To our minds, trained to a rigorous logic, nothing could be stranger than these Rabbinical cavillings, from which, arguing from some vague similarity in names or circumstances, or from any resemblance more or less remote, they draw their conclusions by analogy, and infer something from the text which it does not contain.[3]

---

[1] Eccli. xxxix. 1-5.
[2] These seven rules for arguing (the *Middoth*) can be found in the Introduction to *Sifrâ*, tos. *Sanhedrin*, c. vii.; Rabbi Nathan's *Aboth*, c. xxxvii. See article under HILLEL in Kitto's *Biblical Cyclopædia*.
[3] A passage from the Talmud of Jerusalem (*Pesachim*, vi. 1) shows how the Rabbis employed these various forms of argument: "Once when the 14th of Nisan chanced to fall on a Saturday, a difficulty arose, whether,

As yet they had not gone to the excesses of the Talmudists, who sought for the meaning hidden in words and even in the smallest fragments of words, "from the corners of every letter picking a bushel of decisions."[1] But already at this early date, if one could discover any uncertain likeness, some distant relationship between two things, sufficient to admit of a comparison, that was quite enough to warrant any conclusion drawn from one to the other.

The subtility of such proofs, and their lack of solid foundation, could not escape the minds of men as eminent as Hillel and Gamaliel; accordingly, they bent their efforts, not so much towards establishing the existing forms of reasoning as to maintaining their right to interpret the Law freely. In the schools frequented by the aristocracy, there was but one way of determining the meaning of a text known to the teachers, — the authority of the ancient Doctors. The leaders of the people found it an easy task to transform this learning of theirs into an infallible Tradition, to which they alone kept the key. Hillel did not dispute the real worth of this Tradition, but he refused to accept it as unchangeable; by fostering among his followers the use of his Seven Rules, he suc-

---

despite the Sabbath, it was lawful to perform the sacrifice of the Paschal lamb. Hillel was appealed to, and was asked, " Hast thou ever heard tell whether or not it be our duty to celebrate the ceremony of the Paschal lamb when the 14th of Nisan falls on a Saturday ? " " Do we not hold," Hillel replied, "that this Passover alone excels the Sabbath in dignity ? Have we not a great number of sacrificial victims similar to the Paschal lamb, which the Sabbath must give place to ? " . . . Thereupon Hillel proceeded by basing his decision upon analogy, upon a conclusion *a fortiori*, and on the similar use of a word. — From analogy : The daily sacrifice is a sacrifice offered by the community, and so too is the Passover ; as the former excels the Sabbath, the latter must excel it also. — From an *a fortiori* conclusion : If the daily sacrifice, whose neglect does not involve the penalty of extermination, excels the Sabbath, much more the Passover, whose omission is punished by extermination, must excel the Sabbath. — From the similar use of a word: In the case of both these sacrifices the Law reads that the act must be performed in its due time (במועדו) ; as in the case of the daily sacrifice this term signifies, " despite the Sabbath," so this term should be understood to mean in the case of the Paschal lamb that it likewise must be immolated "despite the Sabbath." Quoted by Dereubourg, *Histoire de la Palestine,* p. 178.

[1] *Menahot,* 20 b.

ceeded in making a place for reason in the teaching of the Law, and managed to reconcile the letter of the Sacred Text with the necessities of the times. In this way, among other points wisely modified by him, Hillel pointed out to his hearers a way of escaping that cancelling of all debts which was one of the commandments Israel must needs fulfil every seventh year. Such a law as this practically prohibited all commerce with Pagans. By wise expedients he made the Law practicable, in a way which satisfied the people's conscience and their business interests at the same time.

However much attention Saul may have paid to these dialectics, he certainly attached only a secondary importance to them; what kept him in Gamaliel's school was the faith he breathed there,— the master's ardor in dealing with the words of the Prophets, and the enthusiasm which this sort of preaching provoked among the companions of his age and studies. In this centre of eager life, the young scribe developed without hindrance; from the lessons of Gamaliel he gathered what was most fitting for his fiery nature, disdaining the more temperate thoughts which the former interspersed amid his warmest exhortations. Like this great Doctor, Saul too longed for the triumph of the Law, but of an inflexible Law, unforgiving as in its earliest days. When it came time for the youth to leave these classes, where he heard the most tolerant of Jews speaking only of conciliation and peace, Saul had become a stern zealot of the Mosaic law, prepared to assail any one who did not share his beliefs.

The impulse to undertake extended mission journeys was felt very generally by the scribes of this epoch; not content with preaching in Judea alone, they "ran over land and sea"[1] to gain proselytes for the coming reign of the Messiah. Apparently Saul was of this number, and remained away from Jerusalem during the few years of Jesus' Ministry, for he never saw the Saviour, and was not present either at His trial or upon Mount Calvary. When he returned to the Holy City, the disciples of the

[1] Matt. xxiii. 15.

Christ had come to be a notable and important part of the people. The spirit of freedom which breathed through the Deacons' preaching, and in Stephen's particularly, had liberated them, little by little, from the heaviest yoke of the Law; every day they broke some one of the bonds which at first had kept the Christians so united with the Jews to all appearances that it was hardly possible to distinguish the Church from any one of the numerous synagogues of Jerusalem. Saul saw the danger ahead in this city where a spirit of revolt against the Law was rife in the people; the thought excited him wellnigh to madness, and, acting in concert with the princes of Israel, he resolved to destroy the Christians.

Stephen, noted for the boldness of his speech, was marked out for their first victim. We have seen Saul, sitting in the tribunal before which the Deacon appeared, giving in his vote against him, following him to the place of execution, and standing guard over the garments of the men that stoned him.[1] His mind inflamed by this first murder, he fancied himself one raised up by God for the extermination of the innovators. "I conceived the idea," he says, " that there was nothing which I ought not to do against the name of Jesus of Nazareth."[2] The Pontiffs who swayed the Sanhedrin councils were not slow to encourage this hatred, and gave the scribe full powers.[3] Thereafter his passion knew no bounds; he hastened from synagogue to synagogue, forced his way into private houses, compelling the weak and timorous to deny their faith in Jesus' Name.[4] Every one who resisted was thrown into prison or constrained to blaspheme the Saviour by whippings, torture, and death.[5] According to Paul's expression, his persecution was "an outburst of fury,"[6] and in this spirit he ravaged the Church of Jerusalem. But his rage redoubled when he learned that though the faithful fled into the neighboring towns, it only resulted in spreading their beliefs more speedily; he heard that the new Faith had converts farther afield, and that even at

[1] Acts vii. 5, 9; xxii. 20; xxvi. 10. [2] Acts xxvi. 9. [3] Acts xxvi. 10.
[4] Acts xxvi. 11; viii. 3. [5] Acts xxii. 4. [6] Gal. i. 13.

Damascus there were numbers of Jews who invoked the Crucified Christ. " Full of threats, breathing out slaughter against the Lord's disciples, he went in search of the High Priest[1] and asked of him letters to the synagogues of Damascus, so that in case he found there any persons of that sect, men or women, he might bring them back bound to Jerusalem."[2]

This commission granted by the Sanhedrin, the deeds of violence perpetrated with such impunity, and the terrible bloodshed, all go to show how the government of Judea had changed since Caligula began to reign. To pull down everything which his predecessors had built up, seemed the sole ambition of this mad Cæsar. Tiberius had held the distant provinces under his yoke: Caius left them unnoticed, and allowed the magistrates of the country to administer the laws. Tiberius, continuing the policy of Augustus, seized every opportunity to reduce the allied powers into provinces: Caius chose only the maddest means of flinging away these conquests. Not content with releasing Herod's grandson, Agrippa, whom his predecessor had held as a captive in order to put a stop to his intrigues in Judea, this Emperor went so far as to make him a present of a part of Palestine;[3] he granted Commagenë to Antiochus, Iturea to Soæmus, to Cotys he gave Lesser Armenia, and a part of Thrace to Rhæmetalces.[4] About the same time, we find Damascus in the hands of Aretas, king of Petra. This was another piece of extravagance on Caligula's part, and one which, in the sequel, led to events already known to our readers.[5] It will be remembered that Herod Antipas, John the Baptist's murderer, had not succeeded unscathed in substituting the adulteress Herodias for his legitimate wife. Aretas took up arms to avenge his outraged daughter, and so

---

[1] This High Priest was probably Theophilus, son of Annas, who exercised the functions of the office from the year 37 to 42. Josephus, *Antiquitates*, xviii. 53 ; xix. 6, 2.
[2] Acts ix. 1-2. [3] Josephus, *Antiquitates*, xviii. 6, 6-11.
[4] Suetonius, *Caius*, 16; Dion Cassius, lix. 8, 12; Josephus, *Antiquitates*, xviii. 5, 3 ; 6, 10.
[5] See *The Christ, the Son of God*, vol. i. bk. iii. ch. ii. ; bk. iv. ch. vii. 2.

thoroughly defeated the Tetrarch that the latter was forced at last to appeal for help to Rome. Tiberius, who always favored Antipas, ordered Vitellius, his legate for Syria, to go to his aid; and his legions were marching against Petra when the Emperor's death stopped them on the way.[1] Here again, as everywhere else in the East, Caligula made haste to take the opposite policy to that pursued by Tiberius; he left a free field for the conquering Aretas, who took possession of Damascus, — it is possible that he received it as a gift from this whimsical Cæsar,[2] for the lack of any Damascene coins bearing Caligula's[3] name would seem to indicate that the town never regarded itself as belonging to that Emperor. Accordingly, from the year 37, Aretas was King there, and appointed an Ethnarch to administer its affairs.

The consent of this Idumean official was necessary to allow Saul to execute his commission. So then we should be utterly at a loss to explain why the Sanhedrin should have addressed letters authorizing their delegate to act for them, not to this governor, but to the synagogue, were it not for the well-known power of the Jewish community of Damascus. According to the likeliest calculations, the number of Israelites settled in this town went as high as fifty thousand,[4] and their influence was such that they had attracted almost all the women of the city to the worship of Jehovah.[5] Consequently, they formed at this time the most considerable body in the town, one which it behoved the rulers to gain over if they wished to make them, not only obedient subjects, but zealous partisans as well. Aretas had been led by his own politi-

---
[1] Josephus, *Antiquitates*, xviii. 5, 1-3.
[2] The latter hypothesis seems all the more likely to be the true one, because Aretas would find a natural ally in Agrippa, the favorite of the new Emperor, and who shared the King of Petra's hatred of Herod Antipas. Josephus, *Antiquitates*, xviii. 7, 2.
[3] In fact we possess Roman coins of Damascus bearing the names of Augustus, Tiberius, and Nero.
[4] According to Josephus they could muster ten thousand men capable of bearing arms, which supposes a total population of about fifty thousand souls. Josephus, *Bellum Judaicum*, ii. 20, 2.
[5] Josephus, *Antiquitates*, xviii. 5, 1, 3.

cal views to grant the Jews of Damascus the same liberties which their brethren enjoyed all over the Roman Empire. Not content with respecting their faith, he allowed them a practical autonomy, with courts of their own where the leaders of Israel decided religious questions and punished offenders by whippings, imprisonment, and excommunication; he even allowed the community at Damascus the right of immediate appeal to Jerusalem. One proof of this is the event we are occupied with at present, — these letters and instructions addressed directly to the synagogues of the city. The leaders of Israel were too wary to expose their authority to the risk of a rebuff. When they bade Saul bring back the rebels in chains, they knew that their orders would be respected, and that, if need be, Aretas' officers would lend a helping hand in their execution.

CHAPTER VII.

THE CONVERSION OF SAINT PAUL.

SAUL marched straight to Damascus, without a glance at the smaller Christian bodies along his way. Whichever road he may have taken on leaving Jerusalem,[1] before reaching the city he had to traverse Iturea, over a lava soil strewn with jagged rocks and seamed with deep crevasses. Coming out of this desert, the valley, watered by the Pharpar and Abana,[2] gleams like a vision of paradise. With the peaks of Anti-Libanus towering over it to the north, and on the east the snowy sides of Hermon, girt about by a sea of sand, this oasis seems like an immense orchard. Walnut, fig, and apricot trees on every hand intertwine their branches and rustle their foliage together; here and there in the sweet-smelling thickets the fruits of a warmer climate are ripening, — oranges, citrons, and pomegranates; vines are festooned from tree to tree; everywhere under these domes of greenery you hear the waters ripple and plash. The town lies like a huge oval in this forest of a thousand hues. In the Apostles' time it had neither cupolas nor

---

[1] Three Roman roads led from Jerusalem to Damascus. One, crossing the Jordan at Jericho, ascended by Heshbon, Bosra, and Trachonitis. The second spanned the stream to the south of Lake Genesareth, and reached Damascus by way of Gadara. The third and most travelled passed by Samaria, Tabor, Capharnaüm, crossed the Jordan "at the Bridge of Jacob's Daughters," and skirted the southern slopes of Hermon.

[2] The Pharpar (Nahr-el-Awady), flowing to the south of the city, waters only the plain of Damascus. It is the Abana (the modern Barada), which falls in countless brooklets about the city and the gardens which encircle it. The Greeks called it the Chrysorreas, the River "with Floods of Gold," and with good reason, for it was the very wealth and life of Damascus; rising in a gorge of the Anti-Libanus, it transformed the fiery desert along its course into the loveliest valley to be found in all Syria.

minarets; but the white houses glittered in the sunshine then as now, the surrounding plain too had the same rich garb. Then as now, Damascus was most like to what the Arabs sing of her to-day, — a handful of seed-pearls on an emerald carpet.

It was high noon when Saul, surrounded by his escorting band, traversed the roads which wind through the orchards.[1] A fierce sun blazed in the sky; here on the outskirts of the city, oppressed by the heat of the day, there reigned an unbroken silence. In the quiet of these last few miles of the journey[2] Saul's dreams were of

---

[1] The tradition common among the Latins locates the scene of his conversion in the midst of the Christian cemetery, to the southeast of the town, and not far from the ramparts.

[2] S. Luke gives three accounts of S. Paul's conversion: the first in the ninth chapter of the Acts (3-19), where he himself relates this event; the two others in discourses delivered by Paul to the Jews and to Agrippa (xxii. 5-16; xxvi. 12-20). The little pains taken by an historian usually so careful to eliminate the variations in these narratives, shows that he did not regard them as contradictory, but as different details going to complete one and the same picture. S. Paul often referred to that wondrous apparition which had turned the course of his whole life; what could be more natural than that his mind should recur now to one circumstance, now to another! We have gathered together above the scattered lines from the three accounts; although we have borrowed from the speech before Agrippa only the words of Jesus, "Arise and stand upon thy feet," and omitted the instructions which follow: "I have appeared unto thee that I may make thee a Minister and a Witness of those things which thou hast seen, and of those also which I shall show thee when appearing unto thee anew; and I will deliver thee from this people and from the Gentiles unto whom now I send thee to open their eyes, that they may be converted from darkness to light, and from the power of Satan to God, and that by the faith which they shall have in Me they may receive forgiveness of their sins and have part in the inheritance of the Saints." That I have not referred these long instructions to the day when Jesus struck down the Apostle on the road Damascusward, is because it does not seem to accord so well with the concise order of events as recorded in the two other narratives: "Rise up and go into Damascus; there it shall be told thee what thou must do;" but a still more important reason is that it does not agree with the two first reports, which describe Saul on his entrance into the city as still ignorant of God's plans in his regard. So then the words which we have left out from the discourse before Agrippa appeal to our mind as an oratorical development, whereby the Apostle sums up the Saviour's teachings, which he had heard at different times, — some in the residence of Judas, some during his long retreat in Arabia, and some even later, when on his return to Damascus he found the Jews still obstinately rejecting the Gospel; for those words, "I will deliver thee from this

his glorious mission and coming triumphs, the town resounding with the news of his advent, the acclamations of the Jews, the dismay and destruction of the Christians. Suddenly, a great light coming from heaven enveloped the travellers. Those who have experienced the fierce glare of noontide in Syria will appreciate the force of those words: "At midday I saw a light burning in heaven more dazzling than the sun." Thunderstruck by this sudden brightness, all fell to earth;[1] and on the instant Saul heard a voice saying in the Hebrew tongue:

"Saul, Saul, why persecutest thou Me?"[2]

"Who art Thou, Lord?" he answered.

And the Lord said to him, "I am Jesus of Nazareth, Whom thou persecutest. It is hard for thee to kick against the goad."

Thereupon, trembling and terrified, "Lord!" he cried, "what wouldst thou That I should do?"

"Rise up," the Lord made answer, "and go into the city; there it shall be shown thee what thou must needs do."

Now, Saul's companions were still overcome with the first stupor, for they heard a voice and saw no one. Their leader arose, stretched out his arms, and began groping his way; his eyes were wide open, but he could see nothing. They took him by the hand, led him along, and entering under the gate of Damascus, came to the street called Straight. This avenue was one of the splendors of the town, traversing it from east to west, an hundred feet in width, divided into three roadways by

people and from the Gentiles to whom I now send thee," leave us to infer that Saul had already encountered the Synagogue's hostility to his doctrine.

[1] Paul, in his address to Agrippa, notes expressly that all fell to the earth (Acts xxvi. 14). The account given by S. Luke in chapter ix. 7, would seem to indicate that some, if not all, of Paul's companions had recovered from their first fright before he did, and that they were on their feet (the pluperfect εἱστήκεισαν has this meaning) when the voice of Jesus was heard by their leader lying prone on the ground.

[2] In the three accounts of the Apparition the Hebrew name Σαούλ is given as Jesus pronounced it; elsewhere in the Acts, S. Luke uses its Greek form : Σαῦλος.

lines of Corinthian porticos,[1] and crowned midway with an arch of victory. Here the whole city gathered for pleasure, citizens as well as strangers. Paul had looked forward to his triumphal entrance along this way, and now he was walking the street, unable even to see the crowd which gazed at him as he entered, guided by the hands of his men, an object for astonishment and pity.

They conducted him to the house of a Jew named Judas, and he stayed there three days, deprived of his sight, without eating or drinking. The Christians, shuddering at the mention of Saul's name, avoided his dwelling; the Jews shunned him. Paul lay there all alone in fasting and in prayer. The memory of the faithful ones he had tortured, Stephen's last words, his last heavenward glance, his blood spilt on the earth, were themes for poignant remorse. "Why persecutest thou Me?" he heard the voice of Jesus saying, for indeed it was Jesus Whom Saul had heard; 'twas He Whom he had seen, not such as he had imagined Him, but with only tender reproaches for His persecutor, like His humble followers in whom the Saviour lived and suffered again. Why had this Jesus stricken him down by the wayside, and what punishments would he inflict upon his fallen foe? In his anguish, Saul turned to Heaven; he prayed, and his soul, calmed at last, was fain to hope again. At the end of three days his spirit was rapt in an ecstacy; a man appeared to him laying his hands upon him and curing him. This Vision was the herald of his salvation, now near at hand. Throwing himself upon God, he awaited His good time in recollectedness and peace.

"Now there was a disciple at Damascus, Ananias by name, to whom the Lord said in a vision: 'Ananias!'

---

[1] A modern street (Tarik el-Mustekim) follows the track of this road; but, narrow, irregular, and lined with leprous stalls, it has nothing about it to recall the ancient Corso; here and there, however, some fragments of columns are still visible, now half hidden by the houses or furnishing support to the bazar-stalls. Paul's companions, entering the city from the southeast, led him into this great street by the eastern gate, the Bâb-Sharki.

"And he answered: 'Here am I, Lord.'

"And the Lord added: 'Rise up, and go into the street which is called Straight; seek in the house of Judas for a man named Saul of Tarsus, for behold, he prayeth.'

"'Lord,' Ananias replied, 'I have heard this man spoken of many a time, how many woes he hath caused Thy Saints in Jerusalem, and he hath power here from the High Priests to carry back captive all such as call upon Thy Name.'

"'Go!' the Lord repeated; 'for this man is an instrument to My hands, whom I have chosen to bear My Name before the Gentiles, before Kings, and the children of Israel. I will show him how great things he must suffer for My Name's sake.'

"Then Ananias went his way and entered the house where Saul dwelt; laying his hands upon him, he said:

"'Brother Saul, the Lord Jesus, Who hath appeared to thee on the way by which thou camest hither, hath sent me that thou mayst receive thy sight and be filled with the Holy Ghost.'

"Immediately there fell from his eyes, as it were, scales, and Saul recovered his sight."

His first glance was for Ananias. Trusting himself entirely to the guide sent him by the Lord, Saul speedily learned what it behoved him to know, — that Jesus was the Messiah foretold by the Seers of Israel. This testimony from Prophecy was the proof most esteemed by baptized Hebrews, and with it doubtless ended Ananias' instructions, for he remained a true son of Israel. "He was a man according to the Law," it says in the Acts,[1] "to whose virtue all the Jews of the city bore witness."

"The God of my fathers," Ananias said to him, "hath chosen thee aforehand, that thou shouldst know His will and see the Just One, and hear the voice from His mouth; for thou shalt be a witness unto Him before all men of what thou hast seen and heard. And now, why

[1] Acts xxii. 12.

dost thou tarry? Rise up, be baptized,[1] and wash away thy sins, invoking His Name."[2]

There was abundance of water in Damascus; every house had its fountain, surrounded by flowers and orange-trees. Saul arose and received baptism in the Saviour's Name. After he had eaten, he regained his strength and remained some days with the disciples who were in town. The majority, if not all, had hastened to find out the truth of this rumor concerning the circumstances of his healing, and they thronged about the man so dreaded by them a little before. From them Saul heard the Glad Tidings much as we get them from Saint Matthew's Gospel,—the principal acts of the Master, His Miracles, Parables, and Sermons compressed into short sentences and remembered sometimes very confusedly. For the catechumen, just "born again of water and the Spirit,"[3] this was the milk of his tenderest age, he was nourished thereby; partaking ever more eagerly of this food divine, his faith becoming so ardent that he at once began preaching in the synagogues, asserting and affirming that Jesus was the Son of God.

Every one who listened was filled with astonishment, and the people said: "Is not this the man who, in Jerusalem, exterminated those who invoked this Name? and who came here to bring all such back in chains to the Princes of the Priesthood?"

But Saul grew stronger every day, and overwhelmed the Jews by proving to them that Jesus was the Christ. After the first surprise, their anger and implacable hatred burst forth; whereupon Saul, exposed now to pressing dangers, heard the voice of Jesus calling him into solitude; accordingly, he quitted Damascus and withdrew into Arabia.

The name Arabia, which we use nowadays only for the peninsula which lies between the Red Sea and the Persian Gulf, in olden times had a much wider mean-

[1] Although called to be an Apostle by Jesus Himself, Saul only became a Christian by baptism.
[2] Acts xxii. 14-16.   [3] John iii. 5.

ing, designating not only Idumea and the eastern side of Jordan,[1] but Upper Syria as far as Apamea[2] also and even the neighborhood of Damascus. Many think that Saul tarried in the lands outlying the city, among the rocks of Trachonitis, or in the fields of Hauran. Others suppose that his journey into Arabia was a protracted mission, — that Bostra[3] and Petra, Aretas' capital, received the Good News at this time. But the latter hypothesis does not agree very well with what the Apostle wrote later: "When it pleased God to reveal His Son to me, that I might preach to the nations, forthwith I conferred with no man, but I went into Arabia."[4]

Another manifestation of Jesus, distinct from that which overthrew the persecutor in the Damascus road, seems to be referred to in this passage from the Epistle to the Galatians. Thereby the Saviour revealed to Saul his mission as Apostle to the Gentiles, showed him that he need not look to any man for help, calling him into solitude, there to be his sole Master. Consequently, the place to which the new Christian retired must have been some secluded spot, and according to the likeliest supposition, it was Sinaï, in Arabia Petrea. It is true that ever since the Lord had appeared to Moses there, amid the crash of lightnings and thunders, the Holy Mountain had never ceased to be an object of great terror to the children of Israel. During fifteen centuries, history mentions only one pilgrim as having gone up from Judea to the region where Jehovah once gave them the Law; that pilgrim was Elias, and he went thither only to find himself face to face with God, the ground quaking beneath his feet, and girt about with fire and "with hurricanes so mighty as to overthrow the mountains and shatter the rocks in pieces."[5] But if such memories made Sinaï awful ground, they also marked it out as the scene for great

---

[1] Eusebius, *Onomasticon*, Ἰορδάνης. — Josephus, *Bellum Judaicum*, i. 4, 3; *Antiquitates*, xii. 4, 11.
[2] Arrianus, ii. 20; Strabo, xvi. 2.
[3] Βόστρα, ἡ νῦν μητρόπολις τῆς Ἀραβίας. Eusebius, *Onomasticon*, Βοσώρ.
[4] Gal. i. 16–17.   [5] 3 Kings xix. 8–15.

revelations. Saul might well have trembled as he was led thitherwards by the Holy Ghost; he could not, however, feel any astonishment, for it was that he might be initiated into the Mystery whereof he was never more to cease speaking, — "that Mystery hidden unto all generations and to all ages,"[1] "that Mystery of the Christ, veiled hitherto to the children of men, . . . how that the Gentiles are called to the same heritage as the Jews, that they are of the one same body, co-heirs in the selfsame promises of God in Jesus Christ."[2] That salvation is offered to the Pagans by another door than the one opened to them by Judaism; that their justification is the gratuitous work of Divine Mercy, to be won by grace and faith in Jesus, — such were the truths revealed to Paul during these days. It was what he called "his Gospel,"[3] as to which he proclaimed everywhere that "he had neither learned nor received it of any man, but by the revelation of Jesus Christ."[4]

Besides these principal dogmas there were many others which he was instructed in. The mystery of the world's latter days was explained to him;[5] the institution of the Eucharist was related to him by the Saviour Himself;[6] in a word, the deposit of Faith was placed in his keeping with such fulness of detail that Paul had no need to receive aught from the disciples of the Saviour. When he went up to Jerusalem to see Peter, and later again to take part in the First Council of the Church, "the great Apostles had no new thing to teach him;"[7] and on his part, he was content to communicate to them the Gospel which he preached to the Gentiles,[8] and no one censured him in anything.

We do not know the length of this sojourn in Arabia, during which Saul, "separated from flesh and blood,"[9] saw and heard Jesus, even as Moses had talked with Jehovah. It may be that this retreat was prolonged for

[1] Col. i. 26.
[2] Ephes. iii. 5-6.
[3] Rom. ii. 16; xvi. 25.
[4] Gal. i. 12.
[5] 1 Thess. iv. 15.
[6] 1 Cor. xi. 23; xv. 3.
[7] Gal. ii. 6.
[8] Gal. ii. 2.
[9] Gal. i. 16.

the greater part of the three years that elapsed between the conversion of the Apostle and his escape from Damascus, which we shall relate shortly; for the Acts testify that it was a considerable time [1] after his first preaching there, that the Jews, seeing him once more present in their synagogues, resolved to kill him. And, furthermore, in God's dealings with the Saints is there any commoner occurrence than just such periods of obscurity, whereby He annihilates the old that He may create a new man in its stead? In Saul's case, this transformation of character was most wonderful; out of a fanatical and bloodthirsty scribe, it brought forth a vessel of election, so true a reflection of the Master's virtues that the Apostle could say, "I live no more, but Jesus liveth in me." [2]

At the same time that Paul's soul was lifted to these heights, his body, shaken by sudden emotions, breaking down under the struggles which were the price of his virtue's hardihood, this poor body of his grew daily weaker till it became a sore burden to him. Thereafter his life was to be a lengthened martyrdom, "a daily death." [3] Not one of his letters but speaks of his infirmities and the afflictions of his flesh. "I bear about in my body," he says, "the death of Jesus Christ." [4] Some chronic disease seized on him, cramped his ministry, and reduced him to such a humiliating state that later on he thanks the Galatians " for not having either scorned or disowned him because of the trials which he suffered in his flesh." [5]

The Apostolic documents, which often speak of this infirmity, nowhere let us know its nature. Great pains in the head, is the explanation of certain Fathers; gout or gravel, according to others, was the cross which Paul must carry with so much bodily pain.[6] But these mala-

---

[1] Acts ix. 23. 'Ως δὲ ἐπληροῦντο ἡμέραι ἱκαναί. [2] Gal. ii. 20.
[3] 1 Cor. xv. 31.   [4] 2 Cor. iv. 10.   [5] Gal. iv. 14.
[6] Cornelius a Lapide, *in* ii. *ad Cor.* xii. 7 : " Anselmus, Beda, Sedulius, et Hieronymus putant fuisse corporis ægritudines, sive capitis perpetuum dolorem, ut vult Hieronymus ; sive viscerum iliacos dolores, ut alii, apud S. Thomam ; sive renum infirmitatem et podagram, ut vult Nicetas; sive, ut alii, stomachi ægritudiuem ; sive aliquem alium morbum."

dies would not explain the disgust which he dreaded to inspire.¹ Accordingly, it would seem that the likeliest hypothesis is the one proposed by several modern writers, — that the Apostle suffered from inflammation of the eyes. In the Orient, ophthalmia has effects unknown in our climate; little by little it extinguishes the sight, at the same time rendering the organ so sensitive that the light pierces it like a knife; as it consumes the eyelid, it forms angry scars: leprosy alone is more hideous. Without any knowledge as to how far this malady distressed the Apostle, there is reason to believe this was really that "affliction of his flesh"² he so often alludes to. During a more than usually grievous attack while staying with the Galatians, he testifies that these faithful followers "were ready, if that had been possible, to tear out their eyes to give them to him."³ This is a hint worthy of note. And again, when in writing to these same Christians, he exclaims, "See what big letters I am tracing here with my own hand!"⁴ it seems evident that Paul, obliged to make use of a secretary, can only sign his name with difficulty and in awkward characters. It would seem that the organ of sight in his case was seriously injured. This is why when in the Sanhedrin he could not distinguish the High Priest from those about him;⁵ hence, too, his apprehensions lest he should be left alone, without companions to assist him.⁶

Grievous as this affliction was, Saul had a yet more humiliating trial within himself, for the concupiscence of the flesh still burned in his ailing body. He himself avows the violence of these struggles. "I do not the good which I will, but the evil which I hate, that do I. . . . I delight in the law of God according to the inward man, but in the members of my body I feel another law which fights against the law of my mind and makes me prisoner to the law of sin that is in my members. Unhappy man that I am, who shall deliver me from this body of

---

[1] Οὐκ ἐξουθενήσατε οὐδὲ ἐξεπτύσατε. Gal. iv. 14. [2] Gal. iv. 13.
[3] Gal. iv. 15. [4] Πηλίκοις γράμμασιν. Gal. vi. 11.
[5] Acts xxiii. 2–5. [6] 1 Thess. iii. 1; 2 Tim. iv. 16, etc.

death?"¹ This, then, was the cross which Jesus laid upon him, — a frail and rebellious body; yet it was imposed as a counterweight to the favors showered upon him, — the sublime mission which made him Apostle of the Gentiles, as Peter was Apostle of the Circumcision. And yet the trial continued to be so poignant that Paul never could grow used to it; twenty years later he bemoans it again to the Corinthians, calling it the spur which pierces his flesh, the angel of Satan which buffets him. "Thrice," he says, "have I besought the Lord to deliver me from it; and He hath answered me, My grace is sufficient unto thee, for My power is made more evident in thy weakness."²

This feeling of humiliation was reflected in the outward appearance of Paul. From the first he shows that he is distrustful of himself, timid, and self-conscious. His sorry mien was against him. All ancient authorities agree in depicting him as homely and small, with a pale complexion, grayish beard, a bald head, aquiline nose, and heavy eyebrows which darkened his face.³ The Corin-

¹ Rom. vii. 15-24.
² 2 Cor. xii. 7. S. Thomas seems to us to give the true interpretation of this text when he understands it as referring both to the physical ailments which the Apostle was afflicted with, and to the concupiscence of the flesh which tormented him : " Datus est, inquam, mihi stimulus carnis, crucians corpus meum per infirmitatem corporis, ut anima sanetur; quia ad litteram dicitur quod fuit vehementer afflictus dolore iliaco; vel stimulus carnis meæ, id est concupiscentiæ surgentis ex carne mea, a qua multum infestabatur" (*Comment. in* 2 Cor. xii. 7).
³ Nicephorus Callistus is the only one in whose writings this portrait, as a whole, can be found; although he wrote at a recent date (xiv. century), he merely sums up the testimony of very ancient authors; for even now, without the resources then furnished him by the Library of Constantinople, we can still trace, scattered through the documents of the first centuries, all the features here gathered together by this historian (Nicephorus, *Historia Ecclesiastica*, ii. 37). In the sixth century John Malala thus describes the Apostle : " A man with stooping shoulders, his hair and beard grizzly, an aquiline nose, blue eyes, eyebrows almost meeting, a blotchy complexion, and a heavy beard " (*Chronographia*, p. 257). S. John Chrysostom calls him ὁ τρίπηχυς ἄνθρωπος, " the man only three cubits in height " (Or. xxx. *In Princip. Apost.*). An apocryphal document of the same period (fourth century), the *Philopatris*, speaks of him as the Galilean " with a bald head and arched nose, who ascended into the third Heaven, and there learned wondrous things " (Lucian, *Philopatris*, § 12). The Acts of SS. Paul and Thekla, composed in the third century (Tischen-

thians, with their refined tastes, considered his discourses as low in style, his person mean and contemptible.[1] Paul had a lively appreciation of the disadvantages of such an exterior, and he begged his believing hearers not to judge him by appearances, but to be mindful of his charity for them.[2] And, indeed, it was by his great heart that he went forth to conquer the world. No man ever loved and none was ever loved like this man. By one of those contrasts we see so often in ardent natures, Saul with his unruly, irascible temper, prone even to bloodshed when mastered by passion, this same Saul had a compassionate soul, was easily moved to tenderness, and ready with his tears. He gave his love without reserve, but he demanded a response to his feeling. No one has put affection on a higher plane, or shown himself more sensitive, more grateful to kindness; but ingratitude and separation tortured him. Heedful himself of others' needs, and respectful towards their customs, he looked to find in them the feelings which animated him; he loved mankind as much as he loved the truth, and he won men to it by making himself so dear to them.

Another no less powerful charm in the man was the humility with which he let others see his weaknesses, his fears, often trembling and in tears, as accessible to discouragement as other men, praying day and night, finding no strength in aught save the Christ, Who had become to him "all in all."[3] This saintliness, whereby God's handiwork was made so manifest, gave Paul's preaching much of that marvellous efficacy which we shall soon have to note. Undoubtedly the Apostle did not attain, at the very first, the perfection to which he rose later; but it was during the long retreat which accompanied his conversion that God transformed his heart and turned

---

dorf, *Acta Apostolorum Apocrypha*, p. 41), describe the Apostle as "small of stature, bald, with heavy eyebrows, and an aquiline nose." It is easy to recognize the most striking features of this portrait in the medallion found in the Cemetery of S. Callixtus, a well executed work which belongs to the second century. Northcote and Brownlow, *Roma Soterranea*, vol. ii. p. 310.

[1] 2 Cor. x. 1, 10; xi. 6.   [2] Gal. iv. 13, 19, 20, etc.   [3] Col. iii. 11.

those traits of character which were defects in his nature, into a source of splendid virtues. It will be well to recall just here what they were, in order to facilitate our study of a life which had a foremost influence upon the infant Church.

Paul left Damascus a neophyte, walking with unsteady feet in unwonted paths, still staggering under the blow which had lately overwhelmed him; but in solitude his eyes grew accustomed to the light which had dazzled them at first. Once more he felt that he was master of himself, knowing his mission in life, since during this time he received the teachings of Jesus under precise dogmatic forms, as they stand to-day in Christian Theology. However, even while giving him the Gentile world as the field set apart for his labors, the Saviour bade him, as He had bidden the Twelve, to proffer the Gospel first of all to the Jews. He was given to know also how that the Keys of God's Kingdom had been placed in Peter's hands, and that the Gentiles might not enter therein until such time as the Head of the Church should open the door to them; and Saul awaited that hour with perfect submissiveness and respect. So, in fact, on his return to the city of Damascus, we see that he preaches to the Jews alone; but he told the words of Jesus with such power that none could withstand him. In the Israelitish communities, when reasonings failed, they made up for it by physical arguments; the dungeon, the scourge, and excommunication were the weapons with which they avenged every semblance of an attempt against the Law. It is more than likely that from the very first, Saul had to stand these tests, and probably it was because they found them unavailing that the chiefs of the Synagogue resolved among themselves to put him to death. Secret as were their plans, however, the Apostle got warning in time, and disappeared from his enemies' sight, who, not knowing where to look for him, and fearing that he would escape them altogether, kept the city gates guarded day and night. In their search they were aided by the Ethnarch of Aretas, who employed his soldiers in tracking the innovator.

Paul, now hounded down on every hand, saw no way of escaping death save by leaving Damascus; and nevertheless, fearing to draw down the fury of the Jews upon his brethren, he refused this means of safety, as it appears, for the text of the Acts leaves us to infer that the disciples alone prepared him for his flight and forced their plans upon him: "they took him and during the night they let him down in a basket from a window in the side of the wall."[1] For many centuries the traveller was shown, in the eastern quarter of the town, one of the houses which jut out over the ramparts, and in this house an opening through which the panier of rushes descended long ago. This landmark disappeared some years ago. In the same place, however, there is a cave still venerated as the first refuge of the Apostle, and close beside it stands the tomb of Saint George, the good gate-keeper who was put to death for having helped the fugitive to escape.[2] Whatever historical basis there may be for these legends, they make us realize better the circumstances of this flight, which were especially painful to the Apostle, — the vengeance to which he left his brethren exposed, and the humiliation of hiding away like a criminal. This trial seemed so grievous to Saint Paul that, twenty years later, he still recalls its bitter memories, and ranks it among the great sorrows of his life. "So then, if I must needs glory over aught,[3] I will glory in my pains and in my sufferings. God the Father of Our Lord Jesus Christ, Who is blessed unto all ages, knoweth that I lie not. Being at Damascus, he who

---

[1] Λαβόντες οἱ μαθηταὶ αὐτοῦ is the reading given by the oldest manuscripts (A, B, C, ℵ). S. John Chrysostom translates it thus: "Paul's disciples besought and induced him to descend," etc. The Vulgate, with the Syriac, Coptic, and Ethiopian Versions, have the lection αὐτόν, which we find in the *Codex Laudianus* (sixth or seventh century), in the *Mutinensis* (ninth century), and in the *Angelicus Romanus* (ninth century). The latter reading gives a more plausible sense to the text, for it is hardly probable that S. Paul had any disciples of his own at this time.

[2] The Christians of Damascus, as a sign of their veneration, used to deposit the dead they were bearing to the neighboring cemetery at the feet of the Saint.

[3] 2 Cor. xi. 30–33.

governed the province in the name of Aretas had the city guarded that I might be made prisoner; but I was let down in a basket through a window in the side of the wall, and so I escaped his hands."

On leaving Damascus, Paul betook himself to Jerusalem. Certainly there was everything to call him thither, — Gethsemani, where the dying Stephen had prayed for him, and Calvary, bathed with the blood of Jesus. In the very places which were like dumb witnesses of his blasphemies, the penitent scribe could confess his Faith and proclaim the Christ to be his God; but most of all he wished "to see Peter,"[1] the Head of the Church, the Foundation on which was laid the Apostleship of the Gentiles as well as of the Jews: "to see him, such is the force of the original text, as one goes to gaze on something wonderful and worthy of being sought after, contemplated, studied," says Saint John Chrysostom,[2] "and to behold him as one greater as well as older than himself."[3]

No one who saw this Jew broken down with fatigue as he entered Jerusalem had any inkling of the high counsels for the fulfilment of which he had been led back to the cradle of the Church. Most of the faithful were not aware of the marvels Jesus had wrought in their persecutor; even those who had heard tell of his conversion did not know what had become of the fanatical scribe struck down at the gates of Damascus and almost immediately disappearing, now three years ago. Accordingly, when Saul sought to join the company of believers, they shunned him; they recalled only too vividly how they had seen this very Pharisee spying upon their words and actions, forcing his way into their houses, to drag out their brethren and hand them over to the torturers. All were afraid of some secret

[1] Gal. i. 18.
[2] 'Ανέρχεται ὡς πρὸς μείζονα καὶ πρεσβύτερον . . . 'Ιστορῆσαι, φησὶ, Πέτρον. Καὶ οὐκ εἶπεν ἰδεῖν Πέτρον, ἀλλ' ἱστορῆσαι Πέτρον, ὅπερ οἱ τὰς μεγάλας πόλεις καὶ λαμπρὰς καταμανθάνοντες λέγουσιν. S. John Chrysostom, *Commentarius in Epistolam ad Galatas*, i. 11.
[3] Bossuet, *Sermon sur l'unité d l'Église*, premier point.

scheme, and they "could not believe that Saul was a disciple."[1]

There was one generous man, however, in the timorous throng; this was Joseph, surnamed Barnabas, the Levite from Cyprus whom we saw, in the first days of the Church, selling all he owned, to put it in the common purse. There is a very old tradition[2] which relates that he had known Saul at the School of Gamaliel, and ever since had tried in vain to bring him to a knowledge of the Christ. Meeting him again here in Jerusalem, and ignorant of what had taken place at Damascus, he renewed his appeals, whereupon Saul threw himself at his feet and told how Jesus had made an obedient disciple of the furious blasphemer. It is indeed a touching story, and one might well wish it had some solider foundations, for it is a fitting and natural prelude to this passage in the Acts: "Then Barnabas, taking him by the hand, brought him to the Apostles, and told them how the Lord had appeared to him on the road, and what He had said to him, and how thereafter he had spoken openly in the city of Damascus in Jesus' Name."[3]

Saint Paul informs us[4] that the Apostles to whom he was conducted were not the Twelve gathered together, but only Peter and James the Lord's brother. Following the usual make-up of the synagogues, the Church had its Head, assisted by Elders, who governed its actions; after them the "Angel of the Synagogue," specially appointed to direct divine service and act as the representative of the community. Everything seems to point to the conclusion that Peter and James filled these two offices and represented the Twelve, receiving converts, speaking and acting in their name. They made no difficulty about accepting Barnabas' word for the new member, and they welcomed Saul gladly, who, thereafter, "went back and forth[5] with them in Jerusa-

---

[1] Acts ix. 26.   [2] Tillemont, *Mémoires*, t. i. p. 214.
[3] Acts ix. 27.   [4] Gal. i. 18, 19.
[5] The expression "went in and came out" with them is a Hebraism,

lem, speaking freely in the Lord's Name." The whole Church followed the example set by their leaders, and cherished as a brother this man whom not long before they had stood in so much dread of.

That burning zeal which had impelled Saul to strive against Stephen in the synagogues, led him to the same places in order to confess the faith there where formerly he had been known as its persecutor. Passing by such gatherings as were exclusively Jewish, and where he would have encountered only obstinate resistance, he found his way to Israel of the Dispersion, the self-same Hellenists before whom the holy Deacon had preferred to speak : " he argued with them, and spoke to the Gentiles also." [1] The fact that all Jerusalem had seen this scribe raging against the Christians, made his preaching in Christ's Name all the more remarkable ; on the other hand, his knowledge of the Scriptures, wherein he showed them the Life of Jesus foretold, gave great weight to his words. The princes of the city were so alarmed at this new turn of events that within fifteen days after his arrival they were looking for an opportunity to kill him. The brethren, considering that he was in imminent danger, urged the Apostle to leave the city, but in vain. Saul felt that his testimony was a proof of the Almighty power of the Christ, and he continued to bear witness to Him from synagogue to synagogue. Word must come from the Lord Jesus Himself if he was to be snatched from the teeth of his enemies.

One day, when he had gone up to the Temple to pray,[2] his soul was caught in an ecstasy, and he saw the Saviour, Who said to him,—

" Make haste and depart quickly out of Jerusalem, for they will not receive the testimony which thou wilt give of Me."

So ardent was his desire to repair somewhat of the

יָבוֹא עֵת, meaning that during these fifteen days Saul dwelt in familiar intercourse with the Apostles.

[1] Acts ix. 29.
[2] Acts xxii. 17-21.

wrong he had done, and so great his hopes, that he longed to stay here a while.

"Lord," he cried, "they know that I have thrown those that believed in Thee into prison, and have had them whipped in the synagogues; and while the blood of Stephen, Thy witness, was shed, I too stood by and consented to his death, and kept the garments of those that killed him."

"Go forth," repeated Jesus, "for I will send thee afar off, unto the Gentiles."

And Paul resisted no longer; he trusted himself wholly to the direction of his brethren, who "brought him down to Cæsarea, and sent him away to Tarsus."[1]

When recounting this journey to the Galatians,[2] Saint Paul tells them that he went thereupon "into the lands of Syria and Cilicia. But," he adds, "the churches of Judea that believed in the Christ knew me not by face. They had heard only this, 'That he who persecuted us in times past now publishes abroad the Faith which he once destroyed.' And they glorified God because of me." These words of the Apostle show with sufficient clearness the road the Apostle took in going from Jerusalem to Tarsus: he did not tarry in Judea; the little ship which bore him away from Cæsarea skirted the shores, stopping, as was the custom, at the various harbors along the coast, — Tyre, Sidon, and Seleucia. From one of these cities the Apostle probably continued his way on foot, telling of the Saviour's coming, and gaining even in this first mission journey the numerous disciples whom we shall find him revisiting later on, both in Syria and in Cilicia.[3]

In whatever field Saul may have been sowing the word of Life, he certainly did not, at this time, give token of that wonderful activity which we shall soon have to note. While waiting for Peter to open the way to the Gentiles, he usually dwelt in his native town of Tarsus. There he came in contact once more with the most flourishing

---

[1] Acts ix. 30.   [2] Gal. i. 21-24.
[3] Acts xxi. 4; xxvii. 3; xv. 23, 41.

schools of Paganism, with illustrious scholars, almost all Stoics, who filled the whole world with the teachings of Zeno. It is very probable that Saul did not shun their lectures as he once did when, with his sole ambition to be a scribe in Israel, he held the Gentiles and their learning as accursed. Though he still retained his contempt for the arts of Greece, he seems, however, to look upon their philosophies with less disdain; his writings have a certain coloring taken from their doctrines, and he has even appropriated certain terms used by them, which he deemed likely to make the divine revelations more striking to his new audiences. Doubtless this accounts for the expressions common to Saint Paul and the Stoics, which we are astonished to find so frequently, in writers so far apart in matters of race, education, and beliefs. Both Apostle and Philosophers have drawn from the same springs, only the Christian purifies what he has gathered from the wise men of the ages, often, too, re-clothing their words and figures with a new meaning. Thus for two or three years Saul continued to dwell in his birthplace, still preparing here in the shadow to go forth on his Apostleship. He was arming himself against his time of war; that style of speech which is so peculiarly his own was likewise in process of formation, — rude, peculiar, incorrect, nay, oftentimes obscure, but gifted with an impetuosity, a nobility, a power, which was to overawe the hardiest rebels against God's grace.

CHAPTER VIII.

THE PEACE OF THE CHURCH.

THE plot against Saint Paul's life was one of the last acts of that persecution which, beginning with the execution of Stephen, lasted for three years (37–40). After telling how the Apostle withdrew from Jerusalem into Cilicia, the Acts go on to say that thereupon the Church enjoyed a season of great peace, which was not disturbed until two years later, in 42, when Agrippa fell upon the Christians once more. These changing periods of tempest and calm were but the natural result of events which at first allowed the Jews to give full rein to their fanaticism, but soon after turned their thoughts in other directions.

We have seen how Caligula, abandoning the policy of Tiberius, restored to the Oriental peoples their independence, with many of their privileges, and to some even their kings. The Jews partook more largely than the rest in these favors, for they had a powerful protector at Rome in Herod Agrippa, the friend of the new Cæsar. Brought up in company with Drusus, Tiberius' son, afterwards driven from court and reduced to extreme poverty, this grandson of Herod the Great had managed to reinstate himself in the tyrant's good graces before the latter died at Capri. His sole thought on his return was how to gain over Caligula, the future Emperor, to his side. One day when they were driving out in the same chariot, Agrippa was so imprudent as to wish the Prince a speedy change in his position as ruler. This speech was overheard and carried to Tiberius, who had the indiscreet courtier thrown into prison forthwith. There Agrippa languished for six months, till one morning his freedman Marsyas rushed to him, saying in Hebrew, "The lion is dead!" On the morrow Caligula delivered his friend; some few days later he proclaimed him king, and gave him Cœlesyria and the regions lying to the south of Damascus as his domain.[1]

There was great joy among the Jews on learning that one of their princes had received such gifts, and enjoyed the confidence of the Emperor. In the height of their triumph they offered holocausts for the prosperity of the new monarch, and fancied themselves freed at last from all servitude. The death of Stephen and the sufferings of the Christians have shown us how prompt and bold the Jews were in reasserting their right to administer justice. Maryllus, who was sent in Pilate's place, knew Agrippa's power at court too well to take issue against the fellow-citizens of the favorite. He tolerated these encroachments on his power, which a little later, encouraged by the presence of the new King, grew the more audacious. This prince, in fact, after obtaining permission to visit his kingdom, made his royal entry about the middle of the year 38 with a pomp and noise that resounded from Upper Syria all over Judea and Galilee. To the Jews it seemed that this grandson of Herod and descendant of Mariamne, daughter of the Machabees, was about to restore the throne of his ancestors; they dreamed of nothing less than seeing him King of Jerusalem. In Galilee the emotions excited by his coming were of another sort altogether. Antipas, who was its ruler, realized that it was all over with him if Caligula's favorite continued to eclipse his authority in this manner. His fears were fostered in every way by Herodias, whose influence over her weak-willed husband was now all-powerful; she urged that it was an unbearable thing that they should have to submit to the high fortunes of this adventurer, who had once been only too glad to be received in their

[1] Philip's Tetrarchy, and that of Lysanias. Josephus, *Antiquitates*, xviii. 6, 10.

palace at Tiberias when, driven from Rome and overwhelmed with debts, his only refuge had been their liberality. One thing alone could reconcile them to his insolent new fortune, — the title of King, which their rival flaunted so insultingly. In Rome alone could this favor be obtained; accordingly, the Tetrarch hastened thither, accompanied by Herodias, and together they did all in their power to overreach the Emperor. But Agrippa had been beforehand with them by denouncing their intrigues with the King of the Parthians. Tried and convicted of treason, Antipas was banished into Gaul, and his tetrarchy of Galilee added to the domains which had fallen to the share of Caius' friend. Everything smiled on the Jews; the shattered members of their ancient empire were being knit together; the body politic seemed to be regaining its pristine form and strength. To restore the unity lost after the death of Herod the Great, all that was needed now was that the Emperor should add Judea to the new kingdom; but in the very hour when these hopes were at their highest pitch, the tyrant's caprice sent them tumbling to the dust.

Three years before, some disease had suddenly attacked the master of the world and deprived him of his reason, leaving him the creature of his naturally cruel disposition. It was no longer a man, but a bloodthirsty fool, a monster, that sat upon the throne, says Suetonius. Going from one folly to another, Caius finally conceived the notion that he was God. He had the most illustrious divinities brought from Greece, even the Olympian Jupiter, that masterpiece of Phidias,[1] and without a thought for either art or religion, he ordered their heads to be removed, and his own placed in their stead. He had his temple and priests, with victims all of brilliant plumage, — peacocks, pheasants, guinea-hens, and scarlet flamingos. Frequently he feigned to be engaged in long conversations with the Capitoline Jupiter, sometimes chatting

[1] If we are to believe Josephus, fearful prodigies prevented Memmius Regulus from executing the orders of Caligula, and Phidias' statue remained on Olympus. *Antiquitates*, xix. 1.

familiarly with him, sometimes threatening him. One day he was heard to cry out in a rage,[1] —

" Kill me, or I kill thee ! "

Then came the order for the whole world to worship the new God, and the Jews alone refused to bend the knee. This action of theirs is one of the glories of their race, but it changed the favor which had given rise to such high hopes into the bitterest hatred. We must allow, furthermore, for the fact that the imperial protection had puffed them up with pride, and consequently had deepened the antipathy of the Pagans among whom they lived. Caligula's impious command was eagerly used by the latter as an occasion for wreaking their spite; in every city the Jewish population became the sport of informers and bullies. In the synagogues they set up statues of Caligula and altars to the almighty Cæsar, thus obliging them to offer sacrifices to the divine majesty of their prince. Everywhere cruel persecutions ensued, but nowhere worse than in Alexandria: the Israelites, shut up in a narrow quarter of the town, perished of hunger and pestilence; those who fled from this living tomb were hewn down and cut in pieces; whole families were burned by slow fire; even the head men of the community were dragged to the theatre, and there, before the eyes of the populace, were whipped to death. Such were some of the awful scenes which encrimsoned the beautiful capital of Egypt.

The Jews, perishing under the severity of their sufferings, deputed Philo, with some of the most venerable men of their nation, to beseech Caius to spare them. The only result of their embassy was a new series of outrages and insults. Summoned from Rome to Pozzuoli, remanded to Rome, then for a long time left unnoticed, they finally got leave to plead their cause in a country house where the Emperor was visiting. But the mighty ruler met them with sarcasm and scorn.

"So," he said, grinding his teeth, "these are the enemies of the gods who refuse to adore me, and prefer to

[1] Suetonius, *Caligula*, xxii.

worship a divinity whose name they dare not pronounce!" and in the face of the horror-stricken Jews he shouted the ineffable name of Jehovah.

Then he began to rush about the house, going up and down the stairways, dragging after him these old men, now trembling with fear and out of breath, — Philo, their leader, being over eighty years of age. When he did turn back to address them, there were new taunts to be borne.

"Why don't you eat pork?" he asked.

The courtiers burst out laughing, while the ambassadors responded timidly that every nation had its customs, and that some peoples would not eat sheep.

"Oh, so far as mutton is concerned, they are quite right," Caius retorted; "it is certainly an insipid meat."

In the great hall of the villa he seemed inclined to hear them; but hardly had they uttered the first words of their speech when he began to run about, this way and that, giving orders to the workmen. Utterly dismayed at such a reception, the Jews expected every moment to hear him order their execution. But for the nonce the monster had no appetite for bloodshed; he dismissed them with insulting sympathy.

"Why, after all," he said, "these folks don't seem as bad as they are made out to be. What poor fools they are not to believe in my divinity!"

But what did this humiliation of the Alexandrians matter when compared with the sacrilege with which Caligula threatened the whole race? The enemies of Judaism counselled him to give it its death-blow by dedicating the Temple at Jerusalem to his imperial majesty, and at once the order went forth that a colossal statue of the Emperor should be erected in the Holy of Holies. Petronius, a new prefect for Syria, left Rome to take in hand the accomplishment of this decree. His orders were that he should not recoil before any act of violence, but enter Jerusalem at the head of his troops, and, if need be, call on the two legions of the Euphrates. Petronius went into winter quarters at Ptolemaïs (St. John of Acre), and from there he communicated the wishes of Cæsar to the Sanhedrin and High Priests of Jerusalem. He was only waiting for the statue, as yet not out of the workmen's hands at Sidon, before executing his orders.

At this news thousands upon thousands of Jews thronged about him, all covered with sackcloth, their heads sprinkled with ashes; princes of the people, women, children, without distinction of class in this common grief, declared that they were ready to die rather than allow their Temple to be profaned. Petronius repulsed them with great harshness, alleging their ruler's edict as his excuse for what he was about to do; and the throng made answer that they feared God's wrath more than the Emperor's.

Before this earnestness of despair the Governor comprehended the awfulness of a mission which could only be accomplished by the extermination of a whole people. In great perplexity of mind, he withdrew with his officers to Tiberias; but the Jews followed him thither. He tried over and over again to calm them, reminding them that these were the orders of an all-powerful master, and contrasting their conduct with the prompt obedience of others.

"Then will you make war against your Emperor?" he demanded.

"No war," replied the Jews; "but he who would violate our Law must first slaughter us!" And falling with their faces to the earth, the whole multitude made ready for the executioners.

For forty days the same scenes were renewed; spring and the seed-time came, but none thought of earthly cares. Petronius was too humane to wish a flourishing land to be changed into a wilderness watered with blood, and ravaged by famine and robbery. At the risk of his own life he promised to intercede with the Emperor, — a courageous decision, which Heaven blessed forthwith, for hardly had he uttered it than the rain, after a long drought, came to prosper the sowing.[1]

At Rome, however, Agrippa was not unmindful of the anguish suffered by his brethren; he was on the watch

[1] Josephus, *Antiquitates*, xviii. 8, 2–6.

for a favorable opportunity, and managed to find his chance at a banquet which he offered in Caius' honor. The Emperor was pleased to promise his favorite, during the feast, that he would grant him anything he might desire. Whether from policy, or moved by sincere feeling, the son of the Asmoneans thought only of his imperilled Faith; he besought that the edict might be revoked. Caligula kept his word, but with a bad grace; turning to wreak his anger on some one, he sent an order that Petronius should be put to death. Happily the vessel which bore his mandate was delayed by storms. When it touched the shores of Syria, the news had already reached there that Chæreas had slain the tyrant (Jan. 24, 41).

This year of terror had at least called a truce to the sufferings of the Christians, for the sacrilege with which the Temple was threatened, absorbed the thoughts of their persecutors. Doubtless on this point the disciples of the Christ shared in the feelings common to all Israel, and said their prayers daily for the safety of the sanctuary where they still offered prayers and sacrifices. But their anxiety was tempered by joy at regaining their peaceful existence, — with many, too, by a presentiment that even if the Temple were to be closed to them, the Supper Room would suffice for the celebration of the New Passover and the worship of their Heavenly Father. And so, in this season of great trouble, the Acts tell us that the little flock of Jesus prospered. "The Church was at peace all through Judea, Galilee, and Samaria, waxing strong, walking in the fear of the Lord, and filled with the consolation of the Holy Ghost." [1]

Here, for the first time, Galilee is mentioned as among the provinces to which the Kingdom of Jesus had extended. Certainly it had not waited this season to give birth to more than a few Churches, for this was the region above all others where Jesus had sown the Glad Tidings, and where after His Resurrection He appeared to more than five hundred disciples. A number of these believers had followed the Apostles to Jerusalem; but most of them

[1] Acts ix. 31.

remained in their own country and made up devoted companies here and there, from whom the Christians, driven out of the Holy City, were wont to find a brotherly greeting. During the persecution these communities scattered over the land of Israel seemed to the Jews no more than the wreckage of a vast ruin ; none the less these broken blocks were the makings of an edifice, Christ's Holy Church, whose foundations were already laid deep and strong, hereafter to grow and increase forever, and destined soon to cover the face of the earth.

Peter profited by the peace to visit the faithful settled outside the Holy City,[1] journeying over Judea, Samaria, and Galilee. But in no part of his travels did his mission-work bear better fruits than in the plains of Sharon, which border the Mediterranean from Carmel as far as Jaffa. To the southeast of these fields, and a half hour's walk from Ramleh, rich orchards surround the city of Lydda.

The Apostle, "upon coming to visit the saints that dwelt there,"[2] found a man named Eneas, who had been a paralytic since his eighth year, lying upon a bed.

"And Peter said to him, 'Eneas, Jesus the Christ healeth thee. Arise and make thy bed.' And immediately he arose."

Thrilled by this miracle, the Jews in those parts deemed that this was the time foretold by Isaiah wherein the earth should bud forth like the lily, and attire itself in the beauty of Carmel and of Sharon. "God shall come," the Prophet had said, "and He shall save you. Then the eyes of the blind shall see the light, and the ears of the deaf be opened. The lame man shall leap like the hart, and the tongue of the dumb be loosened." The healing

[1] Ἐγένετο δὲ Πέτρον διερχόμενον διὰ πάντων κατελθεῖν καὶ πρὸς τοὺς ἁγίους τοὺς κατοικοῦντας Λύδδαν, may be translated : "It came to pass that Peter, journeying *over the whole coast*, came likewise to the saints who dwelt in Lydda," thus putting πάντων in the neuter ; but there is good reason to prefer the Vulgate reading, which refers this adjective to ἁγίους : "Petrus dum pertransiret universos," for the καὶ which precedes τοὺς ἁγίους : "he came likewise to the saints in Lydda," supposes that the writer had already alluded to certain disciples in the church.
[2] Acts ix. 32-34.

of Eneas declared the fulfilment of the Prophecy, and from all sides they came to Lydda; not only "those who lived in the town, but all Sharon came to see this man, and they were converted to the Lord."

At the same time, among the disciples in Joppa, there was a Jewish woman, a Hellenist, whose name is given in the Acts in the Aramean form as "Tabitha," and in the Greek translation as "Dorcas."[1] Each of these words signifies a gazelle, — the perfect model of grace to which the Orientals were fond of comparing the beauty of women.[2] This lady was possessed of some wealth apparently, and "was full of good works and alms-gifts which she made." She had fallen sick of late, and died just at this time, her death causing great mourning in the Church of Joppa, for the holy widow supported the poor, wove their garments, and showered her bounties upon all alike. Her body, after being piously washed, was wound in cerecloths and perfumes, then borne into the upper hall of her house. The widows, towards whom Tabitha had a mother's heart, clung close about the bier, and hung the garments she had made for them on the walls of the room.[3] Then, seated round about the body, they began the wail, beating their

---

[1] The word Tabitha, טָבִיתָא, is Aramean, and corresponds to the Hebrew צְבִי.

[2] Cant. iv. 5.

[3] M. Renan sees in the words of the Greek text, ὅσα ἐποίει μετ' αὐτῶν οὖσα, a reference to the fact that Tabitha had formed a company of holy widows, who, with her, spent their days in making garments for the poor; and hence he concludes that Jaffa "saw the beginning of that race of veiled women, clad in linen, who were to perpetuate the tradition of such charitable secrets all down the ages" (*Les Apôtres*, p. 200). Nothing in the context authorizes this interpretation. Tabitha is there represented as charitable towards all (Acts x. 36); nowhere is it so much as hinted that she supervised an association of women folk; the widows display to Peter, not their own work, but the gifts made to them by Tabitha (x. 39); finally, when Peter raised the pious lady to life, he restores her, not to any holy sisterhood, but "to the saints and the widows," that is to say, to the whole Church of Jaffa. The Vulgate gives the real meaning of this passage: "Circumsteterunt illum omnes viduæ flentes, et ostendentes ei tunicas et vestes, quas faciebat illis Dorcas." M. Renan is no less beguiled by his own fancies when he considers "the saints and the widows" as being "a sort of *bégards* and *béguines*, — *fraticelli* [pious lay folk living in community] dearly loved by the people." To satisfy one's self that S. Luke means all Christians by the term "saints," one has only to glance through

breasts, weeping, and uttering long-drawn cries. Nevertheless, the disciples had not given up all hope; many a time their Master had made death obey His commands, and had He not promised that the Apostles should do still greater things? Joppa is only a few hours' walk from Lydda. "Hearing that Peter was there, they sent two men thither to beseech him to come. Forthwith Peter rose up and went with them. And when he arrived there they conducted him to the upper chamber, and all the widows stood about him weeping, showing the coats and garments which Dorcas made them. Now, when Peter had put them all without, and knelt down himself, he prayed; then, turning towards the body, 'Tabitha,' he said, 'arise!' She opened her eyes, and, seeing Peter, she sat up. At once he gave her his hand and lifted her up; then, calling the saints and the widows, he restored her to them alive."[1]

The dwelling where this wondrous deed took place stood among the orange-groves which surround the city,— there, at least, is the spot where tradition[2] venerates its ruins to-day. But the miracle was soon known through the whole city, and many believed in the Lord. These numerous conversions, Tabitha's restoration to life, and a presentiment of even more splendid favors in store for the Church, made Peter decide to stay for some time at Joppa. Accordingly, he went into the city and took lodgings at the house of a tanner named Simon.

That he should have chosen such a host is enough to show that the Apostle, taking pattern by his Master, had begun already to free himself from the Pharisaic Rules, for in the eyes of the rigorists this man's house was unclean, and none of them would have entered it willingly.[3] "The world," says the Talmud, "cannot exist

---

the Acts (ix. 13, 32; xxvi. 10). In this he simply follows the example of his master, S. Paul (Rom. i. 7; xii. 13; xv. 25–26, 31; xvi. 2, 15; 1 Cor. i. 2; vi. 1; xiv. 33; xvi. 1, etc.).
[1] Acts ix. 38–41.
[2] "Non longe a ruinis Joppes, versus Jerusalem eundo, monstrantur fundamenta et residuum domus Tabithæ" (Quaresmius, *Elucidatio Terræ Sanctæ*, t. ii. p. 6). [3] *Kidduschin*, f. 82, 2.

without tanners; but woe unto him who chooseth this trade!" The necessity of handling dead beasts made their condition one of perpetual impurity, and, to a certain degree, put these artisans outside the Law. Again, some held that the Law of the Levirate did not oblige so far as they were concerned, and that a sister-in-law might refuse to marry one of them. The same privileges were granted a woman married to a tanner,— she was allowed a divorce if she had not been forewarned of the kind of industry her husband was engaged in.[1] The disgust of the Jews for this class of men went to such lengths that they had tanneries removed at least fifty cubits outside the town limits.[2] So we must suppose that Simon's workshop was not in the house where he lived, for the native traditions locate his dwelling inside the walls.[3] The mosque which occupies its site to-day has nothing about it to recall the look of things in the olden times when Peter sojourned there. But from the housetops, whither the Apostle went up to pray, our eyes take in all that he saw then, — a stretch of sea bluer than the skies above, the waves dashing their white spray over the reefs, a pleasant hill-side covered with white dwellings, the water lapping at its base. From her beautiful site, overlooking the shore so proudly, fragrant and gleaming with fruits and flowers on every hand, Jaffa did indeed look like what her Hebrew name signifies,— Yapho, "a Look-out place of Joy."[4]

But such lovely sights could not hold Peter's attention long, for always and in all places his only thought was of Jesus. This harbor, whence Jonas once set sail for Tharsis, — that long reef where he had been thrown back after three days spent in a living tomb, — this

---

[1] *Kettouboth*, f. 77, 1.   [2] *Baba-Bathra*, f. 25, 1, 16, 2.
[3] See Guérin, *Description de la Judée*, t. i. p. 7.
[4] "Having abandoned the Watchtower of Joy (for this is the meaning of the word Joppa among the Hebrews)." . . . S. Gregory Nazianzus, *Apologet. Orat.* i. 42. According to certain writers, Noë's son Japhet founded Joppa and named it after himself; but Pomponius Mela and Pliny make this city antedate the deluge: "Est Joppe ante diluvium, ut ferunt, condita" (Pomponius Mela, *De Situ Orbis*, i. 12). "Joppe Phœnicum antiquior terrarum inundatione, ut ferunt" (Pliny, *Historia Naturalis*, v. 14).

"Sign of the Prophet Jonas" recalled to his mind the Resurrection which the Seer had thus prefigured;[1] then again, how he had preached repentance for sins at heathen Nineveh, even as the Master had promised that they too should carry salvation unto the ends of the earth. What were the paths then by which they were to lead the Gentiles into the Kingdom of Jesus? This Peter did not know as yet, for on Pentecost day the Holy Ghost had not seen fit to reveal to them the great truth that, according to the Master's own words,[2] the Gospel gave the Law its only perfection, at the same time dispensing mankind from its practices. This revelation, more amazing than any other to the sons of Israel, was now about to be made to the Prince of the Apostles in the despised abode of Simon the tanner.

Howbeit, Jaffa was not the spot where God's designs were first to be made manifest. At Cæsarea there was an officer named Cornelius, centurion of a cohort of Italian volunteers stationed there in garrison. He was a Roman citizen, which was a requisite quality for the commander of auxiliary troops,;[3] indeed, his name seems to imply

---

[1] "As Jonas was in the whale's belly three days and three nights, so shall the Son of man be three days and three nights in the bosom of the earth" (Matt. xii. 40).

[2] Matt. v. 17; vi. 5, etc.

[3] There were three kinds of troops under arms in the Roman army: the Legion, composed exclusively of Roman citizens; the Auxiliary Cohorts, made up of provincials who were not citizens of Rome, together with various allied peoples and kingdoms; finally, the Volunteer Cohorts, which originally were open only to Italians exempt from militia duty, but afterwards included all such as desired to bear arms without enduring the severe discipline of the legionaries. We read in Josephus that the garrison at Cæsarea usually comprised five Auxiliary Cohorts (*Bellum Judaicum*, iii. 4, 2; *Antiquitates*, xix. 9, 2), almost all levied from Syria itself (*Bellum Judaicum*, ii. 13, 7). On the other hand, there is an inscription which mentions a cohort of Volunteers in Syria: "Cohors militum Italicorum voluntaria, quæ est in Syria." (Gruter, p. 434, 1.) It may be that the force under Cornelius' command was really a troop of Volunteers from Italy, or that, though coming originally from that country, it had received so many recruits from among the Syrians that at last it numbered very few foreigners; indeed this seems to be the inference S. Luke means us to draw, for he speaks, not of the Italian Cohort, but of a Cohort called the Italian. Whatever the nationality of the soldiers, their officers, according to custom, were certainly Romans.

that he could boast of some kinship — that of a client at least — with the "Gens Cornelia," the illustrious family of the Scipios, Sylla, and the mother of the Gracchi. Born and bred in Italy, he had embraced the career of arms with all a youth's dreams of military glory, but without foreseeing that more lasting greatness which has raised him upon our altars.[1] It was at Cæsarea that he came to know the Jews and felt himself strongly attracted towards them. Soon he began to share their faith in the Eternal, their worship and fear of God, and their practices of virtue. He prayed to God always, gave large alms to the people, and brought over to the worship of Jehovah, first his own household, and thereafter certain ones of his command. This high-souled man, "praised by all the Jews" of the city,[2] still lacked the character which in their eyes would have made him perfect, — the pious Centurion was uncircumcised, and albeit an Israelite at heart, from that one fact he remained outside the Synagogue. Why did he hesitate to take this step? What was he asking of God? Did he, like many other Gentiles, shrink from bearing on his body the seal of the children of Abraham? Or was he wavering between the Pharisees' Law and the Glad Tidings brought to Cæsarea by Philip? for "he knew what had taken place in Judea"[3] and all that had been noised abroad concerning Jesus. Whatever the motives of his uncertainty, Cornelius was one of those who ardently desire the truth, ready to do all things in its service.

Now, one day when he was praying, about the ninth hour (three in the afternoon), an Angel of God appeared to him and called him by his name, —

"Cornelius!" said the voice.

The Centurion was seized with terror. "Lord," he answered, "what wouldst Thou with me?"

And the Angel replied, "Thy prayers and thine alms

---

[1] His name is in the old Roman Martyrology, and in that of Usuard, under the date of February 2, and in the Armenian Calendar for the tenth of December.
[2] Acts x. 22.   [3] Acts x. 37.

have ascended into the presence of God, and He is mindful of them. And now send men to Joppa, and call hither one Simon who is surnamed Peter. He lodgeth with a certain Simon, a tanner, whose house is by the seaside. He will tell thee what thou must do."

With these words the Angel disappeared. Cornelius straightway summoned two of his house-servants with one of his soldiers who feared the God of Israel, and, after telling them all that had taken place, he despatched them to Joppa.

On the morrow, about midday, just as the Centurion's messengers were nearing the city, Peter, faithful to the Jewish custom, went up on the housetop to pray. Once there, he was seized with such great hunger that he immediately asked for something to eat. But while the food was being prepared, he was rapt in an ecstasy. Heaven opened before his eyes; a great cloth descended thence, knotted at the four corners, and suspended from the firmament by invisible hands. Looking therein, he saw all sorts of four-footed animals, with reptiles and birds of the air,[1] and he heard a Voice from Heaven, —

"Arise, Peter," it said; "kill and eat."

"Far be it from me, Lord," Peter replied; "for I have never eaten anything that is impure or unclean."[2]

Once again he heard the Voice, —

"What God hath cleansed, do not thou call impure!"[3]

This same thing occurred three times,[4] then the cloth was withdrawn into Heaven. Peter was once more alone on the housetop; but he was greatly troubled as to the meaning of this Vision, because abstinence from unclean flesh was considered so sacred a duty that, in order to

---

[1] The addition found in the received text, τὰ θηρία καὶ, "and wild beasts," is omitted in the critical editions (Griesbach, Lachmann, Tischendorf, Alford).

[2] There were both clean and unclean animals in the cloth, but the combination made each one a contaminated thing which Jews must abstain from partaking of; hence Peter's refusal.

[3] These words of God abrogated the Law.

[4] 'Επὶ τρίς: this threefold repetition was meant to make the doctrine now revealed absolutely certain.

observe it faithfully, the Jews separated themselves from the Gentile world, even refusing to enter their dwelling-places, soiled as they always were by the presence of impure animals. Daniel[1] in the palace of Nabuchodonosor, Eleazar, the seven brethren, and their mother,[2] preferring death rather than violate the Great Precept, — these were some of the heroic examples which were wont to kindle the zeal of even the lukewarm. We need not be surprised to find the Apostles still sharing Israel's attachment to this observance. It is true the Master had said "that nothing from without entering into a man's body can defile him;"[3] but this was just one of those sayings which seemed obscure, in the deposit of Faith, and Peter did not turn to them for light to help him understand the mysterious invitation which had so shocked him.

In the mean time Cornelius's messengers had entered Joppa, and, inquiring their way to Simon's house, came at last to his door. They knocked, and asked if this was the place where Simon, surnamed Peter, was lodged. But the Apostle heard nothing, saw nothing, lying prone upon the terraced roof, his mind filled with the emotions roused by his Vision.

Then the Holy Spirit said to him, "Behold, here are three men who seek thee. Arise, get thee down and go with them, doubting nothing, because it is I Who have sent them."

Peter descended to the street, approached these men, and said, "Lo, here am I! Am I he whom you seek? What is the cause for which you are come?"

"Cornelius, the Centurion," they replied, "a righteous man, and one that fears God, to whom the whole Jewish nation bears testimony of his good deeds, has been bidden by a holy Angel to send for thee into his house, and to listen to thy words."

At these words the bandage fell from the Apostle's eyes; enlightened by the Holy Ghost, he beheld the designs of God, — the old Covenant, which was but for a

---

[1] Dan. i. 5-19.   [2] 2 Mac. vi. 18-31; vii.   [3] Mark vii. 15.

figure of the New, now vanishing as the latter outshone it in brilliancy ; how that the rites of Judaism were become superfluous since what time the Blood of Jesus had consummated the Eternal Sacrifice; how, by baptism, the Gentiles might enter into the kingdom of the Christ without submitting to circumcision ; finally, that this distinction between clean and unclean beasts, with all the legal Observances, must be cast away, as the yoke of a slavery unworthy of men whom Jesus called His brethren and His friends. At last it seemed as if that wall which for so many centuries had divided Israel from the Gentile world was crumbling under Peter's eyes ; and so, renouncing, once again, everything of his own, — prejudices, opinions, all, — in order to follow his Master, the Apostle awaited only the promptings from on High.

The messengers were too weary to return to Cæsarea at once. Peter made them enter, found them lodgings for the night, and on the morrow departed with them, resolved that, as God had commanded, he would not look upon either the dwelling or the person of a Pagan as unhallowed or profane. Nevertheless, taking precautions against any scandal which might arise from such an unheard-of thing, he wished to have some of the brethren from Joppa as witnesses of his actions, and so he begged six of them to accompany him.[1]

It is only an eleven hours' walk from Jaffa to Cæsarea. The little band must have walked slowly, since it was three o'clock in the afternoon of the second day's journey when they reached the Centurion's residence.[2] Cornelius had assembled his kinsfolk and friends, and was now awaiting them. So soon as Peter stood on the threshold, the officer fell down at his feet and worshipped him.[3] But the Apostle made him stand erect.

"Arise," he said ; " I too am a man." And still con-

[1] Acts xi. 12.   [2] Acts x. 30.
[3] In Beza's Codex and in a marginal correction of the Syriac Version we read the following additional words : " As Peter was approaching Cæsarea, one of the servants ran ahead to announce his arrival. Forthwith Cornelius hastened out, and, meeting him, fell at his feet and worshipped him."

versing with him, he entered the house, where he found a number of persons gathered to meet him.

The six believers from Joppa, belonging to the Circumcision, followed their pastor; but they were much troubled to find themselves introduced into an unhallowed dwelling, while the Pagans, accustomed to the Jews' scruples, displayed no less astonishment. Peter quieted their uneasiness.

"You know," he said, "that it is an unlawful thing for a Jew to league himself with a foreigner, or to go with him; but God hath showed to me that I ought not to call any man impure or unclean. This is why, since you sent to seek me, I came without hesitating. I ask, therefore, for what cause you have bidden me come."

"Four days ago," Cornelius replied, "I was fasting up to this hour;[1] and as I was praying in my house at the ninth hour,[2] all at once a man clad in white apparel stood before me and said, 'Cornelius, thy prayer is heard, and God is mindful of thine alms. Send, therefore, to Joppa, and call hither Simon, who is surnamed Peter;

---

[1] That is, the hour wherein Cornelius addressed S. Peter in these words: 'Ἀπὸ τετάρτης ἡμέρας μέχρι ταύτης τῆς ὥρας ἤμην νηστεύων καὶ τὴν ἐννάτην ὥραν προσευχόμενος. . . . The words νηστεύων καί are not in the manuscripts of the Vatican, Sinaï, and Ephrem; in the Alexandrian, after being effaced by some early corrector, they have been reinserted in a later revision. None of the translators of the Vulgate, Coptic, Ethiopian, or Armenian Versions found it in the original copies which they made use of. But there are weighty reasons notwithstanding why we should not reject this lection, which we find in Beza's manuscript, in the *Codex Laudianus* (5th century), that of *Mutinensis* (9th century), the *Angelicus Romanus* (9th century), in the Italic, Syriac, Sahidic, Arabic, and Slav Versions, as well as in very many Fathers (S. John Chrysostom, S. Epiphanius, Tertullian, S. Augustine, etc.).

[2] This passage has been variously interpreted. Meyer translates it thus: "For four days up to this hour I have taken no food." Neander and De Wette understand it in another sense: "For the last four days I have fasted daily up to this hour" (the hour wherein I saw the vision). Alford proves that grammatically both these translations are inadmissible. Ἤμην can only refer to an action already accomplished, which is not prolonged until the moment whereat Cornelius uses the word. Furthermore, ταύτης τῆς ὥρας, which means "this hour of the day," cannot be rendered by "up to the present hour," for in that case we should have τῆς δὲ τῆς ὥρας. The translation adopted above is the only one which harmonizes with the context, as Cornelius' intention was plainly to tell what he was doing when the Angel appeared to him.

he lodgeth in the house of Simon the tanner, by the sea-side.' I sent immediately to you, and you have done well in coming. And now we are all here, in the sight of God, to hear everything which has been commanded unto you by the Lord."

In these few words the pious soldier reveals the loyalty of his character, as ardent as he was whole-souled and generous in his faith, ready to sacrifice everything at God's command. His family and his friends about him, moved by his example, like him, longed only for the truth. To turn away from such a household, where God's grace was working so powerfully, would indeed have been " to call unclean that which Heaven itself had purified." [1] This Peter boldly declared.

" In very deed," he said, " I perceive that God regards not the condition of persons,[2] but that in every nation he who feareth Him and doeth righteousness is acceptable to Him." [3] Thereupon he yielded to his host's request and spoke to them of the Word of Life, first recalling what they already were acquainted with, whether through Philip or from the Jews of Cæsarea, concerning " Jesus, the Lord of all, how through Him God hath manifested Himself unto the children of Israel, and hath published forth tidings of peace." As he had no new thing to tell them, he was content to bring the Saviour's mortal life briefly before their eyes,[4] — " how God anointed him with the Holy Ghost and with power; how that this Jesus of Nazareth passed from place to place healing all those whom the Devil had made slaves to his power, for God was with Him; His death upon the Cross, His Resurrection and appearance to the Twelve, " who did eat

---

[1] Acts xi. 9.   [2] Deut. x. 27 ; Job xxxiv. 19, etc.
[3] The truth hereby unveiled to the Apostle's eyes was not that the Gentiles are called to a share in the good things promised to Israel, for this point was already clear to them all, but that Pagans are in noways disqualified, not even the uncircumcised, from entering the Kingdom of Heaven. Nevertheless, such was the force of received opinions at this time that, in depicting the man well-pleasing to God under the New Law, Peter still holds to the two features which embodied their idea of the perfect Jew : " He who *feareth God* and *worketh righteousness.*"
[4] Acts x. 36–43.

and drink with Him after He was risen again;" how the Apostles were bidden "to bear witness that He is that one Who is appointed by God Judge of the quick and the dead."

Then, coming down to the practice of a Christian life, he was going on to prove from the Prophets that all those who believe in Jesus receive remission of their sins through His Name, when suddenly his discourse was interrupted. The Holy Ghost descended upon those that listened, and the wondrous signs of the Supper Room were witnessed again at Cæsarea;[1] there was the same outpouring of graces, the same ecstatic rapture among the hearers; while under the influence of the Holy Spirit they were heard speaking in divers tongues and glorifying God.

The faithful who came from Joppa with Peter were astounded at seeing these supernatural gifts showered upon Gentiles. Then the Apostle seized the opportunity to fulfil the behests of Heaven.

"Can any man," he said, addressing his companions, "refuse water, that these should not be baptized, who have received the Holy Ghost as well as we?" And he commanded that they should be baptized in the Name of the Lord Jesus Christ.

Nor was he content with giving these uncircumcised folk, in this way, all the privileges of Israel; he went farther, and yielding to their entreaties, he consented to remain some days with them. Living under their roof, and eating at the same table with them, he showed by his example what he meant by teaching that there was now no middle wall between Jews and Gentiles, but that henceforth all were to be of one body and one soul in Jesus Christ.

The rumor of so unforeseen a change in his practice quickly spread throughout Judea, and excited the liveliest emotions; for by this sudden blow the Church realized that it was cut off from the ancient stem of Jesse. In Jerusalem especially, the feelings of anxiety were intense. The Apostles, well assured that the Lord would be

[1] Acts x. 44–46.

Peter's guide and counsellor unto the end of time, waited in humble expectation; but such was not the case with very many of the Jews, who were not a whit less zealous for the Law because leagued by their faith with the Christians.

The latter gave free rein to their indignation, and when Peter returned to Jerusalem, gave utterance to their complaints.

"Why did you enter in among the uncircumcised?" they demanded.

"And why did you eat with them?"

Peter braved the storm, for he had acted only as he had been prompted by the Spirit of God. His companions from Joppa had seen it all, and could witness thereto. Surrounded by these men, whom he had brought with him to the Holy City, the Apostle presented himself before the assembly of the faithful, and needed but to tell the story of all he had done, in order to confound the murmurers. He related the Vision on the terrace of Simon's house, how the Angel appeared to Cornelius, and how the Holy Ghost descended upon the Centurion's household, as at Pentecost in the Upper Chamber. Was not this the baptism of the Spirit promised them by the Saviour?

"So then," Peter concluded, "since God hath given to them the same gift as to us who have believed in the Lord Jesus Christ, who am I that I should withstand God?"

This defence silenced the objectors. The Lord had spoken too plainly to leave any doubt as to His holy will; and by its presence the Holy Ghost had justified, nay, consecrated, Peter's act. The faithful of the Holy City recognized all this, and they glorified God, saying:

"Thus hath God granted to the Gentiles also that gift of penitence which leadeth unto life!"

However, though the majority of Christians bowed beneath the hand of the Head Shepherd, nevertheless for long years after there remained a certain number of Judaizing converts to Christianity in Jerusalem, who felt that by their brethren's actions they were wounded in their dearest convictions; nor did they take any great pains to conceal their bitterness. For a time they appeared to acquiesce before the revelation at Cæsarea; but we shall soon hear them recriminating the new doctrine again, fighting not only against Paul, but against Peter and the Apostolic College. "These men of the Circumcision,"[1] as Scripture calls them, were to bring about the first schism which rent the Church.

[1] Acts x. 45; xi. 2; Gal. ii. 12; Col. iv. 11; Tit. i. 10.

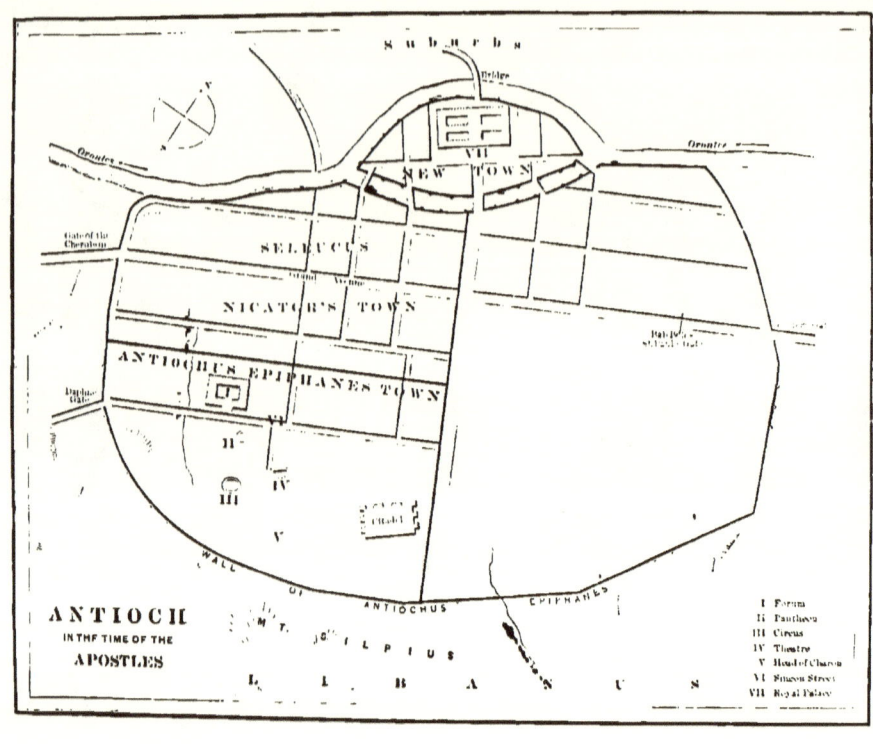

CHAPTER IX.

ANTIOCH.

WHILE the Faith was thus waxing strong in Judea, the Church's progress was not less rapid beyond the frontiers. The disciples from the Holy City, who were scattered by the storms which ensued upon Stephen's death, had made their way northward little by little; from Galilee they passed over into Phœnicia, some set sail thence to Cyprus, while others, following the course of the Orontes, pushed on as far as Antioch.[1] Did Peter act as guide for the latter, and did he as early as the year 37 establish that Church in the capital of Syria of which he was the first Bishop? So certain historians have held,[2] but with little likelihood; for we know that not one of the Apostles left Jerusalem at the beginning of the persecution.[3] Consequently Peter did not go to Antioch before the year 40;[4] only then did he establish there his Apostolic seat, which he transferred to Rome[5] two years later. The Acts do not mention the

[1] Acts xi. 19.
[2] See Tillemont's *Mémoires*, t. i. note xxv. on S. Peter. S. Gregory relates (*Epistolæ* l. vii. 40), that S. Peter's episcopate at Antioch lasted seven years. Now, as the common opinion holds that his Pontificate at Rome was prolonged for twenty-five years and began in the year 42, in order to obtain the seven years of his episcopacy at Antioch before this epoch, we should be obliged to date the foundation of this See in 36 or 37. But this is so out of harmony with the series of facts recorded in the Acts that it seems to us quite impossible to accept it. We must either sacrifice S. Gregory's testimony altogether, or understand him as meaning, by these seven years, the time which elapsed before S. Evodius succeeded the Prince of the Apostles in the See of Antioch.
[3] Acts viii. 1, 14–25.
[4] This is the date adopted by Tillemont (*Mémoires*, t. i. note xxv. on S. Peter).
[5] S. Jerome, who had the aid of so many documents now lost to us, summarizes the testimony of tradition as to S. Peter's Apostleship, and

foundation of this episcopate, but Tradition has preserved a record of it,[1] and it is this fact which has given Antioch its title of Metropolitan city of the East.[2]

Peter made this choice before the vision at Joppa,[3] though he had small conception of the Church's future, or that the Gentiles were to be co-heirs of the promises, or that Jerusalem was doomed to speedy destruction. At a time when the Holy City still held its supremacy in the eyes of all Jews, to forsake it in order to bear the sovereign pontificate into the most Pagan of Oriental cities, was indeed a surprising act, which must have been prompted by some express order from the Master. But, as always, the Apostle obeyed, and established the Chair of Peter in the place marked out for it, but without at first understanding whither God's Spirit was leading him. It is easier for us, freed from the prejudices which then darkened the disciples' vision, to perceive the wisdom of

---

sets down certain dates which have never as yet been seriously impugned.' Consequently it seems the wisest plan to accept his chronology as the most plausible we know of, though, of course, not absolutely certain : " Simon Petrus, . . . princeps Apostolorum, post episcopatum Antiochensis ecclesiæ et prædicationem dispersionis eorum qui de circumcisione crediderant, in Ponto, Galatia, Cappadocia, Asia, et Bithynia, secundo Claudii anno (42), ad expugnandum Simonem Magum Romam pergit, ibique viginti quinque annis cathedram sacerdotalem tenuit, usque ad ultimum annum Neronis, id est decimum quartum (67)." *De Viris illustribus*, i.

[1] The bare fact of this foundation cannot be considered as doubtful, for the evidence of S. Jerome just quoted : " Petrus . . . post episcopatum Antiochensis ecclesiæ. . . . Romam pergit," is confirmed by the traditions of the Roman Church and by the entire Eastern half of Christianity. To represent the former we have a succession of Sovereign Pontiffs, notably S. Leo (*Serm.* lxxxii. 5) and S. Gregory the Great (*Epistolar*. l. vii. ep. 40 ; l. viii. ep. 2) : for the latter, Origen (*In Lucam Hom.* vi.) ; Eusebius (*Chronicorum*, l. ii.; *Historia Ecclesiastica*, iii. 36) ; and S. John Chrysostom (*Hom. in Inscript. Act.* ii. 6). We shall show elsewhere (Appendix IV.) that no difficulties can be raised from the fact of a feast being celebrated on the 22d of February in honor of S. Peter's Chair at Antioch.

[2] *Conciliorum collectio*, éd. Labbe, t. ii. p. 1269.

[3] If he went there, as we suppose, about the year 40, he had not as yet been enlightened by this revelation ; for, two years later, the Church which he instructed in the Faith and left behind him in this city was still as Jewish as ever, — indeed, its members were astonished at the idea that Pagans should be bidden to enter freely into the new realm of the Christ. Acts xi. 19-23.

the divine Counsel which had foreordained that Antioch should become the centre of Christianity in the East.

Jerusalem, lying so far distant from the great world of men, perched among the hill-tops of Judea, with no means of communication with the outlying regions save by mountain roads, — certainly Jerusalem could never become the focus of a religion which was to spread over the whole globe. Antioch, on the other hand, was eminently fitted to take this important place. Situated on the borders of Asia Minor and Syria, the meeting-point of the ancient world with the new, she occupied that valley where the Orontes, after flowing north from its sources, turns to the west, between Taurus and Libanus, to empty itself into the Mediterranean. By means of this stream, she could reach the great sea which washed all the coasts of the Empire, while from the East there were numerous roads which brought the caravans to her gates. This advantageous situation was for a long time overlooked. Kings of Nineveh and Babylon, the Medes, Persians, and Pharaohs, from Memphis and Thebes, passed by without a glance at the Valley of the Orontes. Alexander, too, rode through it on his way to Egypt, on whose shores he founded the city which perpetuates his name. But, after him, Seleucus, one of his lieutenants, perceived the advantages of the place, and built there a city in memory of his father, Antiochus. A divine inspiration guided him, we are told, for an eagle darted from the skies to mark the birthplace of Antioch; then, in its second flight, winging its way to the mouth of the Orontes, indicated the spot where the Prince should build the harbor, which he afterwards called Seleucia, — for, besides his passion for great building works, he owned a pious devotion for his family names. A little later, Laodicea was erected in honor of his mother; Apamea was dedicated to his wife. At the death of its first king, Syria counted no less than sixteen Antiochs, nine Seleucias, and six Laodiceas.[1] Of all these cities, the most

---

[1] Vaillant, *Seleucidarum Imperium.*

magnificent, unquestionably, was Antioch,[1] the capital of the realm.

This city extends from the base of Mount Silpius, the last link in the chain of Libanus, as far north as the Orontes. The town grew so rapidly that under Augustus it was only second in importance to Rome and Alexandria. Strabo depicts it as a gathering of four cities:[2] to the northwest, between the mountain and the river, stood the primitive foundations built by Seleucus Nicator; on an island in the Orontes was a quarter of the town called after Callinicus;[3] on the brow of Mount Silpius was the town of Antiochus Epiphanes, — the "Epiphania;" to the east of these three cities, a fourth covered the valley and continued to grow with the increase of population. There were ramparts reaching from the river to the summits of Silpius, rising now to the crest of the mountain, here climbing steep ascents, now spanning the mountain-streams, and descending again to the bottom of precipices only to climb new heights. Though it is only a ruin to-day, this wall still stands like a rude crown over the brow of Silpius.[4] The effect must have been far more imposing when the city of Epiphania rose in terrace upon terrace along the mountain-sides. From the midst of the streets and houses great rocks towered up to the height of many hundred feet; the chasms festooned with laurel and myrtle, gardens hanging over the hill-sides, dark caverns and deep ravines, — all these met the traveller's wondering gaze; while on every side the woodland

---

[1] For an account of Antioch, consult Ottfried Müller (*Antiquitates Antiochenæ*), who has gathered together all that the ancients tell us of this city. The principal sources whence he draws his facts are the following: Josephus, *Bellum Judaicum*, vii. 3, 3; *Antiquitates*, xii. 3, 1; xvi. 5, 3; Philostratus, *Vita Apolonii*; Libanius, *Antiochicus*; S. John Chrysostom, *passim*; Julian, *Misopogon*; Pliny, *Historia Naturalis*, v. 18; and the *Chronographia* by John of Antioch, surnamed Malala.

[2] Strabo, xvi. 2.

[3] There remains not a vestige of this island; one arm of the stream which encircled it had been widened, artificially doubtless, and little by little the current wore it away.

[4] The existing enclosure dates from the time of Justinian; but this Prince, when strengthening the city fortifications anew, followed the lines of its ancient walls.

brooks fell in shower and spray, filling the air with their refreshing coolness. Greek art contributed its marvels of architecture to add to the strange beauty of this site. Seleucides and Romans had raised stately piles in the "Epiphania," — a pantheon, temples, the forum, circuses, theatres, basilicas, baths, buildings for business and for pleasure; while at the foot of the mountain ran the great avenue which traversed Antioch from east to west a distance of thirty-six stadia.[1] Bordered by covered porticos with four lines of columns,[2] this avenue was finally paved with flag-stones by Herod the Great,[3] and ornamented with statues as well.[4] Every day along this thoroughfare the stranger could watch one of the most varied throngs ever met together in the world. There were Macedonians, Jews come up from the banks of the Euphrates, native Syrians,[5] Phœnicians, Greeks, merchants from far-off regions who had landed at the harbor of Seleucia, while there were always great caravans from the east, come thither from the ends of the earth. A law of Seleucus gave the rights and title of a citizen to every foreigner who settled in the city; at the end of three centuries Antioch numbered more than five hundred thousand inhabitants.[6]

Her prestige was largely increased when, after the Roman conquest, she became the capital of the province of Syria. The Governor made his residence, according to custom, in the palace of the Seleucides; and the island of Orontes, where Callinicus had built that royal residence,[7] became the meeting-place for all proconsular personages, with the knights and officers who assisted the pro-Prætor in the rule of the country. Besides these there

---

[1] About three and three fourths miles. Dion Chrysostomus, *Or.* xlvii.
[2] Palmyra, Gerasa, Gadara, and Sebaste had porticos similar to this; their long colonnades are still standing.
[3] Josephus, *Bellum Judaicum*, i. 21, 11; *Antiquitates*, xvi. 5, 3.
[4] Malala, *Patrologie grecque*, t. xcvii. pp. 313–315; Pausanias, VI., ii. 7.
[5] Libanius, *Antiochicus*, p. 348; S. John Chrysostom, *Ad Populum Antioch, Hom.* xix. 1; *De Sanctis Martyr.* 1.
[6] The modern *Antakieh* numbers scarcely 6,000 souls.
[7] Libanius, *Orat.* xi. *Antiochic.*

was a large sprinkling of rich and idle Romans, who were attracted thither by the lovely climate and the natural charms, but especially by the great license of manners; for so many races could not come together without corrupting each other. The banks of the Orontes held forth novel enticements for the Western world. Juvenal deplores the infamies which the Syrian stream disgorged upon the mud of Rome, — unspeakable depravations, courtesans flaunting mitres of many colors,[1] choruses of lutes and lyres and tambourines, whose sensuous airs, accompanied by a long-drawn bass, intoxicated the people and drove them to every extreme of passion. Antioch eclipsed Corinth. Men quitted their orgies only to indulge in dissolute games; at the theatre they lost all feelings of shame;[2] at the circus were furious races, with the strifes of rival factions; in the public squares there were dancers, jugglers, sorcerers, and their like, ready to infatuate a population always as greedy for impostures as they were prone to debauchery. The general aspect of certain Feasts of Islam to-day, or the great fairs of Tantah or Dosseh at Cairo, may give us some idea of the populace of Antioch, — a motley mass, with representatives from every race, without family or national honor; a restless and seditious throng, witty rather than well educated, devoted to their orators and comedians, fond of impertinent foolery and senseless songs.

Religion offered them no protection against this profligacy, for neither Syrians nor Greeks had kept any remnants of their respective beliefs, save some stupid superstitions. Once, when the pestilence was raging, Epiphanes conceived the curious idea of having one of the high crags of Mount Silpius hewn out into the form

---

[1] Jam pridem Syrus in Tiberim defluxit Orontes;
Et linguam, et mores, et cum tibicine chordas
Obliquas, nec non gentilia tympana secum
Vexit, et ad circum jussas prostare puellas.
Ite, quibus grata est picta lupa barbara mitra.
JUVENAL: *Satiræ*, iii. 62-66.

[2] S. John Chrysostom records the fact that at the Festival of Maiouma, consecrated to the worship of Bacchus and Venus, naked courtesans were seen bathing on the stage. *Hom. VII. in Mat.* 5, 6.

of a colossal statue of Charon,[1] hoping by this to recall their minds to graver thoughts of death and the worship of the gods. When the plague had passed, the gloomy ferryman of the dead continued to cast his shadow over the voluptuous city, yet without disturbing its round of pleasure. The numerous temples dedicated to the Nymphs, to Phœbus, and the deities of Greece, are enough to show what gods they chose to serve, and what homage they offered them.

Antioch's own and favorite sanctuary was that of Daphnë, lying in a delicious valley some two hours' walk outside the city,[2] where thickets of laurel and cypress amid the many rivulets invited them to a life of soft delights. Here among the fragrant groves they worshipped Phœbus and Artemis, with rites much like those of Baäl and Astarte; on every hand you could hear nothing but choruses of music, shouts of joy, licentious rites, with every extravagance of a luxurious throng.[3] "Their religion," says the Pagan Libanius, "consisted in defiling themselves with a thousand shameful deeds, and stripping themselves of every last shred of virtue."[4]

Though surrounded on every hand by this torrent of impurity, the Jews did not allow themselves to be carried away by it; steadfast in their faith, they held themselves aloof and far above the throngs which surged about them, by their high standard of morality. In Syria they enjoyed the same rights that their brethren had obtained in Egypt, for it was to the interest of the kings of both these rival countries to conciliate their numerous and powerful quota of Jewish subjects. All that the Ptolemies had conceded to the Jews of Alexandria, was granted to those of Antioch: they had equal privileges with the

---

[1] Malala, *Patrologie grecque*, t. xcvii. p. 320.
[2] Strabo, xvi., ii. 6. Beit el-Ma marks the site of Daphnë. This lonely valley, surrounded by mountains, is watered by very many springs which interlace the laurel-thickets. The only vestiges of the past left standing are a few half-ruined mills.
[3] "Legiones Syriacæ diffluentes luxuria et Daphnicis moribus agentes" (*Scriptores Historiæ Augustæ*, Vulcatii Gallicani *Avidius Cassius*).
[4] Libanius, *Op*. ii. 456, 555 ; iii. 333.

Greeks,[1] — full permission to practise their religious rites, to build synagogues, and to live according to their customs. A head man from their own race governed the community, and a council of elders judged all matters pertaining to the Law.

Such prerogatives as these attracted a goodly number of proselytes to join the sons of Israel. One hundred years after their first settling in Antioch, they wielded so much influence that Antiochus Epiphanes felt obliged to make them some public reparation for his persecutions in Judea, and accordingly offered the ornaments torn from the Temple at Jerusalem as a peace-offering to the synagogue of his capital.[2] Under the Romans, not only were their franchises confirmed, but their influence was in every way augmented; for the decay of Paganism made every one who cared aught for honor and virtue turn their eyes towards them. So, then, when the disciples who were dispersed by the persecution came as far as Antioch, they found many souls in every synagogue who were thirsty for the truth, and on whom the Glad Tidings fell like a grateful dew. In a short time the believers in Jesus composed a considerable body. At this juncture Peter came to establish that episcopal seat which was to be celebrated throughout all Christian antiquity. We have no details relating to this part of the Apostle's ministry; however, we may easily believe that he at once gave the community of Antioch its hierarchical organization, and while he remained the real Bishop of this city, in order to govern its affairs in his absence he founded that College of Priests which we shall soon see consecrating Saul and Barnabas.[3]

The Church which Peter left at Antioch about the year 40 was altogether Judaic in its characteristic features, for "as yet they preached the word to the Jews alone."[4] But shortly after this, the Head of the Twelve, as he pursued the course of his Apostolic visits, arrived at

[1] Josephus, *Antiquitates*, xii. 3, 1 ; *Bellum Judaicum*, vii. 3, 3.
[2] Id., *Bellum Judaicum*, vii. 3, 3.
[3] Acts xiii. 1–3. [4] Acts xi 19.

Joppa, and there had the Vision which changed the whole face of the Church. Jerusalem was not the only one to feel its effects; to the most remote Christian gatherings news came shortly that God had bidden Peter "to share with the Gentiles that gift of repentance which leadeth unto life."[1] At Antioch these wonderful new tidings were brought by some of the faithful who were natives of Cyprus and Cyrenë. On entering the city, these missionaries were not content, as others had been before them, with preaching the Gospel to the Jews; "they spoke to the Greeks also,[2] and published unto them the Lord Jesus."

The Greeks mentioned here by the Acts are not the proselytes whom the Christians met at the entrances of the synagogues; the latter had received the Good News some time previous to this, since among the very first Deacons we noticed one who was a proselyte from Antioch, — Nicholas.[3] It was to the Pagans that the brethren from Cyprus and Cyrenë preached the Saviour Jesus. "And the hand of the Lord was with them; insomuch that a great number of Gentiles believed and were converted."[4]

Rumors of all this reached Jerusalem and disquieted the Church in that city. They had bowed in reverence for the revelation given their Chief at Joppa; but this throng of the uncircumcised, entering the infant Church with such freedom, re-aroused all their prejudices. Was there to be no barrier left between Israel and the profane world? Had the Synagogue no longer any right to their reverence and respect? Peter was not among them now, as everything seems to indicate, and the flock was without its shepherd. The Elders of the community resolved

---

[1] Acts xi. 18.
[2] The reading "Ελληνας certainly ought to be preferred to 'Ελληνιστάς. True, we find it only in the Alexandrian manuscript and Beza's Codex; but it has been adopted by Eusebius and by S. John Chrysostom in his commentary, while furthermore it is so imperiously demanded by the context that no modern editor has hesitated to adopt it. It is accepted alike by Griesbach, Lachmann, Scholz, Tischendorf, Meyer, and Alford.
[3] Acts vi. 5. [4] Acts xi. 21.

to send some one to Antioch to watch and report the new preaching. Howbeit, far from shutting the door which their Apostle had opened, their only anxiety was to prevent any indiscreet haste, and yet avoid any rupture; for instead of choosing a believer from the Circumcision, who would have been zealous for the Law, they selected a Hellenist from Cyprus, Barnabas, the friend of Paul.

On his arrival at Antioch, Barnabas "beheld the grace of God."[1] By the breath of His mouth the Spirit had caused rich fruits of holiness to spring up from out the very filth of Paganism. There was nothing to distinguish the Gentile from his Jewish fellow-believer; their only rivalry was in the pursuit of virtue. Delighted beyond measure at this spectacle, Barnabas could find no better exhortation to address them withal than " that they continue in the Lord with hearts firm and unshakable."[2]

His approbation produced all the more effect owing to the fact that they had feared lest the Church should censure their conduct in regard to the Pagans. Furthermore, the personal position of Barnabas added great weight to his testimony, for " he was a truly good man, full of the Holy Ghost and of faith."[3] Accordingly, the number of conversions grew irresistibly in Antioch; all such as felt a repugnance for the Circumcision and the Observances, were now absorbed in the study of this sublime religion, in which man adores his Maker "in spirit and in truth."[4] " Many believed and were added unto the Lord."[5]

While the Gentile world was dimly being moved towards Jesus, the man who was to spread this feeble impulse until it shook the whole world, Paul, was hidden away at Tarsus, wrapped in solitude and recollection of soul. Barnabas could not witness this awakening of life in a Pagan city without recalling "this instrument chosen by God to bear the Name of the Christ before the Gentiles and the kings of earth."[6] Never thinking of himself, he only longed to place the Apostleship of the Gentiles into

[1] Acts xi. 23. [2] Acts xi. 23. [3] Acts xi. 24.
[4] John iv. 24. [5] Acts xi. 24. [6] Acts ix. 15.

ANTIOCH. 167

the hands of the one whom Jesus had set apart for it. Consequently, he betook himself to Tarsus, there searched for Paul, and after discovering his retreat,[1] brought him back with him to Antioch. For an entire year the two friends remained in this Church, where they instructed large numbers of persons. To their preaching, Barnabas — "the Son of Consolation" — brought all the persuasive sweetness implied in his name, while Paul brought that fiery speech of his, now all the more ardent because it had been so long restrained.

If we may credit the account given us by Malala,[2] the place where he usually preached was in a street called "Singon," not far from the Pantheon and the Forum, in the upper portion of the city, which Epiphanes built along the slopes of Mount Silpius.[3] So, then, the Apostle began the battle with Paganism in the very heart of the gay city, right in the midst of the theatres and public buildings, and upon the great avenue along which the crowds were ever passing to "Epiphania,"— pleasure-seekers, eager business men, and worshippers at the shrines of the gods.

Any preacher who would arrest the attention of men who had strayed so far from the truth, and bring their souls to a knowledge of the Saviour, must needs seek for new methods of presenting the facts, and appeal not so much to the Tables of Sinaï as to "the law written in their hearts;"[4] only thus could he convince mankind that they were languishing in the toils of sin, with no hope of salvation save in God's grace. This imperative need of making himself understood by Pagan minds was the final experience that ripened Paul for the mission for

---

[1] The words καὶ εὑρών (Acts xi. 25) seem to imply that he had some difficulty in finding him.
[2] John of Antioch, surnamed Malala, or the Orator, wrote at the close of the sixth century, but he ascertained this fact from certain learned chronographers *Patrologie grecque*, t. xcvii. p. 371.
[3] Later on, the Mussulman conquest forced the Christians to move back to the east, to the region about the Aleppo Gate, which to this day bears the name of S. Paul, *Bâb Bolos*.
[4] Rom. ii. 15.

which the Spirit of Jesus had been preparing him during these last six years. Stripping off the garb of Judaïsm, he cast aside the yoke of slavery to the Synagogue and vindicated the claim of all men to that liberty of the children of God. Thus, while Jerusalem and the other Christian communities observed the exterior forms of Mosaïsm, Antioch stood out every day in stronger contrast to them. Of the law they retained only the pure morality of its teachings, — that sap which had kept Israel alive through so many untoward seasons. But they would not adopt what was only the coarse bark of the tree, such as circumcision, ablutions, and the rules concerning meats. The proselytes no longer belonged to the one Jewish race, as they had hitherto; they were drawn from every class of Pagan society, from every quarter of the city, — consequently, their virtue was not marred by that appearance of scorn for mankind which from his horror of any contact with unbelievers had distinguished the Hebrew even when but a convert to the Faith. But now, mingling with the people and joining in all the duties of public life, Paul's uncircumcised disciples let the whole populace feel somewhat of the warm brotherly love which he had kindled in their hearts.

Noticing these new features, the Pagans of Antioch were not slow to perceive that this was something different from the ordinary synagogues; and so, to distinguish the Church from the common run of Jews, they gave it the name of the Christ Whom they heard preached therein, and called the new converts "Christians."[1] The termination of this word[2] is enough to indicate that

[1] Acts xi. 26.
[2] As we know, the termination *anus* is peculiar to the Latin tongue. Thus: "Diocletianus, donec imperium sumeret, Diocles appellatus, ubi orbis Romani potentiam cœpit, Graium nomen in Romanum morem convertit" (A. Victor, *Ep.* 39). This form was generally made use of to indicate the partisans or disciples of some illustrious man Cæsariani, Pompeiani, Ciceroniani, Sertoriani, Cassiani, Brutiani, Vitelliani, Flaviani. The Greek adjective derived from χριστός would be χριστεῖος. Very likely the name "catholic" also came from Antioch, for we find it for the first time in S. Ignatius' letter to the Christians of Smyrna (viii.). It is likewise employed in the account of S. Ignatius' martyrdom (viii. 1; 16, 2; 19,

it was coined by Latins who resided in Syria, — indeed, it may have been stamped on the new community by the Governor himself; thereby to distinguish it from the many other sects over which the police of Rome kept strict watch. Catching up this expression in their turn, the citizens of Antioch used it as a term of insult and contempt,[1] — so much so that for a long time the disciples shrank from adopting it among themselves, and continued to call the faithful "brethren, elect, saints, disciples, believers, those of the Way."[2] But the Church could not always neglect a name which recalled the glories of Jesus, — that divine anointing whereby He is made King and Pontiff unto Eternity; this royal name could not be relinquished to the opprobrium of the mob. Accordingly, Saint Peter, in his First Epistle, exhorts his flock to accept it, not as an insult, but as their splendid title.[3] His word was obeyed; and in the centuries that followed, we see Sanctus, one of the Martyrs of Lyons, answering his judge with only the words: "I am a Christian."[4]

2), an account which was long believed to be by a contemporary of the saintly Bishop, but in which unmistakable traces of fourth or fifth century workmanship have been discovered. See the Prolegomena of Funk's *Les Pères Apostoliques*, t. i. lxxviii.

[1] "Quos vulgus christianos appellabat" (Tacitus, *Annales*, xv. 44).

[2] The term "brethren" was most commonly used; to prove this we need only glance through the Acts and S. Paul's Epistles. Ἐκλεκτοί: Rom. viii. 33; xvi. 13; Coloss. iii. 12; 2 Tim. ii. 10, etc. Ἅγιοι: Rom. viii. 27; xv. 25, etc. Πιστοί: Ephes. i. 2; Coloss. i. 2. Μαθηταί: Acts ix. 26; xi 29, etc. Πιστεύοντες: Acts v. 14, etc. Τὴν ὁδόν: Acts xix. 9, 23; xxii. 4, etc.

[3] Εἰ δὲ ὡς χριστιανός, μὴ αἰσχυνέσθω, δοξαζέτω δὲ τὸν θεὸν ἐπὶ τῷ ὀνόματι τούτῳ (1 Peter iv. 16). We find the word "Christian" in only one other verse of the New Testament (Acts xxvi. 28), in Agrippa's reply to Paul: "Almost you persuade me to be a Christian." Doubtless the Prince attached the same significance to this name as did the populace of Antioch.

[4] Eusebius, *Historia Ecclesiastica*, v. 1. The common folk disfigured this word, pronouncing it *chrestiani* (whence the French word *chrestien*). The popular notion was that Chrestus was the name of the religious leader who founded the new sect. "Judæos impulsore Chresto assidue tumultantes Roma expulit" (Suetonius, *Claudius*, 25). Fervent believers soon began to glory in this new title, which they chose to consider as derived from the Greek χρηστός, "excellent," referring, they said, to the surpassing gentleness and goodness of Christian hearts: "Sed quam et perperam Chrestiani nuncupamur a vobis (nam nec nominis certa est notitia penes

Though at first this circumstance may seem of little importance in the history of the Church, it does indeed mark one of its most solemn hours, wherein the branch first grafted on the trunk of Jewry is now so plainly severed from it that it is no longer possible to confound the two. The Jews conceived an implacable aversion to the authors of what seemed to them a wretched schism, and thereafter they never ceased persecuting them. Theirs was a keen and far-seeing hatred, for this new division between them was to be the deliverance of the Church, which had been prisoned in the womb of the Synagogue hitherto, but now and forever after was to move and breathe with a life altogether its own.

Jerusalem, permeated with Judaic prejudices as she was, could not watch the independent actions of the converts she had hoped to fashion in her own likeness, without a thrill of anguish. This marvellous child she had borne to the world was too great for the mother's strength, and Jerusalem was soon about to die. God chose this time to make Antioch the foster-parent of Christianity. There Paul first essayed his splendid gifts, and from thence for many a hundred years those noted missioners were to start forth to conquer the Eastern world to Jesus Christ. By the grace of her divine Saviour, the voluptuous Antioch was to become for ages an inexhaustible spring of holiness, the city of Ignatius Martyr, Saint John Chrysostom, and the pious Stylites, who fled a too-seductive land to take refuge on their pillars, whence Heaven alone was to be seen.[1]

vos) de *suavitate* et *benignitate*, compositum est " (Tertullian, *Apol.* 3). Οἱ εἰς Χριστὸν πεπιστευκότες χρηστοί τέ εἰσι καὶ λέγονται. Clement of Alexandria, *Stromata*, ii. 4, 18.

[1] It was in the neighborhood of Antioch that S. Simeon first went to such lengths, impelled by the "holy folly" of the Cross; for many years he remained upon his column, exposed to every extreme of heat and cold, dying there in 459 (Evagrius, *Historia Ecclesiastica*, i. 13). His disciple Daniel (489) lived near Constantinople, but it was in the region lying around Antioch that Simeon the Younger (596) perpetuated the traditions of the Stylites.

CHAPTER X.

THE PERSECUTIONS UNDER HEROD AGRIPPA.

DURING the time Paul and Barnabas were preaching the Gospel at Antioch certain Seers arrived there. They came from Jerusalem, the Mother Church, where they had been distinguished on account of the grace of Prophecy, whereby, at that time, was meant, not only the gift of foretelling the future, but the right to instruct as well, and the gift of adapting their teaching to the needs of their hearers.

In Paul's eyes no supernatural favor could be esteemed of greater value than this, none more to be desired than that of prophesying, or, in other words, as he himself explains it, "speaking unto men to edify, exhort, and comfort them."[1] The Apostle welcomed these favored souls all the more gladly because, in all probability, they were Priests of the Lord, — in fact, it would seem that the Twelve, while reserving the right of jurisdiction to themselves, were wont to confer the plenitude of priestly powers upon these Prophets, for at Antioch we are told that the latter consecrated Paul and Barnabas;[2] at Jerusalem they are mentioned as foremost among the brethren;[3] while at Ephesus they are ranked with the Apostles as the foundation-stones of the Church.[4]

These venerable men were pressed to speak, as was their custom, in the public meetings. Now, one of them, Agabus by name, foretold that there would be a great famine over the whole world, and drew such a picture of the approaching sufferings of Jerusalem that it was re-

[1] 1 Cor. xiv. 3, 5.   [2] Acts xiii. 2–3.
[3] Acts xv. 22, 23, 32.   [4] Ephes. iii. 5; iv. 11; ii. 20.

solved that each one, according to his ability, should send alms to the brethren in that city. This was a wise precaution; for now that the renunciation of individual property had become such a general practice among the first disciples, almost all members of the Mother Church were poor in this world's goods,[1] living on their daily toil, and sometimes forced to appeal to the distant Christian congregations for their support.[2]

Although the famine foretold by Agabus was not to come to pass until two years later,[3] namely, in 44, " under Claudius," yet, as the Prophet had not declared the exact date, they felt that the need of aid must be urgent. A collection was taken up and intrusted to Paul and Barnabas, who were to put it into the hands of the Elders of Jerusalem.

The two messengers reached the Holy City some time in Paschal tide of the year 42.[4] Herod Agrippa was then just beginning a persecution of the Church, made doubly terrible by the fanatic spirit which this Prince inspired in the Jews, and by the arbitrary powers which he had obtained. We have related how he, as Caligula's favorite, had been given the tetrarchies of Philip and Herod Antipas. Claudius' accession to the throne was the climax of his good fortunes. Over and above the supple spirit notable in his race, Agrippa had a wide

---

[1] This was not the case at Antioch, where those of the wealthy Jews (Josephus, *Antiquitates*, xviii. 6, 3, 4; xx. 5, 2) who believed in the Christ, kept their great riches, and afforded the Church invaluable assistance in times of need.

[2] Until the destruction of Jerusalem, we continue to see the Apostles soliciting charity for the poor of the Holy City from all the churches which they visited.

[3] The verse in the Acts: "He foretold that there would be a great famine over all the earth, *which came to pass thereafter under Claudius*," plainly implies that the narrator supposes the prediction to have been realized a long while after the events just related. Josephus mentions this great famine as occurring in the time of the Procurators Cuspius Fadus and Tiberius Alexander (*Antiquitates*, xx. 5, 2); that is to say, during the period intervening between the year 44, the date of Fadus' entry into office, and 47, at which time Tiberius Alexander was replaced.

[4] In Appendix II. the reader will find the weighty reasons which have induced me to determine on this date for the martyrdom of S. James and the deliverance of S. Peter

knowledge of men, joined with the duplicity and insinuating flattery fostered in him by the vicissitudes of his youthful career. In the troublous times following the assassination of Caius (January 24, 41), he employed his talent for intrigue, acted as a go-between for Claudius and the Senate, which was bent on regaining its liberties, and finally succeeded in foisting upon the throne a Prince who was far too sluggish to have forced his way thus far unaided.[1] For these services he received large pay. Agrippa was already master of the eastern Jordan and Galilee; he now obtained Judea and Samaria from Claudius. Thus he managed at last to restore the Empire of Herod the Great in its entirety.[2]

His first acts showed that he was as able to use his powers as to acquire them. Far from trying, like his grandfather, to force Israel to adopt the manners of Greece and Rome, Agrippa passed by Sebaste and Cæsarea, Herod's Pagan cities, and made his royal residence in Jerusalem. This re-establishment of the real seat of the monarchy was doubly prized by the inhabitants of the Holy City, for it not only increased their power in the nation, but gave them many privileges as well, — among others, the tax paid for each town house was taken off.[3] A new suburb, called Bezetha, had grown up outside the city enclosure, and, consequently, was left defenceless. Their new monarch surrounded it with a wall.[4] But more than these favors lavished on the city, what won the hearts of the people was the piety whereof Agrippa gave so many tokens. Not content with performing the customary sacrifices in thanksgiving for his accession to the throne, on that occasion he consecrated a goodly number of Nazarites[5] and made an offering in the Temple of those golden chains which Caligula had

---

[1] Josephus, *Antiquitates*, xix. 3 and 4.
[2] Id., *Antiquitates*, xix. 5, 1.
[3] Id., xix. 6, 3.   [4] Id., xix. 7, 2.
[5] The Nazarite's vow, whereby he devoted himself for a season to a life of penance, entailed certain costly sacrifices. Wealthy Jews regarded it as a pious duty to assume these expenses, and thus became instrumental in consecrating Nazarites too poor to pay for themselves.

given him, in memory of his captivity.¹ Soon an hundred such traits were noised abroad in his honor. He was seen carrying his basket filled with the first-fruits of the harvest up to the Sanctuary, just like the lowliest Jew among them.² He yielded place to the passing marriage or funeral processions.³ One day, when making a burnt offering of a thousand victims at once, he permitted a poor man to add his modest oblation of two pigeons to this regal holocaust.⁴

What he dreaded more than anything else was that the people might despise him as an Idumæan. "On the evening of the Feast of Tabernacles," the Talmud tells us,⁵ "Agrippa took in his hands the Book of the Law, and standing up out of respect, began the reading of Deuteronomy (xvii. 14-20). When he came to the words, 'Thou shalt not set a stranger, who is not thy brother, over thee to be thy King,' tears streamed from his eyes; but all the people cried aloud to him, 'Fear not, Agrippa, thou art our brother!'" This was no bit of flattery, but an outburst of popular feeling. Israelites loved this Prince who gave them a last glimpse of royal splendor. His Idumæan ancestry was forgotten, and they only told men that his grandmother was the beautiful Mariamne, daughter of the Machabees, whom Herod had compelled to share his throne.

There is no stronger testimony to the esteem Agrippa won from the Jews than his conduct towards the priesthood. Jerusalem never once murmured while he deposed their Sovereign Pontiffs even more frequently than the Roman procurators had done. In three years he set up five High Priests, — Issachar of Kefar-Barkaï, Simeon Kanthera, Jonathan, Mathias, and Elionas. Every one of them, indeed, turned out to be unworthy of his high functions, for the priestly aristocracy had become so unbelieving and worldly as to dishonor the Temple by their

---

¹ Josephus, *Antiquitates*, xix. 6, 1.   ² M. *Biccourim*, iii. 4, 2.
³ *Ketoubot*, 18 a.   ⁴ M. *Vayyikra-rabba*, iii.
⁵ M. *Sota*, vii. 8. This solemn reading of the Law took place every seventh year, on the recurrence of the Sabbatic Year.

shameless luxury. The Pontiffs decked themselves in robes of fabulous price;[1] others wore garments of such fine texture that underneath them their bodies appeared as if naked.[2] The stories told of their gluttony, however exaggerated we may suppose them to be, justified the disgust of the populace,[3] and those maledictions which we read in the Talmud, —

"The Porch of the Sanctuary uttereth four cries: —
"Depart hence, ye descendants of Eli, ye who soil the Temple of the Eternal!
"Depart hence, O Issachar of Kefar Barkaï, thou who profanest the hallowed offerings ; for he hath swathed his hands in silk, lest he should stain them in performing his office.
"Open wider, O ye gates, and let Ismaël ben Fabi, the disciple of Phinehas, enter in![4]
"Open wider, O ye gates, and let Johanan, son of Nedebaï, the disciple of gluttons, enter in, that he may feed himself to the full with the flesh of victims!"[5]

Against such priests as these, the King could dare do anything The facts in regard to Issachar of Kefar-Barkaï are proof of this. One day he went so far as to make an unseemly gesture in the Prince's presence, whereupon the latter ordered his guard to strike off the Pontiff's right hand, which he took such dainty care of. Issachar bribed

[1] Ismaël ben Fabi's tunic is said to have cost 100 mina; that of Eliezer ben Harsom the incredible sum of 20,000 mina. (See *Ioma*, 35 b.) The Greek silver mina was worth about $14.00.
[2] *Ioma*, 35 b
[3] The Talmud (*Pesachim*, 57 a) relates that Johanan, son of Nedebaï, demanded for his daily maintenance 300 head of veal, the same number of casks of wine, and 40 hampers of pigeons. Without putting too much reliance on these figures, we are warranted in the belief that such luxury prevailing at their tables must have been a scandal to the people and a disgrace to the priesthood.
[4] Evidently this Phineas is not the grandson of Aaron who put a stop to the intercourse between Israel and the daughters of Madian, but the son of Elias the High Priest, called in the First Book of the Kings (ii. 12) "that son of Belial who knew not the Lord." By their abominable crimes, he and his brother Ophni seduced the people from the sacrifices and involved them in evil practices.
[5] *Pesachim*, 57 a; *Keritot*, 28 a.

the executioner to cut off the left instead; but Herod, on learning this, had the other taken off as well.[1] This cruel deed is worthy of note, because the whole incident gives us the clearest notion of Agrippa's character, — full of clemency and moderation when he yielded to the influence of the Law, but unrestrained in his violence when swayed by the instincts of the councillor of Caligula, by religious fanaticism, or by his passion for pleasing the populace.

To the last-named motive the Acts attribute the persecution he now began against the Church. The Passovertide of the year 42 was just at hand. From the time Agrippa took up residence in Palestine, his reign had been an unbroken series of prosperous events. One stain alone obscured his glory in the eyes of the orthodox, — the obstinate zeal of the Christians in spreading their schism through Israel, and their preaching of the new Faith. Agrippa resolved to win another triumph over these men. "And at the same time," we read in the Acts, "he laid hands upon some of the Church to work evil on them, and James, the brother of John, he put to death by the sword."[2] Brief as the record is, it shows us that the persecution was directed, not so much against the body of faithful, as against their pastors. The influence of the latter over their flock was very evident: it was thought that a blow aimed at them would suffice to scatter all the rest.

And so the first victim to be brought before Agrippa was one of three disciples and intimate friends of the Master, — the brother of John "the Beloved." The burning zeal of this "Son of the Thunder,"[3] his thirst for martyrdom,[4] had marked him out for the hatred of the Zealots of the Law. The King, without deigning to inform himself further in the case, ordered him to be beheaded, — thus testifying his contempt for any disciples of the Nazarene, since decapitation was not used among the

---

[1] *Pesachim*, 57 a. [2] Acts xii. 1-2.
[3] Mark iii. 17; Luke ix. 54. [4] Mark x. 38, 39.

THE PERSECUTIONS UNDER HEROD AGRIPPA. 177

Jews, and was held as the lowest depth of ignominy.[1] Borrowing the custom from the Romans, along with its accompanying horrors, this Prince made it the punishment for the objects of his especial scorn. Saint James had to undergo the cruel preparations: his head was veiled, his hands were tied behind his back, he was stripped, and then flogged;[2] so that it was not until he had endured a prolonged torture that he received the death-stroke.

About the end of the second century the Elders of Alexandria[3] wrote an account in which we are told that the man who had informed upon the Holy Apostle, touched by the firmness with which he confessed the Faith, cried out that he repented and believed. Instantly he was seized by the enraged Jews and dragged to the same scene of torture where the Martyr had suffered, and as the two men passed each other on the way, he besought him to forgive his baseness. James stopped.

"Peace be with thee!" he said, and embraced him; a few minutes later, both heads fell under the sword.[4]

"Now it was in the days of unleavened bread,"[5] and the Pasch, which was beginning, had drawn Israelites thither from every land. As this throng applauded the execution of the Apostle, Agrippa, as always, hungering for popular favor, resolved to win greater gratitude from the Jews by sacrificing a still more august victim to their hatred, — Peter, the Head of the Twelve. He had him arrested and thrown in prison; yet, remembering that the

[1] *Sanhedrin*, fol. 52, 2.
[2] Livy, i. 26; ii. 55; Seneca, *De Ira*, i. 16; Suetonius, *Caligula*, 26; Heyne, *Opuscula Academica*, vol. iii., comment. xi.: "Cur virgis cæsi Romano more, qui mox securi percutiendi essent. I, lictor, colliga manus."
[3] Eusebius, *Historia Ecclesiastica*, ii. 9.
[4] 'Ἀνεῖλεν μαχαίρῃ. Acts xii. 2. In early days the lictors beheaded the condemned with the axe which surmounted their bundles of rods, but in the time of the emperors a sword was used instead of the axe. Ulpianus, i 8, § 1, *D. de pœn.* (48, 19): "Animadverti gladio oportet, non securi, vel telo."
[5] Acts xii. 3. Beginning at the sixth hour (noon) of the fortieth day of Nisan, none but azym bread was used. At that hour all leaven must be burned, and none left in any house wherein the children of Israel abode. *Pesachim*, iv. 1-8.

Jews considered it a religious duty not to disturb the Sabbatic rest of their feast-days [1] by capital punishments, he deferred the prisoner's death-sentence until after the Passover, when he could announce it before the whole people.[2]

During these few days nothing was neglected to prevent an escape. Four watches, of four soldiers each, kept guard, turn and turn about; when a new band came on duty, two men were fastened to the Apostle's chains, while the two others did duty as sentinels,[3] one in the dungeon itself, the other a little farther off, — probably between the inner grated door of the prison and the iron gate which gave upon the street.[4] Guarded in this fashion, Peter remained many days without the possibility of any of his brethren getting word to him; all that they knew was that, like James, he was doomed to die.

Gathering together in the dwellings which served as their first sanctuaries, the whole Church gave itself up to prayer; and yet it seemed as if it was to be all in vain, for the last day of the Feast was at an end, and on the following morning the Prince of the Apostles was to be beheaded. As evening drew on, Peter put off his mantle, loosened his belt and his sandals, and, still held fast by his two heavy chains, lay down to sleep between the

---

[1] "Non judicant die festo" (*Moed Katon*, v. 2; *Sanhedrin*, fol. 89, 1).
[2] Acts xii. 4. Wieseler thinks that Peter's arrest and rescue took place on the same day, and that Herod had him incarcerated on the last evening of the Pasch, intending to put him to death on the morrow in presence of the people. He bases this opinion principally on the fact that one and the same squad of soldiers appears to have kept guard over the Apostle; now, each squad did duty only during twelve hours. I do not share his conviction, for, taking the narrative as a whole, so restricted a space of time seems most unlikely; and, further, the words "on that night" in verse 6 manifestly imply that the Apostle had already passed several days in prison.
[3] Τέσσαρσι τετραδίοις. Acts xii. 4-16. Herod had adopted the Roman organization for his troops. The night was divided into four watches, each of three hours, during which four soldiers at a time were kept on duty. Τὸ δὲ φυλακεῖόν ἐστι ἐκ τεττάρων ἀνδρῶν (Polybius, vi. 31); and, accordingly, the squad on duty was called a τετράδιον (Philo, *In Flaccum*, 13).
[4] Verse 10 clearly indicates that, in escaping, the Apostle had three successive obstacles to pass, — the first guard, then the second, finally the iron gate.

soldiers, while the other guards kept watch at the doors.

And lo, at the fourth watch[1] of the night (between three and six in the morning), an Angel of the Lord entered there, and a resplendent light filled Peter's dungeon. Then the Angel struck him on the side and waked him, saying, —

"Arise quickly!"

At the words the shackles fell from his hands. And again the Angel spoke, —

"Gird thyself and put on thy sandals." When he had done so, the Angel added, "Wrap thyself in thy mantle and follow me."

He went forth then and followed his guide, not believing that what the Angel had done was real, but fancying that all he had seen was but a dream.

After passing the first and second warden,[2] they came to the iron gate which was the entrance from the street, and now it opened of itself before them; thereupon they stepped forth, descended a stairway of seven steps,[3] and walked together the length of one street. Then the Angel suddenly left him standing there alone. At last Peter came to himself and said, — [4]

"Now indeed do I understand that the Lord hath truly sent His Angel, and hath delivered me out of the hand of Herod, and from all the expectation of the Jewish people."

Alone, at night, in the middle of Jerusalem, the Apostle was at a loss for a moment whither to direct his steps;

---

[1] It was not until after this watch (γενομένης ἡμέρας . . . Acts xii. 18) that his escape was discovered. The soldiers, who came on duty at three o'clock in the morning, would have given the alarm, had they not found Peter still in the prison when they began their watch.

[2] By the first and second guards is meant two soldiers stationed, one within the cell itself, the other probably in a vestibule which was divided off by the iron gate beyond the inner door of the prison.

[3] This reading is found in Beza's Codex, which, after ἐξελθόντες, adds the words κατέβησαν τοὺς ζ' βαθμοὺς καί. This original addition has some very strong marks of authenticity.

[4] Συνιδών, "considerans" (Vulgate), — coming to full consciousness of what had taken place.

nevertheless, he must needs take the readiest means of flight before the alarm should be given in the prison. And so, among the various houses where the disciples were wont to gather, Peter doubtless chose the nearest, — that of Mary, the mother of John Mark.[1] The head men of the Church were not there, it is true, but there were many brethren watching and praying during this night of anguish. Suddenly some one knocked at the gate. A maid-servant named Rhoda went to answer the summons. Recognizing the voice of Peter, and beside herself with joy, she never stopped to open the door for him, but running back to the rest, she brought the news that Peter was there.

" You are mad," they cried.

The girl continued assuring them that it was he.

[1] John Mark, whom we find again during the first mission journey of SS. Paul and Barnabas, appears to be the same person as Mark the Evangelist. To this it is objected that the oldest documents never give the Evangelist the name of John, and that he is spoken of as the companion of Peter, not of Paul. But it is easy to answer the first difficulty by saying that John was the Jewish name, Mark the Roman. The latter alone was generally used; just as Paul took the place of Saul. John Mark in the Acts (xii. 12, 25), and John in chapter xiii. (5, 13) of the same book, is not called Mark till later on (Acts xv. 39; Col. iv. 10; 2 Tim. iv. 11; Phil. 24). His impetuous character seems to have lacked somewhat of steadiness; he goes from Peter to Paul, but he is especially devoted to S. Peter, whose interpreter and evangelist he is. It is not until near the end of Paul's life that we find him reconciled with the Apostle (Col. iv. 10; 2 Tim. iv. 11; Phil. 24). To suppose the existence of two Marks, one attached to S. Peter, the other to S. Paul, is a superfluous and unnecessary hypothesis. The only authority which seems to favor it is taken from a passage in which S. James says that Mark Evangelist died in 62: "Mortuus est octavo Neronis anno, et sepultus est Alexandriæ succedente sibi Aniano" (*De Viris Illustribus*, viii.). As a disciple named Mark is mentioned in the second Epistle to Timothy, written in 66 or 67, one might conclude therefrom that this Mark, S. Paul's companion, should be distinguished from Mark Evangelist, who followed Peter and founded the Church of Alexandria. Although at first sight this difficulty may seem a serious one, to do away with it we have only to recall the fact that here S. Jerome is simply translating Eusebius. Now, in the text of that historian there is no question of the death of S. Mark; it is merely said that Anianus was put in his place. In his *Chronicle* (62), Eusebius says the same. There is every reason to believe that S. Jerome mistook, for the date of S. Mark's death, the year in which he appointed his successor, and so ceased to govern the Church of Alexandria.

"It is his Angel,"[1] replied some of them.
In the mean while Peter was still knocking. They opened the gate, and, seeing him enter, they too were transported with joy.

With a gesture of his hand, the Apostle commanded silence, telling them how the Lord had delivered him, and at the end bade them "Make this known to James and the brethren;" whereupon he set forth at once, and before dawn had left Jerusalem behind him.

With the daylight there rose a great clamor among the soldiers. "What has become of Peter?" was their cry, and they set to work searching everywhere. They lost no time in informing Herod of the event, and no one resented it more keenly, for he had counted upon this punishment to make a display of his zeal for the Law. How could he confess to the Jews that the Chief of these Galileans had disappeared miraculously? He ordered a search to be made all through the city, and not finding him, he turned his wrath against the guards, who were put to the torture, but without result, for they had seen nothing. Howbeit, in order to keep the truth from the multitude, Agrippa could find no better means than that of declaring them guilty, and he commanded that they be put to death. This wretched expedient did not prevent the truth from becoming known; the happiness and the accounts of the Christians spread the story far and wide. Herod was so disgusted at the turn of affairs that he decided to quit Jerusalem and make his royal residence in the various cities of the realm in succession.

Josephus tells us how he bore himself in all these places, ever intent upon dazzling the people's eyes. Beyrouth was his first stopping-place. The situation of this city is not to be compared with that of any other in Phœnicia. Lying along the slopes of a headland between Sidon and Byblos, it rises from the blue waters to the

---

[1] From this we see that the Primitive Church not only treasured the belief in guardian Angels as expressly taught by the Master (Matt. xviii. 10); they even believed that the Angels assumed the appearance and the voice of the mortals of whom they had charge.

brow of Libanus, with its snowy houses towering over a forest of flowers; high up above, perched on the purple soil of the mountain, are little hamlets, patches of mulberry-trees and wide-spreading pines, while the white mountain-peaks crown the whole scene. Herod was fain to raise some monument that would rival this wonderful site in beauty; he had an elegant theatre built, an immense circus, baths, porticos, sparing no cost to make them splendid. Nor did he leave until after he had inaugurated them with much pomp and festival, with scenic representations, musical competitions, and contests of gladiators.[1]

From Beyrouth, Herod Agrippa transferred his court to Tiberias, where the noise of his royal progress drew thither the neighboring kings, Antiochus of Commagene, Sampsigeramus of Emesa, Cotys, Polemon, and Herod of Chalcis. All these princes were received in such magnificent state that Marsus, Governor of Syria, took offence and ordered them back to their own provinces.[2] This humiliation, which he felt most keenly, was the first check to the persecutor's power: a more awful punishment awaited him.

In the early part of 44, Agrippa left Tiberias and made his residence at Cæsarea. It was just at the season of the anniversary festivals to celebrate the accession of Claudius to the throne (January 24).[3] On this occasion, a large number of Jews and foreigners visited the city, and among them was a solemn embassy from Tyre and Sidon. These towns, with which Agrippa had broken off rela-

[1] Josephus, *Antiquitates*, xix. 7, 5.
[2] Id. xix. 8, 1.
[3] This cannot refer to the quinquennial games instituted by Herod in memory of the foundation of Cæsarea. As this city was consecrated in the year 10, the games celebrated every five years could not have taken place in 44, which was certainly the date of Herod's death. Nor can there be any question as to its being the solemn service of thanksgiving which followed the fortunate expedition of Claudius into Britain (Dion, lx. 19-23; Suetonius, *Claudius*, 17). The games spoken of here by Josephus were celebrated either on the Prince's birthday (August 1), or on the anniversary of his accession to the throne (January 24). The latter is the only admissible hypothesis, for we have seen (Appendix, II.) that Herod died in the beginning of the year 44.

tions,[1] doubtless on account of certain commercial treaties, were wont to get their provisions from Judea;[2] under the present regulations, and distressed by the famine which was already beginning to make itself felt, they saw that they were forced to come to some understanding with the angry ruler. No diplomat knows the power of gold better than these merchants knew it. They gained over to their side a certain Blastus,[3] the King's intimate friend, and obtained a solemn audience the second day of the feast. According to a custom quite common in the East, this reception took place in the theatre. Herod made his appearance there at almost high noon, attired in a robe of sparkling gold. Seating himself on the throne, he began his address to the Tyrians; but he had hardly spoken when the people shouted their acclamations, crying, —
"It is the voice of a God, and not of a man!"
"On the very instant, an Angel of the Lord struck him, because he had not given the honor to God, and he was eaten by worms."[4]

The historian Josephus tries to cover over the horror of this decease: he tells of an owl, the foreboder of misfortune, which the King saw hovering over his head, and puts into the prince's mouth words which are more Stoical than Jewish in tone; yet he confesses that the tyrant was struck down for his impiety, and that dur-

---

[1] Θυμομαχῶν does not mean that Herod was at war with Tyre and Sidon, which would be a quite incomprehensible statement, since these cities were then a part of the Roman Empire. Θυμομαχῶν must be understood to mean "much exasperated against them."

[2] Phœnicia furnished hardly any products to Judea save cedar and fir, while it obtained its grain, oil, honey, and balm from Israel. 1 Kings v 11; Ezek. xxvii. 17; Esdr. iii. 7.

[3] This is a Roman name. Herod doubtless brought Blastus with him from Rome and made him his *Cubicularius*, — *Præfectus Cubiculo*. Suetonius, *Domitianus*, 26.

[4] The Acts do not say that the Angel appeared visibly, but that this death-stroke, coming from the wrath of God, was dealt the king by an Angelic Minister. So in the Fourth Book of the Kings (xix. 35) it is related that the Angel of the Lord struck the Assyrians of Sennacherib; in the Second Book of the Paralipomenon (xxi. 15-30) that an Angel put to death certain Israelites in punishment of the pride displayed by David in the numbering of his people.

ing five days his bowels were torn with unsupportable torments.[1]

The death of Agrippa put an end to the independence of Judea. Immediately after, a Roman Procurator, Cuspius Fadus, resumed the office left vacant since Pilate's banishment.[2] This ruler assured every security to the new Faith, and ended by putting a stop to the persecutions; for Rome, having no reason to be prejudiced against the Church, extended to a body, which seemed to outsiders as merely a sect of Judaism, the same protection which all her subjects enjoyed. To molest the Christians thereafter was regarded as a breach of the public peace, and exposed any one attempting it to a very rigorous code of justice; naturally no Jew ventured to withstand it. The Acts describe this return of peace and prosperity in a few words: "The word of the Lord made great progress,[3] and was spread abroad more and more."

But aside from the fear of Rome, the famine which was then ravaging Judea was enough to turn the most fanatical minds from any thought of persecution. According to Josephus' account,[4] it was under Fadus that the scourge foretold by the Prophet Agabus devastated the cities of Israel. It swept away many victims, among whom more Jews than Christians were numbered; for the latter received aid from their brethren in foreign lands, while the gifts sent by the Israelites from all over the world often remained in the hands of the sons of Levi. Left uncared for in this way, the populace would have suffered the worst horrors of hunger, if God had not provided them with unlooked-for succor in the person of the Princes of Adiabenë. This royal family seemed raised up to be the providence of Jerusalem.

Izates, its Chief, was then reigning, on the banks of the Tigris, over a province whose boundaries are not easily

---

[1] Josephus, *Antiquitates*, xix. 8, 2.
[2] Marcellus, appointed by Vitellius Prefect of Syria, to take charge of the affairs of Judea (Josephus, *Antiquitates*, xviii. 4, 2), and Maryllus, deputed by Caligula (*id.* xviii. 6, 10), cannot be reckoned in the number of Procurators properly so called.
[3] Acts xii. 24.   [4] Josephus, *Antiquitates*, xx. 5, 2.

traced, though they were within the limits of what is now Khurdistan.[1] He was bred at the court of Abennerig, King of Kharacenë,[2] and there became acquainted with a Jew named Ananias, whose commercial affairs had given him access to the palace, and who had converted almost all the women living there. Through their efforts Izates came into intimate relations with the pious Israelite, and learned to revere God according to the custom of the Jews. A little later, when recalled to Adiabenë by his father's death, he showed such striking proofs of virtue upon mounting the throne that his brother Monobazes and his mother Helen were anxious to share his faith.[3] However great the fervor of these two Princes, they were not circumcised, for Ananias had dissuaded Izates from this humiliating ordeal. "But one day, as these proselytes were reading Genesis, they came upon the verse where it is said,[4] 'Ye shall circumcise your flesh for a sign of the Covenant between Me and you;' whereupon one of them turned his face to the wall and began to weep; the other, turning about in like manner, shed tears. Then both together went forth and received circumcision."[5]

Helen, whose zeal outran even that of her sons, resolved to leave her native land in order to dwell close by Jehovah's Temple. About the year 44 she came to Jerusalem and built a palace there for her family, and afterwards the beautiful mausoleum known to-day as the

---

[1] At this period the Parthian Empire, like the Roman, included a large number of petty vassal kings. Of these Pliny mentions eighteen, but in such vague terms that it is impossible to determine the boundaries of their principalities. Adiabene, one of these provinces, lies along the left bank of the Tigris, in the plains which surround Nineveh. See Strabo, xvi. 1-19; Josephus, *Antiquitates*, xx. 2, 4.

[2] As to Charax, Spasinu, and Mesene, see Reinaud's article in the *Journal Asiatique*, August–September, 1861, Fifth Series, vol. xviii.; *Mémoires sur le Commencement et la Fin du Royaume de la Mésène et de la Kharacène*.

[3] Josephus, *Antiquitates*, xx. 2.   [4] Gen. xvii. 11.

[5] *Bereschit Rabba*, xlvi. 15 d. Josephus says (*Antiquitates*, xx. 4, 3) that it was a Galilean, named Eleazar, who persuaded Izates to undergo circumcision.

"Tomb of the Kings."[1] Her generous deeds are praised both by the Mischna and the historian Josephus. In the time of the famine she redoubled her efforts, ordered great supplies of corn from Egypt, with dry figs from Cyprus, and had the happiness of seeing large numbers of poor folk saved by her bounty.[2] Her sons seconded her in her charities; to help the sufferers in the Holy City, they sent sums of money which were so large that their kinsfolk met together and reproached them for wasting the treasures left by their forefathers. Then Monobazes made this answer, as it is preserved in the Talmud: —

"My fathers laid up treasures for earth; I lay up treasures for Heaven. . . . A thousand dangers imperilled their riches; mine I place where they are secure for evermore. . . . Their goods produced nothing; mine bear fruit, . . . They heaped up money; I am gathering souls."[3]

Such sentiments seem to warrant the tradition which tells us that this family became Christian,[4] — at least we are led to infer that Helen must have tended the wants of all the inhabitants of Jerusalem alike, without distinction as to their faith; nor could she have turned her back upon men who, when pleading for some largess at her hands, might well have had those words of their Master on their lips,[5] —

---

[1] I know how earnestly M. de Saulcy has contended that this mausoleum contained the remains of David and his successors; yet his opinion has not prevailed with the critics. It seems more and more certain that this monument is the sepulchre of Helena, described by Pausanias (*Græc. Descript.* 8, 16), and located by Josephus and S. Jerome to the north of Jerusalem (Josephus, *Antiquitates*, xx. 4, 3; *Bellum Judaicum*, v. 22, 42; S. Jerome, *Epitaph. Paulæ*). See Robinson, *Biblical Researches*, vol. i. pp. 356-364, 610; vol. iii. pp. 251, 252. Fortunately the zealous efforts of my learned fellow-countryman resulted in placing this admirable tomb in the hands of the Péreire family, and thus rescued it from the devastators of antiquities. It has recently passed into the possession of the French Government.
[2] Josephus, *Antiquitates*, xx. 2, 6.
[3] *Baba-bathra*, 11 a.
[4] Orosius, vii. 6; Moses of Khoren, ii. 35.
[5] Matt. vi. 19-20.

"Lay not up to yourselves treasures on earth, where rust and moth consume, and where thieves break through and steal; but lay up to yourselves treasures in Heaven, where neither the rust nor moth doth consume, and where thieves do not break through nor steal."

CHAPTER XI.

THE DISPERSION OF THE APOSTLES.

No fact is more worthy of note, in these first years of the Church, than the obscurity which envelops the eleven companions of Peter. He alone appears in the sacred Record, speaking and passing judgment in the name of the rest; his Vision at Joppa at once dissipates their most inveterate prejudices. Although the Eleven also wrought signs and miracles, yet it is to Peter the people bring their sick, and lay their beds along the way he had to pass; they recognized some superior power in him, — his shadow alone had healing in its touch.[1] John is mentioned three times as accompanying him;[2] but at the Beautiful Gate of the Temple, as before the Sanhedrin, the Beloved Disciple is only the companion of him who had taken Jesus' place in their little band: he only speaks in the words of Peter, — he acts and suffers with him.

Concerning the other Apostles the Acts give still fewer details; we are given to understand that their ministry in Jerusalem, while not equal in importance to that of Peter, nevertheless bore rich fruit. "And with great power did they bear witness to the Resurrection of Our Lord Jesus Christ, and Grace was mighty among all the faithful."[3] "Every day they ceased not to teach and to proclaim Jesus,"[4] "in the houses, yea, even in the Porches of the Temple," fortifying their words "with many signs and wonders."[5] The work of preaching so absorbed all their efforts that they left the temporal cares of the Church to the Deacons, in order to devote them-

---

[1] Acts v. 15. [2] Acts iii. 1-11; iv. 1-21; viii. 14.
[3] Acts iv. 33. [4] Acts v. 42. [5] Acts ii. 43.

THE DISPERSION OF THE APOSTLES. 189

selves unhindered to prayer and teaching. In the latter duty, their main thought was how best to preserve the unity commanded by Jesus, wishing to be, for their own part, simply His "Witnesses."[1] The Acts do not speak of the preaching of James, or John, or Thomas, but of "the Doctrine of the Apostles."[2] From this its collective form their testimony gathered its irresistible force, — it was the very language of the Master, almost as powerful as when it fell from the lips of Jesus.

Their anxiety to stand as one body, one voice, and one man in everything they did under Peter's headship and direction, is a feature that is constantly manifesting itself. The Apostles everywhere appear as acting in common; when arrested and dragged before the Sanhedrin, they suffer their unrighteous scourging together; all are present at the election of the Deacons, and together they lay their hands over them; when persecution scatters the flock, they remain, as a united College, in the Holy City.[3] This community of thought and action sets the Apostolic body in such a striking light that in looking at the Church of Jerusalem we can see nothing, so to say, but this one fact. Thus, when Saint Luke describes the feeling caused by Cornelius' conversion,[4] he says, "the Apostles, and the brethren who were in Judea, learned that even the Gentiles had received the word of God." In his mind, the word "Apostles" was enough to designate the Mother Church, as distinguished from the Christian communities scattered over Judea.

Such is the Apostolic College, from all we can gather from the first chapters of the Acts, — a body occupied solely in directing and instructing the Church of Jerusalem. This government by twelve head men had the one great advantage, that outwardly it was in conformity with the customs of the Synagogues. In fact, we know that the latter had at their head a council of elders, called either *priests, pastors,* or *overseers*.[5] The number of these dig-

[1] Acts i. 8, 22; ii. 15, 32; v. 32, etc.
[2] Acts ii. 42; v. 28. [3] Acts v. 18, 29, 40; vi. 2, 6; viii. 2.
[4] Acts xi. 1. [5] Kitto's *Cyclopædia:* SYNAGOGUE, 3.

nitaries, which varied according to the importance of the city or community, always comprised a President, assisted by two Councillors, three Almoners, who took care of the poor, with the Angel of the Congregation, who took charge of divine service and interpreted to the people from the Hebrew of the Holy Books. Consequently, no Jew would feel any surprise at seeing Peter acting as the chief man among his brethren, or when hearing him speak of the Twelve as *Priests, Pastors, Bishops, Angels of the Church*, or to find that the Deacons acted as almoners, whose duty was to give relief to the needy. Though persecuted again and again for its teachings, the Church at Jerusalem was never an object of suspicion on account of its external forms; and for twelve years it preserved them as we have described above.

But after this lapse of time we find in the Acts that their affairs are no longer directed by the Apostles alone. When Paul and Barnabas bring the offerings of the Antioch Christians, they hand them over "to the Elders;"[1] and the latter wield such authority that at the first Council of Jerusalem they are named, along with the Apostles, as heads of the Church of Jerusalem and judges in matters of doctrine.[2] A document of the first centuries gives us the reason for this change. Apollonius, a man worthy of belief, — such is the opinion of Saint Jerome,[3] — "had been informed by the Elders of the command which the Lord had given the Apostles that they should leave the Holy City twelve years after the Ascension." At the end of the second century Clement of Alexandria sets down the same commandment of the Lord, as preserved by tradition, under this form: —

---

[1] Acts xi. 30.
[2] "Statuerunt ut ascenderent ad apostolos et presbyteros in Jerusalem super hac quæstione. — Suscepti sunt ab Ecclesia et ab apostolis et senioribus. — Convenerunt apostoli et seniores. — Placuit Apostolis et senioribus cum omni Ecclesia. — Apostoli et seniores fratres, his qui sunt Antiochiæ ... salutem" (Acts xv. 2, 4, 6, 22, 23).
[3] "Vir disertissimus (ἐλλογιμώτατος) scripsit adversus Montanum ... insigne et longum volumen" (S. Jerome, *De Viris Illustribus*, xl.). Apollonius wrote about the year 210.

"If any man in Israel be willing to do penance and believe in God for My Name's sake, his sins shall be forgiven him; but after twelve years you shall depart from Jerusalem, going forth over the world, lest any one should say, 'We have not heard the word.' "[1] The hour had now come when they were to carry " even to the ends of the earth "[2] that testimony which the Master had bidden them to reserve at first " for Jerusalem, Judea, and Samaria."[3] The Apostles resolved to separate and go forth to evangelize the world. Everything seems to show that their departure preceded the Passover of 42, for at that period the Acts mention only three of them as remaining in Jerusalem, — James, the brother of John, who was soon to perish by the sword; Peter, not long after imprisoned by Agrippa; and James, son of Alpheus, to whom, as we have seen, the Head of the Twelve bade his hosts report his deliverance by the Angel.[4] Thus the Church in the Holy City passed into

---

[1] I have translated this passage according to the punctuation adopted by Crave and Grabe: " Propterea dicit Petrus Dominum dixisse apostolis: si quis ergo velit ex Israel duci pœnitentia et propter nomen meum credere in Deum, remittentur ei peccata. Post duodecim annos egredimini in mundum, ne quis dicat: Non audivimus" (*Stromata*, vi. 5: *Patrologie grecque*, t. ix. p. 263). These words, here put in S. Peter's mouth, are probably borrowed from some apocryphal writing; but the fact that Clement and Apollonius agree that the Apostles stayed in Jerusalem for these twelve years, plainly indicates the existence in the second century of a well-authorized tradition, going back, so says Eusebius (*Historia Ecclesiastica*, v. 18), to the elders, who had heard it from Apostolic men and Peter himself.
[2] Acts i. 8. [3] Acts i. 8.
[4] It is most likely that the founding of the Church of Antioch took place in the year 40, and before the Vision at Joppa (see page —). On the other hand, the Apostles never thought of adventuring the Pagan world until after the revelation then made to Peter; consequently the date of their separation cannot be earlier than 41. Many Martyrologies set down the feast of the *Separation of the Apostles* for the fifteenth of July: " Ex Beda Plautiniano, Adonis appendice, et auctuariis Usuardi colligo illius Divisionis memoriam Idibus Julii annua festivitate celebratam fuisse " (*Acta Sanctorum*, fifteenth of July). It is just possible that in the above date we have an indication of the season of the year to which Antiquity attributed this event. The feast of the *Separation of the Apostles*, instituted before the twelfth century, was celebrated by very many churches, and especially at Paris, in the Collège de Montaigu.

the hands of the " Elders," under the authority of James, who from that time became the Bishop of Jerusalem. Hegesippus, and after him Clement of Alexandria, Eusebius, and Saint Jerome, all certify to this fact.[1] The Chronicle of Alexandria records that Peter himself enthroned[2] the new Bishop before his departure for Rome; but there is anterior testimony, — that of the first Roman Martyrologies,[3] — which attributes this act to the whole College of the Twelve ; for it fixes the 27th of December as the feast of the *Ordination of Saint James by the Apostles.*[4]

Here we mark for the first time the government of one shepherd over a whole flock ; and to Saint James belongs the honor of having been the first Bishop of the oldest of all Churches.[5] Undoubtedly, when founding the see of Antioch, Peter had given his flock a distinct outline of episcopal rule, but without filling out the idea inspired in him by his Master, with any degree of fulness; for he quitted this new community very soon, leaving it to be governed in his absence by a college of "Prophets

---

[1] Clement and Hegesippus, quoted by Eusebius, *Historia Ecclesiastica*, ii. 1; xxiii.: *Patrologie grecque*, t. xx. pp. 133, 195; S. Jerome, *De Viris Illustribus*, ii.: *Patrologie latine*, t. xxiii. p. 609.

[2] "Ὃν ἐνεθρόνισεν ὁ ἅγιος Πέτρος. *Patrologie grecque*, t. xcii. p. 592. The *Chronicon Paschale*, or *Alexandrinum*, a summary of the world's history from the Creation down to the twentieth year of the reign of Heraclius (630), appears to have been composed somewhat about the last-named date, by the aid of earlier documents.

[3] *Acta Sanctorum*, die 1ª Maii, t. xiv. p. 24.

[4] Like his companions, James had received from Jesus Himself the priestly office in its plenitude. The terms *ordain* and *enthrone* cannot, therefore, be construed too rigorously here, but rather as borrowed from the customs of the period in which the Author of the Chronicle and the Martyrologies was writing. Inaccurate as they may seem, these expressions are worthy of note, for they show that the ancients recognized the innovation implied in the ordination which made James pastor of the Church of Jerusalem. This novelty seemed so exceptional that it was commonly attributed to the Saviour Himself. Eusebius (*Historia Ecclesiastica*, vii. 19), S. John Chrysostom (*Hom*. 38 in 1 Cor. xv. 7), S. Epiphanius (*Hæreses*, lxxviii. 7), and Nicephorus Callistus (2 *Histor*. 38), all assert that Jesus ordained James Bishop of Jerusalem. Eusebius, together with some later Fathers, would seem to have read this tradition in an apocryphal work called the *Recognitions* (*Recognitiones*, i. 43).

[5] S. Jerome, *In Epist. ad Galat.*: *Patrologie latine*, t. xxvi. p. 331.

THE DISPERSION OF THE APOSTLES. 193

and Doctors."[1] And thus Jerusalem, which had been the cradle of the Church, beheld also the growth of its foundations, with the establishment of that Hierarchy which was to spread everywhere after the death of the Apostles, thus making the Christian Society the most solid edifice of all time.

In James they had the perfect model of a Bishop. His life beyond reproach, his faithfulness to the traditions, the authority breathing in his language, with all outward dignity, and animated by the spirit of prayer, his saintliness might well make an impression on all beholders. Nevertheless, beneath the Apostle's perfect life, so Christian in every sense of the word, one feels the influence of Judaism; and this fact gives a singular note to the character of Jerusalem's first Shepherd, which is unprecedented in the Apostolic age. The rigorous life to which he subjected himself from childhood was precisely that of the Nazirites, — abstinence from flesh, wine, and fermented liquors. Never had a razor touched his hair; he used neither baths nor oil; he wore no sandals; while his only garment was a tunic under his linen mantle.[2] His limbs were as if dead, says Saint John Chrysostom,[3] and he remained so long kneeling that his knees were hardened like the callous hide of the camel. The Law was a fitting rule of life for so stern a nature; he loved its implacable discipline, bloody rites, and minute Prescriptions which shackled body and soul; all his life long he never lost this predilection for it, which even the new spirit that came with Jesus could not destroy. In the Council of Jerusalem we shall find him upholding the legal Observances; seven years later, he imposes his respect for circumcision and the Mosaical customs upon Saint Paul, at which time he obtains a promise from the same Apostle that he would purify himself legally in the Temple in the company of four Nazirites.[4] The Church at Jerusa-

---

[1] Acts xiii. 1.   [2] Eusebius, *Historia Ecclesiastica*, ii. 23.
[3] S. John Chrysostom, *Hom.* 5 in *Mat.*
[4] Acts xv. 13-21; xx. 20-26.

lem, formed thus after the example of its pastor, remained Jewish in all outward aspects to the very last, — that is, to the year 70 after Christ.

Among the Gentiles, this clinging to a moribund rule of life would have fettered the preaching of the Gospel; in the Holy City it was an efficient aid. Many Israelites who would have been repelled and angered by Paul's freedom of speech, yielded to the influence of a man of their own blood, who, like the holy men of the Old Testament, spoke the language of their Sacred Books, exalting "the royal Law, the perfect Law, which condemns the untruthful, a Law so holy that to violate one point thereof makes a man guilty of breaking the whole."[1] James showed the penitents who came to him how perfect was the agreement between the New Faith and the Oracles of their Prophets,[2] but without asking them to renounce their allegiance to Moses; so it came about that thousands of Jews were converted by his preaching, all of whom remained filled with zeal for the Law, faithful to the circumcision, worshipping in the Temple of the God of Israel, "that Father of lights Who had revealed Himself to them in His Son Jesus."[3] Certainly there were other higher Mysteries, — and most of all the Breaking of the Bread, — to bring them together in the Supper Room; but even there everything was modelled after the manner of a service in the synagogues. In order to give an outward evidence of the Priesthood with which he was invested, James had chosen the garb of the priests of Jehovah, — a linen tunic, without folds, drawn together about his loins. To add to the dignity of his presence, he went so far as to adopt one of the insignia of the High Priest, — the golden plate bearing in Hebrew characters the words "Holiness of Jehovah."[4] Strange as this custom may seem, there are very weighty authorities who attribute it to Saint Mark and the Apostle

---

[1] James i. 25; ii. 8, 9, 10, 12.   [2] Acts xv. 15.
[3] James i. 17.
[4] Epiphanius, *Hæreses*, xxix. 4; lxxviii. 14.

John as well.[1] However, James did not wear this symbolical ornament before the Jews, who would not have tolerated such an act; he used it only in the privacy of Christian assemblies. There, too, he took his seat upon the Episcopal throne that Eusebius speaks of, which was venerated down to the fourth century.[2] This faithfulness to the Law, taken together with his exceptional uprightness, won for James the reverent respect of all Jerusalem. During twenty years, Jews and Christians rivalled each other in their admiration for this ascetic worn to a shadow by a life of self-denial, as they saw him pass by daily, with bare feet, speaking always with burning faith "of that Door, which is Jesus crucified,"[3] whereby man must pass into the Presence of Jehovah. Every one spoke of him as "The Just," "The Bulwark of the People."[4] They would throng about him just to touch the hem of his tunic;[5] it was related that once, in a time of drought, he had stretched forth his hands Heavenward, and immediately rain fell on the thirsty earth.[6] He was ever praying; prostrate on his knees in the Temple, he made unceasing intercession for the people; when he could, he made his way to the limits of the Holy Place, while Hegesippus declares[7] that

---

[1] Polycratus of Ephesus, who wrote at the close of the second century, certifies as to the truth of this fact in S. John's case. Eusebius, *Historia Ecclesiastica*, v. 24 : *Patrologie grecque*, t. xx. p. 494. So far as concerns S. Mark, we have only the testimony of later and less reliable documents. See Tillemont, *Mémoires* : S. JACQUES LE MINEUR, art. iv.

[2] Eusebius, *Historia Ecclesiastica*, vii. 19 ; *Patrologie grecque*, t. xx. p. 681.

[3] This expression, original with him and repeatedly animadverted to by the Scribes and Pharisees (Eusebius, *Historia Ecclesiastica*, ii. 23), doubtless recurred very frequently in the sermons of S. James.

[4] Eusebius, *Historia Ecclesiastica*, ii. 23.

[5] S. Jerome, *In Gal.* i. 5.   [6] Epiphanius, *Hæreses*, lxviii. 14.

[7] Εἰς τὰ ἅγια, in other words, into the galleries set apart for the Levites, and not into the Holy of Holies, as Rufinus and Epiphanius believed, — an hypothesis altogether impossible. This passage from Hegesippus is certainly good evidence, and was accepted unhesitatingly by Eusebius and S. Jerome; but it has been wrongly concluded that therefore S. James belonged to a Levitical family. The saintly life of the Apostle, and the extraordinary veneration displayed towards him by all the citizens, are quite sufficient to explain the great privilege which he enjoyed. So then

he even entered therein, and the Levites dared not expel this son of Israel, whom they found in their Porches, face downward on the ground, lost in God.

This form of government in the Church of Jerusalem, under the distinct authority of a single Shepherd, for a long time continued to be an exceptional fact. The Apostles, indeed, although scattered over the world, kept their authority, in common, not over one region, but over the whole body of Christian folk. In this arrangement, which is peculiar to the first years of the Church, there was all that was necessary for its government by the Apostles, because for this end they were given a sovereign Grace,— that of the Apostleship. The heavenly prerogatives which it carried with it, will suffice to show us how this gift of God to certain chosen servants supplied the place of the whole Hierarchy. These men, we must remember, were the custodians of the Faith, infallible Doctors, and universal pastors of the people : such are the principal notes which mark the difference between the Apostles and those who received the Christian Priesthood from their hands.

The last words of Jesus before He rose up into Heaven were, "You shall be My Witnesses,"[1] — Witnesses to all My teaching. This the Master's doctrine, they had received during His Ministry and the forty days which followed the Resurrection; this they received once again at Pentecost, and at all times, according to the Saviour's promise, the Holy Ghost was with them to move their minds to a right understanding of the Truth.[2] And this indicates that God's Spirit not only enlightened their minds as to those words of Jesus which still remained obscure in their memory, it went further, and guided them step by step in their utterance of the Message, and

---

he entered these precincts "to pray, not to sacrifice : *orandi, non sacrificandi causa.*" This addition to the text of Hegesippus, which we read in a manuscript in the Church of Reims, shows in what sense our forefathers construed it. See D. Ruinart, *Acta Martyrum Sincera ;* MARTYRIUM S. JACOBI, p. 5.

[1] Acts i. 8; ii. 32.   [2] John xiv. 26.

gave them to know things that were to come.[1] This whole body of revelations, covering the period of the Apostles' lives, all together make up the Deposit of Faith, whereof they are the authentic mouthpiece, and which they have transmitted to their successors. They were chosen of God to distribute this His treasure throughout the world: hence their name of *Apostles*, *Envoys*, endowed, as they were, for the fulfilling of their mission, with such lofty powers that they never dreamed of communicating them to others on their own responsibility. On two occasions it became necessary to complete the number of the Apostolic College. On the first event happening, Peter prayed the Lord to point out the man of His choice, and the lot fell on Mathias. Later again, the Holy Ghost in Person bade them set apart Barnabas and Paul for the office; and we know how insistently the latter glories in the fact that he was called, not by man, but by God Himself. That Paul thus indicates his claim to this high privilege, is only because he regards it as the mark of his Apostleship, — the title which conferred on him the extraordinary prerogatives reserved to the Twelve.

Besides their commission to guard the Faith, — which carried with it infallibility in the teaching of it, — the Apostles were universal pastors; that is to say, they had full power over the whole earth to bind and to loose, to found Churches, to ordain pastors and priests, — in a word, to perform all spiritual functions whatsoever. There were no limits set to their authority, save the pre-eminence of Peter, who alone held the Keys, and was the sole foundation wall, giving the Church its firmness; the only one charged to confirm his brethren, to feed the sheep and the lambs. And so, albeit the Apostles enjoyed the same rights as he, though they were infallible like him, and were given the power of ruling the whole world, nevertheless they possessed these powers only when in

---

[1] ‘Οδηγήσει ὑμᾶς ἐν τῇ ἀληθείᾳ πάσῃ . . . καὶ τὰ ἐρχόμενα ἀναγγελεῖ ὑμῖν (John xvi. 13).

communion with Peter and under his Headship. Thus, forming one single body under one and the same Head, they linked together all the Churches founded by them unto the Centre of Unity.

This community of action is especially noteworthy in the first chapters of the Acts, where we are told of but two distinct ranks in the Church,—the disciples, and above them the Twelve, governing together. At the death of Ananias and Saphira, we find for the first time some indications of a ministry exercised under their orders. Certain young men perform a duty which, later on in the Catacombs, was done by clerks called "Grave-diggers;"[1] they carried forth the dead bodies and buried them. But these are clearly but material tasks, and the same is true of the powers granted to the Deacons, according to the first design in appointing them. Distribution of alms and the superintendence of the common tables, were the usual daily cares of these men, whom Saint Luke never speaks of as "Deacons," but "the Seven."

Nevertheless, it cannot be doubted that, though the Apostles reserved the principal duties of the Priesthood to themselves, they were already thinking of confiding its less important acts to the care of the seven elect, for they chose such as were known to all as upright and holy, and then laid hands upon them. Very soon, indeed, these men, after being consecrated to these humble ministrations, take their part in much higher functions: they are teaching, exhorting the faithful, and step forward to take very perilous positions. Stephen makes his way into the most fanatical synagogues, to preach the Christ there.[2] Philip travels as far as Samaria, proclaiming the Gospel tidings and giving baptism.[3] The administering of this Sacrament naturally devolved on them, when the Twelve ceased to confer it themselves. Thus,

---

[1] See Krauss, *Real Encyclopädie der Christlichen Alterthümer*, FOSSORES. Sig. de Rossi thinks that at first the *fossores* belonged to the order of Porters.

[2] Acts vi. 9–14.   [3] Acts viii. 5, 12.

THE DISPERSION OF THE APOSTLES. 199

as we have seen, when Peter converts Cornelius and his family, he deems it enough to command others to baptize them.[1] And so everywhere, at Cæsarea as well as in Jerusalem, we begin to descry something like an order of Christian Levites, under obedience to the Apostles, and giving them active aid.

It is not so easy to distinguish the two higher degrees of the Hierarchy, — the Priesthood and the Episcopate. The line of demarcation between these two ministries, which later on we find so sharply defined, seems hard to trace out in the course of the New Testament.[2] In the Acts, the early Epistles of Saint Paul, and in those of Saints Peter and James, the same persons are called sometimes Bishops, sometimes Priests or Deacons.[3] The name of "Apostles" is given to simple helpers, sometimes to women.[4] Peter speaks of himself as a Priest.[5] This confusion of titles shows plainly that, outside of Jerusalem, the Hierarchy was not as yet established. The Apostles, as we have said before, while reserving to themselves universal jurisdiction, — in other words, the power of ruling the whole Church, — only entrusted to the ministers they left behind them in the new-born Christian communities, the duty of preaching, offering the Holy Sacrifice, and conferring the Sacraments. With this, doubtless, was connected some rights of administration, for no Christian congregation ever existed in a state of anarchy; but this right was established in various ways, and shared according to circumstances.

Wherever there chanced to be some disciple of the

---

[1] Acts x. 48.
[2] In setting forth the historical development of the Christian Priesthood, the fact has not been lost sight of that the order and subordination of the ministers composing it is of divine institution, and that Jesus inspired the Twelve to put over each Church a hierarchy which included, first, a Bishop, their governing head, beneath him the priests, then the inferior ministers (*Concilium Tridentinum*, sess. xxiii. can. vi.). The Apostles knew that this was to be its definitive constitution, but they comprehended also that this body, though completely organized in its germ, must grow very gradually, according as circumstances demanded.
[3] 1 Cor. iii. 5; 2 Cor. iii. 6; Acts xx. 17, 28, etc.
[4] 2 Cor. viii. 23; Rom. xvi. 7.   [5] 1 Peter v. 1.

Lord, who had received the Good News from His lips, and had meditated upon it for many years, such a one was given the highest rank as a matter of course. With the aid of a few Deacons he taught and directed the Church. But it happened oftenest of all that a body of Christians received only such care as the Apostles could bestow on it when on their journeys, and thus all were but novices in the Faith: how then could they select the one man capable of governing them? The easiest and surest method seemed to be to choose a certain number of Elders, whose combined wisdom and virtue, together with their recollections of the Apostles' preaching, would suffice to constitute a ruling authority for the Church.[1] The fire of Christian charity, then burning so brightly, swept away all rivalry and ambition which might have given rise to serious disorders in these bodies of ministers.

Everything points to the conclusion that the majority of these dignitaries, as they had received the fulness of sacerdotal power,[2] performed, under the Apostles' jurisdiction, the functions now reserved to the Episcopate. Indeed, the Elders of Antioch ordain Paul and Barnabas;[3] the head men of the Church of Ephesus are called in the Acts Priests and Bishops;[4] later on we shall find Saint Paul writing to the Bishops and Deacons of the Philippians with no mention made of Priests, while in his letter to Timothy he reminds his disciple that he

---

[1] "When the Apostles first began to preach," says S. Epiphanius, "they did not create priests and bishops everywhere, but in certain places only priests, elsewhere a Bishop alone. When they could find no one worthy of the episcopal authority, they ordained priests, who ministered to the wants of the Church with the aid of the deacons. When but one person could be found worthy of the episcopal dignity, and there was a lack of subjects for the priesthood, they were content to confide the Church to the care of this Bishop" (*Hæres*, lxxv.).

[2] By this word is meant the sum of the spiritual powers conferred by the sacrament of Holy Orders, especially that of consecrating priests and bishops, and thereby perpetuating the fecundity of the Christian Priesthood. Together these rights constitute "the power of Orders," distinct from "the power of jurisdiction," whereby the Church governs her subjects and binds them by her laws.

[3] Acts xiii. 1–3. [4] Acts xx. 17, 28.

had been consecrated by the laying on of the Priests' hands.[1] The "Elders" and Priests here referred to must therefore have been given the power of exercising every ecclesiastical function : they confirmed the faithful and ordained Priests ; but they did not have jurisdiction over any one flock which was intrusted to their care exclusively; and hence they were not, properly speaking, Bishops in the full sense of the word. It was not until their life-work was drawing to a close that the Apostles gave each Church a pastor of its own, assisted by subordinate ministers, and thus constituted the Hierarchy very nearly as we find it to-day.[2]

By that time, some such regularly established authority became necessary in order to continue the Apostolic ministry and transmit to posterity the Deposit of Faith. Heretofore, on the contrary, besides the difficulty alluded to above, of finding men capable of taking the whole power in their hands, their anxiety not to offend against the customs of the Synagogue led them to leave the Christian congregations to the direction of a body of Elders;[3] and in fact every Christian gathering was generally a mixed assembly of Pagan and Jewish converts. Which of these classes could be expected to furnish a Bishop who would be acceptable to all, free from prejudices, and able to preserve perfect harmony between the different parties in his flock ? To choose a man from the number of those who still observed

---

[1] Philip. i. 1 ; 1 Tim. iv. 4. Some trace of this primitive liturgy has come down to us in the ceremonies of Ordination, where all the priests present join the Bishop in laying their hands upon the newly ordained.

[2] " Et si episcopalis ordo jure divino in Ecclesiam introductus est, non eodem tamen illo jure decretum est ut unus in singulis civitatibus et ecclesiis esset episcopus, sed Ecclesiæ auctoritate, conciliorumque sanctionibus, quarum ex apostolica traditione origo descendit " (Petavius, *Dissertationum Ecclesiasticarum*, lib. i. cap. iii. 5).

[3] If it be a fact — unlooked-for and contradictory as it may seem — that Jerusalem, the very stronghold and centre of Judaism, was the only city at that time which possessed a completely constituted Hierarchy, it was because James was so zealous for the Law that he could not be suspected of desiring its overthrow, — most of all it was because the virtue of the holy Apostle had so impressed his fellow-citizens that no Jew would feel any surprise at seeing him attended and revered as a common father.

the prescriptions of the Law, would have been a virtual sacrifice of the liberty of the children of God born among the Gentiles; while to have chosen one of the latter class, would have been looked upon as an affront to the Jews of the Dispersion, who in their chagrin at seeing the Pagans made co-heirs with them in the Kingdom, would have found it still harder to bear if they had had to accept as their leader a man whose nation they looked upon as reprobate and condemned. The surest means of surmounting these difficulties was to choose from the two parties a college of Priests subordinate to the Apostles' authority and controlled by them.

One circumstance in particular rendered the exercise of this government an easy matter, though shared among so many heads, — that was the outpouring of singular and special grace, which ever since Pentecost never ceased to vivify the Church. These gifts of God, which the Apostles communicated by the laying on of hands, abounded in every community and in all alike, pastors and people, with such striking effect, with such plentiful fruits of holiness, that greater respect was paid to this power than to the various duties of the ministry. "In His Church," says Saint Paul, "God hath established, first Apostles, secondly Prophets, thirdly Doctors, after that the power of working miracles, then the graces of healing the sick, giving aid to the needy, interpretation, and diversity of tongues."[1] Not one word about obedience to authority or the priestly dignity. Evidently these spiritual gifts were then the life of the Church, and esteemed above everything else. Each one received some grace peculiar to himself, which he employed for the good of his brethren; each one spoke in the meetings of the disciples. One, who was a Prophet, would reveal what he had seen in his ecstasy; another interpreted strange tongues; while the Doctor and the Evangelist taught them what was the true and what the false doctrine. "But all these things one and the same Spirit worketh,

[1] 1 Cor. xii. 28.

dividing His gifts according to His good pleasure."[1] Under such extraordinary conditions no need of an organized ruling body was realized. Indeed, what could the leaders of a Christian body, — itself born of the breath of God's Spirit, — what else could they do but bow before the wondrous effects of Grace, simply leaving to the Apostles the responsibility of trying the spirits, whence they came? In this mighty wind from Heaven which was bearing the Church on its first course, it was fitting that one sovereign hand should hold the helm. Only when this first speed slackened, when the signs and wonders declined somewhat in splendor, then only the Twelve were moved to intrust the direction of the Christian communities to a regular order of pastors.

We shall have an opportunity of watching this transformation, step by step, in the work of Saint Paul; in fact it is from him we get all these details in the history of the Primitive Church, for just as his ministry is more easily studied in the twenty years which are to follow, so that of his brother Apostles fades into the darkness. Outside of Peter, John, and James of Jerusalem, the rest of the Twelve have left so few traces of their individual work that a few lines will suffice to tell all we know of them.

On leaving Jerusalem they preached from town to town, until drawn onward from one Jewish colony to another, scattered to the very ends of the earth, they finally reached the most distant lands. Origen recounts that Saint Andrew spread the Gospel to Scythia, along the banks of the Danube and by the Black Sea, while Saint Thomas penetrated into that part of the Parthian realm lying between Tigris and Euphrates.[2] In the Indies, or, to speak more exactly, in the southern part of Arabia,[3] an Alexandrian philosopher named Pantænus found the Hebrew Gospel of Saint Matthew, which had

[1] 1 Cor. xii. 11.
[2] Origen, in the third volume of his *Commentaries on Genesis*, quoted by Eusebius (*Historia Ecclesiastica*, iii. 1; *Patrologie grecque*, t. xx. p. 216).
[3] See p. 218.

been brought thither by Saint Bartholomew.[1] Simon the Zealot is credited with a still wider field for his Apostleship. Nichephorus and the Greek calendar writers describe his travels along the African shores of the Mediterranean, from Alexandria to the Pillars of Hercules, thence crossing the ocean to carry the Gospel to Great Britain. But this tradition is hardly worthy of our notice, since it is contradicted by the testimony of the oldest Martyrologies, which bear the name of Saint Jerome. There we read that Simon preached and was martyred in Persia.[2] There is the same division of opinion about Saint Matthew's career: Rufinus and Socrates, with other historians, speak of him as having labored in Ethiopia; while Saints Paulinus and Ambrose, the Martyrologies by Saint Jerome and the Menologies, assign him to the region of the Parthians and Medes.[3]

There is less uncertainty as to Saint Philip. He evangelized Phrygia, died there, and was buried in the city of Hierapolis. A Bishop of that Church, Papias by name, relates that he saw the Apostle and heard his daughters tell the story of how he raised a person from the dead in their time.[4] Clement of Alexandria informs us that several of these girls were married;[5] and Polycratus of Ephesus says that two of them lived a life of virginity and were entombed with their father. "And indeed," adds this writer of the second century, "these were great lights in the Church of Asia."[6]

Saint Jude, the Saviour's cousin, is especially noted for his Catholic Letter. Hegesippus speaks of the martyrdom of his grandsons;[7] hence he was married, and

---

[1] Eusebius, *Historia Ecclesiastica*, v. 10; *Patrologie grecque*, t. xx. p. 455.
[2] Tillemont, *Mémoires*: S. SIMON, t. i. p. 424.
[3] Id., S. MATTHIEU, t. i. p. 3.
[4] Papias, quoted by Eusebius (*Historia Ecclesiastica*, iii. 39; *Patrologie grecque*, t. xx. p. 298).
[5] Clement of Alexandria, *Stromata*, iii. 6; *Patrologie grecque*, t. viii. p. 1158.
[6] Polycratus, quoted by Eusebius (*Historia Ecclesiastica*, iii. 3; *Patrologie grecque*, t. xx. p. 280).
[7] Hegesippus, quoted by Eusebius (*Historia Ecclesiastica*, iii. 20; *Patrologie grecque*, t. xx. p. 252).

following the example of Jesus, had holy women in his company, who served him and assisted him with their goods. From all appearances it would seem that Saint Paul is speaking of him, and not of his brother James of Jerusalem, when he says, " Have we not power to carry about with us a woman who may be our sister, as do the Lord's brethren ? "[1] The only detail we have of Saint Matthew's life is found in Clement of Alexandria, which is that "he never ate meats, but partook only of beans, fruits, and herbs."[2] As for Saint Mathias, all we have is a single sentence from his lips on the necessity " of subduing the flesh by mortification."[3]

It is plain to be seen that we know almost nothing about the majority of the Twelve. Their ministry is lost in the darkness of the ages, and the same obscurity envelops their death.[4] In the fourth century only the tombs of four Apostles[5] were known, — at Rome those of Saints Peter and Paul, that of Saint John at Ephesus, and of Saint Thomas at Edessa. The three first expired in the places where their ashes now repose. But Saint Thomas's body was transported from the Indies, where he suffered martyrdom,[6] to Mesopotamia, apparently by the efforts of Thaddeus, to whom he intrusted the duty of evangelizing the country.[7]

We say nothing here as to those great disciples of the Christ, — Peter, James son of Alpheus, John and Paul; for, very different from the rest of the Apostles, their deeds and the field of their preaching are known, and it is by following in their footsteps that we shall trace the history of the new-born Church.

[1] 1 Cor. ix. 5.
[2] Clement of Alexandria, *Pædagogus*, ii. 1 ; *Patrologie grecque*, t. viii. p. 406.
[3] Clement of Alexandria, *Stromata*, iii. 4.
[4] In the second century Heracleon (Clement of Alexandria, *Stromata*, iv. 9; *Patrologie grecque*, t. viii. p. 1282) wrote that SS. Mathias, Philip, Matthew, and Thomas died a natural death ; but his testimony contradicts by far the greater number of authors and martyrologies that recount their last sufferings and execution.
[5] S. John Chrysostom, *In Hebr.*, xxvi.
[6] Tillemont, *Mémoires* : S. THOMAS, t. i. p. 396.
[7] Eusebius, *Historia Ecclesiastica*, i. 13.

CHAPTER XII.

SAINT MATTHEW'S GOSPEL.

I. — THE EVANGELICAL PREACHING.

WHEN a branch grows forth on the parent stem, even though it be destined to absorb all the sap and life of the latter later on, still meanwhile its organs differ in no wise from those which help to nourish the trunk, — it is of the same fibre, with the same channels reaching down to the very roots. So was it with the Church. We have seen how its Hierarchy was modelled after that of the Synagogue; its methods of teaching were borrowed, in like manner, from the Doctors of Israel. Tradition handed down by word of mouth was its distinctive trait. "Put nothing in writing," their old masters had said; and all obeyed their precept, even Hillel and Gamaliel, as well as the rigorist Shammaï. To repeat the lesson word for word was the mode of instruction, which Papias has so aptly termed "the living and lasting Voice."[1] In every Jewish community this voice of the Rabbi could be heard, ever repeating the same precepts of the ancients, applying the same commandments of the Law to individual cases, and giving the rules for the interpretation of sacred literature. It was the doctor's glory that he possessed all his learning by memory, without owing anything to books. One written thing alone sufficed, — the Bible, the unsullied spring of Truth, the brightness of the Wisdom of God. Any commentary by the hand of man written upon these inspired pages would have

[1] Ζώσης φωνῆς καὶ μενούσης. Papias, in Eusebius (*Historia Ecclesiastica*, iii. 39; *Patrologie grecque*, t. xx. p. 297).

seemed like a profanation ; no master ever set down his thoughts, no scholar wrote any notes ; their doctrine was transmitted from mouth to mouth. It was not until after the fall of the Temple, when they began to fear lest the treasures they had gathered through the ages should be scattered and lost,— then only could they bring themselves to consent that the lessons which the scribes of Israel had recited for the last two centuries should be gathered together in the Talmud.

It is hard for us to imagine how they could have recollected such a mass of decisions and maxims with any degree of accuracy. But the memory has infinite resources, and when spurred to it by Faith, has accomplished marvels. In India, the Vedas for a long time remained as an oral tradition, and its thousands of verses were all known by heart. So too with the Koran in the beginning of Islamism, while even in our day very many of the Mussulmans quote it without using the text. The schools of Jerusalem, and consequently the Doctors of the Primitive Church, had no other method of teaching. The disciple's heart was the only book whereon they inscribed the Master's lessons ; but they remained there graven in ineffaceable characters.

"While still young," writes Saint Irenæus to Florinus,[1] "I saw thee in Lower Asia, with Polycarp, diligently seeking his approbation. Even yet I can point out the spot where the blessed Polycarp used to sit and teach. I see him walking and coming in among us ; his manner of living and his outward demeanor are well remembered by me. I can hear him telling how he had lived familiarly with John and other men who had been in the Lord's company. He would repeat their words and everything he had heard from them touching the Christ, His miracles, and His doctrine. As he had gathered these traditions from the very persons who had touched the Word of Life,[2] Polycarp never made any

---

[1] S. Irenæus, quoted by Eusebius (*Historia Ecclesiastica*, v. 20 ; *Patrologie grecque*, t. xx. p. 485).
[2] Παρὰ αὐτοπτῶν τῆς ζωῆς τοῦ λόγου παρειληφώς.

statement which was not in accordance with the Scripture. For my part, I listened carefully to these lessons, which strengthened the grace of God within me. I imprinted them, not upon paper, but in my heart, and by the same grace of God I constantly repeat all these memories and turn them over in my mind." An Ebionite document of the second century attributes the same custom to Saint Peter. "In the middle of the night," it makes him say, "I wake up of myself, nor can I go back to sleep thereafter. This is the result of a habit I formed of repeating to myself the words of the Lord, in order to retain them faithfully in my memory."[1]

In confining themselves to oral teaching, the Apostles were not only following the customs of their nation, they were fulfilling the Master's precept. "Go forth and preach the Gospel."[2] For very differently from Moses bringing back the Law graven on tables of stone from Mount Sinaï, and ordering the Jews to keep it ever written before their eyes, the Twelve had received from Jesus nought but the living word of the Father, with His bidding that they should bear it to the ends of the earth. Of set purpose, the Master chose them out of Galilee, a rude and uncultured province, knowing well that the art of writing, rare enough everywhere in the East, was a most uncommon accomplishment among fishermen of Genesareth. So by vocation as well as by race customs and early bringing up, they all became simply preachers of the word.

The first chapters of the Acts give us some inkling as to the usual form of their teaching. In Christian sanctuaries, as in the Jewish assemblies, two very different sorts of instruction were to be heard, — the "Halaka," and the "Hagada," the dogmatic interpretation of the text, and the moral homily thereon. The "Halaka" formed the principal part of the divine service in the Synagogues. "In every city," says Saint James, "Moses

[1] The *Recognitiones* (ii. 1), composed, according to M. Renan, about the year 135.
[2] Mark xvi. 15.

is read and preached every Sabbath day."[1] The scribes treated this commentary as if it was meant to be all a piece of dry and tedious casuistry, making it a series of decisions which laid an unbearable yoke on every action of man's life. Certainly this was not the Christians' manner of using the Scripture, for in every line of it they found something to remind them of Jesus. For them Isaiah sang the Saviour's birth of a Virgin; Micheas pointed out His crib in Bethlehem of Juda; when those words of Osee were read, "I have brought back My Son out of Egypt," some one would exclaim, "It is He, returning from the banks of the Nile in the arms of Mary!" He was the Corner-Stone foretold in the Psalm; and again, that Stumbling-Block of which Isaiah speaks was Jesus.[2] His Passion shone forth in all its details, and every act in the Divine drama lived again in the minds of the faithful hearers, overwhelmed with wonder and love: they recognized Judas and the thirty shekels, the stupefying drink which our Lord refused, the garments divided by lot, the feet and hands pierced with nails, the awful thirst, the sponge soaked in vinegar, the bones left unbroken,[3] — everything had been foretold. What tears were shed as they listened to these divine oracles they had revered so long without understanding the Mystery enshrined therein! The Old Testament, read in this new light, still keeps its place in our Liturgy; the Law and the Prophets are recited at the beginning of Holy Mass, just as they once were in the first Churches of Jerusalem; under the name of the Epistle they precede the Gospel in the same way that the "Halaka" preceded the homily in the Synagogue.

In fact, the "Hagada," the second form of Judaic preaching, was likewise in use among Christian gatherings. But what a difference between the Rabbis' sermonizing and these words of the Apostles which have become our Gospel! The Twelve had but one single end in view, —

---
[1] Acts xv. 21.
[2] Is. vii. 14; Mich. v. 2; Os. xi. 1; Ps. cxvii. 22; Is. vii. 14.
[3] Zach. xi. 12; Ps. xxi. 17, 19; lxviii. 22; Exod. xii. 46.

to inspire greater love for Jesus in the disciples' hearts; and for that they had no need to do more than rehearse His words and deeds. Assuredly they did not neglect "the Holy Law" of Israel, "which converteth the soul,"[1] and they repeated it to the faithful in that language of the Psalms and the Prophets which is to-day the proper speech of Christian piety; but the great end, the turning point of their discourse, the Good News which they were bringing to the world, was, using the words of Ignatius of Antioch, "the Flesh of Jesus,"[2] God Incarnate for the salvation of Humanity. The Truth has taken our flesh so to "dwell amongst us;" and it behoved them to show mankind just how God had revealed Himself to them, conversing like a Man with men. "The Living Word which was from the beginning, Him we have heard, we have seen Him with our eyes, we have gazed upon Him, our hands have touched Him, for the Life hath made itself manifest. We have seen Him, and we do bear witness of Him; Him we announce to you, that Life Eternal, Which was with the Father and hath manifested Himself to us."[3] In this testimony of Saint John we find the substance of the Homily as it was generally preached by the Twelve. Here the didactic order of the Philosophers is as unknown as are the Rabbis' futile discussions. The disciples of the Master were content to be nothing more than His Witnesses, repeating what He had said.

However, we must not fancy that this preaching was a mere echo, a string of parables, sentences, and precepts of the Lord put together according to each one's taste. No collection of His discourses, however divine, could have given an idea of all that Jesus was to them, for the Saviour's Ministry had this peculiar character that the action ever followed the word; what He taught He forthwith put into practice. Thereby giving "breath and life"[4] to His lessons, He transformed them into deeds

---

[1] Ps. xviii. 8.
[2] S. Ignatius, *Epist. ad Philippenses*, v.
[3] 1 John i. 1-3. [4] John vi. 64.

more persuasive than any exhortation. And accordingly to make the Saviour known aright, the Apostles took care to fill out His teachings with a portrayal of the circumstances which had accompanied them, setting forth "that which Jesus began to do and to preach."[1] Thus their own preaching came to be truthful biography, reflecting as in a mirror the living figure of Him Who is the Pattern proposed for all mankind. Only to recount the Life of the Master was enough to thrill their souls with love, and spread the conquest of God's grace. They never tired of returning to this Theme, and consequently their preaching very early assumed a definite form, which is easily recognized, not only in the three first Gospels, but in the Book of the Acts as well.

The first and foremost object of this Narrative was always to establish the fact of the Resurrection beyond all shadow of doubt, for the principal duty of their Apostleship was to attest the triumph of the Christ over the power of death. This Peter declared to his brethren when assembled in the Supper-Room;[2] but at the same time he reminded them that as this victory was but the fruit of a long combat, every incident of the Saviour's public life had been a preparation for its glorious issue. So then to be what Peter called "a Witness of the Resurrection,"[3] one must have a personal knowledge of the doings and sayings of the Saviour during the three years in which He manifested Himself to the world, and consequently must have "followed Him from the Baptism of John up to the Ascension."[4] The beginning and end of the Apostolic testimony are here, as we see, very clearly marked out. The biography of Jesus opened with the appearance of His Forerunner; then came the Baptism of the Christ, His Temptation, and His Ministry in Galilee. Out of feeling for the Jews, they passed over the description of His appearance in Jerusalem, and the obstinate hard-heartedness of the Holy City; they only told how He entered there as a conqueror five days before

[1] Acts i. 1. [2] Acts i. 21, 22.
[3] Acts i. 22. [4] Acts i. 21, 22.

His death. But after that event the pious narrator followed his Divine Master step by step, recording day by day, hour by hour, His words, His sufferings, His last cry of anguish, everything that would heighten the contrast of the marvels which consummated and crowned His Sacrifice. "He is risen, He is not here!"[1] this the Angel's Message was the fitting climax to which the Story tended; this, more than all else, was the Glad Tidings, the Gospel[2] foretold by Isaiah.[3]

With its grand outlines drawn so clearly, the whole framework of the Gospel Story was at first filled in by each Apostle according to the inspiration of the moment, the opportunity or the needs of his audience. But the repeated reiteration of the same narrative very soon gave it a uniform character, particularly for what concerned the Saviour's teaching. The Apostles had been promised that the Holy Spirit would recall to their minds everything that Jesus had said,[4] that is to say, not the very words used by the Master, but the exact meaning of His thought. As for many years they were preaching the Gospel in the same city, and could lend each other mutual assistance, the Twelve bent all their efforts to reproducing as exactly as possible what they had heard. The precepts of the Christ, coming thus from their mouths, took on a hallowed form, very rightly regarded as the utterance of the Divine Word, and consequently treasured up and repeated with great care. Not only the discourses of Jesus, but certain important facts, such as the institution of the Last Supper and the principal acts of the Passion, in like manner assumed an unchangeable form. But for the rest of the Story, they allowed themselves perfect liberty as to its treatment; the Narrative continued ever varying, sometimes more, sometimes less circumstantial, according as memories crowded back upon them, and feeling was more or less intense.

It would be impossible to deny that in this evangelical

---

[1] Matt. xxviii. 6.
[2] In Greek, εὐαγγέλιον; from εὖ, "well," and ἀγγέλλειν, "to announce."
[3] Is. lxi. 1; Luke iv. 18.   [4] John xiv. 26.

preaching we have an oral Gospel, the first form and the model of those we now possess. Indeed, the four sacred writers, known by the name of Evangelists, had only one plan in mind, — that of setting down the verbal teaching of the Apostles. This Saint Luke affirms at the outset; he is about to follow the footsteps of the "eye-witnesses of the Word,"[1] and to write down what they had recounted in spoken words, in order to "catechise"[2] the first Christians. "As a faithful companion of Paul," says Saint Irenæus, "he put down in a book the Gospel preached by the Apostle."[3] This evidence is confirmed by the whole body of traditions. Saint Mark's work had precisely the same origin, being a summary of the Good News which Saint Peter proclaimed to the world. At the opening of the second century, Papias learned this fact from the priest John, who had lived with the Apostles;[4] after him, Clement of Alexandria, together with all the Fathers, speak of it in the same way.[5]

With such weighty authorities for it, the fact can be regarded as settled; but were they wanting, the Gospels of Saints Matthew, Mark, and Luke, set side by side and compared, would suffice to give us an idea of how the Good News was told in the Primitive Church, — that spoken Gospel, which served as a pattern for them in their work. These three documents are very properly called the "Synoptic Gospels," because, as there is a certain conformity in the arrangement of the main events, they can be put side by side, so that one can embrace all the facts at a glance. Furthermore, their agreement does not consist merely in chronicling the same events in the same order; often it results in their using similar expressions. To explain such harmonious treatment, only two hypotheses are tenable, — either that the Evangelists copied from each other, or that they all give a free reproduction of the same original text.

[1] Οἱ ἀπ' ἀρχῆς αὐτόπται . . . τοῦ λόγου (Luke i. 2).
[2] Luke i. 4.   [3] S. Irenæus, *Hæreses*, iii. 1.
[4] Papias, quoted by Eusebius (*Historia Ecclesiastica*, iii. 38).
[5] Clement of Alexandria, quoted by Eusebius (*Historia Ecclesiastica*, vi. 14).

The first supposition is generally abandoned, for it makes no account either of the divergences or the points of agreement which we discover in the "Synoptic Writers." Why should one Evangelist, writing at a later date, have neglected certain circumstances related by his predecessor? What reason could there be why one of them should have adopted the expression used by another for a part of a phrase, and curtly omit what followed? How could the two later have allowed so many seeming contradictions to stand between their narratives and the one they had before their eyes? To such difficulties as these there is no plausible solution.

Thus we are bound to admit that, as Saint Epiphanius has pointed out, the first three Witnesses who have revealed to us the Life of the Christ, drew their materials from the one same source.[1] About this mooted point, modern writers have given their imagination full sway. Some have conjectured that a Greek version of the Gospel Story, which soon went out of use, furnished the historians of Jesus' Life with those details which they appropriated in common. According to others, the primitive Gospel was written in Aramean, and the free translation made by the sacred writers gives the reason why their works show so many contradictory passages along with so much that is similar in all. An hundred combinations of these various conjectures have been proposed in order to solve the problem; but the more ingenious and better adapted to fit the question they may seem, the less we can credit them: for who will believe that in the age of the Apostles, in Judea, where the only learned task was that of hearing and repeating immutable traditions, these Evangelists could have made their extracts, compared and discarded texts borrowed from this and that source, quite after the fashion of our scientific scholars? How are we to be convinced that from the threads so laboriously collected they could have woven a cloth of such stout weft that it needed all the subtlety of our modern critics to pierce the secret

[1] Ἐξ αὐτῆς τῆς πηγῆς ὥρμηνται (S. Epiphanius, *Hæreses*, li. 6).

of its texture? On the other hand, is it not enough to read one of these narratives without prejudice to recognize the fact that this is no tedious effort of some compiler of facts, but a work wrought by one man's hand and at one time, inspired to the doing of it by memories which the first Christians held in common?

For the rest we must beware of exaggerating the harmony between these writers. In their general plan the three narratives move in nearly parallel lines: the Mission of John Baptist, the Baptism of Jesus, His Temptation, the return into Galilee, the Saviour's Ministry in that province, His journey Jerusalemward, the entry into the Holy City, His preaching during the following days, the Passion, and the Resurrection, — these in like manner have their place in each Gospel. But if we go farther, and calculate the number of minor incidents which go to fill up these divisions, we find that in most cases [1] the narrator has not scrupled to omit or to add certain details. Still more rarely do the Historians of Jesus employ the same words in reporting the same facts. Their agreement, infrequent as it is in the purely narrative portions, has a valid and plain reason for its existence in the teachings and conversations of the Lord, when there is a question of some Prophecy fulfilled in Him, or when they are treating of some great event, like the Institution of the Eucharist, certain circumstances in the Passion, the Multiplication of Loaves, — all figuring forth the most sacred of the Christian Mysteries. Even in these portions, though there are many verbal coincidences, the number of words changed or omitted without any motive proves that each author retained his own independent method, even as to those points where a formal tradition would have seemed rather to restrict them to a more scrupulous fidelity to what they had heard.

But over and above this freedom which they allowed

---

[1] An examination of any Harmony of the Synoptic Writers will suffice to show the reader that only two fifths of the facts related are common to all three Evangelists.

themselves in the preaching and compiling of the Gospel, there is another cause which explains many of the divergences we find in their work; they arose in great part from the fact that the Good News was delivered to very various audiences, even in Jerusalem. As the majority of pilgrims from the Dispersion understood Greek only, they were obliged to preach the Saviour to them in that language. And thus from the very first, the Twelve were led to give a twofold version of the Life of Jesus, — one in Aramean for the native-born Christians of Jerusalem, the other in Greek for the Israelite strangers who knew no Hebrew. We have seen how the latter, after changing many of their customs and opinions from frequent contact with the Pagans, came to differ very widely from their brethren, still strictly observant of the Mosaïcal rites. To meet and conquer minds of such opposite tendencies, it was necessary for the Apostles to adapt their preaching to their various needs. Thus it came about that with a theme common to all three Synoptic Writers, we find certain individualities which distinguish one from the other, — a personal treatment, which, taking Saint Matthew's Gospel, will give us an insight into the Hebraïc preaching in Jerusalem.

II. — The Gospel of Saint Matthew.

As long as the Apostles remained in the Holy City, no one dreamed of asking them to set down in written words the Good News they were repeating day after day; for how could a book replace these living fervid Witnesses? The need of such a substitute was not felt till the time came for them to separate. It would seem that Matthew was especially noted for the charming character of his recital of the Divine Story, his talent for adapting the deeds and words of Jesus to the understanding of the children of Israel, above all for the pains he took to show how the Master was foretold and prefigured in the Old Testament. For all these reasons, his story of the Gospel stood in high repute among the Jews. The latter obtained his promise that before leaving them "he would set down in writing the Gospel which he had preached to them, and thus supply the want which would be felt in his absence."[1] Such, according to Eusebius, was the origin of the first manuscript containing the Life of the Christ. His testimony is but an echo of Tradition. From the time of the Apostles, in fact, we have an unbroken line of Fathers who declare that the Gospel of Saint Matthew was written in Aramean and destined for the use of the Hebrews.

The first to attest this fact is a Bishop who lived in the beginning of the second century, Papias of Hierapolis, the friend of Saint Polycarp. A man versed in tradition, he had gathered together from older men who had conversed with the Apostles, and in particular with the Priest John, many bits of testimony which he solemnly affirms "are true."[2] Here is what he says concerning our Gospel. "Matthew composed the Oracles in Hebrew, and each one interpreted them as best he could." It is the opinion of the best critics that the word "Oracles" is used here to designate the long discourses[3] which are a peculiar feature of Saint Matthew's work. The Bishop of Hierapolis marks three distinct periods in the diffusion of this

[1] Eusebius, *Historia Ecclesiastica*, iii. 24.
[2] Διαβεβαιούμενος ὑπὲρ αὐτῶν ἀλήθειαν. Papias, quoted by Eusebius (*Historia Ecclesiastica*, iii. 39).
[3] Schleiermacher and others give this word a restricted meaning, and translate it by "certain utterances of the Lord." But it is manifest that λόγια has a larger signification. In the Epistle to the Romans (iii. 2), τὰ λόγια τοῦ Θεοῦ refers, not merely to the Law, but to the whole body of Scripture, and in the Epistle to the Hebrews (v. 12) the same word embraces "all divine Revelation." It cannot be said that Papias means by τὰ λόγια simply a collection of sentences without an accompanying narrative. Certainly, when commenting upon the λόγια κυριακά, he would have no occasion to treat of anything in his Preface save what nearly concerned his subject. His expression applies very aptly to a Gospel comprising both the deeds and words of Christ. Speaking of S. Mark, he says that his work contained τὰ ὑπὸ τοῦ Χριστοῦ ἢ λεχθέντα ἢ πραχθέντα Compare Plato, *Phædo*, 2. But this did not deter him from calling the same book Σύνταξις τῶν κυριακῶν λόγων. Indeed, Papias' own work, entitled, Λογίων κυριακῶν ἐξηγήσεις, contained the narratives as well. See Routh, *Rel. Sacræ*, p. 7 et seq.

Gospel: the first when only the Hebrew text was in existence; during the second each reader exercised all his learning in translating it as he went along; finally, after alluding to these efforts of days gone by,[1] Papias gives us a third epoch, which is his own, when these individual essays at interpretation had yielded place to an authentic translation, accepted by all in place of the original.[2]

The same tradition was held by the Church of Alexandria. About the middle of the second century Pantænus, one of the Doctors of that city, was sent by the Bishop Demetrius to preach along the borders of the Red Sea in Araby the Blest.[3] But he found "that certain of the dwellers in that region already knew of the Christ, and possessed the Gospel of Matthew. In olden times Bartholomew had brought them the Good News, and left in their hands this Book of the Apostle written in Hebrew characters, and this they had preserved up to that day."[4] Pantænus certainly had no doubts as to the authenticity of this document; his teaching in regard to the matter has been handed down to us by Origen, one of his disciples: "Here is what I have learned from tradition concerning the four Gospels, the only ones of incontestable authority in the Church of God which is under Heaven. Matthew, who was first a Publican, afterwards an Apostle of Jesus Christ, wrote the first; he intended it for the use of those who came over from Judaism, and com-

[1] Ἡρμήνευσε, and not ἑρμηνεύει.
[2] Hence it follows that the second generation of Christianity already possessed the authentic translation of S. Matthew's Gospel as it stands in our modern editions.
[3] The text of Eusebius has it that he started forth to preach in the Indies, but by this name the ancients sometimes designated Araby the Blest (Mosheim, *De Rebus Christ ante Constantin. M. Commentarii*, 6206). According to the tenth chapter of Genesis, this region was peopled by the children of Chus and Joktan. Now, the Syrians and Hebrews call the former Chusites, the latter Indians (Assemani, *Bibliothec. Orient.*, t. i. p. 359). On the western coasts of Arabia, washed by the Red Sea, there were numerous Jewish communities which could only have used a Hebrew version of the Gospel. And it was there, so Socrates asserts, that Bartholomew preached the Gospel, "in India, which is nigh unto Ethiopia" (*Historia Ecclesiastica*, i. 19); "in India called the Blest," adds Sophronius.
[4] Eusebius, *Historia Ecclesiastica*, v. 10.

posed it in the Hebrews' language."[1] Along about the same time, Saint Irenæus speaks of it in the same terms to the Christians of Lyons.[2] To their testimony we may add that of Eusebius, Saint Epiphanius, Saint Jerome,[3] and the Fathers of later times ; all are unanimous as to the point in question, and we must come down to the sixteenth century to find in Erasmus the first one to gainsay them. Following his example, certain modern writers strive hard to prove that Saint Matthew wrote in Greek ; but none of their arguments will bear a searching examination.

Whether we attach little or no weight to the voice of tradition in this matter, the character of the work alone is enough to show what sort of readers Saint Matthew had in mind. Always beneath the Greek version one feels the presence of a Jewish author, writing in his native Semitic speech. The first page contains one of those genealogies,[4] so common in the Old Testament, where symmetry of numerical form is one of the first objects in view. From the opening of the Gospel down to its last line, the author's dominant thought is to show his readers, who rest all their hopes in the Messiah's coming, and put their whole trust in the Law and the Prophets, that Jesus embodied all that these Seers had foretold, and thereby manifested Himself as their Saviour and Christ. It would seem that no events had any importance in his eyes unless they verified some prediction, while the deeds and words of the Master are chosen with the single aim of showing that, " These things were done that it might be fulfilled which the Lord spake by the Prophets."

Furthermore, the audience our writer is addressing is not one of Jews merely, but of Jews who speak the Aramean tongue, — witness the many words of that language,

---

[1] Origen, quoted by Eusebius (*Historia Ecclesiastica*, vi. 25).
[2] S. Irenæus, *Hæreses*, iii. 1.
[3] Eusebius, *Historia Ecclesiastica*, iii. 24; S. Epiphanius, *Hæreses*, xxix. 9; S. Jerome, *Præfat. in Matt. De Viris Illustribus* 3.
[4] In Hebrew, SEPHER TOLEDOTH. It is worthy of note that in this genealogy the transcriptions of proper names are not always those which we find in the Septuagint.

such as *raka, corbona,* [1] employed without further explanation; note the interpretations he gives, which suppose a knowledge of Hebrew, as, for example, of the name Jesus, and Nazarene.[2] It is no less plain to be seen that these Israelites were living in Jerusalem before its destruction, and that they were daily witnesses of the sacred ceremonies, the Temple, the Altar laden with its offerings,[3] "the City of the Great King" just as the Saviour knew it, its courts,[4] its prejudices,[5] the Laws peculiar to Palestine, with the political and social organization of Judea while it was still intact. Scribes and Pharisees are seated in the chair of Moses, broadening their phylacteries and the fringes of their garments. To them belong the first places in the banquets, the front seats in the synagogues, and the tithes of mint, anise, and cumin. They pray noisily at the street-corners, standing upright and surrounded by a crowd which greets them with cries of "Rabbi! Rabbi!" Around about the walls, and in the valleys of Hinnom and Josaphat, these hypocrites erect white tombs to the ancient Prophets; they adorn the sepulchres of the righteous dead, and meanwhile they whip the living saints in their synagogues, crucifying and killing those whom the Lord sends to them in His Name.[6] The Jerusalem of the time of Agrippa stands forth so strikingly in Saint Matthew's work that the Rationalists have not ventured to give it a later date than the years which followed immediately upon the destruction of the Holy City.[7] Otherwise they would

---

[1] Matt. v. 22; xxvii. 6.   [2] Matt. i. 21; ii. 23.

[3] "If thou offer thy gift at the altar. . . . Whosoever shall swear by the gold of the Temple . . . by the altar . . . by the gift which is thereon" (Matt. v. 23; xxiii. 16, 18).

[4] Matt. v. 22.

[5] The word "Gentiles" is always used in a bad sense; the Apostles are commanded not to go among them. The Samaritans are an abhorred race, etc.

[6] Matt. xxiii. 2, 6, 7, 14, 23, 27, 29, 34; vi. 2, 5.

[7] "As near as we can conjecture, it was about the year 75 when, for the first time, the hand of man attempted to sketch certain features of that figure before which eighteen centuries have knelt and adored. . . . The language used was the same wherein the very words of Jesus were first conceived, — those words which we all know by heart; that is, it was

be at a loss to explain how the vanished city could have left so vivid a memory in the minds of men.

These critics have only one reason for assigning the compilation of the First Gospel to a later date than the year 70 :[1] that reason is that they find the destruction of Jerusalem foretold therein ; and as every Prophecy is an historical impossibility, to their thinking, we must suppose that the event had already occurred. This argument is not enough to counterbalance the evidence of antiquity, which agrees in dating the appearance of Saint Matthew's text, not only before the time when Titus devastated Judea, but considerably earlier. In fact, the general feeling among the Fathers seems to be that the Apostle composed his Narrative some ten years after the Ascension,[2] when he was making ready to leave the Holy Land. It is impossible to explain why Matthew, if he had been living among Gentiles who neither spoke nor understood Hebrew, should have written in that language; whereas at the time when he was still in Jerusalem his reason for doing so is easily conceived. It was to the Christians of that city, to whom his departure was such a blow, that he left the Glad Tidings he had preached to them, and " thereby left a substitute in his absence."[3]

When assigning so early a date to this Gospel, we have in mind the Aramean text alone, now lost to us. As to the Greek translation, it is impossible to determine the

written in the Syro-Chaldaic, then called, by an abuse of terms, Hebrew " (Renan, *Les Évangiles*, p. 97).

[1] These two verses from the last chapters in S. Matthew are sometimes quoted as indicating a later date : " And for this cause that field has been called, *even to this our day*, Hakeldama; that is, The Field of Blood" (xxvii. 8). " And this saying is spread abroad among the Jews *even unto this day* " (xxviii. 15). Everything goes to show that these two remarks were added at some later date, when the original Aramean was translated into Greek.

[2] Theophylactus and Euthymius hold for the eighth year after the Ascension; Nicephorus and the Chronicle of Alexandria, the fifteenth, — 45. As regards the passage in S. Irenæus which seems to give 61 as the year in which this Gospel was composed, " when Peter and Paul were preaching the Gospel in Rome," see Appendix III.

[3] Eusebius, *Historia Ecclesiastica*, iii. 24.

time of its publication with any degree of assurance. Papias and the other Fathers of the second century had it before them, and quote it as the authentic work of Saint Matthew. Hence we know that it was made in the first century, but without any evidence to indicate the year or the author of this part of the work. Saint Jerome confesses that he could discover nothing bearing on this point.[1] Some credit it to Saint John,[2] others to Saint Barnabas,[3] others again to Saint James.[4] Papias informs us that at first each one translated the Aramean as best he could. How did it happen that so many versions should have disappeared without leaving any trace? What translator enjoyed such a reputation that his work should have superseded all the others? To these questions we can find but one simple and plausible answer, — to wit, that Saint Matthew himself was the author of both texts. The same reasons which led the Hebrews of Jerusalem to beg him for a summary of his preaching, must have induced the communities of Greek Christians which he afterwards established to beseech him to grant them the same favor, and certainly he would not have refused their request.

We can get some inkling as to the manner in which this translation was made from what we know of the Apostles' preaching of the Good News.[5] Saint Matthew's work may be divided into two parts, — first, the general plan, and certain details proper to it; and secondly, numerous extracts from his spoken version which he had selected and then inserted in this frame-work. Now, in

---

[1] S. Jerome, *De Viris Illustribus*, iii.
[2] Theophylactus, Euthymius.
[3] Isidore of Seville, *Chron.*, 272.
[4] *Synopsis Sacræ Scripturæ* in the Works of S. Athanasius, vol. ii. p. 202. The last-mentioned tradition is rather curious in that it describes the Bishop of Jerusalem — an Israelite of the Israelites — circulating among the Greeks of his flock a work which S. Matthew destined for the use of Hebrews alone.
[5] Here I have drawn largely upon the labors of the many learned scholars who have thrown so much light on the origins of the Gospel; notably Westcott's *Introduction to the Study of the Gospels*, and Norton's *Genuineness of the Gospels*, etc.

Jerusalem the preaching was of a twofold description, — one in Aramean for the Israelites who used that tongue, the other in Greek for the Hellenist Jews, both similar at bottom, but presenting some divergent characters; for instance, in the quotations from the Old Testament, where the Hebrews referred to their original text, whereas the Greeks followed the Septuagint. Since Saint Matthew wrote his first Narrative in the Aramean tongue, he must have taken all he wished to preserve of the Apostles' preaching from the oral Gospel of the Hebrews; but the material of all these extracts was to be found, word for word, in the oral Gospel of the Greeks, which was a faithful reflection of the former. Thus, then, when it was simply a question of the one same text delivered daily in two different languages, Saint Matthew had only to substitute one idiom for the other in order to put his work into the hands of Hellenists; and a translation, properly speaking, became necessary only for those parts of his Gospel which belonged exclusively to himself.[1]

---

[1] Certainly this is but an hypothesis, yet a very likely one, since it explains how the Greek copy, the only one which has come down to us, preserves all the charm and vividness of the original. Also it gives a reason for the verbal coincidences in S. Matthew with the text of SS. Mark and Luke, who alike drew the substance of their story from the spoken Greek Gospel. But what goes still further to support our supposition is this peculiarity; to wit, that all the quotations which S. Matthew makes from the Old Testament follow the Hebrew text (Matt. i. 23; ii. 15, 18; iv. 15, 16; viii. 17; xii. 18–21; xiii. 35; xxi. 5; xxvii. 9, 10), while those in the discourses which are spoken by the Saviour or other personages, are conformed to the Septuagint Version (Matt. iii. 3; iv. 4, 6, 7, 10; xv. 4, 8, 9; xix. 5, 18; xxi. 42; xxii. 32, 39, 44; xxiii. 39; xxiv. 15; xxvii. 46). Just this would be the case according to the supposition adopted above. Certainly, when translating into Greek those passages of his work which belonged exclusively to himself, S. Matthew would prefer to revert to the Hebrew text, which he possessed in the original Aramean, for all his own quotations from Scripture; on the contrary, when he had only to transfer to his earlier work those precious gems of thought which he treasured in common with all who knew the spoken Greek Gospel, he would prefer to keep them just as the people were accustomed to hearing them, giving all the quotations according to the Septuagint. The fact that he borrowed thus from the oral Gospel of the Greeks is made still more manifest because in cases where S. Matthew adopts the Septuagint wording, SS. Mark and Luke do so likewise; and when the first makes any change, the other Synoptical writers do so too.

Saint Matthew's work, after being put into an available form, remained the only one in use in countries speaking the Greek tongue; that is to say, among the Gentiles and Jews scattered over the world outside of Palestine. The original Hebrew version was left to the disciples of the Holy City, who preserved it, without alteration, up to the year 134. In that epoch the Jewish Church of Jerusalem, after being banished from the city, together with all the children of Israel, finally ceased to exist;[1] in its place there grew up a community of Christian colonists, Greek in race and speech. The Aramean Gospel, therefore, continued to be used only by a certain number of Hebrews, who stubbornly insisted upon mingling the practices of Mosaism with the New Faith. These Judaisers took refuge beyond Jordan, and there were known by the name of Nazarenes. In the time of Saint Justin, their attachment to the Law was tolerated by some, condemned by others; but keeping aloof from the Church and without any regular Hierarchy, they soon dwindled to an obscure sect. Saint Epiphanius, who is the first to rank them in the number of heretics, says "that what separated them from the Christians was their obstinacy in keeping the Circumcision, the Sabbath, and the rest of the Mosaical Observances."[2]

---

[1] It is true that in 70 the faithful of Jerusalem had withdrawn with S. Simeon, their shepherd, over beyond Jordan, but they returned to the ravaged city as soon as Titus had departed. They re-entered it firm in their Christian faith, and no heresy had its rise among them before the year 108; they still clung to Jewish customs. During the century of their Church's existence, they had fifteen Bishops, all of the circumcision, all faithful to the Law (Eusebius, *Historia Ecclesiastica*, iii. 32; iv. 5, 6, 22; S. Cyril of Jerusalem, *Catech.* xiv. 15; S. Epiphanius, *Hæreses*, lxvi. 20). As there was nothing to distinguish them from other Jews to Roman eyes, they were included in the proscription which befell the children of Israel after the defeat of Barcochebas (135). Those whom Adrian's soldiers were unable to slay or sell, were forbidden to approach Jerusalem; only once a year, and at a great price, they extorted permission to enter and weep over the Holy City, which the Conqueror had pillaged and stripped of everything, even its name, — for the decree had gone forth that thereafter it was to be known as *Ælia Capitolina*. This rigorous banishment put an end to the Jewish Church of Jerusalem.

[2] S. Epiphanius, *Hæreses*, xxix. 7.

SAINT MATTHEW'S GOSPEL. 225

In their hands Saint Matthew's Hebrew Gospel did not remain long intact. Without going so far as to alter and mutilate[1] the text, as the Ebionites did, they made very many additions to it. We have seen, from the example of Papias and Saint Irenæus, with what care men gathered up every word of Jesus and His Apostles. The Nazarenes went farther, and inserted many traditions into their Hebrew Gospel. However, they did not accept them lightly or without consideration; for the Fathers, without conceding any canonical authority to these fragments, nevertheless quote them with respect. Hegesippus, a man of scrupulous orthodoxy, Clement of Alexandria, and Origen, often allude to the Gospel of the Nazarenes;[2] Saint Epiphanius contents himself with saying that it is very complete.[3] Saint Jerome went further: finding it at Aleppo, he copies and translates it; and although he calls it "rather the Gospel according to the Apostles, than according to Saint Matthew,"[4] he does not fail to recommend its use.[5] Such fragments as we possess do not justify his esteem for it; the influence of Gnosticism

---

[1] S. Epiphanius, *Hæreses*, xxx. 3, 13. Νενοθευμένῳ καὶ ἠκρωτηριασμένῳ. They had abbreviated the genealogies. S. Jerome says that, on the contrary, the Gospel of the Nazarenes began with the two first chapters as we have them in the Greek text of S. Matthew.

[2] Eusebius, *Historia Ecclesiastica*, iv. 22; Clement of Alexandria, *Stromata*, ii. 9; Origen, *In Mat.* xv. 14.

[3] S. Epiphanius, *Hæreses*, xxix. 7, 9.

[4] S. Jerome, because he found this text at Berea (Aleppo) among the Nazarenes of that city, at first believed that he had in his possession the original Aramean version of S. Matthew. "Ipsum Hebraicum habetur usque hodie in Cæsariensi Bibliotheca, quam Pamphilus Martyr studiosissime confecit. Mihi quoque a Nazaræis qui in Berœa urbe Syriæ hoc volumine utuntur, describendi facultas fuit" (*De Viris Illustribus*, iii.). But a few years later he modified his opinion, and expressed himself thus: "In Evangelio quo utuntur Nazaræi et Hebionitæ, quod nuper in Græcum de Hebræo sermone transtulimus, et quod vocatur a plerisque Matthæi authenticum" (*In Matt.* xii. 13). And still later, in his *Dialogue against the Pelagians* (iii. 2): "In Evangelio juxta Hebræos, quod Chaldaico quidem Syroque sermone, sed Hebraicis litteris conscriptum est, quo utuntur usque hodie Nazareni, secundum Apostolos, sive, ut plerique autumant, juxta Matthæum, quod et in Cæsariensi habetur Bibliotheca."

[5] S. Jerome, *In Matt.* xv. 14; *Contra Pelag.* iii. 1.

is plainly felt in the tedious turns of the sentences and the vagueness of the thoughts.[1]

The Greek text, on the contrary, faithfully depicts Jesus as He was preached in the Church of Jerusalem. Here is no misty verbiage, no long preambles; the word stands forth simple and luminous, in vivid sentences such as the Oriental mind loves, and with scanty regard for dates or the order of events. All the author cares for is to make us see and hear the Master, in the streets of Jerusalem, upon the mountain and by the shores of the lake, evermore evoking the memory of the Prophets who from His Birth to the tomb had foretold of Him, the Messiah and King of Judea. Whether this likeness of Jesus was drawn fifteen years after His death, as we believe, or twenty-five years later, as our opponents contend, it matters little after all. Jesus lived as no man ever lived in the memory of His companions. It was one of them who wrote the text which has remained unchanged since then.[2] This one man alone stands between us and the Christ as His holy interpreter, — this Publican who loved Him so dearly as to leave all to follow Him, and here paints Him for us in words of love.

[1] A collection of them is to be found in Grabe (*Spicilegium Patrum*) and in Anger (*Synopsis Evangelica*). A slight comparison of certain passages — as, for instance, Matt. iii. 14-17; x. 2-4; xviii. 21, 22 — will suffice to show how far the Nazarenes' Gospel disfigures and weakens the force of the original.

[2] "We may feel certain that, even if we now possessed the Hebrew Gospel as S. Jerome saw it, our Matthew would still be preferred to it; for our Matthew, indeed, has been preserved intact since its definitive compilation in the last years of the first century, while the Hebrew Gospel, owing to the absence of any jealous orthodoxy to act as guardian of the text in the Judaizing churches of Syria, had suffered by overmuch handling from century to century, in so far that in the end it was not much superior to any other apocryphal document" (Renan, *Les Évangiles*, p. 104).

CHAPTER XIII.

THE TEACHING OF THE CHURCH OF JERUSALEM.

THE APOSTLES' CREED.

THE Church had lived for now fourteen years, and by virtue of that never-ceasing progress which is the very law of life, her growth had developed until she had put forth all that was needful for her existence, not only outward forms, such as her Hierarchy, worship, and methods of government, but most of all the truth which illuminated her path, the divine guide of Revelation. Wonderful as was the descent of the Holy Ghost on Pentecost Day, it had not shown them in a flash of light all they were to discern later on. We have seen how his ecstasy at Joppa unveiled to Peter's gaze many things which had hitherto seemed mysterious to him, — the Gospel freed from the servitude of the Law, and Gentiles entering into the new Kingdom of Jesus without passing through the narrow door of Judaism. Yet other points of doctrine were still wrapped in shadow, and only emerged into the full light successively and one by one. "When the Spirit of Truth shall have come," the Master had said,[1] "He will lead you into the knowledge of the whole truth." This pouring-forth of the Spirit, begun on the day of Pentecost, was to continue until the death of the last of the Twelve. During all this period, — that is to say, during more than sixty years, for Saint John did not die until the end of the first century, — the domain of Faith never ceased to extend its boundary-lines. Step by step, God's Spirit guided each Apostle through this

[1] John xvi. 13: 'Οδηγήσει ὑμᾶς εἰς πᾶσαν τὴν ἀλήθειαν.

supernatural world,[1] according as circumstances and the needs of the disciples demanded His aid. When Peter and Paul were taken from them, the light of the New Day was certainly far advanced and the noontide brightness drawing on; nevertheless John was empowered to shed a clearer radiance on the heritage which they left to the Church. It is the Jesus Whom he depicts for us, Who alone can say, "It is finished; I am the Alpha and Omega, the Beginning and the End."[2] Thus, then, it was not until the second century that the Church was in possession of the whole truth which had been promised to her; only then, and under their implicit form, did she hold all the dogmas which shall be proclaimed unto the end of time.[3] Let us beware, however, of fancying that this slow growth of Revelation left the Apostles in a state of confusion or uncertainty at times; the Holy Ghost laid bare the essential truths of Faith that early morning in the Upper Chamber. Doubtless it was but the dawn; yet the dawning light knows no change, and needs only time to grow and spread abroad till it is broad day.

This gradual manifestation of the truth is more and more perceptible, the longer one studies the works of the Apostles. In the two letters written towards the close of his life, Peter has a different manner of speaking from that which we note in his discourses in the Acts. When he stepped forth in the Supper Room he confined himself to affirming the Resurrection of Jesus, with intrepid spirit calling to witness the testimony of the Prophets who had foretold the sufferings, death, and triumph of the Saviour. He is eloquent only when he utters the exclamations of a soul transported by grace. "Better by far

---

[1] "Non utique ipso die Pentecostes, sed tempore adventus Spiritus sancti paulatim ac per gradus inducti sunt in omnem veritatem, ut ex manifestis factis et ex ipsis verbis constat: Inducet in omnem veritatem. Joan. xvi. 12-15" (Franzelin, *De Divina Traditione*, sect. iv. th. xxii. p. 272).

[2] Apoc. xxi. 6; xxii. 13.

[3] "Quamvis tempore apostolico revelatio catholica nondum fuerit conclusa, attamen nulla nova revelatio in depositio fidei suscipienda erat, quæ non esset ab ipsis Apostolis vel promulgata vel confirmata" (Franzelin, *De Divina Traditione*, p. 276).

to obey God rather than man!" "We cannot but speak that which we have heard and seen!"[1] Thirty years later, the Apostle dictated the pages of the New Testament which bear his name, wherein we hear his great voice resounding with a majesty like that of Paul: there is a like abundance of thoughts, the same forcefulness in his words, and a depth of meaning not to be fathomed by our minds.

Evidently, during this long lapse of time Peter was not content to remain inactive, relying on the greatness of his estate. His first task was to search the Scriptures, which he and John had understood so little even on the day of the Resurrection.[2] Whether he applied himself to the Law, the Prophets, or the Hagiographies, everywhere he would find the Name of Jesus, and thus be able to show forth the truth. In those early days, his teaching reduced itself to that single thought; when the Princes and Doctors of Israel have him brought before them, they see in him only "a man of the common folk and without education;"[3] these arrogant scholars, despising the people, are astonished that an ignorant Galilean dare answer them with such audacity. The Gospel of Saint Mark, which is but the echo of Peter's preaching, gives us a clear idea of how the Apostle delivered his Message in the middle stage of his career as a preacher. But his two Epistles disclose a still more surprising progress for the last years of his life; the humble Fisherman is become the man who, with a word, sheds a flood of light upon the whole theology of Grace: "Unto us Jesus Christ hath given great and precious promises, in order that through them you may participate in the Divine Nature."[4] These gracious admonitions are his too: "Purify your souls by obedience to the truth. . . . Love one another earnestly from a pure heart, being born again, not of a corruptible seed, but of an incorruptible, — by the word of God, Who liveth and remaineth forever."[5] And, again, does not this picture

[1] Acts v. 29; iv. 20.　　[2] John xx. 9–10.　　[3] Acts iv. 13.
[4] 1 Peter i. 4.　　[5] 1 Peter i. 22–23.

of the first heretics show that the Apostle's words have become as mighty as his thoughts? "Fountains without water, clouds tossed by the storm, to whom the mists of darkness are reserved for evermore; speaking words puffed up with vanity, they allure, by the covetousness of the flesh and by their lewdness, those who a little before had escaped unto men tainted by error; promising them liberty, whereas they are slaves of corruption, for he is a slave to him by whom he is vanquished."[1] Nothing that the Gospels or the Acts relate of Peter could have prepared us for such commanding power. This transformation is indeed wholly the work of Grace, whose movements were never more wondrous than in Peter's case.

We witness the same splendid spectacle in the career of Paul. And the development of his mind is all the more striking, inasmuch as we can follow it from day to day, from his conversion up to the last hours of his life. Those great doctrines to which he gave a definite form are only in their germ in the discourses delivered during his first Mission journeys. His combats with the Judaisers bring his teachings to their full maturity. This is the middle period in his Apostolic career, — the time of his letters to the Galatians, Romans, and Corinthians. Then Gnosticism appears, and Jesus manifests Himself to Paul with a new and brighter radiance, which illumines every page of his later Epistles.

And so it was with the other Apostles. Little by little the Holy Spirit opened up to their gaze the Faith which they were to leave to the world. This it did in a threefold manner, accomplishing first in its fulness their presentation of the teachings of Jesus; then recalling to their minds those other lessons which the Twelve remembered only imperfectly; and finally adding to the doctrines uttered by the Saviour those which it was the Paraclete's mission to reveal to them.[2] The Master

[1] 2 Peter ii. 17-19.
[2] " Efficientia Spiritus sancti est quidem multiplex, sed quatenus spectatur munus a Christo impositum authentice docendi et testificandi, quod

had foretold this in express terms:[1] "The Comforter, the Holy Spirit, Whom the Father will send in My Name, He will teach you all things and bring all things to your minds, whatsoever I have said unto you. . . . I have yet many things to say to you, but you cannot bear them now. But when He, the Spirit of Truth, shall have come, He will bring you unto the knowledge of all truth."

It follows from this that Revelation has likewise its History, though interwoven with that of the inspired Witnesses, — a divine History, since God dictated to them the truths they were to teach ; a human history, because, under the mysterious workings of the Spirit, the Apostles still retained everything that was individual to them, — style, genius, character. The irresistible breath of the Most High enveloped the sacred writer, and bore him where it listed, but without extinguishing his personality. It exalts his life and gives a power to his every act such as is unknown to us ; but it is always a man who thinks and speaks and utters the word of God. The preaching of the Twelve is therefore the faithful expression, waxing more perfect from day to day, of the Divine Revelation. Do we know this preaching so well in all its details and at every point of time as to be able to trace a complete chart of the manifestations of dogma ? Assuredly not. In the Deposit of Faith have come down to us, under a twofold form, Oral Tradition and the writings of the New Testament.[2] Now, only in the latter do we find the historical movements portrayed, with a series of facts and discourses, wherein we can follow

est proprium Apostolorum, eis immediate promittitur Spiritus Veritatis, ut doceat omnia, et suggerat omnia quæcumque dixerat eis Christus ; ut doceat omnem veritatem, etiam eam quam, Christo adhuc cum eis visibiliter versante, nondum potuerant portare" (Franzelin, *De Divina Traditione*, sect. i. cap. i. th. v. p. 31).

[1] John xiv. 26 ; xvi. 12-13.

[2] In Session iv. (Canon of Scripture), the Council of Trent teaches that it behoves us to recognize two sorts of traditions in the Deposit of Faith, — certain ones which are to be referred to our Lord Himself ; others to the Apostles, inspired by the Holy Spirit : "Omnem salutarem veritatem et disciplinam contineri in libris scriptis, et sine scripto traditionibus, quæ, ipsius Christi ore ab Apostolis acceptæ, aut ab Apostolis, Spiritu sancto dictante, quasi per manus traditæ, ad nos usque pervenerunt."

the development of beliefs. There is nothing of the kind in oral traditions. The Church simply transmits them to us as the voice of the Apostles, without attempting to tell us at what hour this or that inspired word was spoken.

So, then, in order to follow the course of the current which never ceased to grow in volume and power until it filled up the measure of Revelation, we should have to have been present at the preaching of the Apostles, along with the early Christians. To-day, with only the books of the New Testament to give us an idea of the progress of doctrine, we can but venture our conjectures, and even then with extreme caution, for the greater number of the Epistles are occasional documents, written under peculiar circumstances and for a particular object. To maintain that they contain everything which was taught to the faithful would be to delude oneself to no purpose.

In this respect we get more light from the Gospels. Though they do not contain in express terms all the truths afterwards made known to the Apostolic body, they at least give us their substance, and show us what points of doctrine were commonly held at the time of their appearance. Thus the Gospel of Saint Matthew marks the highest point in the revelations made to the Church about the year 42. Taken together with the twelve chapters of the Acts which contain the history of these first years, it forms a twofold piece of evidence, sufficient to give us an idea of the preaching heard at Jerusalem and the Faith professed by the disciples there.

According to a tradition for long years held in high repute, we have in our possession a still more precise summary of the doctrine of that date. "We have received it from our fathers," says the priest Rufinus,[1] a contemporary of Saint Jerome, "how that after the Ascension, . when the Holy Spirit had come down in tongues of fire upon the Apostles, . . . it was ordained by the Lord that

---

[1] Rufinus, *Comment. in Symbolum*, 2; *Patrologie latine*, t. xxi. p. 338.

THE APOSTLES' CREED. 233

each one should go forth to preach to the various nations. Before separating, they compiled in common a rule for their future instructions, that so they might not set forth a different belief unto them whom they should call to the faith of the Christ. They gathered together, therefore, and being filled with the Holy Ghost, they communicated their opinions one to another, then composed this abridgment of the truths which they were to publish, and resolved that it should be given as a rule to the believers." While Rufinus, living on the Adriatic sea-board, thus sets forth the tradition of the Church of Aquileia, Saint Ambrose uses much the same terms in speaking to the Christians of Milan. "The twelve Apostles, he says,[1] "like skilful workmen, well knew how to construct this Key. I call this Symbol[2] a key which opens the dark realms of the demon, that so the light of the Christ may shine therein." At the end of the fourth century, therefore, it was generally believed in the north of Italy that the Apostles' Creed was composed by them before their separation; that is to say, about the same time that the Gospel of Saint Matthew was written. Saint Ambrose adds that this *Credo* was preserved in all its purity by the Holy Roman Church.[3] This is the form in which Rufinus has handed it down to us: —

I believe in God the Father Almighty,
And in Christ Jesus His only Son, our Lord,
Who was born of the Holy Ghost, of the Virgin Mary,
Was crucified under Pontius Pilate, and buried,
The third day He arose from the dead,
Ascended into Heaven,
Is seated at the right hand of the Father,

[1] S. Ambrose, *Serm.* xxxviii.
[2] The Fathers give to the word "Symbol," as designating the formulary of our Faith, the same significance it has in Classical Greek, — "a preconcerted mark" (from συμβάλλειν, to cast, or put together), "a distinctive sign," or "password." "Symbolum Græce indicium dici potest . . . indicium vel signum . . . ut si forte occurreret quis de quo dubitatur, interrogatus Symbolum prodat, si est hostis an socius" (Rufinus, *Expositio in Symbol.*; S. Augustine, *Serm.* ccxiv. 12, etc.).
[3] S. Ambrose, *Epist.* xlii. 5.

And in the Holy Ghost,
The Holy Church,
The forgiveness of sins,
The resurrection of the flesh.[1]

It will be seen that this ancient formula differs in several points from our Creed. To the first article, "God the Father Almighty," the attribute, "Creator of visible and invisible things,"[2] was added by Saint Augustine, and in the sermons of his disciples received its present form, "Creator of Heaven and Earth."[3] The wording "conceived by the Holy Ghost, born of the Virgin Mary,"[4] which is much clearer and more precise than the terms of the Roman Creed, "born of the Holy Ghost, of the Virgin Mary," does not appear until the fifth century in a *Credo* attributed to Faustus of Riez.[5] This same *Credo* contains the additions, "Who suffered" and "died;" to the words "is seated at the right hand of the Father," it adds the qualification "God Almighty;" it applies the note "Catholic" to the Church; pronounces the two dogmas of "the resurrection of the body," and "life everlasting;"[6] in a word, it gives to the ancient Roman "Symbol"

---

[1] "Credo in Deum Patrem omnipotentem, — Et in Christum Jesum unicum filium ejus Dominum nostrum, — Qui natus est de Spiritu sancto, ex Maria Virgine, — Crucifixus sub Pontio Pilato et sepultus, — Tertia die resurrexit a mortuis, — Ascendit ad cœlos, — Sedet ad dexteram Patris, — Inde venturus est judicare vivos et mortuos, — Et in Spiritum sanctum, — Sanctam Ecclesiam, — Remissionem peccatorum, — Carnis resurrectionem" (Rufinus, *Patrologie latine*, t. xxi.).

[2] "Visibilium et invisibilium Creatorem" (S. Augustine, *Sermo* cxxii. 1, ed. Gaume, t. v. pars prior, p. 1361). The holy Doctor borrowed these words from the formularies of the East, which were worded with the idea of refuting the Gnostic theory of the Demiurge.

[3] "Creatorem cœli et terræ." S. Augustine, *Serm.* ccxl., ccxli., ccxlii., ed. Gaume, t. v. p. 2971 et seq.

[4] "Conceptus de Spiritu sancto, natus ex Maria virgine." These words are in ccxiii. Sermon of S. Augustine (t. v. p. 1365); but the authenticity of this document is doubtful.

[5] Caspari, *Quellen zur Geschichte des Taufsymbols und der Glaubensregel*. Faustus, born in Britain near the close of the fourth century, was successively Abbot of Lérins and Bishop of Riez, in Provence. He died in 492.

[6] The word "passus" and the article "vitam æternam" are commented on by S. Augustine, and consequently must have been in the Symbol of the African Church. S. Augustine, *De Symbolo*, ed. Gaume, t. vi. pp. 291 et 930.

the form under which we know it to-day, always excepting the article "he descended into Hell," which Rufinus read a hundred years earlier in the Rule of Faith of Aquileia, but is not to be found in this version.[1] The present form of the *Credo* is to be found for the first time in the sermons attributed by mistake to Saint Augustine, and composed, so far as we can ascertain, about the middle of the sixth century.[2]

These changes, which each Church inserted in the Creed so freely, show that this formula was not regarded as unchangeable. As for the Scriptures, on the contrary, the slightest alteration was considered to be a sacrilege. When Tryphillus, Bishop of Ledra, in Cyprus, in reading Saint John substituted the word "bed" for "cot,"[3] the latter seeming to him rather vulgar, at once Saint Spiridion started up from his episcopal chair, and, before the whole people, rebuked him for his affected delicacy. Their scrupulosity went so far as to make them unwilling to accept any modifications of the received version of the Holy Books. This is the reason why Saint Jerome experienced such great difficulty in getting his Vulgate accepted. Saint Augustine himself tried to dissuade him from making this translation, and, as a convincing argument, adduced the following fact: "One of our brethren in the Episcopate endeavored to read your version in his Church. He quoted a passage from Jonas in words other than those which were graven on their memory, having been repeated by them for so many generations. So great a tumult arose among the people, the Greeks crying out at him, and exclaiming that it was a forgery, that the Bishop was constrained to call the Jews to testify in

---

[1] Rufinus, *Patrologie latine*, t. xxi. p. 356 : "Sciendum quod in Ecclesiæ Romanæ Symbolo non habetur additum: *descendit ad inferna*, sed neque in Orientis Ecclesiis habetur hic sermo."

[2] S. Augustine, *Opera, Serm.* ccxl., ccxli., ccxlii., t. v. p. 2971 et seq. The third of the above sermons was held in great esteem in Gaul; they were read three times to the catechumens before baptism was administered. D. Martène, *De Antiquis Ecclesiæ Ritibus*, lib. i. p. 95.

[3] Σκίμποδα instead of κράββατον. Sozomenus, *Historia Ecclesiastica*, lib. i. cap. xi. : *Patrologie grecque*, t. lxvii. p. 889.

his favor. The latter, whether through ignorance or malice, made answer that they read the text in the original Hebrew just as it stands in the Greek and Latin. The Bishop was obliged to give way as gracefully as he could, lest he should be left without a flock."[1] Certainly it would be difficult to give a more striking proof of attachment to the letter of Scripture than this one left us by Saint Augustine; howbeit, the great Doctor, who is so fearful of the least alteration of the Apostolic traditions, allows himself almost absolute liberty in dealing with the Creed. We have many explications of the *Credo* from his pen, wherein we can study the workings of his thought; in all of them he appears bent, not on preserving it as an inviolable text, but on giving a more perfect form to this Rule of Faith.

We find similar liberties taken in the three great Metropolitan sees of the East. At the same time that Rufinus gives his interpretation of the *Symbol* of Antioch, and tells us what he knows concerning that of Rome, Cassian translates a part of the formula of Antioch; again, Saint Cyril treats of the one in use in his Church during the fourth century, while the Coptic creed, older than all the others, bears witness to the accustomed form in Alexandria. In each of these bits of evidence, which together declare the belief of all Eastern Christendom, we find the same Faith, though very variously expressed. Long commentaries are appended to the concise dogmatic statements of the Roman creed. It will be enough to quote the first article in these Confessions, in order to show how freely each Church and each generation treated this formal utterance of their belief.

" I believe in the one and only true God, Father Almighty, Creator of all creatures visible and invisible " (Creed of Antioch).[2]

" I believe in one only God, Father Almighty, Who hath made Heaven and Earth, things visible and invisible" (Creed of Jerusalem).[3]

[1] S. Augustine, *Epist.* lxxi. 5, ed. Gaume, t. ii. p. 240.
[2] Latin translation by Cassian, *De Incarnatione Domini*, 1, vi. c. iii.
[3] From the *Catechistæ*, by S. Cyril of Jerusalem.

"I believe in the only true God, Father Almighty" (Creed of Alexandria).[1]

Rufinus, who with us remarks these notable differences, seeks to explain their origin. "So far as can be ascertained," he says, "it was owing to certain heresies that these additions were made, in order to prevent innovations in doctrine."[2] But he assures us, at the same time, that Rome never acted after this fashion, and that there the Creed of the Apostles was cherished in its integrity. For this he gives two reasons: first, that "no heresy had had its birth in the bosom of that Church; and further because she had always kept up the olden custom of having the *Credo* recited publicly before the catechumens in presence of the whole people. Now, no one of those who had received the Faith at an earlier date would have tolerated the addition of a single word."[3]

Whatever the cause of these variations, they are incontestable, and make it impossible for us to accept without reservation the tradition which credits the composition of the *Symbol* to the Twelve on the eve of their separation. Furthermore, the time was not one likely to produce formularies. The Church, being still oriental to all outward seeming, preached and meditated, without feeling any need of dogmatizing on her beliefs. The disciples' only anxiety was to treasure up every one of the Master's words, and thus embrace the whole body of truth, not to compress it into a precise form. When Rufinus credits the Apostles with so much anxiety lest they should fail to teach the one same doctrine, after their dispersion, he forgets that the Holy Spirit spoke by their mouth, and was to assist them to the very last hour of their lives. So then we conclude that the Creed had its origin, not in Jerusalem, but, at a later date, in Rome, when Peter and Paul were nearing the close of their lives.

[1] *Constitutiones Copticæ*, ed. H. Tattam, § 46.
[2] Rufinus, *Comment. in Symbolum : Patrologie latine*, t. xxi. p. 339.
[3] Ibid.

Here place and time alike had changed. Difficulties and divisions came to trouble the unanimous faith of the first days. "Ravening wolves fell upon the Shepherds, nor spared the flock; men arose, speaking perverse things to draw disciples after them."[1] The doctrines of these innovators were not so much to be feared as was their speech, for "it spread like a canker," masking its inward corruption "under a profane show of new words."[2] To shun these pitfalls of speech, these uncertain and equivocal expressions, which could be made to teach error and truth alike,[3] it behoved their leaders to arm themselves with certain fixed terms, precise in their significance and hallowed by use. Hitherto, the Apostles' preaching had aimed solely at making Jesus better known and loved. Now the hour was come for embodying their teaching in a few essential dogmas, which all could commit to memory, and hold as a safeguard against heresy.

To this work Saint Paul applied all that energy which is the glory of his character, and proceeded to establish this "Deposit of the Faith," which he so earnestly recommended to the care of Timothy, before his death. "Preserve the summary[4] of sound words which thou hast heard from me in the faith and the love which is in the Christ Jesus. Keep the good deposit committed to thy trust by the Holy Ghost Which abideth in us." So then, besides the ordinary teaching of the Gospel in its widest extent, Timothy had received from Paul an abridgment, a summary of the Faith.

---

[1] Acts xx. 29, 30.   [2] 2 Tim. ii. 17.
[3] Τὰς βεβήλους κενοφωνίας καὶ ἀντιθέσεις τῆς ψευδωνύμου γνώσεως (1 Tim. vi. 20).
[4] 2 Tim. i. 13. Ὑποτύπωσις signifies the abridgment of a doctrine or philosophy. It is the name Sextus Empiricus gives his summary of Pyrrhonism. Πυρρωνείων ὑποτυπώσεων, a title borrowed from Œnesidemes. Proclus had called his epitome of Astronomy by the same name. "Passim Sextus negat se prolixius posse singula persequi . . . quoniam ὑποτυπωτικῶς, hoc est compendiose, summatim, omnia tradere instituit. Itaque συντόμως et ὑποτυπωτικῶς conjungit, p. 65, et Simplicius in *Categor.*, p. 196, ὑποτυπωτικὴν διδασκαλίαν opponit τῇ ἀκριβεστέρᾳ παραδόσει" (Fabricius, *Adnot. ad Sextum Empiricum*, p. 1).

Peter alludes to this formula in one of his Epistles, and at the same time tells how it came into use in primitive times. Speaking of the men saved from the Deluge by means of the floods which floated them in the Ark, "This same water," he adds,[1] " is for a figure of the Baptism which saveth us. Now, baptism consisteth, not in a cleansing of the impurities of the flesh, but in the examination [2] of a good conscience towards God." [3] What " examination" is the Apostle speaking of here? We have seen, in the passage from Rufinus quoted above, how it was the custom at Rome to put certain questions to the neophyte before baptizing him, that so he might make public confession of his faith in the Father, Son, and Holy Ghost. In the Coptic Church, at Carthage, and later on among the Gauls, the priest questioned the catechumen on the essential truths as well, and the latter made answer to each, " I believe. " Elsewhere he declared his belief of his own motion, but everywhere some profession of faith preceded the sacramental rite and was regarded as inseparably united to it.[4] There

---

[1] 1 Peter iii. 20–22.

[2] The Greek commentators explain the word ἐπερώτημα by the synonyms ἐξέτασις, ἐκζήτησις, and the Vulgate translates it by "*interrogatio.*" De Wette and Huther (in Meyer's Commentary) recognize the fact that this is an allusion to the baptismal interrogation, and consequently to the Profession of Faith,—the *Credo* demanded of every catechumen. It is worthy of note that three articles in the Apostles' Creed are mentioned here by S. Peter as making part of " this interrogation of a good conscience before God," this interrogation which saveth us " by *the Resurrection* of Jesus, Who . . . *is ascended into Heaven and sitteth at the right hand of God.*" " Anima non lavatione, sed responsione sancitur," says Tertullian (*De Resurrectione Carnis*, 48).

[3] S. Peter does not demand simply faith in God : πίστεως εἰς Θεόν, but a still deeper sentiment,—the consciousness that the soul has given itself wholly to God : συνειδήσεως εἰς Θεόν. Cf. Acts xxiv. 16.

[4] " The soul," says Tertullian, " is consecrated, not by ablution, but by the reply " of the catechumen (*De Resurrectione Carnis*, xlviii.). The consecration by the Symbol is of such importance that he calls baptism " the compact, the testimony of the Faith, the promise of salvation." " Testatio fidei et signaculum Symboli . . . Sponsio salutis " (*De Baptismo*, vi., xi., et passim). Origen employs analogous terms: " The Symbol of Purification " (*Contra Celsum*, iii. 51). Finally, the very etymology of the term " Symbol," meaning a mark, a distinctive character, would alone establish the fact that the first Christians treasured it as a sign, the rallying word by which, before receiving baptism, the soldier of Christ pledged himself to combat the common enemy.

is nothing to show that this mode of initiation, certainly practised by the Church in the third century, could have been introduced, or even modified, during the preceding hundred and fifty years. The *Credo* of the baptismal liturgy, therefore, must be referred to Apostolic times: if this be granted, then what could be more natural than to hold that the " examination " which Saint Peter speaks of, and the " summary " recommended by Saint Paul, allude to this Christian Creed? The words of the latter to Timothy leave hardly any doubt that he had some part in the making of this abridgment. It seems likelier to us, however, that the plan is due to the Chief of the Apostles, because his letter, written from Rome, gives us an idea of the manner of baptizing as it was administered under his eyes and by his orders; consequently, it is more natural to attribute the idea of making a formula of belief to him rather than to any other, as he was founder of the Roman Church, and drew his inspirations from the customs and traditions of the people among whom he lived.

Indeed, it is impossible not to recognize the imprint of the Roman genius in this baptismal examination which he speaks of. On his coming to that city, Peter found a very different society from any which he had frequented heretofore,—a world of soldiers, politicians, and lawmakers, to whom external forms were everything. In the army discipline was inexorable and religion was reduced to certain rites scrupulously observed. In the law there was the same slavery to the letter; just such facts, such and such terms, with such other forms of writing, were requisite to give any value to their agreements. Every day the Apostle was a witness to their public acts. He heard the sacramental words which the lawyers decided were necessary for the validity of a stipulation.[1] He listened to these questions and their answers.

[1] Any agreement in which the terms fixed by custom and law were not employed, was regarded as null and void. The words " Polliceris ?

"Do you promise?"
"I promise."
"Do you pledge your word?"
"I pledge my word."[1]
The sacred and irrevocable form which these few words gave to their engagements, must have made an impression upon his mind; and from this ceremony, apparently, he took the idea of adding an analogous form of consecration to the ablution of Baptism,— that solemn examination which we find in use from the earliest times. "Believest thou in God, the Father Almighty?" "I believe," and the rest.

As it was continually being repeated in the presence of the faithful, who never allowed the slightest changes to be made, the Roman formula was preserved in its integrity. Such is the tradition, as we have seen, left us by Rufinus and Saint Ambrose; but we should be at a loss if we were to look for some copy of this Creed of an earlier date than the fifth century to confirm their statements, for it was forbidden to preserve this formula otherwise than in the memory. Only eight days before baptism was this Profession of Faith confided to the ear of the catechumen, who must needs retain it word for word and engrave it on his mind without help of written characters. Accordingly, the Apostolic *Credo*, during eight centuries, remained as a Mystery, a secret known to the initiated alone, — the password which distinguished a true believer from the pretended brother, the heretic, or the Jew creeping into the fold to slay the sheep.

We shall never know precisely what this testimony which they so carefully concealed, contained in the beginning, and what it grew to be in the ages to follow. Hence we confess that it is impossible absolutely to identify the existing Creed with the primitive formula;

Polliceor," used instead of "Promittis? Promitto," or any other change in the consecrated expressions, robbed the contract of its verbal obligation. "Verbis obligatio fit ex interrogatione et responsione, velut: Dari spondes; Spondeo," etc. Gaius, iii. § 92.

[1] Spondes? Spondeo. — Promittis? Promitto. — Fidejubes? Fidejubeo.

but in default of such unassailable certitude, we can appeal to a probability so strong as to support us in our belief. In the first place, it is useless for those who deny the Apostolic origin of our Creed to pretend that it contains doctrines unknown to the Apostles. There is not a single dogma of the *Credo* which is not found in Saint Matthew's Gospel, the speeches and letters of Saint Peter, and, even more notably, in Saint Paul.[1]

In the second place, though the Fathers of the first centuries are so careful to keep the formula of initiation a secret, here and there they give us a glimpse beneath the veil. In two passages in the letters of Saint Ignatius of Antioch we are given a sketch of the principal acts of the Saviour very much like that drawn out in the Creed.[2] Towards the end of the second century, Saint Irenæus speaks very often of the Canon of the Faith which he received at baptism, and which was always repeated at the meetings of Christian people. He gives a few fragments from it in five parts of his book, from which we can collect the following Articles: " One only God, Father Almighty; one only Lord, Jesus Christ,

---

[1] The series of texts which follows are almost all borrowed from S. Peter's letters or his speeches in the Acts, and contain the whole doctrine of the primitive Symbol of Rome. "Accipiens a *Deo Patre* honorem." 2 Peter i. 17. "*Pater Domini nostri Jesu Christi.*" 1 Peter i. 3. "Jesum a Nazareth quomodo *unxit eum* Deus *Spiritu sancto.*" Acts x. 38. "Noli timere accipere *Mariam* . . . quod in ea *natum* est de *Spiritu sancto* est. Ecce *virgo* in utero habebit et *pariet filium.*" Matt. i. 20, 23. "Jesum quem vos *crucifixistis.*" Acts ii. 36. "Quoniam Christus *mortuus est* pro peccatis nostris . . . quia *sepultus* est et quia *resurrexit tertia die.*" 1 Cor. xv. 4. "Hunc Deus *suscitavit tertia die.*" Acts x. 40. "*Profectus in cœlum.*" 1 Peter iii. 22. "Jesum *stantem a dextris Dei.*" Acts vii. 55. "*Qui est in dextera Dei.*" 1 Peter iii. 22. "Reddent rationem ei qui paratus est *judicare vivos et mortuos.*" 1 Peter iv. 3. "*Spiritu sancto* misso de cœlo." 1 Peter i. 12. "Salutat vos *Ecclesia.*" 1 Peter v. 13. "Secundum eum qui vocavit vos *sanctum*, in omni conversatione *sancti sitis.*' 1 Peter i. 15. "*Sacerdotium sanctum*, gens *sancta.*" 1 Peter ii. 5, 9. "Ut exhiberet ipse sibi *Ecclesiam* non habentem maculam . . . sed ut sit *sancta.*" Eph. v. 27. "Baptizetur unusquisque vestrum in *remissionem peccatorum.*" Acts ii. 38. "*Surget corpus.*" 1 Cor. xv. 44. In a majority of these cases the verbal coincidence with the text of the Creed is very striking.

[2] S. Ignatius, *Ad Trall.*, ix. et x.; *Ad Smyrn.*, i. et iii. These letters were written about the year 107.

only Son of God, Who hath deigned to be born of a Virgin, suffered, was crucified under Pontius Pilate, rose again from the dead, ascended into Heaven, whence He shall come to judge the whole world and raise all human flesh from the dead. To such as, having sinned, shall have repented, there shall be given life incorruptible. The Holy Ghost, by the mouth of the Prophets, hath foretold these things divine."[1] "And this," pursues the holy Doctor, "is the greeting which all those who belong to the Christ keep written in their hearts, without paper or ink."[2] In this summary, only one line is lacking to make it a reproduction of the primitive Creed of Rome,—that is, "the Holy Church."

If we pass over from Lyons to Carthage, we find a contemporary of Saint Irenæus, Tertullian, writing down what he calls the Rule of Faith, in three different passages.[3] Here again we find the various Articles expressed in the same terms as in the Roman Creed; but the existence of "the Church" is passed over in silence, just as in Saint Irenæus' Canon; and so, too, is "the forgiveness of sins," whereof the Bishop of the Gauls makes mention. In both cases, these omissions were made purposely, in order to conceal the knowledge of the whole Creed from profane readers; for we know that the *Credo* of the African Churches contained these dogmas, which Tertullian does not mention in his formularies. "Three times," says this Father, "are we plunged in the waters of baptism, answering somewhat

---

[1] S. Irenæus, i. 3, 6; 10, 1; iii. 4, 2; iv, 23, 2.
[2] Ibid. iii. 4, 2.
[3] Tertullian's Three Rules of Faith are to be found: (1) in his *De Præscriptionibus*, xiii.; (2) in the book styled *Adv. Praxeam*, ii., and (3) in the *De Virginibus Velandis*, i. If we take the last-mentioned form and insert two phrases from the others, we shall have a textual copy of the primitive Symbol of Rome: "Regula quidem fidei una omnino est, sola immobilis et irreformabilis, credendi scilicet in unicum Deum omnipotentem . . . et filium ejus Jesum Christum natum ex Maria Virgine ("delatum ex Spiritu . . . in Virginem Mariam . . ." *De Præscriptionibus*, xiii.), crucifixum Pontio Pilato ("sepultum . . ." *Adv. Praxeam*, ii.), tertia die resuscitatum a mortuis, receptum in cœlis, sedentem nunc ad dexteram Patris, venturum judicare vivos et mortuos per carnis etiam resurrectionem."

more than that which the Lord hath decreed in the Gospel."[1] What the Lord had decreed was that they be baptised in the Name of the Father, Son, and Holy Spirit. What, then, was the "somewhat more" they added to what the Lord had decreed? Tertullian himself answers the question, in another place where he is not giving the Rule of Belief. "Inasmuch as our Profession of Faith and the promise of our salvation have been vouched for unto us by the Three Divine Persons, the mention of the Church follows necessarily; for where the Father, Son, and Holy Ghost are, there is also the Church, which is the Body of the Three Divine Persons."[2] Like the dogma of the Church, that of the forgiveness of sins is also to be found in the African Creed. Tertullian mentions it in the following passage, where he is alluding to the different articles of the baptismal profession of Faith: "Let none feel astonished that the Lord did not Himself baptize. For in what Name would He have baptized? For repentance? But then what would have been left for His Forerunner to do? For the forgiveness of sins? He granted that with a word. In His own Name? Nay, He concealed it in His humility. In the Holy Spirit? It was not yet come down to us from the Father. In the Name of the Church? She was not yet founded."[3]

Certainly, not one of the pages we have quoted contains the actual Creed of the Apostles, but they suppose its existence; and if we take into consideration that believers were forbidden to put this secret formula in writing, we must confess that it would be impossible to discover more striking evidences of it than those we have here.

So, then, from the time of Rufinus we can go back from century to century, to the very origin of the Creed, and recognize the work as being, not a preconcerted test made by the Twelve to guide them in their preaching, but as the ripe fruit and abridgment of their teaching.

[1] Tertullian, *De Corona Militis*, iii.   [2] Tertullian, *De Baptismo*, vi.
[3] Ibid. xi.

The Roman influence, and consequently Peter's handiwork, seem to us to be visible in it; and for that reason, at least, this *Credo* deserves its title to Apostolicity. Nevertheless, let us call to mind the fact again, that it was never regarded as an inspired witness, an immutable text, in the same sense as are our Holy Books. It was a formula of initiation, a Profession of Faith, hence Christians were careful in preserving its exact terms; but it was not a document of Revelation, and hence the perfect freedom with which, outside of Rome, in the first centuries, and later on in Rome itself, they proceeded to modify its primitive form.

CHAPTER XIV.

SAINT PETER AND THE JEWS OF ROME.

AFTER his deliverance from prison by the Angel, Peter did not tarry for any length of time in the dwelling of John Mark. "He departed," says the Scripture, "and went forth into another place."[1] What region or what city are designated by these words? The Acts furnish us with no hint on the subject; for thereafter Peter appears only once, when the Head of the Twelve gathers together a few of his brethren to consider the affairs of the Christians at Antioch.[2] During this long interval our only evidence as to his whereabouts, is the tradition preserved by Eusebius, which tells us that, after leaving Jerusalem, Peter preached the Gospel to Jews scattered through Pontus, Galatia, Bithynia, Cappadocia, and proconsular Asia.[3] Going from town to town, after the fashion of needy Jews, he asked the hospitality of his brethren of Israel, and in return spoke to them of Jesus. Doubtless it was more like a series of conversations than set sermons, sometimes carried on in their houses, sometimes in the public squares and marketplaces. Again and again he told them of the Saviour's Life, wept as he spoke of His death and his denial of the Lord, and bore witness to the truth that He had died only to rise again in glory. The ardor of his faith kindled the souls of men everywhere, and Peter then formed the numerous communities which he was to revisit later on, and to whom he addressed this greeting: "Peter, Apostle of Jesus Christ, to those of the Disper-

[1] Acts xii. 17.   [2] Acts xv. 7–31.
[3] Eusebius, *Historia Ecclesiastica*, l. iii. c. i.: *Patrologie grecque*, t. **xx**. p. 216.

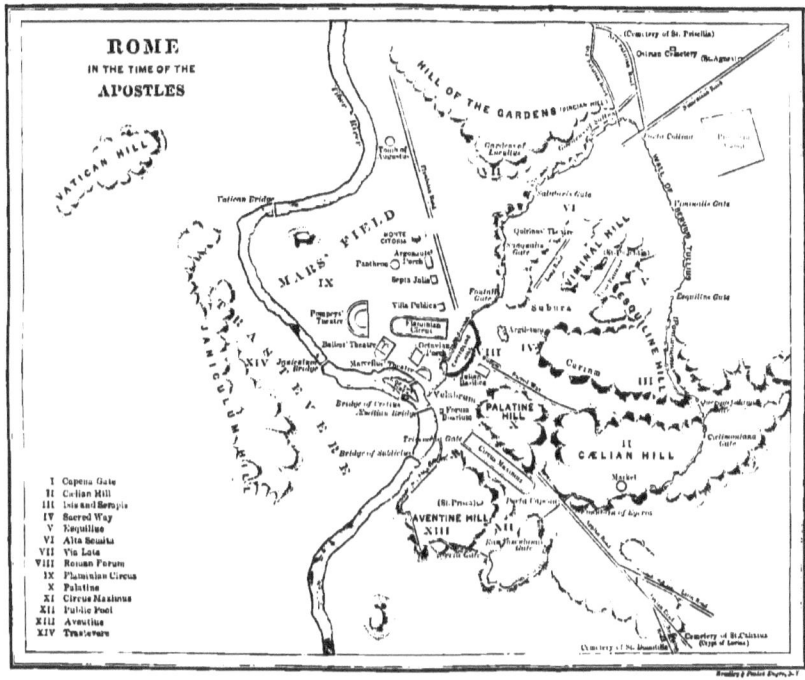

sion, in Pontus, Galatia, Cappadocia, Asia, and Bithynia, who sojourn among the Gentiles. . . . May grace and peace abound among you more and more."[1]

We have no details as to the establishing of these first Christian congregations in Asia Minor; even the names of the towns which Peter evangelized are unknown today. Two Churches in Pontus, Amasea and Sinope, glory in the belief that he was their founder.[2] This tradition, taken together with Saint Epiphanius' testimony that the Apostle returned several times to revisit Bithynia and Pontus,[3] gives us some reason to believe that he traversed chiefly the shores of the Black Sea. From Antioch he probably went up to these regions by way of Cappadocia, returning thence across Galatia towards one of the harbors whence he could sail for the Italian coasts. Saint Paul, who journeyed over Asia Minor at different times, never followed this route, ever faithful to his rule "of not building upon the foundations of another;"[4] in other words, not to preach the Gospel where others had published it before him.

In the course of these mission journeys it is said that Peter exercised his trade of a fisherman.[5] Like Paul, and like all the Apostles,[6] he took care not to become a burden upon any one, and thus maintained the word of God in all freedom, respected by all, without any suspicion of sordid or ambitious motives. Howbeit, there were always pious hands to minister to his needs, for he did not dwell alone. Saint Paul tells us that certain "sisters" accompanied the Twelve, notably Peter and the cousins of the Lord.[7] In Israel no scandal would arise from this, for the people were accustomed to seeing their Rabbis surrounded by fervent followers, who considered services rendered to their masters as a special source of favors from Heaven.[8] Jesus Himself had

[1] 1 Peter i. 1.
[2] Tillemont, *Mémoires:* S. PIERRE, art. xxviii. t. i. p. 169.
[3] S. Epiphanius, xxvii. 6.   [4] Rom. xv. 20.
[5] *Constitutiones Apostolicæ*, ii. 63.
[6] S. Jerome, *Epistol.* iv. *ad Rusticum.*   [7] 1 Cor. ix. 5.
[8] Gfrörer, *Das Jahrhundert des Heils*, i. 114.

authorized this practice, by allowing a band of Galilean ladies to follow Him and assist Him with their goods.[1]

Their aid afforded the Apostles very precious opportunities, since it made it possible for the Gospel to find its way into places where they could not have entered along with their holy companions. The latter, gladly welcomed by the women, spoke to their hostesses of the Saviour who had raised up the fallen Magdalene and comforted so many sorrow-stricken mothers; thus they won them over to the Faith, and finally to baptism. As total immersion was then the ordinary rite of this Sacrament, it was more in keeping with their ideas of decorum that the "sisters" should dip the catechumens of their own sex in the water. We may believe that Peter's own wife was one of the number of those who aided him. It is true, the Apostle once said to the Lord, "Lo, we have left all things to follow Thee," and the reply of Jesus shows what a wide meaning He attached to the words "all things,"—"home, brethren, sisters, father, mother, wife."[2] But though the wife of Simon the fisherman did not accompany him during the Master's lifetime, yet after the Resurrection, united to him now by purely spiritual ties, she could have no reason for leaving his side. Doubtless she is the one whom Saint Paul speaks of as "the sister attached to Kephas."[3]

With this devoted little band, Peter travelled through the provinces of Asia enumerated by Eusebius. Though he founded many Churches by the way, he made no long stay in any of them,— indeed, there is a very venerable tradition to the effect that during the same year in which he escaped from Herod's clutches, he arrived at Rome, and there established the Apostolic See, where it was to remain ever after.[4] He must have set sail for Italy

---

[1] Luke viii. 2–3. [2] Matt. xix. 27–29.
[3] 1 Cor. ix. 5. According to a tradition recorded by Clement of Alexandria (*Stromata*, vii. 11), the Apostle lived to see her martyred for the Faith; and as she passed him on the road to the place of execution he greeted her with this virile farewell: "Woman, remember thy Lord." Cf. Eusebius, *Historia Ecclesiastica*, iii. 30.
[4] Appendix IV. *S. Peter in Rome*.

from the eastern coasts, since there is no evidence to show that he travelled across Greece, as Saint Paul did later on. The Israelitish merchantmen had commercial dealings with distant seaports, and it was an easy matter for some one of them to procure a passage for Peter and his associates. On reaching the outskirts of the great Capital, this little company, so humble and mean in outward guise, found their way unnoticed to the "ghetto," where their fellow-countrymen were crowded together. The mighty city had little notion that this poor Jew was bringing her what eight centuries of victories had not been able to effect,— an Empire reaching to the ends of the earth.

The Hebrews' quarter was, accordingly, Peter's first abiding-place in Rome,— the first field wherein he was to display his zeal;[1] and a vast field it was, for the children of Israel already occupied a considerable position in the town, and were multiplying from day to day. Latin literature speaks of them so frequently that we have only to collect the passages referred to, in order to obtain a very fair notion of the origin of their community, its organization, and the parts of the city to which it spread; indeed, they give us a vivid picture of this restless race, keen in the pursuit of gain, industrious and eternal as the city wherein, to this day, it forms a people separate and apart.

The Israelites appear for the first time in Rome 160 years before the Christian era. Deputies travelled thither, in the name of Judas Machabeus, to solicit the protection of the Senate. The response of the Conscript Fathers, graven upon brass, is translated in our Holy Books. The terms are arrogant enough,— conditions of patronage are imposed on the Jews, and obedience to their masters prescribed in set terms; as their recom-

---

[1] There are two very valid reasons for this hypothesis,— the Lord's command, which we cannot doubt the Apostles always fulfilled: "Go first to the lost sheep of the house of Israel" (Matt. x. 6); and S. Paul's words to the Galatians (ii. 7): "I was made aware that to me was intrusted the Gospel of the Uncircumcision, as to Peter was that of the Circumcision."

pense, the Romans engage to defend them against their enemies.[1] On the death of Judas, Jonathas could only obtain a renewal of these arrangements.[2] Simon, more fortunate than his two brothers, succeeded in concluding a real alliance.[3] Lucius Calpurnius, Consul in the year 139 before Christ, addressed letters in their behalf to all kings and peoples who were allies of the Republic. Declaring that the Jews were her friends, Rome took their country under her protection, and prohibited all nations from attacking them or succoring such as made war against them. Orders were issued that deserters from their nation should be handed over to Simon, the High Priest, to be punished according to the Law.[4] Even while the leaders of the embassy were concluding these negotiations, their followers, mingling with the citizens, doubtless tried to gain some proselytes; for Valerius Maximus tells us that in that same year (139) the Prætor Hispallus sent back certain Jews to their homes for having endeavored to attract the Romans to the worship of their God, — urging them to adore Jehovah under the name of Jupiter Sabazius (Sabaoth).[5]

For eighty years after this there is no mention made of the Israelites in Rome, and we must come down to the time of Pompey to find them definitely settled there. This General, after taking Jerusalem, in 63 B. C., carried

---

[1] 1 Mac. viii. 17–32.   [2] Mac. xii. 1–4, 16.
[3] 1 Mac. xv. 16–24.
[4] The letter cited in the First Book of the Machabees cannot be regarded as an exact copy of the original, for it is not couched in the customary forms for such documents; only one Consul is referred to, and only his first name is given; there is no date nor any allusion to the Senate. But if these omissions are enough to prove that the sacred writer did not transcribe the text he had before him literally, there is, however, nothing to suggest a suspicion that he either invents or alters the substance of the commands transmitted by the Consul. *Handbuch zu den Apokryphen des alten Testaments*, von Fritzsche und Grimm, 1 Buch der Maccabaer, cap. xv. 16. Kitto's *Cyclopædia:* Lucius, 1.
[5] "Dominus Deus Sabaoth": "The Lord God of hosts." Valerius Maximus, i. 3. 2. "Idem [prætor Hispallus] Judæos qui Sabazii Jovis cultu simulato mores Romanos inficere conati sunt, domos suas repetere coegit."

away many captives. From that time to the day when Herod took possession of the throne of David without a struggle (37 B. C.), Judea was always in revolt, and oftentimes crushed under the yoke of Roman legions. At each new defeat prisoners were transported to the Capital, and often in great numbers; for it is recorded of Cassius, one of the conquering generals, that in many cities he sold the entire population into slavery.[1]

At first the rich were glad to receive these Hebrew slaves, noble in mien and of great parts; but soon their increasing numbers embarrassed the merchants, who could make nothing of them. It seems that in the wealthy residences, where servants were crowded together by the thousand,[2] some uniform order of life became a necessity. Now, nothing could force the Jews to submit to this; neither threats nor punishments could induce them to touch what was common and unclean. They pushed away the food prepared by their companions, as polluted. They avoided contact with a thousand impure objects. On the Sabbath days they absolutely refused to work. Josephus tells of a captive priest who forced himself to live on walnuts and figs.[3] Such inmates disturbed the orderly Roman households, governed with as much discipline as one of the Legions. So Philo informs us that they were only too glad to get rid of their Jews, and thus these purchased their freedom at a low price.[4] Once free from constraint, they recovered their activity immediately, with all their genius for business, and soon rendered valuable services to their former masters, now become their patrons. The experience of the benefits to be derived from their ability under these altered conditions, resulted in such an

---

[1] Josephus, *Antiquitates*, xiv. 11, 2; *Bellum Judaicum*, i. 11, 2.
[2] "Toward the close of the Republic and under the Empire, it was no rare thing to meet with wealthy Romans owning many thousands. Under Augustus, a mere freedman, C. Cæcilius Isidorus, although he had lost a considerable part of his fortune during the civil wars, still at his death left 4,116 slaves" (Pliny, *Historia Naturalis*, xxxiii. 47). Allard, *Les Esclaves chrétiens*, l. i. ch. i. p. 8.
[3] Josephus, *Vita*, iii. [4] Philo, *Legatio ad Caium*, 568.

increase in the number of Israelites released by their masters that the Jewish population of Rome was commonly designated by the name of Freedmen, — *Liberti*.[1]

The deed of emancipation, set forth in solemn forms, conferred the rights of a citizen.[2] All their brethren, rich or poor, bond or free, gathered about those of their race who had received this privilege. This body of men, animated by the same spirit, grew larger every day. In a few years it formed in the heart of the Roman State something like a foreign State having a separate life of its own, and at the same time so considerable that its members had to be reckoned with in any business which concerned them in any way. As early as the year 59 B. C., Cicero expressed his fears of them. In his defence of Flaccus, — accused, among other crimes, of forbidding the conveyance of the sacred tribute to Jerusalem, — we find the orator complaining that the case was brought up for trial on the *Aurelian Steps*. The tribunal known by this name occupied a part of the Forum where the Jews possessed numerous shops.[3] Attracted by the sound of discussions which concerned their religious tenets, they swarmed into this court, which was arranged in the form of an amphitheatre,[4] and followed the debate with all their usual fanaticism. Cicero felt that his safety was threatened. He lowered his voice until it was inaudible to the public, and then, calling Lelius' attention to the noisy throng, which had

---

[1] Acts vi. 9; Philo, *Legatio ad Caium*, 523; Josephus, *Antiquitates*, xviii. 3, 5; Tacitus, *Annales*, ii. 85.

[2] Pauly, *Real Encyclopädie:* MANUMISSIO.

[3] Nothing so angered the Jews as to see the money they had destined for their Temple consecrated to profane uses. This Cicero recalls in his plea, and then continues in this wise: "It was in order to expose you to their much-dreaded hatred that Lelius selected this spot for the seat of justice" ("Hoc nimirum est illud quod non longe a gradibus Aureliis hæc causa dicitur." *Pro Flacco*, xxviii.). This reference plainly implies that there were many Jews dwelling near the Aurelian Steps, and naturally gathered there in greater numbers than elsewhere.

[4] "Gradus illi Aurelii tum novi quasi pro theatro illi judicio ædificati videbantur" (Cicero, *Pro Cluentio*, 34).

more than once before disturbed the public meetings,[1] he rebuked him for having used their aid to intimidate the defence and influence the judges. These precautions and the fear of the great orator show as well as anything else what influence the Jews had in Rome even then. Cæsar, too, after seizing the imperial power, judged it opportune to attach them to his party. We read in Josephus a long list of measures adopted in favor of the sons of Israel, both by the Dictator and the magistrates working under his orders. It is a succession of privileges,— freedom of worship, exemption from military service, with the numberless taxes, the right to live according to the customs of their ancestors, full license to form an almost independent body in every land, a peculiar city of their own within every city of the Empire, with its own head men, its police, its regulations, and courts of its own;[2] concessions which are all the more astonishing because at this very time Cæsar was exceedingly severe in restricting the rights of associations, and suppressed all *Colleges* which did not date from the most ancient times.[3] The children of Israel appreciated the value of such benefits. In the Field of Mars, about that funeral pyre where the bleeding body of the Dictator had been laid, a plaintive song was heard for many an evening,— it was the nightwatch set there by grateful Jews.[4] Augustus, though he renewed Cæsar's prohibitions so far as other associations were concerned, like him formally excepted the Israelites, declaring their communities legally authorized, and giving them the right to establish such societies in all places.[5] These edicts of Augustus mark the highest point attained by Jewish prestige; thereafter, not only is nothing added to the account, but, on the contrary, the bitter feelings excited by these privileges tend to bring about their removal.

---

[1] " Multitudinem Judæorum flagrantium nonnunquam in concionibus " (Cicero, *Pro Flacco*, xxviii.).
[2] Josephus, *Antiquitates*, xiv. 10, 2-25.   [3] Suetonius, *Cæsar*, 42.
[4] Id. 84.   [5] Josephus, *Antiquitates*, xiv. 10, 8.

The first to take umbrage thereat was Tiberius. In the year 19 A.D., he proscribed the worship of Isis and Jehovah. Accusations were brought against the ministers of these two religions, which were identical in appearance, but of a widely different character in reality. In both cases the conversion of a woman was involved. The Egyptians, after persuading a matron that their divinity desired to espouse her, induced her to enter their temple, and there delivered her into the hands of a young libertine.[1] The crime of the Jews was not of this odious nature. Four Scribes gained over to the Faith a lady named Fulvia. They were some of those Pharisees whom Jesus once branded, wearing the mask of piety, making long prayers to abuse the simple-minded, and devouring the houses of widows.[2] Under pretext of getting offerings for the Temple at Jerusalem, they had extorted from this rich patrician large sums of gold and purple, which they diverted to their own profit. The husband denounced them to the Emperor, who brought the matter before the Senate, and demanded the enactment of rigorous laws against Jewish proselytizing. An innocent throng was involved in the ensuing punishment; for the Consuls, Marcus Silanus and Lucius Norbanus Flaccus, entered the Jewish quarter, and pressed four thousand freedmen into the ranks of the army. They were despatched to fight against the brigands of Sardinia, with the prospect of succumbing speedily to the unhealthiness of the climate. "This," however, Tacitus adds coolly, "would have been a loss of small consequence."[3] But to these four thousand men the danger of losing their lives weighed little in comparison with their fear of violating the Law. They refused to perform military service, as it was forbidden by their religion, and were consequently condemned to the mines. The remainder of the Jews, with their fol-

---

[1] Josephus, *Antiquitates*, xviii. 3, 4.   [2] Matt. xxiii. 14.
[3] "Si ob gravitatem cœli interissent, vile damnum" (Tacitus, *Annales*, ii. 85)

SAINT PETER AND THE JEWS OF ROME. 255

lowing, were given a short space in which they must either renounce their Faith or quit Italy.[1]

Within another thirty years, the Jews had recovered their rights, again disturbed the peace of Rome, and compelled Claudius to expel them in a body.[2] Yet this proscription availed nothing, for Judaism had become too deeply rooted to be so easily extirpated. Many proselytes belonging to the highest classes, to the nobility and among the courtiers, managed to escape the more rigorous edicts. Even those affected by the law stopped at the gates of the city or in the suburban towns. Juvenal speaks of a little colony of these banished folk encamped on Mount Alban, in Aricia.[3] From there, at the first favorable opportunity, they could return unnoticed. "Though so often oppressed, they struggled only the more vigorously, and succeeded at last in obtaining the liberty of living according to their laws."[4] These words of Dion Cassius sum up the whole story of the Jews' career in Rome.

Their numbers, their franchises, and their industry attracted every one's attention. Of all the foreigners who thronged into the Capital of the world, none held a more prominent place in men's eyes: but, generally speaking, the poets and moralists of that time judge them only by external characteristics. Circumcision, the Sabbath, and their horror of pork furnished an inexhaustible theme for witticisms.[5] One Feast Day, Perseus adventures into the dirty and winding streets of the Jewish quarter. He sees wreaths of violets ornamenting the windows, while fat and soot from countless little lamps drip down on the passer-by. Within each house the family is gathered. On a meagrely spread table stands a large loin of tunny, swimming in a red dish,

[1] Josephus, *Antiquitates*, xviii. 3, 5; Tacitus, *Annales*, ii. 85; Suetonius, *Tiberius*, 36.
[2] Suetonius, *Claudius*, 25.
[3] "Judæos qui ad Ariciam transierant, ex urbe missi" (Juvenal's Scholiast, iv. 117).
[4] Dion Cassius, xxxvii. 17.
[5] Horace, *Sat*. l. I. iv. 143; v. 100; ix. 69.

while a white jug contains the wine for this banquet. The poet departs full of disdain for such a sordid life, and rallies the first proselyte he meets. "On with you!" he says to him; "to-day is high festival for Herod's friends. Hasten along and mumble your lips devoutly, while with your pale face you celebrate the Sabbath of the Circumcised."[1]

At other times it is not the novelty of these solemnities, but their noisy tumults, which attract the curiosity of outsiders. The Jews discussed any mooted point in their traditions with all their customary passion,— with a babel of words, cries, threatening gestures, and dust thrown in the air. Sometimes the excitement would degenerate into such acts of violence that the Prætor would be obliged to intervene;[2] generally, however, a majority of Jews would mass together, and by main force oblige the weaker party to give in to their opinion. This fashion of persuading their opponents was well known. Horace alludes to it laughingly in his invective against the man who is a foe to satire. "If thou yieldest not to us in this point, a numerous band of Poets will come to mine aid. We are the great majority. Like the Jews, we will force thee to join our ranks."[3]

They were not content to stop at mockery. Odious pamphlets, like that of Apion, were passed from hand to hand, crediting the Jews with all manner of vices. Not only the populace, but the better-bred people as well, formed their judgment from these vulgar calumnies, and by dint of repeating them continually, managed to get them believed. From the absence of images in the sanctuaries of the Jews, Lucan concludes that their god is of uncertain existence.[4] Florus and Apollonius Molo[5] treat of them as an impious and atheistical race. Petro-

---

[1] Perseus, v. 180.
[2] Suetonius, *Claudius*, 25.
[3] Horace, *Sat.* l. I. iv. 140.
[4] Lucan, *Pharsalia*, ii. 593.
[5] "Vidit illud grande impiæ gentis arcanum" (Florus, iii. 6).
[6] Josephus, *Contra Apionem*, ii. 14.

nius,[1] Plutarch,[2] and Tacitus [3] gravely record that these folk adore the pig and the ass. "This people was born for slavery," says Cicero;[4] "The race is abominable among all the nations," Seneca adds.[5] The picture is already repulsive enough, but the Satirists delight in making it worse. They depict a crowd all made up of tatterdemalions creeping out of the hovels of Jewry. Beggars, pedlers, and rag-pickers block up the streets and besiege private houses, in the hope of selling their tapers or buying broken glass.[6] Dirty, exhaling a sickly odor, tricky as they are servile, this scum of the human race always drags along a troop of ragged children, bundles of clothing, a basket wherein their eatables are kept, out of the way of profane hands, and the straw which serves as a bed for the whole family.[7] Thus the Satirists exaggerated their caricature by attributing to all Jews certain features which only belonged to the most wretched. But then, as now, prejudice ruled the minds of men.

Happy had been the lot of the Israelites if this concert of jeers had not been audible outside the circle of literary men; but everywhere, on the contrary, they heard the same words re-echoed, — in the public baths, along the Forum, in court, and at the theatre, where they offered a rich theme for the buffooneries of the clowns. Rabbi Abahu complains that it takes so very little wit to raise a laugh at the expense of the Jews. The following specimens certainly justify his remonstrance.

A camel crosses the stage, decked in mourning.

"Why this funeral array?" some one cries out. The reply, which drew shouts of laughter from the populace, is surely a very weak joke.

[1] Petronius, *Fragmenta*, ed. Nisard, p. 94: "Judæus licet et porcinum numen adoret."
[2] Plutarch, *Quæstionum Convivalium*, iv. 5, 2.
[3] Tacitus, *Historiæ*, v. 2-5.
[4] Cicero, *De Provinciis Consularibus*, v.
[5] Seneca, quoted by S. Augustine (*De Civitate Dei*, vii. 36).
[6] Martial, i. 42; Statius, *Silv.* i. 6.
[7] Martial, i. 42; xii. 30, 35, 37; iv. 4; vii. 82; xi. 94; i. 4; Juvenal, vi. 542-547; 156-160; xiv. 96-107; iii. 13, 296; Origen, *Contra Celsum*, i. 33; Ammianus Marcellinus, xxii. 5; Rutilius Numatianus, *Itiner.*, i. 3, 89.

"Because the Hebrews want to observe their Sabbath better, and therefore have resolved only to eat picked green-stuff. Now they are eating dates, and the camel weeps because they are robbing him of his food."

Still more insipid is this scene, in which Momus (the god of farce) appears with shaven head. When asked why he has dispensed with his head-dress, he replies:

"Oil is too dear, and the Jews are to blame. On the Sabbath they spend all they have earned during working days. As they have no more wood to cook their eatables, they are forced to burn their beds and lie in the dust; then, to prevent the dirt sticking to them, they spill oil over themselves in profusion. And now you know why oil is so dear and Momus in tears."[1]

Only blind hatred could bring men to applaud such a plentiful lack of wit as we have here.

This unpopularity, even more than their peculiar rites, obliged the Jews to live by themselves, having no intercourse with Pagan society except through commercial or banking connections. Accordingly, though dwelling in the midst of the Romans, they were looked upon as a separate world, almost unknown to their nearest neighbors. About their origin and worship, the most absurd ideas obtained, even among the educated classes; as witness the picture Tacitus has drawn of them. We may well feel some surprise at finding this great historian, who is so exact when speaking of the most barbarous peoples, mingling so many calumnies with a few truthful lines when treating of the Jews. Evidently he never deigned to converse with the leading men of Jewry, nor did he ever enter their residences; for there he would have found those books in which we of to-day read the true history of Israel, — the writings of the Alexandrians, the Rabbinical commentaries of Jerusalem, and the Bible translated by the Seventy. His prejudices would have vanished, and Tacitus would not have written that extraordinary page, where he paints the Hebrews as a people

---

[1] Grätz, *Geschichte der Juden*, 4, 353.

of infamous manners, hateful as they are full of hatred, of noble, but distorted and gloomy religious views.[1]

The Jews avenged themselves after their own fashion. Merciless in matters of business, they demanded the last farthing from every one not of their blood nor allied to them in any way, and inscribed the names of the mockers, big and little, in their account-books. After wreaking their anger on them in words, the borrowers were forced to treat with this swarm of creditors or abandon themselves to their mercy. Moreover, these much-dreaded competitors were to be met at every turn; for though for preference they adopted commercial pursuits, no employment came amiss to them, even that of the actor[2] or singer[3] in the theatre, and every trade was the same to them. This was notably the case in the literary world, where the Roman, with his easy-going nature, was amazed to see the Oriental, with his acute genius, steal a march on him, while criticising, borrowing, and even plagiarizing his best works. Martial complains of having been plundered in this fashion by a son of Israel, —

"Blighted by jealousy, go on tearing my writings to pieces everywhere. I pardon thee, thou circumcised Poet; thou hast thy reasons. I care little what evil thou mayest say of my verses, even while thou seest fit to filch them."[4]

How are we to explain the tolerant acts of Rome towards this detested nation, if no note of sympathy is to be heard amid this chorus of hatred. From Cicero down to Marcus Aurelius, Latin writers lavish their sarcasm upon everything Jewish; but their object is always to deplore the popular propensity to take up with the Pharisaic Observances. Their doleful complaints are so incessant that we are warranted in concluding that the Israelites could reckon upon almost as many allies as persecutors. Indeed, great numbers of the Pagans, especially of the people, did not halt at the gloomy and dirty outskirts of the "Ghetto," but found their way into the Jewish family-circle, where

[1] Tacitus, *Historiæ*, v. 2-5. [2] Josephus, *Vita*, 3.
[3] Martial, vii. 82. [4] Id., xi. 94.

they discovered a new life of pure enjoyments, peacefulness, good manners, and a touching unitedness of spirit. Not only did they love one another, but they offered the stranger a share in this brotherly charity. The sole condition was that he must embrace the Law of Israel; and in that Law how much there was to attract souls agitated by doubt, remorse, and weariness of life! The Jewish Faith poured balm in all their wounds. To the intellect thirsting after truth, it revealed that God Whose Name is ineffable, — " I am, Who am !" [1] To the heart of man it held forth something that was more than a hope, — the persuasion that a happy age was drawing nigh. Awful calamities were to herald its approach; but Israel and its proselytes might swim the sea of blood without fear; and on the farther shore there awaited them joys without end. The Roman populace, who knew by sad experience that theirs was an age of iron, found it easy to believe in this Golden Age; all listened eagerly to the small shopkeeper when, dropping his task for a moment, he talked to them of God and the Prophecies.

There were not lacking some men among the greater minds — nay, even among the very writers whose scoffs we have quoted — who felt the influence of Israelitish thought. Vergil regarded the Jewish Sibyl as a veracious Oracle; on her authority he announced that after mighty revolutions would come the reign of a Divine Child, Whose advent would thrill the earth with delight, giving the weary world a renewal of its early happy days.[2]

The patrician ladies, especially, were ardent seekers after novelties. One morning Juvenal observes a mendicant Jewess ushered into the presence of some rich matron, to explain her dreams and calm her anxieties.

" Dropping her basket and her bundle of grass, she draws near, wagging her head, and pouring her tale of beggary into the superstitious ear of her listener. She knows well how to explain the rites of Jerusalem, — a High Priestess, she ! . . . faithfully does she translate the

---

[1] Exod. iii. 13.   [2] Vergil, *Ecloga* iv.

messages of Heaven. She must be paid, but she does not come so dear as the [Egyptian] priest. At a reasonable price the Jews will sell you all the air-castles you may chance to desire."[1]

But the Satirists' contempt could not hold back the Roman women when bent upon learning something of the ideal world, or when merely fond of mysteries. Many adopted the Mosaical beliefs, not from caprice, but of set purpose, and remained faithful to them till death. In the Jewish cemeteries at Rome are the tombs of patrician women belonging to the noble families of the Flavii, Fulvii, and Valerii, lying side by side with their sisters of Israel. On one of these sepulchral stones we read that Paula Veturia, upon joining the Jewish community with all her slaves, took the name of Sara. Though seventy-five years of age at the time of her conversion, she lived for full sixteen years in the Synagogue.[2]

Though less prone to enthusiasm than the women, repelled too by the circumcision, there were not wanting many distinguished Romans who let themselves be carried away by the movement. Both Perseus and Horace allude to the fact that many of their fellow-citizens abstain from business on the Sabbath-days; they fast, pray, illuminate their mansions, and deck them with garlands during the Festival seasons of Israel. Others again, without participating openly in the worship of Jehovah, apply themselves to the study of the Law, frequent Jewish sanctuaries, and contribute their offerings to the Temple.[3]

The current seems to have set in with irresistible force, when we find Augustus, on learning that his grandson had not sacrificed to Jehovah[4] during his stay at Jerusalem, go out of his way to praise him for an independent spirit too uncommon in his day. These congratulations show how little faith this ruler had in the Mosaical institutions; none the less he makes it his policy

[1] Juvenal, *Satire*, vi. 542–547.   [2] Orelli, 2522.
[3] Perseus, v. 180; Horace, *Sat.* 1. II. iii. 288; *Sat.* 1. I. ix. 68; v. 100, etc.
[4] Suetonius, *Augustus*, 93.

to protect the numerous adherents of what he regards as a mere superstition. At Rome two synagogues bear his name and that of his friend Agrippa.[1] The sons of Herod, brought up at his court, practise their religion unhindered.[2] This state of things continues during the following reigns: Herod Antipas receives many favors from Tiberius;[3] Herod Agrippa lives in the closest intimacy with Caligula;[4] and we have seen how he helped Claudius to ascend the throne.[5] A Jewess named Poppæa became all-powerful under Nero.[6] More than this, there were always Jews of lower rank who were on the lookout for any opportunity to get within the palace walls and gain the ascendancy there. In the time of Augustus another Jewess, the slave of Livy, formed a terrible conspiracy against Herod.[7] A Samaritan freedman, who had once belonged to Tiberius, rose to such wealth as to be able to lend Herod Agrippa very considerable sums.[8] The inscriptions in the Jewish cemeteries make us acquainted with an Israelitish woman belonging to the house of Claudius,[9] while many freedmen of the same race bear the names of Imperial families; among them those of Julius, Claudius, Flavius, Aelius, Aurelius, and Valerius are the most frequent.[10]

It is so difficult to distinguish proselytes from Hebrews by birth that we cannot be certain as to the total Jewish population of Rome. One fact alone will give us some idea of their number. On the death of Herod the Great (4 B. C. according to our chronology), when the

---

[1] *Corpus Inscriptionum Græcarum*, 9902, 9903, 9907.
[2] Josephus, *Antiquitates*, xviii. 6, 1; Juvenal, *Satiræ*, vi. 157–160.
[3] Josephus, *Antiquitates*, xviii. 2, 1; 2, 3; *Bellum Judaicum*, ii. 9, 1.
[4] Id., *Antiquitates*, xviii. 6; 8, 7.
[5] Id., *Antiquitates*, xix. 4 et 5.
[6] Id., *Antiquitates*, xx. 8, 11; *Vita*, 3.
[7] Id., *Antiquitates*, xvii. 5, 7; *Bellum Judaicum*, i. 32, 6; 33, 7.
[8] Id., *Antiquitates*, xviii. 6, 4.   [9] Orelli-Henzen, 5302.
[10] Schürer notes the fact that the later Emperors often took the names of several of their predecessors; thus Constantine the Great styled himself C. Flavius Aurelius Claudinus Cons. Hence it follows that the Jews mentioned in these inscriptions are not perhaps the freedmen of the first Cæsars. Schürer, *Die Gemeindeverfassung der Juden in Rom in der Kaiserzeit*, p. 7, note 2.

Israelitish deputies came to beseech Augustus to restore the theocratic form of government, they were accompanied by eight thousand of their compatriots who were settled in the city.[1] As this throng was composed of men alone, it must have represented a goodly number of families. But if it is impossible to obtain any exact figures, we can at least enumerate the various quarters where Jews abounded, and follow the marks of their growth and expansion in the great Capital.

At the outset the freedmen, who formed the nucleus of the Jewish community, occupied the district lying along the right bank of the Tiber. This was the spot where Rome piled her heaps of refuse, and thither every foul and offensive industry was banished. According to Martial, the odor of dog-tanneries poisoned the air.[2] The Jews were then so poor that they welcomed this wretched dwelling-place, and despised no kind of trade. The only thing they cared for was the opportunity to live independently; for this purpose the Fourteenth District, reserved to small retail dealers, offered them a thousand resources. They soon peopled it to overflowing,[3] spread over the slopes of the Vatican, and braved the inundations which often submerged the lower bank of the Tiber. There the boats coming up from Ostia unloaded their merchandise, and there the Jewish brokers set up their booths.[4]

This "Ghetto" soon became too narrow and cramped to contain a prolific population, with new instalments of freedmen and Israelites from foreign parts constantly flocking in. All who could not find room in Trastevere overflowed into the town. From street to street, in the squares and cross-ways, they carried their trays laden with provisions, trinkets, or exotic products. From early dawn these itinerant merchants were wont to awaken Martial,[5] who describes them to us pursuing their trade the livelong day, ever keen for a bargain, and indefatigable

[1] Josephus, *Antiquitates*, xvii. 11, 1; *Bellum Judaicum*, ii. 6, 1.
[2] Martial, vi. 93.   [3] Philo, *Legatio ad Caium*, § 23.
[4] Martial, i. 41.   [5] Id., xii. 57.

They were to be met in every place frequented by the crowds, but especially along the Appian Way, which served as a promenade for the wealthy,[1] and where there was always a crush of chariots, litters, and horsemen. The Jews had built their bazaars at the entrance to this avenue, near the Porta Capena, most of them displaying their goods and offering them for sale, while the poorest sort sat by the wayside with outstretched hands. Spying the grove and fountain of Egeria in the near neighborhood, these vagabonds in tatters proceeded to make use of it for their ablutions, and thus contaminated this dainty retreat where Numa was wont to confer with his divine counsellor. " They have driven away the nymphs," says Juvenal, " and, lo, the forest is begging."[2] A little later, Vespasian, renouncing further attempts to expel this rabble, which, as usual, showed itself as tenacious as it was importunate, finally confirmed them in this holding which they had usurped. " The wood which surrounds the sacred fountain, nay, even the Chapel itself, are let out to Jewish beggars, who only bring a basket and a bit of straw to furnish it withal. Every tree is taxed, and pays tribute to the Roman people."[3] Their number in this quarter (First District), though less than in Trastevere (Fourteenth District), was nevertheless very considerable, for two Jewish cemeteries have been discovered near the Porta Capena.[4]

The First and Fourteenth Districts were not the only parts of Rome inhabited by them. Subura, " the clamorous and noisy,"[5] offered them the same advantages as Trastevere, — lodgings at a low price and a large populace to work upon. In the narrow and muddy streets[6] of this region all sorts of trades were followed, but especially the vilest and most bizarre ; travelling cobblers,[7] men who manufactured scourges to whip slaves,[8] masters of the art

---

[1] Horace, *Epod.* iv. 14 ; *Epist.* l. I. vi. 26, etc.
[2] Juvenal, iii. 10–15.   [3] Id.
[4] In the *Vigna Randanini* and the *Vigna Cimarra*.
[5] Martial, xii. 18 ; Juvenal, ix. 51.   [6] Martial, v. 23.
[7] Id., ii. 17.   [8] Id., ii. 17.

of cutting roasts,[1] receivers of stolen food,[2] — all crowded the landings and stairways of these five-story buildings.[3] For the nimble and tireless Jew no field could be more favorable for swift advances in fortune. Many profited so well by their chances that, coming into Subura poor men, they left it to take their rank among the rich merchants in the Field of Mars.

The last-named locality was one of the loveliest spots in Rome, and the meeting-place for the aristocracy. Sumptuous shops[4] displayed to the passer-by their marvels of art and luxury. Here the highborn Romans walked and did their shopping, buying purple or brass from Corinth (more precious than gold),[5] vases from Murrha, sparkling with a thousand lights;[6] here, in the time of Cicero, a table of citron-wood cost 800,000 sesterces ($35,000),[7] and in the following century an embroidered carpet from Babylon cost the unheard-of sum of four million sesterces (about $218,000).[8] Among the merchants capable of handling such an enormous traffic, we find a tribe of Jews numerous enough to form a body by themselves and have their own synagogue.

Porta Capena and the Campus Martius, Trastevere and Subura, occupy the opposite sides of Rome. That the Jews dwelt in these various regions is sufficient to show that they were not then, as formerly, shut up in a single "ghetto," but free to take up quarters where they pleased. So, too, with their sepulchres, which they excavated as they found it convenient round about the city. Three of these cemeteries, discovered in modern times,[9] have fur-

---

[1] Juvenal, xi. 136.   [2] Martial, vii. 19.
[3] Friedlænder, *Mœurs romaines*, t. i. pp. 10-13.
[4] The Field of Mars, being a public domain, no private building could be erected there. The merchants, however, were allowed to keep shops under the outer arcades of the theatres (Ovid, *Ars Amat.*, ii. 165), in the porticos of the Argonauts (Martial, x. 87), and in the courts of the *Villa Publica* (Martial, ix. 60).
[5] Statius, *Silv.* ii. 2, 68.   [6] Martial, ix. 60.
[7] Pliny, *Historia Naturalis*, xiii. 15.   [8] Id., viii. 196.
[9] All trace has been lost of the one discovered by Bosio in 1602, facing the *Porta Portuensis*, near *Collo Rosato*, which was used by the Israelites of Trastevere. But two others have been brought to light on the Appian

nished us with interesting inscriptions, almost all written in that bastard Greek then in use among the Israelites of Rome; only a few are in Latin, none in Hebrew. From the language of their fathers they borrowed but a few hallowed phrases, which they placed at the end of the epitaph, such as "Peace!"[1] But they added certain Mosaical symbols, — the Candlestick with its seven branches, the Ark, and the Book of the Law; we find the boughs of palm and citron which the people carried at the Feast of the Tabernacles, with an array of ornaments, such as the Sea of Brass, etc.

Although the exact period to which these inscriptions belong may be difficult to determine,[2] in general they are to be credited to the period of the Empire, during which the constitution and spread of Judaism went on steadily in Rome.[3] The light they throw on the conditions of Jewry in that city will therefore show us the Israelites much as Saint Peter found them. As to the forms of worship, in particular, and concerning the organization of the community, we obtain from them many details which would otherwise be unknown.

Seven synagogues are mentioned by name. Three — those of the *Augustenses*,[4] the *Agrippenses*,[5] and of *Bolumnus*[6] (Volumnus) — owe their titles to the high personages designated by these names. Were Augustus and Agrippa[7] the protectors of the first two synagogues,

Way, — one, near Porta Capena, in the *Vigna Randanini*, whence come most of our inscriptions; the other is near the Catacombs of Callixtus, in the *Vigna Cimarra*. A goodly number of the Jewish epitaphs which have come down to us were collected from a cemetery in Porto (at the mouth of the Tiber). See De Rossi, *Bullettino*, 1866, t. iv. p. 40.

[1] שלים.

[2] De Rossi, *Bullettino*, t. iv. p. 40.

[3] The period in which Judaism made such rapid progress at Rome, and assumed the position given it above, is the epoch from Pompey to the Antonines.

[4] *Corpus Inscriptionum Græcarum*, 9902, 9903; Orelli, 3222.

[5] *Corpus Inscriptionum Græcarum*, 9907.

[6] Orelli, 2522.

[7] According to all appearances, the Agrippa mentioned here, we have to do, not with one of the kings of Judea who bore that name, but with M. Agrippa, the friend and councillor of Augustus.

or did the appellation come from the fact that their members were for the most part freedmen of the Emperor and his friend? Plausible as the latter explanation may appear, the other seems more likely to be the true one; for it is based on the well-known benefits which Augustus and Agrippa lavished on the Jews, and on the historical fact that such associations commonly took the name of their founder or their patron. Volumnus, some unknown personage, was doubtless an illustrious benefactor, or perhaps the owner of the synagogue called after him.[1] Saint Paul, writing to the Christians of Rome, refers to one of their sanctuaries in similar terms, — "Prisca and Aquila, ... as well as the Church which is in their house."[2]

Two other synagogues, those of the *Campenses*,[3] and the *Suburenses*,[4] are so designated from the quarters of Rome inhabited by the faithful. Should we go farther and conclude that these houses of prayer were set up by the Israelites in the Field of Mars and Subura? We think not. The first-named region was, as we have said, a public domain, set aside for sports, military exercises, and meetings of the comitia. The monuments with which Augustus ornamented it were for the use of the people;[5] a decree of the Senate was required for the privilege of erecting even a tomb thereabouts.[6] We have no reason to believe that they would have tolerated a synagogue on soil consecrated to the god Mars. On the other hand, Subura lay within the limits of the *Pomerium*, a sacred precinct where every foreign worship was interdicted. The *Campenses* and *Suburenses*, therefore, could only have had their counting-houses and residences in those quarters of the town; their sanctuaries stood in

---

[1] In this case the words "Augustenses," "Agrippenses," would have a meaning analogous to the Christian form "of the household of Cæsar," which we find in the Epistle to the Philippians (iv. 22.)
[2] Rom. xvi. 3, 5.
[3] *Corpus Inscriptionum Græcarum*, 9905, 9906; Orelli, 2522; Garucci, *Dissertationes*, 161, n. 10.
[4] *Corpus Inscriptionum Græcarum*, 6447.
[5] Daremberg, *Dictionnaire des Antiquités*: CAMPUS MARTIUS.
[6] Silius Italicus, xiii. 639.

some other district of Rome, which was open to all religions. To these five synagogues, whose titles are to be found in the Jewish epitaphs, we must add that of the *Hebrews*,[1] — so called probably because its members had kept up the use of their own language in the divine service; and finally that of *The Olive*,[2] which had adopted that tree as its emblem.

Besides the seven synagogues whose names are known, many others rose here and there through the Capital, for the Jewish population was divided into parishes, each with its congregation, head men, and its own sanctuary, without any one single power to unite together and supervise these various communities. This is a condition of affairs peculiar to Rome, and quite different from that which existed elsewhere, — notably at Alexandria, where, as we have seen, the chief authority among the Israelites of the city was at first vested in an Ethnarch,[3] later in a Senate.[4] With a settlement in this city which dated from its foundation, and forming a party so important as to quite predominate in public business, the Jews might appear there with impunity as a political body, all the more formidable on account of its unitedness. But in Rome they must needs be wary of arousing suspicion and distrust, and, more than that, they were obliged to model their institutions after those of the sovereign people.

The form by virtue of which the Jewish communities found a place in the social organization of Rome was that of associations, or "*Colleges*," as they were called. There was a goodly number of them, for under the Republic the citizens were granted entire liberty to unite in corporations. They were of all sorts and for every possible end, — trades-bodies, political assemblies, and societies for mutual aid, which assured a certain amount to their members during life, and at death a decent burial. Still others, called "Sodalities," were formed with the sole object of practising the same worship. These brethren assembled in the temple of their god, and participated in

---

[1] *Corpus Inscriptionum Græcarum*, 9909. [2] Id., 9904.
[3] Josephus, *Antiquitates*, xiv. 7, 2. [4] Philo, *In Flaccum*, x.

the sacrifice offered by the priest; the common meal which followed, during which the victim was consumed, constituted the solemn act of these reunions. No foreign religion got a foothold in Rome without the immediate institution of some "Sodality," whose object was to honor the new god.[1] In order to observe their rites and their Law, the Jews had only to constitute themselves after this fashion into religious fraternities; thereby they were entitled, not simply to tolerance, but to the protection which the magistrates owed to every College.[2] The one thing needful for them was to refrain from uniting in a single association. Fifty thousand men joined together as one body [3] would have startled the Roman authorities; parcelled out in a number of corporations, each one with its own leaders and a separate sanctuary, they fell under the common law, and were assured of its benefits.

Thus the Jewish communities already had a regular form and a legal existence when Cæsar accorded them the privileges which we have seen above, — the free exercise of their worship, with power granted the chiefs of the Synagogue to govern and judge the congregation.

This last concession was of the highest importance to the Jews of the Dispersion. Indeed, their Law and the traditional precepts of the Rabbis governed, not religious practices alone, but even the actions of public and private life. Thus it was a sort of special code, unknown to the Pagans; to apply it and enforce its observance, separate courts were necessary, with magistrates, who should be at once judges, doctors, and interpreters of the divine decrees. In the smaller cities of Judea the

[1] Cicero, *De Senectute*, 13. These religious confraternities were distinguished from the official Colleges of Priests in so far as, although recognized by the State like the latter, they could not hold territorial possessions, but were supported by the voluntary contributions of the associates.

[2] Calixtus (189-199) (destined at a later date to ascend the pontifical throne) was once the cause of a disturbance in a Jewish assembly; he was brought before the Prefect of the town, Fuscianus by name, and condemned to the Sardinian quarries. *Philosophumena*, ix. 12.

[3] If their proselytes were to be reckoned with them, the Jews certainly would exceed this number.

heads of the synagogue filled all these functions, and the people, brought up to venerate them from their very position in the sanctuary, treated them with the same respect when they made arrests or issued their orders; their sentence, as well as their preaching, was accepted as the voice of God,—which is more easily understood when we remember that their judgments were pronounced in the synagogue, and the pulpit itself was transformed into a seat of justice. Cæsar saw clearly that this anthority alone could cope with the seditious spirits he was so anxious to conciliate. Accordingly, with due respect for the customs of the nation, he granted full jurisdiction to their religious leaders.

The Jews made use of those rights to build up in Rome, after the example set them by Jerusalem, an aristocracy which retained the government as an inheritance,[1] never allowing either the people or the proselytes to take part in it. To the latter, the subordinate position in which they were kept by the Pharisaic prejudices must have seemed often very odious, for a certain number of these converts, distinguished both by rank and fortune, lavished their benefits upon the community. As some compensation, the titles of "Fathers and Mothers of the Synagogue" were created for them, and we have frequent examples of these in the inscriptions of Rome.[2] The synagogue was said to be the client, or the child, of the proselytes who protected it;

---

[1] Among the Hebrews the head men of the Synagogue were called "Pastors." *Jer. Peah*, 8; *Bab. Chagiga*, 60; *Sabbath*, 17 a. The Jews, when scattered through the lands where Greek was spoken, substituted for this title that of chiefs, "Archontes." We find this name given to children of tender years in the Jewish inscriptions at Rome. Consequently from being elective, this duty finally became an hereditary honor. Garucci, *Dissert.*, ii. 161, Nos. 10, 11; 163, No. 13; Orelli, 3222.

[2] *Corpus Inscriptionum Græcarum*, 9904, 9908, 9909; Garucci, *Cimitero degli antichi Ebrei*, p. 52; *Dissert.*, ii. 161, No. 10; 164, No. 18; Orelli-Henzen, 6145; *Corpus Inscriptionum Latinarum*, v. 4411. The Roman Corporations, whether secular or religious, gave their benefactors an analogous title: "Pater et Mater Collegii." Orelli, 2417, 4134, 2392, 4055, 4056. It was very likely this custom which inspired the Jews of Rome with the idea of creating a similar title.

and by such acts of deference [1] they mitigated the exclusive rigors of the Law so far as it concerned the Gentiles. Thus the barriers between the Jewish world and Roman society were lowered; Israelites by birth and Pagan converts thereafter formed but one family, indissolubly united.

Peter's first preaching, therefore, was not confined to the narrow limits of one "ghetto," nor was it addressed solely to a small group of foreigners divided from the rest of the city by their fanaticism. Israel, as we have seen, numbered more disciples and friends among the Pagans than there were sons born in the Circumcision. In the synagogues, Peter found many proselytes studying the Law, loving it, often even practising it. They were picked souls from among the Gentiles, riper for the Kingdom of Heaven than were the Hebrews of the chosen race, for they had no sympathy with their prejudices, and recognized that the New Law contained in its perfection everything that had attracted them in the Old. Among them, Peter reaped an abundant harvest. Meanwhile in Israel of the flesh there was the same division of sentiments as at Jerusalem; many believed in the Christ, and yet the masses stubbornly clung to the Mosaic system. This conception of the Church of Rome is the same as the one given us by Saint Paul in his letter addressed to the Christians of that city; throughout it he is evidently addressing a mixed community of Jews and Pagans, but it is one in which Pagans predominate, for line after line refers exclusively to them.

[1] This was a merely honorary title, for women could not exercise any functions in the sanctuary, and we encounter one proselyte, Veturia Paulina, who was at the same time Mother of the Synagogue of Campus Martius and of that of Volumnus. Orelli, 2522 "Mater Synagogarum Campi et Bolumni."

CHAPTER XV.

THE RELIGION OF ROME.

BEFORE he left Jerusalem, Peter could have had little knowledge of Paganism. As the "Apostle of the Circumcision,"[1] he had consecrated himself in a peculiar manner to the evangelizing of the Hebrews, and after choosing seven deacons from among the Hellenists, it followed, as a natural consequence, that he should resign to their care those Pagan converts who continued to enter the Church in ever-growing numbers, from the day of his memorable Vision at Joppa. It is more than likely that his conduct was imitated by the greater part of the Twelve. Without raising a hedge of separation round about themselves, like the Pharisaic rigorists, the great Apostles seem to have been regarded as a sacred body, only to be approached with the highest veneration. Paul found that he needed the patronage of Barnabas to gain access to them.[2] Cornelius, on beholding the Head of the Church entering his house, fell at his feet and adored him.[3] So then, with the exception of his short sojourn in Cæsarea, Peter must have had very few opportunities for mixing with foreigners or of becoming acquainted with the genius, religion, and manners of the various peoples among whom the children of Israel had been scattered.

Again, when he visited the Christian congregations of Samaria and Judea, and pushed on as far as Antioch, the Apostle was one of the preachers "who proclaimed the word of God to the Jews only."[4] He followed the same custom in Asia Minor, and his only dealings, while

---

[1] Gal. ii. 7.   [2] Acts ix. 26.
[3] Acts x. 25.   [4] Acts xi. 19.

travelling through that region, were with the Israelites of each city where they stopped.[1] But at Rome the Spirit of God inspired him with very different views. According to his custom, he preached to his compatriots first; but as he very soon found that he was not warmly welcomed by them, he turned his attention to the Gentiles, and consecrated his labors in their behalf.[2]

What a contrast between his former career and the new field which opened out before him! Instead of his Jewish hearers, of indomitable faith, with hopes that were more ardent than ever, all centring in the longed-for Messiah, he encountered a strange compound of all races and every superstition. Vice was enthroned triumphant on their altars, undermining family life and contaminating all public affairs. Rome was sinking in the lap of luxury, abandoning all care of herself to any despot who would allow her " perfect liberty to walk in riotousness, wicked desires, drunkenness, excesses of eating and drinking, and criminal idolatries." [3] Thus the Apostle himself depicts the city towards the close of his ministry; thus too the records of poets and historians describe the great Capital. And yet, worn out and decadent as Pagan society seems to have been at this epoch, it nevertheless contained the principles of its regeneration, — a vague belief in the divine Unity, a serious worship, habits of prayer, and a lively faith in the supernatural prevalent in the people. To obtain any conception of the Roman Church at its foundation, it behoves us to study the

---

[1] At least so much is implied in the opening lines of his first letter addressed "to the foreign Jews of the Dispersion settled in Pontus, Galatia, Cappadocia, Asia, and Bithynia," παρεπιδήμοις διασπορᾶς. 1 Peter i. 1

[2] Indeed, we know that S. Paul's Epistle to the Romans was addressed especially to Pagan converts, and elsewhere we read in the Acts (xxviii. 22) that in 61, when the Apostle of the Gentiles came to Rome, the Synagogue scarcely knew what the Christians really held The natural conclusion from these two facts is that Peter did not long confine his labors to the " ghetto " in Trastevere, but that finding his fellow-countrymen either indifferent or hostile to the Gospel which he preached to them, he devoted himself entirely to the Pagans of the Capital.

[3] 1 Peter iv. 3.

nature of these germs which God's grace was to develop so bountifully.

The mistake is too commonly made of supposing that the religion of Rome was precisely like that of the Greeks; it is popularly believed that these two peoples worshipped the same gods, — that the Zeus of Olympus differs in no way from Jupiter Capitolinus; that Juno, Mars, and Vesta represent in Latin the Hellenic divinities Hera, Ares, and Hestia. The similarity of these two Mythologies came about very gradually, and only when Greece had initiated her conquerors into the arts wherein she excelled, giving them the statues of the Immortals, which she had fashioned after her own likeness, radiant with beauty, but human in form and passions. All that we know of the origin of Rome warrants us in believing that at the outset her religion bore a very different character from that of Greece, and that Bossuet was right in his judgment that it was "as serious, as grave, and as modest as the darkness of idolatry would permit."[1]

We must beware of supposing, on the other hand, that this worship was of so lofty a tone as to conceive the existence of one only Supreme Being. The country-folk of Latium and the Sabine mountaineers who founded Rome brought thither the rustic and coarse divinities of their forefathers. There was Janus, opening and shutting the gates of the firmament at his own good pleasure; Saturn, and Ops, his wife, who were the source of all fruitfulness; Jupiter, best and highest of all, enthroned upon the clouds, lord of light and rain and storms; Mars and Quirinus, protectors of the fields, who did not become patron spirits of the sword and war till after Numa's time. In Vesta men venerated the fire of the domestic hearth, — the sacred centre of the family circle; in Juno they did reverence to the first principle of womanhood, exercising a power analogous to that of Jupiter. These were the great gods of Rome. Unlike those of Greece, they had no seductive

---

[1] Bossuet, *Discours sur l'Histoire universelle*, partie iii. chap. vii.

or splendid stories associated with their names; they did not belong to one family, united by strange alliances, intrigues, and common interests; all that was known of them was the power which each one wielded over the world; but even this division was so vague, and the attributes of each were so numerous,[1] that their domain, and consequently even their persons, were frequently confounded. Janus, Jupiter, and Juno reigned together in the heavens;[2] Saturn, Ops, and Mars were alike all-powerful in fertilizing the great earth;[3] Janus presided at the most important of creative acts, the fecundation of the human race,[4] howbeit they invoked Jupiter also under the name of "The Fostering One."[5]

Often, too, worshippers evince some hesitation as to the nature of the mysterious being whom they are adoring. At the Capitol there was a much-reverenced buckler bearing this inscription, — "Jupiter, best and greatest, or whatsoever title you will."[6] "The real names of the gods are unknown," says Servius.[7] Accordingly, to make more sure of being understood in their solemn supplications, after having given the divinity his ordinary name, the priest added a formula of invocation which comprised a general conception of the gods.[8]

How did the Romans happen to feel this repugnance which kept them from forming any precise image of the celestial powers? Doubtless it was due in part to the

[1] Varro enumerates three hundred different Jupiters, — that is, three hundred attributes of this god. Tertullian, *Apolog.*, xiv.
[2] Preller, *Römische Mythologie*, iii. Abschnitt, 1 JANUS, 2 JUPITER, 3 JUNO.
[3] Ibid., vi. Abschnitt, 3 SATURNUS UND OPS; iv. Abschnitt, 1 MARS. In their processions the Brotherhood of Arvales implored the aid of the latter alone as Guardian of the Fields.
[4] Macrobius, *Saturn.* i. 9, 16; Tertullian, *Ad Nation.* ii. 11; S. Augustine, *De Civitate Dei*, vii. 2, 9.
[5] "Almus Ruminus." Preller, *Römische Mythologie*, iii. Abschnitt, 2 JUPITER; iv. Abschnitt, 12 RUMINUS.
[6] "Post specialem invocationem transit ad generalitatem, ne quod numen prætereat, more pontificum, per quos ritu veteri in omnibus sacris post speciales deos, quos ad ipsum sacrum quod fiebat necesse erat innovari, generaliter omnia numina invocabantur" (Servius, *Ad Georgic.* i. 21; Ovid, *Ibis*, 69-82).
[7] Servius, *Ad Æneid.* ii. 351. [8] Ibid., iv. 577.

poverty of invention which characterized them as a people; but it was likewise due to the fact that among them the Unity of God was not so obscured in their minds as among other peoples. All that they retained of it was but a confused memory of the earliest ages; but it made them conceive a higher idea of the Immortals, and the mystery in which it was shrouded only increased their respect. Monotheism, generally to be found at the beginnings of each race, had indeed left a profound impress upon this religion, whose austere gravity Tertullian admires. "Frugal rites, with no Capitol to rival the heavens, simple altars of turf, the sacred vessels of clay, the smoke from the offering ascending on high, and God Himself in no one place."[1] For a hundred and seventy years, in fact, Rome knew no idols.[2] A lance stuck in the ground was for a symbol of Mars;[3] a fire constantly tended was the only honor tendered to Vesta;[4] a stone marked the spot where the great Jupiter was to be adored.[5]

A still more notable remnant of the primordial faith is the popular inclination to venerate a multitude of inferior spirits in preference to the great divinities. Their Pontiffs have drawn up a list of these indigenous gods in the official registers called *Indigitamenta*.[6] Of these, Varro counted over six thousand names. Every incident in human life, the most trivial phenomena, the growth of plants and animals, all to the Roman mind revealed God present and ever acting upon them; to him they were all supernatural apparitions (*numina*), to whom he gave a

---

[1] "Frugi religio, et pauperes ritus, et nulla Capitolia certantia cœlo, sed temeraria de cespite altaria, et vasa adhuc Samia, et nidor ex illis, et Deus ipse nusquam" (Tertullian, *Apolog.* xxv).
[2] S. Augustine, *De Civitate Dei*, iv. 31; Clement of Alexandria, *Stromata*, i. 15.
[3] Arnobius, *Adversus Nationes*, vi. 11. Clement of Alexandria, *Protrept.* iv. 46; Plutarch, *Romulus*, xxiv.; Justin, xliii. 3.
[4] Plutarch, *Camillus*, xx.; Ovid, *Fastor.* vi. 295–298.
[5] Servius, *Ad Æneid.* viii. 641.
[6] Preller, *Römische Mythologie*, i. Abschnitt, 2 DIE SEMONEN UND INDIGETEN; x. Abschnitt, 3 DIE GÖTTER DER INDIGITAMENTA; Marquardt, *Handbuch*, B. vi. S. 5–23.

name and consecrated a special act of worship. If he cultivated his fields, a troop of divine spirits encircled him. *Vervactor* presided over the beginning of the task; *Reparator* followed next; *Insitor* was the sower; *Obarator* covered over the grain; *Occator* harrowed the ground; *Sarritor* weeded out the bad herbs.

By the family fireside there were ever the same all-powerful aids: *Vagitanus* causes the child to utter its first feeble cries; *Fabulinus* teaches it to emit articulate sounds, *Locutius* to speak distinctly; *Educa* shows it how to eat, and *Potina* how to drink; *Cuba* watches over its cradle, *Abeona* accompanies it when going out of doors, *Adeona* escorts it safely home. Not only outward actions, but sentiments, passions, sicknesses even, are deified. They worship *Peace, Liberty, Hope, Concord, Piety, Modesty, Fever, Pallor,* and *Fear.* We should have to enumerate everything that man can do and suffer, from his conception to his death, his vices and his virtues, his public and his private life, if we would attempt to exhaust this list.

The common character of these lesser gods — and it is one of the most original inventions of the Roman genius — is that they have only the shadow of an existence: they have no history, no other origin than the present need; their names are all that is to be known of them. In the eyes of their first worshippers they were not distinct persons, but manifestations of the supreme power. The qualifications joined to the name of Jupiter, and varying according to the circumstances in which he was invoked, at first expressed these various attributes; later on, when employed by themselves, they came to be regarded by the people as so many divinities.[1] This is the explanation which Saint Augustine found in the most learned Pagan thinkers, and it gives a very fair idea of the *Indigitamenta;* it shows, along with this

[1] " Hi omnes dii deæque sit unus Jupiter; sive sint, ut quidam volunt, omnia ista partes ejus, sive virtutes ejus, sicut eis videtur quibus eum placet esse mundi animum; quæ sententia velut magnorum multumque doctorum est" (S. Augustine, *De Civitate Dei,* vi. 11).

belief, how the feeling that there is but one only God lay at the bottom of the Roman religion. We shall see that it still retained its life at the advent of Christianity, and was one of the sparks which kindled into flame under the breath of Peter.

The *Indigitamenta* make us acquainted with another peculiarity of the Roman cult, which was no less helpful to the cause of Christianity, — this was the care taken to preserve outward ceremonies intact. The slightest details were foreseen and prearranged, and thereafter must be punctually observed, lest any mischance disturb the performance of the ritual. The most trivial accident was enough to compromise the whole religious act, — a wrong turn of the hand which poured out the libation; or if a dancer or flute-player halted in the sacred dances; if the driver of the chariot which carried the divinities dropped his reins and allowed his horse to get out of line.[1] The same sacrifice is known to have been repeated as many as thirty times, in order to make the offering according to the rubric.[2] The words of the liturgy were the object of even greater scrupulosity than the actions. Every sacrifice was accompanied by a special prayer, a sort of magical formula, which must be uttered without passing over or changing a syllable, and without the faintest sound of evil omen marring its delivery. Usually, to avoid being disturbed in his prayers, the Roman covered his head and stopped his ears; but in the solemn functions, Pliny tells us there were numerous helpers about the Pontiff who made the supplication: while one priest dictated to him the words of the ritual, another followed the reading in the sacred volume, a third imposed silence on those present; while all the time a musician played on a pipe to prevent any unlucky noise from being heard.[3] Nor were these idle precautions; since the defective pronunciation of a single word would make the prayer of no effect, and still worse,

---

[1] Arnobius, iv. 31.
[2] Preller, *Römische Mythologie*, ii. Abschnitt, S. 118.
[3] Pliny, *Historia Naturalis*, xxviii. 2, 3.

offend the god, who would not accept any other than the hallowed forms of supplication. Thus it behoved them not simply to begin the invocation over again, they must also expiate the mistake involuntarily committed. Hence the never-ending ablutions and the clouds of incense, all to recover the purity required for prayer and sacrifice.[1]

Tertullian calls our attention to the likeness between this formalism and that of the Jews: in both worships we find the same slavery to the letter, the same heavy yoke, a long list of petty rites, religious practices, sacrifices, vows, and purifications, encompassing human life and impeding every action. Finding such a similarity between these institutions, "might not one believe," says this Father, "that the Devil has copied in the Roman religion the misery and scrupulous constraint of the Jewish Law?"[2] From the rigorism of his ceremonial the Roman reaped the same advantages that the Mosaical Observances procured to the children of Israel, — a strict discipline, which subdued the whole character of a man, his soul swayed by reverence and a fear of something divine, while prayer enters into every public and private act. Even at the time when beliefs, from contact with Greek thought, were undergoing a change, the ritual of Rome stood untouched and in full vigor ; by it the religious sentiment was fostered deep down in the people's hearts, until the day-dawn of Christianity. Cicero witnesses to this fact for his contemporaries: "The Roman people," he says, "in everything else is equalled, nay even surpassed by other nations ; but it excels them all in its pious reverence for the gods."[3]

This testimony, in the epoch in which it was written, did not refer to all classes of society, for if the pre-

---

[1] "Ad divos adeunto caste, pietatem adhibento . . . qui secus faxit, Deus ipse vindex erit" (Cicero, *De Leg.* ii. 8).
[2] "Si Numæ Pompilii superstitiones revolvamus, si sacerdotalia officia et insignia et privilegia, si sacrificalia ministeria et instrumenta et vasa ipsorum sacrificiorum ac piaculorum et votorum curiositates consideremus, nonne manifeste diabolus morositatem illam Judaicæ legis imitatus est" (Tertullian, *De Præscriptionibus*, xl.).
[3] Cicero, *De Natura Deorum*, ii. 2.

scribed forms of worship kept religion still alive among the common people, they had come to be but another source of unbelief for the higher classes. The exclusive possession and management of holy things had brought about deplorable effects among them. For nearly five centuries,[1] in fact, patricians had monopolized the offices of Pontiffs and sacrificers. The heads of the first families were the sole custodians of the sacerdotal books, read from them the acts of the liturgy with the consecrated formulas, and were consequently the only ones who knew the secret names of the gods, by aid of which one could be sure of evoking them and making them listen. They alone also had the right to examine the entrails of victims, the thunderbolts, the flight of birds, their cries and songs, and from these signs discover future events and the will of Heaven. This is what they called taking the auspices, — the foremost branch of learning in Roman estimation, for no important step was decided upon without attempting to fathom its consequences in this way, lest they should be led into some unfortunate course of action. No popular meeting could be held, no resolution drawn up or ratified, unless the auguries were propitious. The patricians were masters in this art of divination, and by that fact alone held the balance of power in the government. They yielded to the temptation of framing the oracles so as to turn them to their own profit, made them another means of fortifying their holdings, and after debasing them in this way, finally ceased to believe in them themselves.

The invasion of foreign fashions in worship hastened this decline of the faith. With the Tarquins, who were of Etruscan race, idols found their way into Rome. Jupiter, that supreme god, whose presence, until then, was made visible to men by a simple stone, now had his image, a human form, and a temple, the Capitol, which towered over the whole city. From year to

[1] Until the Ogulnian Law (452 u. c.).

year, a court of the gods grew up about him. From Greece were imported Apollo, Ceres, Bacchus, Proserpine; from Epidaurus, Esculapius; and from Pessinus in Phrygia, Cybele, the mother of Ida. These new-comers were shrouded in no veil of mystery like the antique divinities of Latium: lowered to the plane of earthly man, born of the flesh like him, they shared his passions and frailties. Their guilty unions with mortals were described, and the names of their children rehearsed.

And yet the poetry and learned works of Greece contributed even more than did the immorality of this Theogony to the destruction of belief. Since the days of the Punic War the aristocracy read their Homer, their Euripides, along with the comic writers of Athens, and from them learned to laugh at things divine. It was not long before the theatre displayed the Immortals to the public view, with plenty of ridicule and abuse. The magistrates, as a general thing very solicitous for the maintenance of religion, tolerated these liberties of the stage folk, giving as excuse that here there was no question involving the gods of Rome, since they were only burlesquing the Olympus of the Hellenes.[1] The danger seemed all the less because these poetical efforts were relished by only a select few. Tragedy, and even comedy, were wearisome to the people, who interrupted the actors with shouts for a bear-fight, or a match between pugilists.[2] Nevertheless, though this contagion of unbelief affected the lower classes very slightly, it wrought havoc in the ranks of the aristocracy. It was spread not only by the stage and the poets, but by the Greek slaves as well, who were so numerous in Rome after the conquest, and who soon held their own in the houses of the great. Many of them were rhetoricians, grammarians, and philosophers. These became secre-

---

[1] As early as the fourth century B. C., a Greek philosopher, Euhemerus, had proved that the gods venerated by his fellow-countrymen were at first mortal men: Ennius translated his *Sacred History*.
[2] Horace, *Epist.* l. II. i. 185, 186.

taries to their masters, educated the young Romans, and insinuated that mixture of scepticism and superstition which was become the peculiar characteristic of their race, into the very bosom of the old families of the nobility.

The spoils of Greece and the Eastern world completed the process of deterioration by filling Rome with the idols of the vanquished. These innumerable statues were bereft of all prestige when taken away from the temples of Syracuse and Corinth; they were nothing after that but trophies of victory, works of human art. The patricians soon learned to appreciate something of their exquisite beauty. They finally became famous connoisseurs, prizing the marbles of Phidias and Praxiteles too highly to render them any other homage than that of cultured admiration. In the time of the Scipios, Polybius, a friend of theirs, giving utterance to the sentiments of the politicians with whom he went, felicitates them upon having invented a religion and superstitious fears capable of holding the common folk in check. "As the multitude," says he,[1] "is fickle by nature, unruly and subject to mad fits of anger, in order to sway their minds we must have recourse to these terrors of the unknowable, and all such tragical fictions." A century later, the decadence appears still more strikingly. The patricians then go so far as to neglect their pontifical duties, and the sacrifices which they had so long claimed as theirs by right; making great fun of the auguries, they never took auspices "except to avoid shocking the masses, or in the interest of the State."[2] Varro, in the opening pages of his *Antiquities*, asks with alarm whether religion "is not doomed to die out speedily, owing to the indifference of believers."[3]

But these are the apprehensions of a man who judges the people by the great men with whom he associates. In the last century, any one who derived his views of France from a study of her philosophers and her nobil-

[1] Polybius, vi. 56.   [2] Cicero, *De Div.*, ii. 33.
[3] S. Augustine, *De Civitate Dei*, vi. 2.

ity, might well have believed that all faith was dead in the land; and, notwithstanding, the major part of the population escaped the influence of the upper classes, and remained a moral and Christian people. Though the head was touched by the malady of the age, the body was still sound and strong. Just so, in the time of Augustus, the little ones of earth kept alive the spirit of faith which an unbelieving aristocracy had thrown away.

This popular faith is known to us to-day, not so much through Latin literature, which rather reflects the thoughts of the upper classes, as by means of the inscriptions, which for the most part are the work of men of the people. Military service, public duties, and commerce carried Romans of the lower classes to the confines of the Empire. Apuleius tells us how the most trivial incidents of the journey would awaken their religious sentiment, — the sight of a sacred tree, or an altar wreathed with flowers; the turf still smoking after the offering of a holocaust, or a stone with the odor of incense clinging to it still.[1] At once they stop, and their piety breathes forth in prayer. At Axima, in the Greek Alps, dwelt a legal functionary of the Imperial domains, who was frequently obliged to travel through the forests and along those mountains; accordingly, he addresses the god Sylvanus, —

"Thy favor is a sure pledge of good fortune, and it hath ever protected me in my journeys across the Alps. I am the guest of these odorous trees which are consecrated to thee. Here I administer justice and right in the Emperor's name. Protect me and mine on our way back to Rome; grant that by thy fostering aid we may cultivate our fields in fertile Italy. If thou wilt but hear me, I will honor thee with a thousand huge trees devoted to thy holy worship."[2]

At dangerous points on the road, these demonstrations of faith are more frequent. More than thirty such inscriptions have been found near the summits of the

[1] Apuleius, *Florid.* i.   [2] Orelli, 1613.

Great Saint Bernard. Soldiers and other travellers have graven in letters of bronze their gratitude to the protector of the mountain, the supreme and most merciful Jupiter Peninus.[1] In other places we find inscriptions which are simple tributes of admiration for the local divinities. At Kalabcheh in Nubia, certain centurions and their legionaries erect a votive tablet in the temple of the sun-god Mandulis.[2] The light of day glows with such splendid radiance under tropical skies that the Romans are overpowered by its beauty, and join in worshipping it. Sick persons coming from Rome to the mineral springs give thanks to the Nymphs who have cured them.[3] In the Pyrenees, two Roman contractors, after successfully transporting some beautiful marbles from the quarries of Martignac, celebrate the praise of Sylvanus and the guardian spirits of the mountain.[4]

Besides such testimony to the Romans' piety, this collection of inscriptions gives us an idea of the large number of temples erected or restored at that time, with their wealth of gold and silver images, which were dedicated to the gods and loaded down with offerings of precious stones.[5] And these bountiful gifts were not inspired merely by vanity and ostentation, for many of the tablets record that the giver is fulfilling commands made by the divinity, either in dreams or in a vision.[6] At a time when religion was at its lowest ebb in Rome, Lucretius laments the existence of these superstitious fears, which have built up new temples all over the world, attracting so many worshippers to their fes-

[1] Promis, *Antichita d'Aosta*, p. 61
[2] *Corpus Inscriptionum Græcarum*, iii. 5042, etc.
[3] Mommsen, *Inscriptiones Regni Neapolitani*, 3513, 3518, Orelli, 1560, etc.
[4] Herzog, *Gallia Narb* app. 283
[5] In honor of her little daughter, a mother consecrates to Isis a diadem of pearls, emeralds, rubies, and hyacinths, costly earrings, a necklace of thirty-six pearls with eighteen emeralds, clasps, bracelets for wrists and ankles, precious stones for every finger, and eight emeralds for the sandals (*Corpus Inscriptionum Latinarum*, ii. 3386). From this one donation of ornaments the reader can fancy what must have been the generosity of certain wealthy givers.
[6] Orelli, 1344, 1790, etc.

tivals.[1] If the objection is raised that many of these monuments were the work of patricians, who let themselves be carried along by the current, for fear of shocking the multitude, none the less the fact remains true that religion was still powerful enough to enforce this outward show of devotion upon indifferent and unbelieving men.

In the people, it not only kept its vigor, but was even capable of giving birth to new cults. When the unrestricted encroachments of the patrician domains had transformed the rich meadows of Italy into a vast pasture land, it so happened that, owing to a delay of the fleets, no more grain was to be had, either from Africa or Egypt, and Rome was thus exposed to the danger of a famine. On these occasions they invoked the aid of the goddess of the wheat-crop, *Annona*, to whom they attributed the abundance or want of bread-stuffs.[2] The old-time belief in the *Indigitamenta* peopled with new divinities every country to which the Empire extended. Every province, every city, laid claim to a protector in the heavens. The corporations, which were then growing to great numbers, made it a prime duty to choose a patron from among the Immortals. The legions, the cohorts, and the bands of hundreds had their own presiding spirit, as well as each family, and every private citizen.[3]

This belief in familiar spirits inspired the thought of worshipping the most powerful *genius* known to them, — that of their Emperor. In this way Augustus became one of their gods, with priests and altars devoted to him. He was given this honor, not from the wish to flatter him, but out of real gratitude; for he had brought peace to the world, delivered Italy from civil wars, and the provinces from the tyranny of the proconsuls. Every city was glad to enroll so beneficent an influence in the foremost ranks of their celestial pro-

---
[1] Lucretius, *De Natura Rerum*, v. 1161-1168.
[2] Preller, *Römische Mythologie*, 10 Abschnitt, ANNONA.
[3] Id., DER CULTUS DER GENIEN, 566-572.

tectors. It was not so much the man that they reverenced in him, it was rather the majesty of the Roman name, the supreme power centred in a single personality. The *Genius* of Rome was already a divinity at the time when Cæsar,[1] and after him Augustus, seized the sovereign authority. It was only that their name was added to that of the city's goddess, and that they were set up side by side in the same sanctuaries. In the first century, this worship was the only one really universal; and its progress was all the more rapid because it responded to the Romans' deepest longing,— to realize God as active and present in their midst.

But neither the worship of a man, though he be both Emperor and god, nor the multitude of *penates* could avail much for minds corrupted by impiety, or disturbed by unspeakable uneasiness. The people especially, despite their vulgar credulity, felt all the time a need of regeneration, and tried to find relief in self-sacrifice and suffering. Did it rise from a consciousness of the unheard-of disorders then ravaging society,— an awful picture, which we shall soon have to study here? Was it the influence of Eastern religions, where bloody rites have always seemed the necessary complement of religious feeling? Or may we not regard it rather as the secret touch of Grace, preparing the Saviour's way to the heart of the Gentiles, as John had made straight the pathways of Judaism "for Him Who was to come"?[2] Whatever its source, the idea of expiation occupied a foremost place in their thoughts. This was what appealed to the multitude in the cults of the Orient, and notably in that of the mother of the gods, the Queen of Ida. Rome could never watch without a thrill of emotion the progress of these priests through the streets, with the sound of drums and cymbals, tearing their flesh with lashes of their whips, cutting their arms and thighs with knives, sometimes going so far, in their

---

[1] Preller, *Römische Mythologie:* DEA ROMA, S. 705.
[2] Matt. xi. 3.

THE RELIGION OF ROME. 287

frenzy, as to mutilate themselves in the sight of all.[1] The belief of these men was that blood washes away all stains. The people understood this when they saw them catching all that flowed from their wounds and eagerly drinking it. But what seemed still more striking to them was the solemn ritual of this religion,— the Sacrifice of Bulls. The initiated stood in a ditch covered over by a planking pierced with holes, while above his head a bull was slain. Prudentius depicts him zealously trying to catch every drop of the warm red shower which fell about him, — throwing himself backwards, so that the drops might wet his cheeks, his hands, his eyes, his ears, his whole body; then opening his mouth to drink it down.[2] When he issued out of the ditch, all crimson and smoking,— a horrible sight,— his co-believers cast themselves at his feet and adored him. "He is regenerated for all eternity!"[3] was their cry. The populace, which flocked to these spectacles, went away persuaded of the mystic virtues of blood. Superstitious as this belief was, it nevertheless opened their minds to receive that redemption which Peter was coming to preach to them in Rome, — the Blood of Jesus Who has redeemed humanity by shedding His life-blood for men.

Another form of worship brought from the East — that of Isis the Egyptian — had even greater attractions for Romans. Like the preceding, it promised justification and peace to remorseful souls, but without repulsive surroundings; ablutions, fasting, and abstinence from sensual joys were sufficient to purify the soul.[4] After long days of trial and austerities, the initiated was conducted to the deepest recesses of the sanctuary, and there, in the silence of midnight, received a revelation which will ever remain a mystery to us, for the authors

[1] Lactantius, *Instit.* i. 21, 16; Lucan, i. 565; Tertullian, *Apol.* ix.; Minucius Felix, *Oct.* xxx. 5; Seneca, *De Beat. Vit.* 27.
[2] Prudentius, *Perist.* x. 1011.
[3] Orelli, 2352; Apuleius, *Metamorph.* xi. 21.
[4] Apuleius, *Metamorph.* xi. 19; Plutarch, *De Isid. et Osirid.* ii.

who have written of this rite carefully refrain from betraying it:—

"You will ask me, perhaps, what was done and said thereafter. I would disclose it all, were I permitted to speak of it. You shall know it, if you are permitted to hear it; but to speak of it here, or to listen to the tale, would be a crime. Nevertheless, if it is religion which inspires your curiosity, I should be too scrupulous to torment you. Hearken, then, and believe; that which I tell you is the truth. I have touched the gates of death and stood upon the threshold of Proserpine. On my return, I traversed all the elements; in the depths of night I saw the sun resplendent. Drawing nigh unto the gods of Hell and Heaven, I beheld them face to face, and worshipped in their presence. I have told you all, and it behoves you to forget even this which you have just heard."[1]

But this is rather an enigma than a description, and as we have nothing more explicit as to the mysteries of Isis, we can indulge only in conjectures as to their nature. From all we can now ascertain, the secrecy in which they were enveloped did not cloak abominable practices, like the voluptuous rites of Syria and Asia Minor. In Rome, it is true, they had achieved an unfortunate notoriety,[2] and Tiberius, as we have seen, ordered the crucifixion of certain priests of this goddess, who had abused the simplicity of a Roman lady.[3] But this was the crime of only a few men, for the initiated have always spoken of the Isiac Mysteries with great reverence. Diodorus assures us that these chosen souls became more righteous and better in all respects.[4] Lucius, in Apuleius' work, lingers for days in the contemplation of the divinity, as one ravished with the thought of her benefits. His heart swells to breaking as the time approaches when he must leave her. Lying prone on the ground, and bathing her feet

---

[1] Apuleius, *Metamorph.*, xi. 23.
[2] Ovid, *Ars Amat.*, i. 77; *Amores*, ii. 2, 25; Juvenal, *Satiræ*, vi. 488.
[3] Josephus, *Antiquitates*, xviii. 3, 4; Tacitus, *Annales*, ii. 85.
[4] Diodorus, v. 48.

with his tears, he utters a prayer to her, in which the adoration seems to be altogether spiritual, and divorced from sensual thoughts:—

"Thou art the Holy, the eternal source of salvation. Thou dost shower thy good things upon mortals, and in their misfortunes thou dost lavish upon them the affections of a tender mother. Not a day, not a night, not a moment, passes which is not marked by some favor from thee. On land, even as on the sea, thou art ever present to lend us a helping hand. . . . Thou dost animate the universe; thou givest to the sun its light, and governest the world, while thou dost encompass Hell. . . . At a signal from thee the winds are set in motion, clouds rise, seeds take root and ripen. My voice is powerless to speak the thoughts wherewith thy majesty inspires me. . . . All that a poor believer, such as I, can do is to cherish thine image graven in my soul, and ever living in my mind."[1]

In this giving of thanks there is nothing to indicate that sensual pleasures stained the worship of Isis. What filled the initiated with his ecstasy was the revelation of the sublime truths which were vaguely hinted under the enigmatical phrases of the ancients. "These borders of death," "the threshold of Proserpine trodden under foot," "that sun shining resplendent in the midnight sky,"[2] evidently indicate that it was an effort to lift the veil which hides the other life from us. The grave was a dreadful thought for the Pagans, who could never look upon it without terror and a sinking heart. Happier far the man admitted to these mysteries, who got from them the assurance that he was to die only to be born anew. The sacred dramas[3] which were played in his presence showed him his place, prepared for him in regions of pure delights among the Immortals. All these gods, multiplied to such a ridiculous extent by the common herd, were worshipped by him as all encompassed in a single Being,— "Isis of a thousand

[1] Apuleius, *Metamorph.*, xi. 25.   [2] Id., xi. 23.
[3] Clement of Alexandria, *Cohortatio ad Gentes*, ii.

names."[1] "O thou, the Only who art all,"[2] they said when invoking her.

Doubtless, neither the divine Unity nor the life beyond the grave became to these initiated what they are for us,— most precious dogmas of faith; but the comfortable promises and the impression of truthfulness, which they brought to souls wearied with doubting, must have lightened their burdens and saved them from dying of despair. Still other minds, which could not rest satisfied with these too vague hopes, found their way to Judáism; and, every day, as we have seen, the number of these waxed greater.

This is the condition in which Peter found the Roman society of that day. The irreligion of the upper classes affected him little. He was not sent to the horde of sceptics, to men of letters or pleasure-seekers, but to God's little ones, in whose name Jesus gives thanks to the Father for having revealed the truth to them.[3] When the Apostle, moving among these poor people, discovered that uneasiness which was attracting them on the one hand toward the Oriental Mysteries, and on the other to Jehovah's Law, he might point them out to his brethren, repeating those words of Jesus, " Lift your eyes and behold these fields; they are already white for the harvest!"[4]

[1] "Isis myrionyma" (Orelli, 1876, 1877).
[2] "Te tibi una quæ es omnia Dea Isis." Mommsen, *Inscriptiones Regni Neapolitani*, 3580. In Apuleius, Isis reveals herself in like manner as the sole Divinity: " I am the Mother of all things, the Mistress of all the elements, the Original Principle of the ages, supreme Divinity, Queen of the Manes, the first among the inhabitants of Heaven; gods and goddesses have but my form. The luminous vaults of the sky, the health-giving breezes of the sea, Hell and the mournful realms of silence obey my voice. Sole Divinity, I am adored throughout the whole universe under divers names and forms and by various sorts of worship. For the Phrygians I am the Goddess of Pessinus and the Mother of the gods; the aboriginal folk of Attica call me Minerva Cecropia. I am the Venus of Paphos unto the people of Cyprus, Diana Dyctinna to the Cretans. . . . But the Egyptians, who possess the ancient doctrine, render me my fitting worship and call me by my true name; I am Isis, the Queen." Apuleius, *Metamorph.* xi. 5.
[3] Matt. xi. 25. [4] John iv. 35.

CHAPTER XVI.

THE CONDUCT OF LIFE IN THE TIME OF AUGUSTUS.

"BABYLON!" Peter cries out, aghast at the depravity of Rome; and in that one name concentrates all his indignation and abhorrence.[1] No word could give a better idea of the corruption which was interwoven with the religious sentiment of this people, thus producing an unprecedented state of disorder. Nowadays it is the fashion to deny the existence of such depravity in morals. Historians who reject our Faith exercise their ingenuity in mitigating the severe language of contemporary writers. They say these sombre pictures must be viewed in the light of that proneness to excess which we know is natural to preachers of morality; and then they contrast with them the noble sentiments of the Stoics, so numerous at that time, acts of virtue which are never lacking in the worst epochs, certain just and clement laws of the first emperors, together with the burial inscriptions which speak the praises of the dead. The conclusion they would have us draw from these evidences is that manners were growing purer; that, far from degenerating, humanity was already on the high road to salvation when Jesus came; and that mankind owes no more to the Gospel than to philosophy and public education, these three causes having had an equal share in the regeneration of the world.[2]

The light in which we view the history of the primitive Church changes the color of every event so com-

---

[1] 1 Peter v. 13. It has been shown elsewhere how this symbolic name came to be used to designate Rome (Appendix IV.).
[2] Renan, *Les Apôtres*, pp. 303, 343; Duruy, *Histoire des Romains*, t. v. chap. lx., lxi., etc.

pletely, according as we accept or reject this theory, that it is impossible to study the beginnings of Christianity without taking one side or the other on this mooted subject. We shall proceed, therefore, by making our estimate from what the Romans of the Empire generally agree in recording of their own times, and from the laws, institutions, and customs of which we have positive proofs. That Juvenal, Seneca, even Tacitus are often extreme in their criticisms, that their indignation leads them to launch forth into exaggerated terms, and that, consequently, we cannot accept without reserve all the evil they say of their fellow-citizens, — all this no one will gainsay. But leaving their invectives unnoticed, certain facts remain settled beyond a doubt. A brief account of these facts will be enough to give us a fair idea of the Roman world, and of the Capital in particular, when Peter began his efforts to reform this corrupt society.

The best days of Rome were in the period which followed her birth. Even then she possessed what was to win her the empire of the world, — family life which was fruitful and strongly guarded; jealous love of liberty; religious reverence for the right and for a man's sworn faith; exact obedience to the laws, even when cruel; a frugal, austere, laborious existence, divided between agriculture and arms; and, finally, no inclination to luxury, nor any taste for the arts. " The paternal majesty "[1] was regarded as the pinnacle of greatness. It was the highest dignity in the reach of man, who thereby obtained his full complement of rights, thus becoming sovereign lord of his household, — wives, children, slaves. With the latter he could do anything he chose. The dependence of the children was but a degree less absolute. At birth the baby was laid at his father's feet, and allowed to live only on condition that the parent accepted him. As the son grew older, he assumed the man's toga, which made him a citizen, rose to high position in the State, became in his turn the

---

[1] Livy, viii. 7; Justin, x. 2.

head of a family, but without escaping the authority of him who, having given him his life, could always dispose of it as he pleased.[1]

Over the wife, too, the head of the house held the same absolute sway. She is generally said to be " in the hands [2] of the husband. " The iron ring slipped on her finger the day of her betrothal gave her to understand that the marriage bond was to be a heavy one. As soon as the solemn sacrifice consecrated their union, she ceased to belong to herself. Henceforth she is treated as a child of the family, the daughter of her husband, the sister of his children. Her lord has complete power over her. He can summon her before his domestic court, chastise, and even kill her, should he surprise her in adultery. In primitive law, the woman never emerged from a state of wardship. It was not till three centuries before our era that she obtained the power of disposing of her dowry and personal effects.

Certainly this was a hard lot; but it had some compensations in the dignity wherewith the Roman Law invested the mother. Though absolutely dependent on her husband, she was still his companion, for marriage constituted an association lasting for a lifetime, the holding in common of all things, divine and human.[3] The wedding festival rites introduce her as its mistress to the family fireside, which is to become a sanctuary for her.[4] When she goes abroad, the mother is no less respected. She is free to appear in public, taking her place at the feasts and shows. The Consuls themselves yield precedence to her, and a law attributed to Romulus

---

[1] In fact the father retained the right of life and death over him; he might, in a criminal case, remove him from the jurisdiction of the ordinary courts, and himself pronounce sentence of banishment, or order that he be put to death by scourging. At all times he was entitled to sell his offspring as often as thrice. According to the primitive law, the father was the rightful owner of everything acquired by his child, as the latter could possess nothing in his own name.

[2] "In manu," was the expression in legal parlance.

[3] "Divini humanique juris communicatio." "Consortium omnis vitæ, individuæ vitæ consuetudo." Dig. xxiii. 2.

[4] Macrobius, *Saturnal.*, i. 15.

punished any improper word or gesture indulged in in her presence.[1] Such, in its primitive organization, was the Roman family: the father, an absolute master, both judge and priest in his own home; the matron, a submissive companion to her husband, but acquiring nobility and authority from the union with him. Under them the child, subject to the father and, until the death of the latter, owing obedience to him.

This stern discipline, which made for the greatness of the Republic, in the Imperial epoch came to be regarded as too heavy a yoke to bear. The depravation of manners undermined family life, and spread with frightful rapidity after the conquest of the East. From those regions, Rome was importing every day, along with their marvels of art and immense stores of wealth, a taste for sumptuous surroundings, a soft and voluptuous life. The change from rugged simplicity to opulence was so sudden that it is small wonder their heads were turned. It took but a few years for the corruption to reach its height.

"Luxury, more to be dreaded than the sword," says Juvenal, "has fallen upon us, and is avenging the conquered universe. All the horrors, all the monstrous sins of debauchery became familiar sights to us, from the day which saw the death of Roman poverty. . . . Venus in her cups no longer has any reverence for anything."[2]

A poet's declamation, this, do you say? We would grant it willingly, were it not that his contemporaries express themselves in the same stern language. "For the most part," says the grave Polybius, "the Romans live a life of strange disorder. The young people allow themselves to be drawn into most shameful excesses. They spend their time at public shows and banquets; indulge in spendthrift tastes and in licentiousness of every description, taking pattern, only too evidently, from what they learned among the Greeks during the

---

[1] Plutarch, *Romulus*, xx.; Tacitus, *Dialogus de Oratoribus*, xxviii.
[2] Juvenal, *Satiræ*, vi. 292–300.

war against Perseus."[1] Cato, Sallust, Livy, Pliny, and Justinian[2] say the same, and depict vice at Rome as devoid of even that surface polish of grace and elegance which made it so seductive in other lands.

Of all excesses, the one which proved most fatal to the Roman family was the ignominious scourge which brought destruction upon Sodom. Greece, indeed, endeavored in every way to palliate this disgraceful feature of her life, to which she has given a name. There the worship and love of Beauty did much to conceal the abominable nature of this crime from men's eyes.[3] Rome knew no such modest scruples; she kept companies of Gitons.[4] The noblest minds — Cicero, Brutus, Cæsar[5] — were stained by these hideous passions. Refined and splendid poets, like Horace, Virgil, Tibullus, and Catullus,[6] boast of their monstrous self-indulgence.

Man becomes accustomed to infamy only too quickly. This is clearly seen in the disgust which marriage and its sterner responsibilities inspired in this worn-out generation. No children, no lasting and fruitful unions. "Their only boast is of their barrenness," says Pliny;[7] "they do not want to have even an only son." Seneca and Tacitus use the same language.[8] In the later days of the Republic the bachelors far outnumbered those who were willing to contract ties generally regarded as unendurable. Day by day the family life declined in influence, and with it the nerve and sinew of Rome.

Augustus finally took alarm at this condition of

[1] Polybius, *Historiæ*, xxxii. 11.
[2] Catonis *Fragmenta*; Sallust, *Historiarum Fragmenta*, i. 9; Livy, xxv. 40; xxxiv. 4; Pliny, *Historia Naturalis*, xxxiii. 18; xxxiv. 3; xxxv. 8; Justin, xxxvi. 4.
[3] Plato, *Phædrus*, *Convivium*, etc.
[4] Seneca, *Epist.* 46, 95, 127; Cicero, *Pro Milone*, 21, etc.
[5] Martial, ix. 51; xiv. 171; Pliny, *Epist.* vii. 4; Quintilian, xii. 1; Suetonius, *Cæsar*, 49.
[6] Horace, *Satiræ*, l. II. iii.; l. IV.; *Od.* i. x.; Vergil, *Bucol.* ii.; Martial, viii. 56; Donatus, *Vita Virg.* v. § 20; Tibullus, *Eleg.* l. I. iv.; Catullus, 48, 81, 99.
[7] Dion, xliii. 25. [8] Pliny, *Epist.* iv. 15.

affairs, and, revising one of Cæsar's projected measures,[1] he prepared, eighteen years before the Christian era, the Julian Law, *De Maritandis Ordinibus*. The people, though ready to abdicate all their liberties, let it be understood that their pleasures were not to be interfered with; they flocked to the *comitia* to prevent the enactment of this reform. Much disheartened, the Prince waited twenty years before taking further action. When he ventured to renew his proposition and encountered the same opposition, he felt himself obliged to enforce his will. But five years had not passed before he realized the futility of this first attempt, and saw that he must look for more effective measures. The law called *Papia Poppæa* is an honor to his reign; and yet what a dismal light it casts on the morals of an epoch when the citizens had to be forced, not merely to have children, but even to bring up those they had! It is true that many were won over by the advantages offered by the Julian Law, and resigned themselves to enduring a married life, but after such a fashion as to derive all its benefits without incurring its duties. Some married none but young girls of a tender age; others, availing themselves of their right as head of the family to either acknowledge or refuse the fruit of their union, sacrificed all their offspring in cold blood. Rarely in the history of the world has human life been held in such contempt. Augustus himself, in barbarous self-contradiction, forbade his attendants to nurture a descendant of his own house whose mother was the infamous Julia.[2] Claudius dashed his son against a boundary-post.[3] The new-born babies were being abandoned continually,— just as is still the custom in China and Africa. On the death of Germanicus, a large number of citizens exposed their children who had come into the world on that unhappy day.[4]

---

[1] Seneca, *Consolatio ad Marciam*, xix. 2; Tacitus, *Annales*, iii. 25; xi. 25.
[2] Suetonius, *Octavius*, 65.   [3] Id., *Claudius*, 27.
[4] Id., *Caligula*, 5.

The law *Papia Poppœa* was a well-conceived remedy against such a corruption of human instincts, relying, as it did, upon one of the commonest tendencies of the age, — the pursuit of inheritances. In those degenerate days, when natural heirs were few, if any, the insertion of one's name in the will of some bachelor was an easy and speedy way of enriching one's self. Cicero boasts of having gained twenty million sesterces[1] in this manner; and no one knew better than Augustus what an important part it played in others' revenues, since he himself drew every year some forty millions from legacies acquired by this means.[2] He made this unlawful for bachelors, by declaring them incapable of receiving any heritage outside of their family. And in the case of married citizens without offspring, the right of succession was limited to a half of the legacy willed to them. The man who had three children, on the contrary, was assured very valuable advantages, — unrestricted right of receiving bequests, a double share in the public distributions, exemption from numerous duties, speedier promotion to honors, a seat in the best part of the theatre, and everywhere the preëminence over men of his own rank and dignity.

These prerogatives constitute the *Jus Trium Liberorum*, — a much envied privilege, but one in which it was possible to participate without observing the law. First it was conceded to the Vestals, then to soldiers, as incapable of contracting marriage;[3] finally, even the bachelors obtained it out of sheer favor. Thus weakened, and left to hold its own against a torrent of opposition, the Poppæan Law lost its efficacy, like its predecessors, and the family continued to crumble and decay.

Another cause hastened its destruction. The matron was a thing of the past. There are times in a nation's history when, even though men sacrifice their fatherhood to pleasure-seeking, if the woman remains pure,

[1] About $800,000. Cicero, *Philipp.* ii. 32.
[2] Suetonius, *Augustus*, 10.   [3] Dion, lx. 24.

the process of decay is retarded at least. Rome had no such resource to rely upon. "Since the censorship of Messala and Cassius (150 B.C.), the chastity of the olden days has perished."[1] This is the sober judgment of Pliny the Elder, a well-informed man of moderate views. His contemporaries, and all the writers of the century preceding, whose works have come down to us, express themselves with equal severity. Horace, Propertius, Ovid, and Martial portray the Roman matrons as sensitive to vanity alone, oblivious of modesty and shame.[2] However exaggerated we may consider the Satires of Juvenal, they are not all the creation of his fancy, and such features as he depicts imply a state of unusual degradation. The historians coincide with the opinions of the poets. In the high praise which Tacitus bestows on the women of Germania, it is easy to read between the lines his judgment on the failings of the Roman women. "They are preserved," he says, "by the safeguards of innocence, remote from the spectacles which contaminate, and far from the festivals which kindle passions. . . . In this land they do not laugh at vices. To corrupt and to yield to corruption is not called living up to one's century. . . . To limit the number of their children, or to kill one of the new-born, is held to be a crime."[3] There is nothing like this in Italy. In the first years of the Empire, the immorality of the Romans was so notorious that Augustus branded them as libertines before the assembled Senate.[4] In the following age, license and luxury had full sway,[5] and Seneca expresses in three words the opinion of his

---

[1] "M. Messalæ, C. Cassii censorum lustro, a quo tempore pudicitiam subversam Piso gravis auctor prodidit." Pliny, *Historia Naturalis*, xvii. 245.

[2] Horace, *Od.* l. III. vi. 17; xxiv. 20; Propertius, *Elegiarum*, l. II. vi. 25; xxxii. 49; l. III. xii. 17; xiii. 23, etc.; Ovid, *Amores*, i. 8, 43; iii. 4, 37.

> Quæro diu totam, Safroni Rufe, per urbem
> Si qua puella negat; nulla puella negat.
> MARTIAL, iv. 71.

[3] Tacitus, *De Moribus Germanorum*, xix.
[4] Dion Cassius, liv. 16.   [5] Suetonius, *Vespasianus*, xiii.

day: "Women are ignorant, unruly creatures, incapable of governing themselves."[1] Surely we are a long way from the good old times when the comic actors never uttered the title of matrons on the stage without saluting "the sanctity of their name!"[2]

Doubtless in this shipwreck there was some salvage from the storm. The same Seneca praises his mother for not having yielded to the impure example set her by the common run of Roman women.[3] Paulina, the wife of this philosopher, loved him so faithfully that she wished to die with him.[4] In the household of Thraseas there were three generations of women who were sublime in their self-sacrificing devotion.[5] Elsewhere, too, we find admirable wives and sisters, especially in the noble families afflicted by the cruelty of the Cæsars, and among whom the traditions of bravery and virtue were still kept alive. With souls purified by misfortune, these patrician women found courage to meet death like the heroines of ancient times; indeed, it is but just to remember their names. But we must not forget that these are but exceptions to the rule; of this we have the strongest guarantee in the disapproval of their contemporaries, — a disapproval which is almost unanimous; for there is one voice alone in this concert of invectives which strikes a less severe note,— that of Pliny the Younger. The evidence of this writer is regarded with great favor nowadays. Many are pleased to conclude from this that women were not as depraved as people have supposed hitherto. Why was it, then, that Pliny himself took such pains to put us on our guard against his over-indulgence? Before this his contemporaries had accused him of painting those about him in too beautiful colors. "I accept the rebuke," he says, "and consider it as an

---

[1] "Animal imprudens, ferum, cupiditatum impatiens" (Seneca, *De Const. Sap.*, 14).
[2] "Tuam majestatem et nominis matronæ sanctitudinem" (Afranius, *Suspecta*).
[3] Seneca, *Consolat. ad Helviam*, xvi. 3; *Ad Marciam*, xxiv. 3.
[4] Tacitus, *Annales*, xv. 63, 64.
[5] Id., xvi. 34; Pliny the Younger, iii. 16; vii. 19; ix. 13, etc.

honor. Even supposing that they are not precisely what I say they are, I am happy in fancying them to be as I have represented them."[1]

What trust can we place in an authority weakened by his own avowals? An effort has been made, it is true, to fortify it by referring to the praises which abound in the burial inscriptions of that epoch.[2] Rome must have been a city of the saints if such epitaphs were taken at their face value, so to say. But the uniformity of these eulogies may very reasonably excite our suspicions, even more than their extraordinary number. The words "innocent," "most chaste," "distinguished," "helpful to all," "married but once," "she spun the linen," and "kept the house,"[3] recur in endless succession. Evidently these are simply the received forms, analogous to those in our cemeteries, where all the women are alike in being good mothers, good wives, and the objects of eternal regret. It is many a long day since the birth of that proverb, "To lie like a tombstone." The husband in his mourning weeds finds such lines as these already graven beforehand on the gravestone he comes to purchase. Rarely we happen upon some such ingenuous substitute as this: "The day of her death I thanked gods and men."[4] Again, one son takes care to put on his mother's tomb an account of the usual way of composing these inscriptions:—

"As the eulogy of all noble ladies is usually couched in simple terms, which are also very similar, since it is under-

---

[1] Pliny, vii. 28.
[2] "Amymona, wife of Marcus, was beautiful and good, an indefatigable spinner, pious, reserved, chaste, and a good housewife." Orelli, 4639.— "Urbilia, wife of Primus, died in her twenty-third year, cherished by all her people; to me she was dearer than life" (Marini, *Inscrizioni delle ville e de' palazzi Albani*, p. 100). "To the most virtuous of wives and the most careful of housekeepers, the object of my soul's deepest regrets . . . I lived with her, and she never gave me cause for complaint . . ." Orelli, 7382. — "Never did she cause me the least trouble . . ." Henzen, 7385. — "Never have I heard an unkind word from her lips." Orelli, 4530.— "Her virtues should be written in letters of gold." Henzen, 7386.
[3] "*Innocens, Carissima, Præstans, Omnibus Subveniens, Lanifica, Domiseda.*"
[4] Orelli, 4636.

stood that the merits which Nature distributes to their sex ought not to attract by the pleasure of variety, . . . even so my dearest mother enjoyed the best of reputations, for she equalled in modesty, uprightness, chastity, obedience, and her work at the loom, her care and faithfulness, all other good women. In nothing did she yield place to any one of them."[1]

A few instances of striking virtues, and the conventional praise of the dead, are not enough to destroy, or even to mitigate, the unanimous censure of their contemporaries, since all the testimony gathered from other sources confirms their view. The strongest proof comes from the changes made in educational systems. Girls were no longer kept secluded in their father's houses during their early childhood; they no longer grew up under their mother's eyes, learning to spin and weave, and forming themselves for the duties of life.

"When I entered one of those schools to which nobles send their sons, I found," says Scipio Emilianus, "more than five hundred young girls and boys, who, in the company of players and infamous characters, were taking lessons on the lyre, or in singing and deportment. I saw one child twelve years old, the son of a candidate, executing a dance unworthy of the lewdest servant."[2]

The young Roman girl who was not sent to the public masters was confided to the care of a slave teacher,—almost always a Greek. They forgot that a servile mind would not be likely to inspire high thoughts, and that in fact all their corruption came from Greece.

"Formerly," says Tacitus,[3] "the chiefest glory of a matron was to keep the house and watch over her children. They used also to select some kinswoman of advanced age, of irreproachable life and unspotted reputation, who should look after the rising generation of the family, and whose very presence alone put a stop to any shameful word or improper action. But nowadays the child is handed over to a

[1] Orelli, 4860. [2] Macrobius, *Saturn.*, ii. 10.
[3] Tacitus, *Dial. de Oratoribus*, 28, 29.

Greek servant-girl, with one or two slaves under her, often taken from the very lowest class, and incapable of performing any serious duties."

Plutarch voices the same complaints.

"A majority of the men of our times fall into a ridiculous error. When they have a good honest slave, they make a laborer of him, or a pilot, or an overseer, or a clerk in their warehouse or bank; but if they find one who gets drunk and over-eats himself, — who, in fact, is good for nothing at all, — he is the man to whom they intrust the care of their children."[1]

If a young girl escaped these corrupting influences of her earlier age, her innocence was but the more imperilled in that voluptuous world which was suddenly unrolled before her eyes; for it was at the period of life when moral courage is oftenest lacking, between thirteen and seventeen, that marriage came, bringing with it the worst of dangers. Very few Roman women of that day contracted those solemn ties of marriage which put them under complete subjugation to their husband. The matron, under the Empire, had her separate establishment, with a troop of slaves trained to consult her every whim. They had their corrupters in the shape of books, which, if they wished, could teach them "the art of loving."[2] In the niches along the walls, under the porticos, and in the dwelling-rooms, were pictures and statues showing forth in action their lessons of vice. Propertius execrates the artist's brush which displays to all eyes what ought to be decently hid.[3]

More dangerous still were the public shows, — coarse farces full of obscenities, adventures of divinities which

---

[1] Plutarch, *De Liberis Educandis*, vii.
[2] Ovid and Catullus were given them to read.
[3] Quæ manus obscœnas depinxit prima tabellas,
  Et posuit casta turpia visa domo,
  Illa puellarum ingenuos corrupit ocellos,
  Nequitiæque suæ noluit esse rudes.
  Ah! gemat, in terris ista qui protulit arte
  Jurgia sub tacita condita lætitia.
        PROPERTIUS, *Elegiæ*, II. vi.

were offensive to any modest mind; Venus and Mars, Danaë and Ganymede playing their parts on the open stage. "The matron who entered the public playhouses a chaste woman came forth a brazen creature."[1] The amphitheatre was as bad. The slaughters of the arena accustomed their eyes to the sight of blood, and their ears were hardened to the cries of pain. Returning home, their slaves are whipped and lacerated for the most trifling faults, thus proving what a woman can become when devoid of pity. And we must not fancy that maidens and good mothers were not to be found in the tiers of the circus and theatre. Ovid describes them flocking to these haunts of pleasure more eagerly than a swarm of ants or a covey of birds. "They come in great numbers to see, but still more to be seen. And there it is that chaste virtue suffers shipwreck."[2]

There were the same reefs and shoals in the harbors of domestic life. At table, where formerly they used to remain sitting, they soon adopted a reclining posture like the men, surrounded by them,[3] and listening to dissolute songs and jests.[4] Syrian and Andalusian women went through dances and pantomimes of revolting indecency.[5] Seneca tells us of the matrons prolonging their drinking-bouts, disputing for the libations with the male companions of their revels, and like them vomiting, only to fall to drinking again.[6] The philoso-

[1] S. Cyprian, *Epist.* i. 8; Lactantius, *Instit.* 6, 30.
[2] Ovid, *Ars Amat.* i. 93–100.   [3] Valerius Maximus, ii. 1, 2.
[4] "Omne convivium obscœnis canticis strepit, pudenda dictu spectantur" (Quintilian, *De Institutione Oratoria*, i. 2, 8).
[5] Juvenal, xi. 162.
[6] "Non minus pervigilant, non minus potant, et oleo et mero viros provocant· æque invitis ingesta visceribus per os reddunt, et vinum omne vomitu remetiuntur" (Seneca, *Epist.* 95). It is so much the fashion nowadays to excuse and dignify the conduct of life during this century that it is natural for critics to try in every way to mitigate the testimony of the ancients concerning even this offensive detail. Friedlænder (*Mœurs romaines*, l. viii. § 1) accumulates quotations to prove that emetics were much used at this time and highly recommended by physicians. To confute such fantasies, we need but refer to Seneca's own words: "Vomunt ut edant, edunt ut vomant, et epulas quas toto orbe conquirunt, nec concoquere dignantur" (*Ad Helviam*, ix).

pher treats of their conduct after marriage, with no less severity. "Among them," he says, "chastity is a synonym for ugliness."[1] However much of exaggeration, or bitterness even, there may be in this attack, and though it is always possible to draw some parallel between the Roman decadence and certain periods of modern history,[2] it nevertheless remains true just the same, that a time in which such an arraignment could be accepted without protest, and further corroborated by all other writers, cannot for an instant be regarded as an era of moral progress.

Another no less striking index of the social laxity is the frivolous spirit in which they assumed and dissolved the marriage tie. Here again, doubtless, Seneca goes too far, when asserting that women reckoned the years, not by the Consuls,[3] but by their husbands; neither is Juvenal serious when he says that they broke every bond before the green bough, set above their door-way on the wedding-day, had withered away.[4] But it is an undoubted fact that lasting unions were become the exceptions. Q. Lucretius Vespillo, Consul in the year 19 B.C., might well write on the tomb of his wife, Turia: "It is a rare thing to see so long a period of life passed in common and not interrupted by divorce before being dissolved by death. Thanks to destiny, our union continued with never a cause for complaint until the

---

[1] Seneca, *De Benef.* iii. 16. M. Boissier, indulgent as he is to the Romans of the Empire, has not hesitated to write these lines, which put the finishing touches to his portrait of their women: " It had been predicted that on the day when they became the equals of men they would try to rule them; nor did the prophecy fail of fulfilment. When they realized they were mistresses of their own persons, and sometimes of others' as well, they waxed violent, haughty, and unbearable. They wielded their domestic authority with pitiless severity, tormenting their husbands and beating their slaves. Some among them, carrying their views of equality to extremes, delighted in invading careers and trades hitherto reserved to men. There were women advocates, lawmakers, and, what is worse, female athletes and gladiators. 'They fled their sex,' says the satirist" (Boissier, *La Religion romaine*, t. ii. p. 232).
[2] Duruy, *Histoire des Romains*, t. v. pp. 348-381.
[3] Seneca, *De Beneficiis*, iii. 16, 2.
[4] Juvenal, *Satiræ*, vi. 223.

forty-first year of our marriage."[1] Many men—Cicero, Ovid, and Pliny the Younger among the number—were married three times.[2] One epitaph mentions a seventh wife.[3] When Messalina wedded Nero, it was the fiftieth honeymoon.[4] There were good reasons why Augustus should seek to limit the legal separations which were completing the ruin of family life. In the face of such social wrecks, how can any one talk of wise legislation and new ideas ameliorating the state of society?[5] What such investigators take for tokens of revival are but the feeble remnants of a dead past. Certainly some virtues remain, the fruits of a healthier, better season; but it is a grave error to mistake them for the heralds of a new spring. Pagan Rome was a field drained of all its strength; if it was ever to be made fruitful again, they had need of another sort of dew from heaven than the enactment of sterile laws.

Public morals lie at the base of public life. If they lose their hold in the family, the whole fabric of the State is undermined. When frugality, moderation, toil, and respect for liberty disappeared, by a fatal consequence the process of dissolution, now working among the Romans, turned their minds to the pursuit of base pleasures and selfish aims. There is here no longer any zeal for the common good,—not even that ambition, so profitable to the community, which impels its greater citizens to strive after an increase of fortune by exerting their own industry.

[1] Mommsen, *Mémoires de l'Académie de Berlin*, 1863, p. 455.
[2] Ovid, *Tristia*, iv. 69; Mommsen, *Hermes*, iii. 35.
[3] Henzen, *Bulletin des inscriptions*, 1865, p. 252.
[4] Juvenal's Scholiast, vi. 433.
[5] "A frightful state of depravity, a shameless course of cynicism, had destroyed private manners. They were no longer fathers, sons, wives, but mere human creatures oblivious of the most natural of all duties, seeking pleasure in every description of debauchery and crime. Marriage, becoming irksome, was discarded, and, to escape its obligations, they lived in celibacy, or worse still, legalized their prostitution by an annual divorce" (Drury, *Histoire des Romains*, t. iii. p. 213). How could the historian who drew this gloomy but veracious picture attempt to prove in the same work (t. v. ch. lx.) that "this moral decadence affected only a small number?" (p. 380.)

The most active agency in this decadence was slavery, which was growing in proportion to their conquests. Every wealthy mansion was getting to be a huge workshop, where thousands of men, following every kind of trade, furnished what the needs and tastes of their masters required.[1] Vanquished in such an unequal struggle as this, the Roman workman saw himself at last doomed to a wretched existence. And at the same period, the country places witnessed the gradual disappearance of the independent laborer,— the very seed and stock of a sovereign people. Lands formerly divided into small holdings, fell finally into the hands of a few lords; the cultivated plains gave place to the immense pasture-lands which still occupy the environs of Rome and exhaust its resources. All that they could no longer procure from the fallow fields of Latium, they must needs seek farther from home,— bread-stuffs from Sicily and Africa, wine from the Isles of Greece or from Spain and Gaul.

The country people, thus driven to the Capital, found few means of earning a livelihood there; for slave labor crushed out all competition. "Laziness was their ruin, because they possessed no ground of their own in the territories which the rich had taken entire possession of, and because they could get no work to do on the land of any one else, in the midst of such great numbers of slaves."[2] One saying of the Tribune Philip (102 B. C.) shows this throng of wretched people in a dreadful light. "In this city there are not more than two thousand of the inhabitants who have private possessions."[3] The rest — that is to say, nearly a million men[4] — was

---

[1] Rich men made it their boast that they could provide everything necessary for their own needs, and thus they increased their wealth by selling what was superfluous, for all the profits of the household industry accrued to themselves.

[2] Appianus, *De Bellis Civilibus,* i. 7.

[3] Cicero, *De Officiis,* ii. 21.

[4] On account of the sudden and numerous variations in the population of Rome, it is difficult to determine upon any exact figures. For the reign of Augustus, the most probable calculations make it 1,300,000 (Dézobry, *Rome au siècle d'Auguste,* t. iii. p. 533), or 1,630,000 (Becker, iii. 2). In

made up of serfs or proletarians. Fifty years later, Cæsar found that the public registers contained the names of four hundred and fifty thousand citizens, of whom three hundred and twenty thousand were supported by the State.[1] Thus three quarters of the populace were paupers. The Dictator sent off eighty thousand of these mendicants to colonies across the seas, and reduced the number of those who were paid out of the treasury to one hundred and fifty thousand. But the troubles which followed Cæsar's death soon brought the number up to the former figure. All that Augustus could do, towards the end of his reign, was to cut down the list of citizens who daily received their few measures of wheat and wine,[2] to two hundred thousand.[3] To add somewhat to this meagre pittance, a few looked for other means of livelihood from their own labors; but the majority were content to put up with the degrading conditions of clientship. In the period before us this state of life was so common that it behoves us to notice some of its features. By this means we can see how far these men, formerly so jealous of their rights, had forfeited their sense of dignity: in the lower classes, among whom Peter was to preach the Gospel, there remained hardly a vestige of their finer, nobler sentiments. To implant the seeds of Christianity among these fawning, slavish souls, he must begin by cultivating anew the very first principles of honor.

Not that the relationship of the client to his patron had anything degrading in itself. With an aristocracy so strongly constituted, it was only natural that the poor citizen should become attached to the patrician who helped him, as a " new man," to take a position in the army, among the magistrates, even in the Senate

the preceding century, the number of inhabitants never touched the million point.
[1] Suetonius, *Cæsar*, 41; Dion, xliii. 21; Appianus, *De Bellis Civilibus*, ii. 120.
[2] By this is meant what they called the *sportula*, — from *sporta*, "a small hamper," — which was used for carrying daily provisions.
[3] Dion, lv. 10.

and in the consular families.[1] The abuse of this advantageous institution began a century and a half before our era, when the nobility, breaking off friendly intercourse with the people, looked down on them as contemptible creatures, only useful as a stepping-stone to power.

Thereafter the wealthy kept a horde of clients about them, not as their protectors, but to gratify their thirst for glory. They never walked out without a numerous retinue of these hangers-on, whose numbers served as a token of their importance. Little by little this fashion came to be absolutely obligatory. Every politician, every man of affairs, if he wished to live up to his state, must take measures to insure an imposing array of followers. The growing multitudes of proletarians made it easy to find recruits; for a slender salary there was any number of needy men eager to offer the homage demanded of them. From early dawn, they were up and on the lookout. "Every night," says Juvenal, "so soon as the stars begin to pale, the poor client wakes up and hastens off, breathless at the thought that perhaps the procession of clients has already passed along on its line of march."[2] This morning visit was one of his obligations, but it did not dispense him from any of the day's drudgery,— going before his lord or following his litter,[3] accompanying him in his visits[4] or to the baths, clearing a way for him through the throngs,[5] applauding his speeches, taking his part with every one and every-

[1] Such was the admirable constitution of Rome, about the time of the Punic wars, when the people had won their civil and political liberty. Then indeed they merited unreservedly Bossuet's high encomium: "Of all nations on earth, the bravest and the hardiest, but at the same time animated by the wisest counsels, most constant to its own loftier maxims, the most circumspect, the most laborious, and in fine the most patient, was the Roman people. And therefore they produced the finest militia of all time, and a political system which was the most foreseeing, the finest, and the most successfully carried out, that was ever known" (*Discours sur l'Histoire universelle*, part iii. chap. vi.).

[2] Juvenal, *Satiræ*, v. 19–22. Cf. Martial, x. 70, 5; x. 74; iii. 4; xii. 68; Statius, *Silvæ*, iv. 9, 48.

[3] Martial, ii. 18, 5; iii. 46.   [4] Id., ix. 100, 3.

[5] Id., iii. 36, 46.

where,[1] sweating and out of breath under his great woollen toga, without which no one was allowed to appear before his patron.[2]

And it was for a petty price, ten sesterces,[3] that the freemen of Rome lowered themselves to such servitude. From time to time, it is true, they might come into a small windfall, in the shape of a cast-off garment or an invitation to supper;[4] but in return for such favors what humiliations were to be endured,— the contempt of the master of the house, and the impertinence of the slaves, even more insolent in their scorn! Juvenal and all his contemporaries tell us that the client never approached his patron without bowing again and again, kissing his hand, calling him lord and king, and begging the honor of a word or a glance.[5] At table, the meats, wine, service, everything, in fact, is intended to show the great difference between the rich man, reclining on the couch of honor, and the parasite with his much torn and mended toga relegated to the farther end.[6] On his plate you find "mouldy bread, hard enough to cut the gums from one's teeth,[7] some ill-looking cabbage soaked in lamp-oil,[8] a sup of wine in a cracked glass, and such wine! . . . your toga wouldn't absorb it if used to take out grease-spots."[9] . . . Then the forced smile at the sarcastic jibes of the footmen or the amphitryon; while at the least murmur they are shown the door.[10] In his picture Juvenal undoubtedly caricatures some features; but no one will object to his indignant conclusion on the score of excess: "The master is

---

[1] Martial, vi. 48; x. 10; xi. 21; Quintilian, xi. 3, 131; Pliny the younger, ii. 14, 4; Juvenal, xiii. 29–31; Seneca, *De Ira*, iii. 8, 6.
[2] Martial, ix. 100; xi. 96, 11; "Sudatrix toga," xii. 18, 5.
[3] About 40 cents a day. Martial, iv. 26; vi. 88.
[4] Juvenal, *Satiræ*, v. 12–18; ix. 159; Martial, x. 11, 6.
[5] Martial, v. 22; i. 133; vi. 88; ii. 68; ix. 92; Seneca, *De Beneficiis*, vi. 34, 1; *Ad Serenum*, 14, 1; *De Brevit. Vitæ*, 14, 4; Juvenal, iii. 184–189; Petronius, *Satyricon*, 44.
[6] Martial, iii. 60; iv. 85; i. 20; vi. 11; x. 49; Suetonius, *Cæsar*. 48.
[7] Juvenal, v. 67–69.
[8] Id., v. 87, 88.
[9] Juvenal, v. 24, 25.
[10] Id., v. 125, 127.

quite right in lavishing his abuse on you. The man who endures all this, deserves it." [1]

In this degraded proletarian the thirst for money was stronger than ever. There was no career he would not take up or invent, if need be, to get gold. Rome, under the Empire, had seen the rise of a new profession, which we have referred to above, one never known in any other age,— the pursuit of legacy hunters. A whole class of intriguers was devoted to this career: getting into the good graces of some testator, inveigling him into making a will in their favor, then waiting for his death, or, if necessary, hastening it. Celibacy and divorce opened a vast field for their manœuvres; the stories told of them by contemporaries would seem fabulous, were it not that they all agree in describing this strange business as the most popular industry of their times.[2] The rich man without children found himself assailed by flatterers, overwhelmed by officious services, favors, presents. His works were applauded and praised extravagantly everywhere. If ill-luck befell him, they emptied their purses to make good his losses.[3] Invited on every hand, caressed by the great, gratuitously assisted by orators of renown,[4] he enjoyed such advantages that "very many fathers disowned their children and, of set purpose, joined the happy lot of people without posterity."[5]

---

[1] Juvenal, v. 160–170.
[2] Pliny, *Historia Naturalis*, xiv. 5.
[3] Martial, iv. 56; v. 39; vi. 27; ix. 48; xi. 83; xii. 90; Horace, *Satiræ*, l. II. v. 12; *Epist.* l. I. 78; Ovid, *Ars Amat.*, ii. 271, 319; Pliny the younger, ii. 20; Juvenal, iii. 221; iv. 18; vi. 38–40, 97; xii. 98, etc.
[4] Plutarch, *De Amore Prolis*, iv.
[5] Seneca, *Ad Marciam*, 19, 2. This reversal of the laws of Nature was not peculiar to Rome alone. Petronius, living at the other end of Italy, witnesses the same deviation from right conduct. "Literary culture is not what is held in highest esteem at Crotona: eloquence is out of place; neither uprightness nor purity of conduct prosper. Here all men that one sees are divided into two parties,— the courted and their courtiers. No one acknowledges his own children, for if a man has natural heirs he is not invited either to festivals or other rejoicings; excluded from all social privileges, he must fain resign himself to be confounded with the lower classes. On the contrary, those who have never had a wife or any near relatives rise to the highest honors; they alone have military ability; only they are brave and innocent in the judges' eyes. This town is like a field

It would be hard to imagine a lower state of decadence in public morals,— the money power in the hands of corrupt millionnaires; grouped about them a half-starved population, at once avaricious and slavish; all sunk to the same low level, effeminate in character, with no strength to strive after something better, seeking only to gratify their base passions. Other ages may seem to be as prone to vice, but there was never any so oblivious of virtue.[1] In the days of its splendor Athens could still give the people great lessons in living. Æschylus, Sophocles, Menander, and Demosthenes spoke to them in noble language, and re-invigorated their hearts. But Rome no longer spoke in the voice of the Forum; her amphitheatres were scenes of butchery and blood; impure spectacles degraded the stage; and the populace was as covetous as it was corrupt.

As some excuse for this epoch, it is pleaded that the Capital was not the whole Empire, and that, away from its influence, there were still great virtues to be found. Indeed, Tacitus and Pliny assert that the distant lands offered an example of stern morality. The deputies from these countries blushed at the sight of wickedness unknown among them.[2] Yet for the few regions untouched by the pestilence, how many provinces appear to have been infected equally with Rome! Greece was destroyed by the same plague-spots. "In our towns," Polybius said, "by reason of debauchery or idleness, men avoid marriage, and if children be born to them, they keep only one or two. . . . Thus are our cities perishing."[3] In the time of Plutarch the land which once sent forth the armies of a Themistocles, an Epaminondas, and an Alexander, could no longer put three thousand soldiers in the field.[4] In Southern Italy there

devastated by the plague, where the passer-by beholds nought but corrupt carrion and birds of prey devouring them" (Petronius, *Satyricon*, cxvi.).

[1] "At Rome, every sort of vice flaunted itself with a revolting cynicism; the public shows, more than aught else, had introduced a terrible state of corruption" (Renan, *Les Apôtres*, 317).
[2] Tacitus, *Annales*, xvi. 5; iii. 55; Pliny the younger, *passim*.
[3] Polybius, xxxvii. 7. [4] Plutarch, *De Defectu Oraculorum*, 8.

was the same dearth of men and virtues.[1] Pompeii and Herculaneum give us an idea of the conduct of life in the smaller places. Egypt was considered one of the most dissolute regions in the whole world; and Rome accused the East of having infected her with its maladies.[2]

The provinces recently conquered were the only ones less affected; but corruption found its way thither with the advent of the legionaries. Tacitus holds that their depraving influence was more efficacious than their weapons in overcoming the vanquished and keeping them under the yoke.[3] Every town where the Romans got a foothold, whether as soldiers, tax-gatherers, or government officials, soon became a nursery of vice, a school of debauchery and cruelty. The first thought of the conquerors was to rebuild their new surroundings after the fashion of the Capital, constructing a host of pleasure-resorts, baths, circuses, and theatres. The ruins of these edifices are scattered over the world, from the Far East to Seville, and from Great Britain to the oases of Sahara.[4] In all these places the gladiators shed their blood, and horrible scenes of cruelty or shame little by little destroyed every sentiment of pity and modesty.

Looking at this summary of the state of the Empire, we note this threefold division at the date of the advent of Christianity: first, a few countries that had as yet escaped the contagion of vice; then the majority of the provinces, and these the loveliest of all, for many a day perverted and depraved; while, finally, Rome herself stands forth as the prey of a corruption which no sophistry can possibly cover or conceal. Granted that dis-

---

[1] Juvenal, *Sat.* vi. 294–297. All Italy, according to Columella's account, was so drained of its masculine forces that the native youth seemed at its last breath. "Sic juvenum corpora fluxa et resoluta sunt, ut nihil mors mutatura videatur" (*De Re Rustica, Præfat.*).

[2] Juvenal, iii. 61–63.

[3] "... Voluptatibus, quibus Romani, plus adversus subjectos, quam armis, valent" (Tacitus, *Historiæ*, iv. 64).

[4] See the list drawn up by Friedlænder, *Mœurs romaines*, l. vi.: LES SPECTACLES.

orders which are common in times of prosperity ought not to be considered more criminal in her case ; let us close our eyes to the excesses in luxury and the orgies at their banquetings ; find some excuse for the slaughters of the circus by remembering that the victims were really prisoners of war and already condemned to death ; let us go farther, if you will, and regard these ferocious sports as a spectacle of courage and noble virtue, [1] — even then you will not have effaced the features on which we have cast the light of history, and which give us the standard of their conduct of life, — men renouncing fatherhood to devote themselves to base pleasures ; women devoid of moral ideas and childless, marriage become by means of divorce no better than legalized prostitution ; these disorders, enervating and degrading the wealthy, and from them reaching the multitude of proletarians, a servile horde, listless and lazy, whose only cry is " Give us bread and sport ! " [2]. Far from being the crime of a small fraction, this deadly depravity rules society, laughs at every reform, sweeps away all attempts at resistance. To deny this, a man would have to confute, not only the writings of moralists, but the laws of the epoch as well, the evidence of their monuments, their inscriptions, and their history.

The meed of praise still due this age, which prevents us from condemning it unreservedly, is won, then, by

[1] Pliny the Younger alleges this reason why Trajan should be praised for affording the crowd such cruel diversions : " This then is no effeminate spectacle, merely good to soften and soothe men's souls, rather it enflames their courage by a fine contempt of glorious wounds and death itself, it shows mankind that the love of glory and the desire to conquer may lodge even in the bodies of slaves and criminals " (*Panegyricus*, 33). Tacitus is less refined in his handling of the subject, and the only excuse he gives is that after all "it is only the shedding of venal blood " (*Annales*, i. 76). Of all the writers of ancient times, Seneca alone, in one of his latest works, rose up to condemn the atrocity of this custom. *Epist. ad Lucil.*, vii.

[2] " In fine, the middle of the first century is one of the worst epochs of ancient history. Greek and Roman society shows a state of decadence as compared with that of the preceding century and is far behind the one which was to follow " (Renan, *Les Apôtres*, p. 343) This is the very same conclusion advanced by Christian scholars. M. Renan is too well acquainted with the period in question not to own frankly that it stood in need of regeneration.

the virtues of a few patrician families, noble characters, whom Tacitus has made immortal,— Cremutius Cordus, Thraseas, Helvidius Priscus, Musonius Rufus. In respect to them we can do no more than repeat what we have said of the matrons of the Empire. By persecuting the highest ranks, the Cæsars restored to them something of their innate nobility of soul. Hunted down, and never sure of what the morrow would bring with it, these men grew more like their forefathers in spirit; but one thought animated them,— how best to steel their souls against suffering, and meet death face to face. The examples of bravery they have given us are admirable indeed, shining out with all the more brilliancy because of the surrounding gloom. But the list of these lofty souls is easily reckoned, and we cannot judge a whole people by a few exceptions to the general rule.

The philosophy which sustained such courage within them was the austere morality of Zeno. Poets, lawmakers, politicians, lived on his doctrine. Seeing the virtues with which it inspired men, one is tempted to believe that no cause could have been more active in seconding the spread of the Gospel; yet, in reality, Simon Peter found very little help from that source. This opinion, hitherto accepted by all writers, is nowadays rejected with great scorn. The new schools, setting up Seneca and Saint Paul side by side, boldly declare that though the restoration of the world is partly due to Christianity, the principal honor is rightfully claimed by Stoicism. The discussion is of lively interest, since our Faith is here at stake. To state the question more frankly, we shall begin by contrasting the great deeds and highest conceptions of the Stoics with the preaching of the Apostles: the facts must speak for themselves.

CHAPTER XVII.

THE STOICS OF THE EMPIRE.

To many Christians of our day the reading of the works of the Stoics of the Roman Empire is fraught with considerable difficulty. As they are very little accustomed to distinguishing the dogmas of Revelation from the truths made known by man's reason, they are astonished at finding Pagans expressing themselves on many subjects in much the same terms as those of our Holy Books. Indeed, Seneca preaches, with no less force than Saint Paul, on the contempt of riches and the consolations of poverty[1] and suffering.[2] To the mind of the Philosopher, as to the Apostle's, life appears as a time of trial, a warfare,[3] the body a prison,[4] and death a deliverance.[5] Both urge the same obligations as binding the wise man. He must shun the world and its pleasures, mortify the flesh,[6] heal the evil which lurks in his soul;[7] and to that end he must live in himself, examine his conscience nightly,[8] purify his heart, and thus rise in higher, freer flight towards Heaven.[9] Both alike have uttered admirable words in praise of charity. " The unfortunate man is a sacred object,"[10] says Seneca; " his misery protects him as do the sacred fillets which the suppliants wear.[11] Is it needful to repeat for the last time that we must lend a hand to the shipwrecked man,

---

[1] Seneca, *Epist.* xxxi., lxxxii., lxxxiii., cviii., cxviii.; *De Vita Beata*, xxiv., xxv.
[2] Id., *Epist.* xcix.
[3] Id., *Ad Marciam*, x.
[4] Id., *Ad Helviam*, xi.
[5] Id.
[6] Id., *Epist.* lxxxix.
[7] Id. *Epist.* lxv., lxxiv., xcii., ciii., cxxii.; *Ad Marciam*, xxiv.
[8] Id., *De Ira*, iii. 36.
[9] Id., *Ad Polyb.* xxviii.
[10] Id., *Epigrammata*, iv 9.
[11] Id., *Ad Helviam*, xiii.

direct the strayed wanderer on his way, and share our bread with the hungry? Why should we use so many words when one sentence is enough to teach us our whole duty. We are members of the one same body, members of God."[1] Even purer of all earthly alloy, more Christian, too, to all outward seeming, is the *Manual* of Epictetus. Saint Nilus had only to change a few words here and there when he made it the rule of life for the monks of Sinai.

Whence came this community of feeling, which often goes so far as to employ the same terms? The Middle Ages answer without hesitation that the Stoics had listened to the Apostles of the Christ, and that they reproduced their teachings. Seneca, in particular, was for a long time regarded as a disciple of Saint Paul. In support of this idea they produced certain letters exchanged between the Philosopher and the Apostle,— letters which Saint Jerome saw in many hands during his life, and to which he too lent some authority by not rejecting them with sufficient resolution.[2] Tertullian contents himself with saying "Seneca is often one of us,"[3]— thus recognizing the fact that the moral doctrines of the Philosopher have much that is in conformity with our Faith. And this is all that it is possible to grant; for in reality the Stoics are only an echo of ancient philosophy. They do but repeat, with less of majesty and eloquence, what the great Schools of Greece had taught long before.

The Pagans, in fact, did not have to await the coming of Seneca and Marcus Aurelius to give utterance to their conceptions of a Supreme Being, man's duty, virtue, and other ideas as lofty as they are clear and precise. Saint Paul acknowledges that they knew all that reason could discover of God,— "His invisible perfections, His eternal power, and His Divinity,"[4]— together with " the

---

[1] Seneca, *Epist.* xcv. [2] S. Jerome, *De Viris Illustribus*, xii.
[3] "Seneca sæpe noster" (*De Anima*, xx.) In his *Apologetica*, Tertullian ranks Seneca as one of the Pagans (*Apolog.* 150).
[4] Rom. i. 19, 20.

moral law written in their hearts;"[1] and he declares that they are inexcusable, because, having known the Lord, they have not glorified Him, but have gone astray in their vain reasonings.[2] The East, especially, from far distant ages, had beheld the radiance of "that true light, which enlighteneth every man that cometh into this world."[3] The sacred books of India and Persia and the writings of Egypt are open to every one to-day. Whoever reads them may well stand amazed at the morality which they teach. Rome, doubtless, seldom went so far afield in search of new light; but Greece was near at hand, with a host of philosophers ever on the lookout to surprise the secrets of true wisdom,— Greece, who, ever since the days of Thales and the Schools of Ionia, never ceased in her bold attempts to scrutinize the Mystery of the Infinite. About the year 150 B. C., when this marvellous effort of man's mind came to an end, they had exhausted (so to say) every resource of human genius, during a period of five centuries; Ionians, Pythagoreans, Eleatics, with Plato and Aristotle, had done their best to lift the veil. Though each one saw truth only in part, yet the heights which they reached had never been climbed before; never before had mortal glance pierced so far above the clouds. So, then, if we group together these scattered rays which they caught, we shall have some idea of the highest that has been thought and said outside the pale of Christianity.

The Romans, though the heirs of this learning, were little adapted to appreciate it; men of action, war, and government, they did not look for sublime thoughts, but for a discipline fitted to regulate human conduct and the present life. The last masters whom Greece produced — Epicurus and Zeno — offered them what they desired. Very different from Aristotle and Plato, who left only a radiant track in their path,[4] these

---

[1] Rom. ii. 14, 15.   [2] Rom. i. 21   [3] John i. 9.
[4] "All of Platonism is in Plato himself, who left no successor. The downward course of degeneration was a rapid one from the master to

two sages had founded veritable sects, which made their way from Greece into the Roman world, and there divided the empire over men's minds. The philosophy of Zeno, which was Stoicism, held the mastery over sterner natures, craving the exercise of strife. Epicurism found favor with softer and less decided characters,— poets and artists, who felt the charm of Greece, and, like her, were content with a state of peaceful serenity.

The age of Augustus wavered between these two doctrines; the age that followed, inclined to the first. Indeed, times were become very hard for any one who could not reconcile himself to the extremes of servitude or pleasure-seeking. Honest men led a precarious existence; finding their life so menaced, they took refuge in the school which taught them to be calm and disdain death. Furthermore, Stoicism was more in harmony with the Roman genius, for this people, despite its incomparable vigor of spirit, was of a mediocre cast of mind ; what pleased them most in the discourses of the Porch, was the absence of any profound speculations; it was, indeed, a summary of practical rules,— virtue shown to consist in justice, courage, temperance, but also in haughtiness and pride of life. They came forth thence insensible to any blows of misfortune, coldly resigned to whatsoever might come, drawing from this high-souled energy a great scorn for suffering : what more could be desired by a race of lawgivers and soldiers ?

Although propounded for the first time in Athens,[1] this severe moral system borrowed nothing from the Greeks. Zeno, who was its author, came of a Semitic race. Born at Citium, a colony founded in the isle of Cyprus by merchants from Tyre, he seems to have re-

---

Speusippus and Xenocrates, and from them to Polemon and Crantor. . . . Peripateticism died with Aristotle and Theophrastus. Straton, Lacon, Lacides, and Hieronymus are not so much disciples as deserters" (Denys, *Histoire des théories et des idées morales dans l'antiquité*, t. i. p. 385).

[1] Zeno did not go to Athens until he was twenty-two years old, according to some (Diogenes Laërtius, 28), thirty according to others (Id., 2), but he remained there the rest of his life.

tained many traits of his origin; indeed, he was called "the Phœnician."[1] His most illustrious disciples came from Babylon, Sidon, or Carthage,[2] and the masters whom the Porch sent to Rome belonged to Rhodes or to Tarsus in Cilicia.[3] Thus the East, more than Greece, has left its mark upon the teachings of Stoicism. This accounts for many peculiarities in that doctrine, — the Pantheism on which it is founded, the Divine Force, which encompasses and permeates the world, investing itself under every known form;[4] Nature, co-equal with God,[5] and finding its perfection in man; truth, a work of intuition rather than of induction;[6] the religious sentiment going hand in hand with materialism; mortification of the flesh joined with a licentious conduct of life. A state of perfect impassibility,[7] that sovereign virtue of Stoicism, always has been the dream of the East. To attain it, any means is lawful, every act allowable. Under color of following the promptings of Nature,[8] the teachers of the Porch authorize even those excesses which they reprove. Zeno himself indulged in the most shameful licentiousness; Chrysippus lauded the immodesty of Diogenes.[9]

Such was the school of thinkers which formed the

[1] Diogenes Laërtius, ii. 120; vii. 1, 25; Cicero, *De Finibus*, iv. 20.
[2] Zeno's foremost disciples were Athenodorus of Soli, Ariston of Chio, Herillus of Carthage, and Cleanthes of Assos; these had successors not less renowned, — Chrysippus of Soli, Zeno of Tarsus, Diogenes of Babylon, Antipater of Sidon, Panætius of Rhodes, and Posidonius of Apamea in Syria.
[3] The most famous Schools of Stoicism were as follows: Rhodes, where Posidonius and Jason taught; Tarsus, which boasted of several celebrated masters who became preceptors in the imperial family; Apollonia, Pergamos, and Alexandria.
[4] Diogenes Laërtius, vii. 137, 148, 156; Plutarch, *De Placitis Philosophorum*, i. 6, 7; Cicero, *De Natura Deorum*, ii. 11.
[5] Cicero, *De Natura Deorum*, ii. 15; *Academica*, ii. 37; Plutarch, *De Repugnantiis Stoicis*, xxxiv.-xl.
[6] Diogenes Laërtius, vii. 51, 53, 54, etc.
[7] Stobæus, *Eclogarum*, ii. 116, 122; Diogenes Laërtius, vii. 116; Cicero, *Academica*, i. 10; ii. 44, etc.
[8] Ὁμολογουμένως τῇ φύσει ζῆν. Diogenes Laërtius, vii. 87, 89.
[9] Stobæus, *Eclogarum*, ii. 118, 230, 238; Plutarch, *De Repugnantiis Stoicis*, 22; Sextus Empiricus, *Contra Mathematicos*, xi. 193; Diogenes Laërtius, vii. 188.

wise men of the Empire. The latter did not adopt their teachings blindly; they first purified the foreign doctrine, and then enriched it with matter borrowed from other Philosophies; for Rome, though she invented so little, willingly accepted from the work of others whatever suited her character. By such fortunate changes she gave to Roman Stoicism that high tone of ideas and feelings which we find in the writings of Seneca and Epictetus. Does their doctrine, thus rehabilitated, deserve the praises showered on it in our day? Does it prove a decided progress in man's reason, conducting humanity into new and higher paths? In the approaching restoration of good morals did it have an influence equal to that of Christianity? Relying on detached texts, men appeal to sentences of the Stoics which are easily given a Christian character. But if we read them in the original works, giving them the sense demanded by the context, we shall stand in amazement at the change of tenor. Reading them thus, Seneca and Epictetus appear as they really are,— inferior to their teachers, corrupting, nay, actually neglecting the splendid legacy left them by their masters. Whichever portion of their work we happen to take up, we find this decadence manifest and undeniable.

To arrive at some knowledge of God they had only to listen to the voice of Greece; there the Poets and Philosophers had spoken of the Sovereign Being in language so perfect that our own theologians have thought they could not do better than appropriate them. "He Who giveth commands to gods and men is One," says Xenophanes of Colophon. "He hath no body like mortals, neither hath He a spirit like unto theirs." [1] Thus the Supreme Good is described in the Hymn of Cleanthes: "That which is ordered, righteous, holy, pious, master of itself." [2] His endless duration was

---

[1] Xenophanes, quoted by Clement of Alexandria (*Stromata*, v. 14: *Patrologie grecque*, t. ix. p. 165).

[2] Cleanthes, quoted by Clement of Alexandria (*Stromata*, v. 14; *Patrologie grecque*, t. ix. p. 168).

known to them. "He hath had no beginning," says Parmenides, "He will have no end; He is one, unbegotten, universal, immutable."[1] "The past and the future," Plato adds, "are the fleeting forms of time, which we do ill to attribute to the Eternal Substance. That *is*,—which is all we can say of it with truth."[2] When the Eternal revealed His ineffable Name to Moses, it was no more than this, "I am Who am."[3]

Not less profound was the teaching of these sages concerning Providence. For them as for us, "God seeth all things at all times, heareth everything, is present everywhere, watches over all alike."[4] "He knoweth the most trifling events and is concerned therefor, . . . nor do these cares degrade His Majesty."[5] Nothing escapes His glance, not even our most secret thoughts. "Oh, thou young man who fanciest that the gods pay no heed to thee, know that neither thou nor any one will escape their justice. Vainly wilt thou try to hide thy littleness in the depths of the earth, or on swift pinions soar into the far-off skies; always thou must needs satisfy the Divine Justice."[6] This God, this just Judge, is at the same time "Father of men." The songs of Homer and the Hymn of Cleanthes invoke Him by that title,[7] and Rome herself, from her earliest years, worshipped a Jupiter who was at once "Best and Greatest."

Instead of building upon this glorious heritage, the Stoics of the Empire concocted a coarse system of theology. Their God is Nature, the soul of the world distributed among created beings, not even a pure spirit, but a fiery substance,—the ether according to Zeno, or according to Cleanthes the sun; for all it was a subtile fire, like that of which our intelligence is composed.[8]

---

[1] Parmenides, quoted in the same chapter (*Patrologie grecque*, t. ix. p. 169).
[2] Plato, *Timœus*, x.   [3] Exod. iii. 13.
[4] Xenophon, *Memorabilia*, i. 4.   [5] Plato, *Legum*, x.   [6] Id.
[7] Homer, *Iliad*, iii. 276; Cleanthes, quoted by Stobæus (*Eclogarum*, i. 30).
[8] Diogenes Laërtius, vii. 139, 148; Plutarch, *De Placitis Philosophorum*, i. 6, 7; Stobæus, *Eclogarum*, i.; Cicero, *De Natura Deorum*, i. 14.

This is the Stoics' idea of God,— the God of Seneca and Marcus Aurelius. Surely we have come a long journey from Socrates and his disciples!

There is the same falling-off in their belief in Immortality. This was a matter of Faith with the Greeks. Enamoured as they were of all earthly delights, sports, honors, and beauty of form, all these gifts of God could not quench their thirst. Beyond the tomb they looked for a new life, eternally serene; and their artists and poets vied with each other in depicting its charms. The philosophers, without contending against these popular traditions, merely endeavored to purify the too material views of the Mystics. To Plato, the happiness of the righteous after death is to consist in the contemplation of Truth and Eternal Beauty, and in the possession of absolute good. These hopes are lofty rather than well founded certainly; but they are set forth in such magnificent language, in such a pure, clear light, that his invisible world dazzles our eyes, and the soul feels itself lifted up to the heights whither his enthusiasm has borne him.

This radiance of hope, which robbed the grave of its terrors for the Greeks, never shone upon the scholars of Rome. With Lucretius many among them looked forward to rising tranquilly from the festal board, "like guests sated with the banquet of life."[1] Over their tombs they carved out sentences devoid of any belief or hope: "Behold me plunged in that deep sleep from which none shall awaken me."[2] "In Tartarus there is neither boat, nor Charon, nor Eacus, nor Cerberus. All we whom Death hath here laid low, we are nought but ashes and fragile bones; nothing more."[3] "I was nothing; I am no longer anything. You, who are still alive, eat, drink, and enjoy yourself,— then come hither."[4] It was said that Sardanapalus once dictated this epitaph to the Romans of the Empire. "What I

---

[1] Lucretius, iii 938.   [2] Stephani, *Tit. Gr.* vi. 18.
[3] *Corpus Inscriptionum Græcarum*, 6298.
[4] *Corpus Inscriptionum Latinarum*, ii. 1434.

have eaten and drunk, that I have with me, what I left behind is lost to me."[1] Several philosophers go farther still. "What accursed folly," says Pliny, "this notion of a life renewed by death! Where would poor creatures ever find repose, if the soul continued to be conscious in those upper regions or in the shades of Hell? Truly this consolation, which is so vaunted, this blessedness of faith, takes away the one virtue of death which is the sovereign good of Nature; and the expectation of a future beyond the tomb does but redouble the dying man's agony. For though it is sweet to live, who can say that it is sweet to have lived?"[2]

It must be said that the Stoics, in general, did not yearn after nothingness with such intensity as this; rather they resigned themselves to the necessity. Seneca, indeed, has certain happy thoughts anent Immortality, and often speaks like a Platonist.[3] But when, on returning to the Porch, he questions his masters and asks them what such hopes are really worth, some answer that the soul, as a fiery substance, shall last until the universal conflagration which is to destroy everything; others tell him that his soul is to remain a little below the gods, among the stars. "Thus they relegate it to the moon," said the scoffers. But even of this dismal existence, only heroes have any share; ordinary mortals are extinguished at death, or if they retain any semblance of life, it is but as ashes scattered upon a whirlwind, which sweeps them round about the world. Such doctrines as these made the expectation of another life so fanciful that the true Stoics, like Epictetus and Marcus Aurelius become confused when speaking of it, and can pretend to know nothing surely.

This uncertainty is all the more striking, because we have only to go among the populace, and we shall find, almost at the same period the very firmest belief in Immortality. The mythological scenes sculptured on

[1] Muratori, 1677, 2. [2] Pliny, *Historia Naturalis*, vii. 188-189.
[3] Denys, *Histoire des théories et des idées morales dans l'antiquité*, t. ii. pp. 253-255.

the tombs symbolize the passing from one life to the other,— Proserpine rapt away into the realms of darkness, but brought back into the light; Adonis dying, only to be born again; Hercules overcoming Hell. Even more numerous are the images symbolical of the elect in their felicity, found on the bas-rilievos and on burial-urns. Bacchantes, Mœnads and Satyrs mingle in merry dance; the Loves fly here and there in playful joy; Nereids pillow their lovely heads upon the waves; everywhere happy choruses, high festival, and every delight of life meet our eyes. Every effort of fancy was exhausted to vary the picture, and add new charms to the subject; for the dead, so they believed, still clung to the handful of ashes gathered from the funeral pyre. The *Shade*, the Soul, still hovered about and took part in the pleasures devised for it. It was fed by the sacrifices and libations, and delighted in the gifts heaped up in the tomb,— the furniture, the garments, and the jewels.

Romans were so fully persuaded of this that they decked out their last abode beforehand with the greatest care, surrounding it with gardens and bosky groves.[1] Their first thought was how best to insure the exclusive possession of the place. The law encouraged this feeling by declaring that of all the goods which had belonged to the deceased, his sepulchre alone was to remain his inalienable property. Numerous inscriptions refer to this right,[2] give the boundaries of the piece of ground,[3] and the damages to be paid to the treasury by any one daring to usurp this immutable domain of the dead.[4] Others again add sundry imprecations against whoever shall venture to violate the rite

---

[1] Orelli, 4374, 4417, 4418, 4456, 4519, 4401, 4456; Petronius, *Satyricon*, lxxi.; De Rossi, *Bulletino*, 1863, p. 95; *Roma Sotteranea*, t. ii. 2ᵉ partie, p. 57. From these documents M. Allard has drawn a vivid picture of the Roman tombs (*Domaines funéraires païens et chrétiens*, Rouen, 1879).

[2] H. M. H. N. S. *Hoc monumentum hæredes non sequitur*, a formula found, with slight variations, in numberless inscriptions.

[3] Wilmanns, *Exempla Inscriptionum Latinarum*, t. ii. p. 692: MENSURÆ SEPULCRORUM.

[4] Jahn, *Spec. Epigr.* p. 28, No. 29; Orelli, 4427, 1175, 4431, etc.

of sepulture. " May he suffer the wrath of the gods! May he die the last of his kin."[1] But it was not enough to be respected in the tomb; the dweller therein longed to be visited too. For this reason the mortuary monuments were set up along the sides of the most frequented streets,[2] and the epitaph became a dialogue with the passer-by. " Young man, hurried as thou art, this stone still asks thee to observe and read what is written thereon : Here lie the bones of the Poet Marcus Pacuvius. Lo, this is what I wished thee to learn! Farewell!"[3] " My friends," says another inscription, " may the gods overwhelm you with good things. You, too, travellers, who do not pass by Fabianus without stopping, may the gods protect you going and coming; and all ye who bring me wreaths and flowers, would that you might do it for many years!"[4] The latter aspiration alludes to the feasts which many times a year brought a throng of visitors to the cemeteries. From the thirteenth to the twenty-second of February they celebrated the *Parentalia*,[5] — a series of sacrifices, terminating in a grand banquet on the last day; in March, they brought violets thither; in May, roses; in autumn, all the fruits of the season.[6] It was useless for the

---

[1] " Quisquis Manes inquietaberit, habebit illas iratas " (*Inscript. Neapol.* 3037). " Qui violaverit, sive immutaverit, deos sentiat iratos " (Henzen, 7340). " Quisquis hoc sustulerit aut læserit, ultimus suorum moriatur " (Orelli, 4790). Elsewhere, instead of threats, we come across a humble prayer : " Hospes, ad hunc tumulum ne meias, ossa precantur tecta homi- nis; sed si gratus homo es, misce, bibe, da mihi" (Orelli, 4781).

[2] "Titus Lollius Masculus lies here by the roadside, that so the passers- by may cry out, Hail Lollius " (Orelli, 4737). All the roads leading out of Rome, notably the Appian, Latin, and Flaminian Ways, were bordered with tombs after this fashion.

[3] Aulus Gellius, *Noctes Atticæ*, i. 24.

[4] *Bulletin de l'Institut Archéologique*, 1864, p. 154.

[5] Marquardt, *Römische Staatsverwaltung*, B. iii. S. 298 ff.; Guther, *De Jure Manium*, l. ii. cap. xii. p. 128.

[6] " Item xi. Kalendas Apriles die violari . . . præsentibus dividerentur sportulæ vinu et pane. . . . Item v. Idus Maias die rosæ . . ." (Wilmanns, *Exempla Inscriptionum*, No. 320). The *Dies Rosationis* is sometimes set down for May : "xii. Kalendas Junias " (Wilmanns, No. 313), sometimes in June : " v. K. Julias " (ibid., No. 95), and sometimes in July (ibid., No. 308). Cf. No. 305, note 1.

Stoics to treat this cult as superstitious, declaring that the grave is an unfathomable mystery.[1] Their words never had any effect on the people, who continued to crowd the funeral solemnities, believed in souls returning to earth,[2] multiplied their charms for driving away or calling forth spirits, good or bad,[3] — in a word, evidenced in every way possible their faith in a future life.

Though less enlightened than their predecessors as to God and Eternity, did not the Stoics have some new and higher ideas at least of human life, duty, justice, honesty? Certainly, morality owes more than one of its dogmas to them. They have discoursed eloquently thereon, and — what is more important — many of them united practice to precept. But neither does their virtue surpass that of the ancient Romans, nor is their doctrine any loftier than that of their masters in Greece.

Long before them,[4] Pythagoras had uttered the maxim proudly repeated by the disciples of the Porch, " Imitate God," " Follow God. "[5] Taking these words literally, it seems as if we heard an echo of our Holy Books. " Walk before Him, and be ye perfect. "[6] " Be ye therefore followers of God, as befits most dear children. "[7] But it is a deceptive likeness, this! The god of the Stoics is nought but Destiny. To follow him, to take him as one's exemplar, merely means to be resigned to the law of fatality which governs the world, to follow the inclinations of Nature, and to live in conformity with them.[8] Plato had conceived a far higher idea of this imitation

---

[1] Cicero, *Tusculanarum*, i. 24, 28 ; Seneca, *Epist.* xxiv. 18 ; Juvenal, ii. 149 ; Lucian, *Charon*, 22. The satirist contradicts himself in his treatise, *De Luctu*, 1–14.

[2] Preller, *Römische Mythologie*, S. 499 ; DIE LARVEN UND LEMUREN.

[3] Friedlænder, *Mœurs romaines*, t. iv. pp. 482–485. In every town there was a deep ditch, called the *mundus*, from which, it was believed, the dead came forth thrice a year to converse with the living.

[4] Boëthius (*De Consolatione*, i. 4) credits this maxim to Pythagoras ; Cicero, to one of the Seven Sages (*De Finibus*, 4).

[5] Seneca, *De Providentia*, v. *Epist.* xcv , cxxvi., etc.

[6] Gen. xvii. 1.   [7] Eph. v. 1.

[8] Seneca, *De Beneficiis*, iv. 7, 8 ; *De Ira*, ii. 16 ; *De Providentia*, 5, etc.

of the divine; for him it meant a contemplation of the Sovereign Good, thereby rising above the contaminations of the world, drawing nearer to God through holiness,[1] and love of Him; for the Platonists had risen even to this great thought.[2] Long before Epictetus, and more eloquently than he, they had preached this lovely code of morals. They called the body a burden, a prison; the present life a long agony, wherein the wise man, by breaking little by little the bondage of the flesh, learns at last how to die.[3] Before Seneca's time, they had proclaimed the dangers of wealth and pleasures,[4] and man's proneness to do wrong.[5] Like him, they taught the necessity of a guide, a director for one's conscience; better than he, they had shown that in the confession of his crimes man finds peace and health for his soul.[6] "To be punished after we have done wrong," writes Plato, "is the happiest of all things, after innocence itself. . . . If we commit any fault, we must go of ourselves to the place where we shall receive the allotted correction, and hasten to the judge as to a physician, for fear lest the malady of wrong-doing, gradually taking up its abode in the soul, should breed a secret corruption, and render it incurable."[7] Even the practice of examining their conscience, for which the sages of the Porch are so highly praised, is by no means a peculiar merit of theirs. Pythagoras, who recommended it to his disciples, received it from the Gymnosophists of India.[8]

The sole glory which the Stoics of the Empire can claim as their own is that they introduced among the upper classes, in that society of law-givers and lawmakers, and thereby into the laws themselves, certain maxims of humanity, of political and social equality,

[1] Plato, *Theætetus*, p. 133 (Cousin's translation).
[2] S. Augustine, *De Civitate Dei*, viii. 5 and 8.
[3] Clement of Alexandria, *Stromata*, iii. 3.
[4] Origen, *Contra Celsum*, vi. 16.
[5] Schneider, *Christliche Klänge*, S. 122 ff.
[6] Plutarch, *Quomodo quis suos in virtute sentiat profectus*, xi.; Seneca, *Epist.* xi., xxv. [7] Plato, *Gorgias*, xxxvi.
[8] Diogenes Laërtius, l. viii. cap. i. 22; Apuleius, *Florid.* i.

never dreamed of by either the Republicans of Rome or the Philosophers of Greece. And yet, here again, these ideas, as generous as they were fruitful of good results, did not originate with them. A conqueror, the peer of any that ever lived, Alexander, had been the first to conceive of an Empire, as vast as the world, where all men with equal rights should be bound together by a community of duties and interests. "He would not listen," says Plutarch, "to his preceptor, Aristotle, who counselled him to treat the Greeks as his friends and his family, but the Barbarians as cattle or vile tools. . . . Thinking rather that he was sent by the Divinity to be an arbiter for all mankind, to unite them together, he used the force of arms only against those whom he could not subdue by his words, and out of a hundred various nations he formed one great body, by mingling in the cup of friendship (so to say) their customs, manners, marriages, and laws. He wished to have every one regard the whole world as a common fatherland."[1]

Alexander died, and his generous visions seemed to have vanished with him. But at the very time when his star was eclipsed in the far-away Orient, Zeno of Cyprus was gathering his disciples beneath one of the porticos of Athens, and there founded a school which embodied the lost hopes of the conqueror in a philosophical system. By this philosophy they were taught that since the true law is reason whereof all mankind participates, this same supreme, universal law establishes the equality of all men, with a community of rights analogous to the ties of blood. By the same title, all are citizens, not of any particular town, but of the world, the general city. This fatherland of all human kind was never more than a splendid fancy among the Greeks; but under Augustus it became a reality, for the Rome of the Cæsars knew no limits save those of the known world:—

"Romanæ spatium est urbis et orbis idem."[2]

[1] Plutarch, *De Alexandri Fortuna aut Virtute*, or. i. 6.
[2] Ovid, *Fastorum*, l. ii. 684.

Thanks to the warlike character of their race, therefore, the Stoics of the Empire found the dream of their Grecian masters realized at last. The Universal City existed, and it was their task to refine its manners and make its laws more equitable and less savage. For this they deserve all honor, which no one can justly deny them. The weak and despised, so pitilessly crushed by previous legislation, were indebted to them for a measure of relief. Without destroying the puissant organization of the family, they recognized that the son and the wife had certain rights, and they even set themselves to work at mitigating the horrors of slavery. On this last head, their efforts merit the highest praise; for the servile code was simply atrocious. On losing his liberty, a man became a beast of burden for the one who bought him. As he was no longer a person, but a chattel, there could be neither justice nor magistrates for him. He could not contract marriage. As the creature of his master's whims, he found all ties of kinship broken, his family scattered to the winds by any hazard of fortune, while his little ones, like those of a brute beast, were the property of his owner. To his master belonged everything that the slave acquired, everything that he was, body and soul, even his honor, which his lord forced him to prostitute to his profit.[1]

From the outset of Augustus' reign, we find more humane influences entering into the councils of the Empire. The Petronian Law forbids any citizen to expose his slaves to the wild beasts of the amphitheatre.[2] Under Claudius, merciful measures are devised in the event of his becoming sick or incurable; should he be cast out into the street, according to the custom, by that very fact he regains his liberty. If his master kills him to get rid of him, the murderer is prosecuted.[3] "There is a judge," says Seneca, "to take cognizance of the injustice of their masters, to set bounds to their

[1] See Paul Allard's *Les Esclaves chrétiens*, liv. i. chap. iv. et v.
[2] *Dig.* xlviii. 8, 12, 12.
[3] Suetonius, *Claudius*, 25.

cruelty, their avarice, their brutality."[1] This judge is the Prefect of Rome. The victim appears before him, "not as accuser, for that is a privilege not to be allowed a slave, but to complain discreetly, if he has been too cruelly beaten, if he has been made to suffer the pangs of hunger, or if any attempt has been made upon his honor."[2] These are but trifling mitigations, doubtless, but in one way they are of capital importance, inasmuch as they are a departure from that hoary maxim, "The servile soul has no rights."[3] The claims of the slave upon humanity were recognized at last; later on he was granted some right to justice.

But this step in advance exhausted the generosity of the Stoics. No one of them dared to follow in his master's footsteps and prove, as Zeno had done,[4] that slavery is a violation of the natural law; for still stronger reasons, none ever thought of destroying an institution which was at the very base of the industry, the agriculture, and, in great measure, of the whole social life of Rome. They set limits to the rights of the slave-owner, but the laws of slavery were still in force. To abolish slavery something more was needed besides the bare idea of equality preached by the Stoics,— there must needs be a revelation that all men are sons of the one same Father, and members of the God-Man by holy baptism. With such claims to brotherhood, the dig-

[1] Seneca, *De Beneficiis*, iii. 22, 3.
[2] *Dig.* i. 12, 1. [3] Id. iv. 5, 3.
[4] The glory of putting forth these claims does indeed belong by right to the founder of the Porch. Before him the wise men of Greece had held that slaves might be endowed with honor and bravery, and they urged men to treat them kindly. But Zeno was the first to transform these vague sentiments into a positive doctrine, branding slavery for what it is, in the name of Reason: "There is a sort of slavery which has its rise in conquest," he says; "another which comes from purchase; for both there exist certain corresponding rights accruing to the master. Now, these rights are evils" (Diogenes Laërtius, vii. 1, No. 122). Neither Seneca nor any of his contemporaries ever wrote anything like this. We have to wait till the second century to hear any similar condemnation,— when the declaration rings forth from the orator's lips that the enslavement of the first human creature was "an act of violence, an unrighteous deed, valueless in the eyes of justice, and that from such iniquity no right can ensue" (Dion Chrysostom, *Disc.* xiv. et xv.).

nity of man is too high, the union too intimate, ever to be degraded to a state of servitude.

A charity so noble as this, divine in its source, was never to be found among the Stoics. We can easily convince ourselves of this by merely studying their essays in philanthropy. They, more than any other Pagans, have exalted mercy and brotherly love. Alms-giving, the care of the infirm and unfortunate, were favorite themes with them. " No sect," says Seneca, " is gentler or more kindly; none so filled with love for mankind, more watchful for the general welfare; since its principal object is to be useful and helpful to all, and to each one in particular."[1] How was it that such beautiful speeches brought forth no fruit? Why did not these sages of the great Empire,— rich men and statesmen, controlling legislation and the public treasury,— why was it that they did not create anything comparable to the works of Christianity? The reason lies in that very difference of first principles. The disciples of the Porch regarded philanthropy as a duty dictated by pure reason; the followers of Christ found the motive deep down in the human heart. Now, the heart of man is the sole source whence spring great thoughts and mighty sacrifices.

And for the rest, it must be said that no one realized the futility of their doctrines more keenly than the Stoics themselves. They did their best in preaching by personal example, and by upholding their virtue in death and exile; still, they saw that they were doomed to remain few in numbers, without either authority or influence. The populace, comprehending the whole philosophical tribe in a common contempt, encouraged every one who made sport of them. Perseus depicts a crowd gathered about an old centurion and applauding the veteran's witticisms. " Well, as for Philosophy, I've got all I want of it. I don't expect to become one of your moody Solons, always walking with head bowed down, eyes fixed on the ground, for-

---

[1] Seneca, *De Clementia*, ii. 5.

ever growling between my teeth and raging inwardly,—one of those fellows who always have their lips pursed out, and act as if they weighed every word they speak, forever chewing some old fool's rigmarole such as '*Nothing is born of nothing ! Nothing returns to nothingness !*' That's what makes you so pale, my man; that's what spoils your appetite."[1] Hearty laughter from the bystanders greeted this coarse caricature.

It is unnecessary to add that the average citizens hardly ever entered the portals of the Schools; they were only to be seen there on rainy days, seeking them as a fine shelter from the storm, or when the lack of any public shows drove them to such insipid distractions.[2] They saw no difference at all between the philosopher and the actor; and it is quite certain that many deserved this want of respect, because of their vices, their secret licentiousness, and their keen pursuit of gain.[3] In the higher classes it was easier to distinguish the hypocrites from the really wise men; but even the latter were often accused of being mere visionaries, wasting in day-dreams the time they owed to public business.[4] Still severer in their judgments were the politicians, who considered the Stoics as a dangerous sect, a hot-bed for ambitious and unruly men.[5] Tacitus himself, who records so many facts in praise of them, does not hesitate to call them chimerical thinkers. During a sedition in the army, he ascribes a ridiculous part to Musonius Rufus, one of the most illustrious of these philosophers.

"Mingling with the soldiers, he went about discoursing on the blessings of peace and the dangers of war, and recited his little lessons to these disciples in arms. He made some of them laugh, but he exhausted the patience of the majority; nor were there wanting some fellows who would have rushed upon him and trampled him under foot, had he not yielded to the advice of the more sensible and the threats of the rest, and discontinued his peace-making propaganda."[6]

[1] Perseus, *Satiræ*, iii. 77–87.   [2] Seneca, *Epist.* xcv.   [3] Id., xxix.
[4] Quintilian, xi. 1, 35; xii. 2, 6, 7; Tacitus, *Historiæ*, iv. 5.
[5] Tacitus, *Annales*, xiv. 57.   [6] Id., *Historiæ*, iii. 81.

The Stoic is drawn from life in this scene; here we see him just as the Roman Empire knew him,— a noble soul, smitten with the love of uprightness and universal brotherly love, eager to spread his ideas, but doomed to a fatal collision with the indifference of his contemporaries. How often this feeling of powerlessness betrays itself in the words of Seneca and Marcus Aurelius! What bitter complaints against our poor weak nature, and the tyranny of evil which enslaves mankind! The perfection whereof they dream is far out of reach of the common herd. They themselves are conscious of the contradictions in their doctrines,[1] of the slight help given the soul by pride and an outward show of virtue. As members of God, according to their theories, they feel themselves crushed by this lying divinity. The future life seems to them uncertain and misty, the present fills them with disgust. Dissatisfied with themselves and with others, despairing of any better state of humanity, most of them are given over to melancholy moods, and look for no peace save only in death. Marcus Aurelius longed for it, that he might no longer stay " amid this darkness and filth ; " and he recommended it as a remedy for men incapable of ever becoming wise. To the Stoic school, suicide was almost a moral precept, the deed and sign-manual of a great soul.[2]

Thus we see the end to which these beautiful speculations of the Stoics tended,— final despair. There we have the dark shadows cast by this Philosophy, which is so luminous from many points of view. We can see it now, not as modern writers too often lead us to fancy it, equally fruitful in good works with Christianity, but just as it has ever been regarded until our day,— nourishing virtue in the hearts of only a chosen few, sterile and ineffective so far as the people are concerned, and utterly incapable of regenerating the world.[3] To convince the

[1] Plutarch has written a whole treatise on these contradictions, *De Repugnantiis Stoicis.*
[2] Seneca, *Epist.* lviii. lxx. lxxvii.; *De Providentia*, vi.
[3] " It is a grave mistake to believe that Philosophy was capable of renewing the world, and that Christianity checked its onward course; every-

Stoics of their powerlessness, God was not content with merely giving them great lights, whereby they could discover remedies for the soul; He had even revealed to them that the one thing needful is to know how to apply them.[1] Accordingly, they exhausted themselves in this search, and we have seen how utterly vain their efforts were. "No one," Seneca confesses, "has strength enough to rise of himself, if no helping hand aids him."[2] This outstretched arm, with power to raise the fallen world, was already succoring Judea and the East. Rome, in its turn, guided by Peter, was to know this Helper from on High.

thing goes to show, on the contrary, that the philosophical movement came to an end in the second century; indeed, it is not likely that it could have produced any other results than those we are acquainted with; and if humanity was ever to be empowered to go further, it was necessary that it should receive a fresh impulse" (Boissier, *La Religion romaine*, t. ii. p. 110).

[1] "The soul's remedies have all been discovered long before our day; only it rests with us to seek how and when to employ them" (Seneca, *Epist.* lxiv. 8).

[2] Seneca, *Epist.* lii.

CHAPTER XVIII.

SAINT PETER'S MINISTRY IN ROME.

THE details of Saint Peter's ministry in Rome are almost entirely unknown. Accordingly, as it is not part of our plan to construct a story out of supposititious events, we shall simply note the circumstances surrounding it, see to what classes of society it was addressed, and finally what parts of the city have preserved any traces of the Apostle's sojourn. Out of these evidences, vague enough doubtless, but at any rate not imaginary, it will be possible to make at least a sketch of the scene which the subjects of the Emperor Claudius had before their eyes.

For the first few Sabbaths which Peter passed in Rome, he was to be seen taking part in the religious services of his nation, praying with his fellow-countrymen to the God of his fathers. There was nothing about the new-comer to attract special notice, neither high rank, nor great learning; consequently, he was not invited to speak in the synagogues, as was generally the custom with strangers of any renown. As his speech betrayed the fact that he was an illiterate Galilean,[1] he got no warm welcome from the head men of Israel. When, later on, Saint Paul came to visit the Jewish congregations of the Roman world, his standing as a Scribe, as well as his learning, opened the doors to any gathering he chose to address; but Saint Peter enjoyed no such advantages. He had to begin by winning souls one by one, telling the Glad Tidings during his conversations with friends, gaining over such as listened to

[1] Matt. xxvi. 73.

him, preaching rather by example than by eloquence, showing towards one and all "compassionate kindness, love for his brother man, a forbearing charity of mingled gentleness and humility."[1] This love of the neighbor, so often insisted upon by the Saviour, was the most striking feature of his preaching. He was listened to, because, while excluding no man from the hope of salvation, he promised it first and foremost to the common people,— to the very men whom the philosophers debarred as incapable of knowing the truth; still more, because he offered an unhoped-for consolation to the poor and suffering. Like all cities devoted to pleasure-seeking, Rome concealed great depths of sadness under her gay exterior. Nowhere else were shed so many tears, because nowhere was there ever so little pity for the unfortunate. Thus Saint Peter made his first conquests among the most wretched. As our warrant for asserting this fact, we have the contempt, which from the very outset was evinced towards the Roman Church by the philosophers. They would have us believe that it was nothing but a rabble of slaves, miserable laborers, and old women.[2] Their jeers are overstrained, undoubtedly, yet they testify that in the beginning by far the greater number of believers belonged to the lowest classes. The formation and the continuity of this current just setting in towards Christianity, have their rise in causes clearly traced and easily understood.

If ever any class of men was disposed by the very conditions of their existence to welcome the Good News, that class was the slaves of Rome. Deprived of all rights, defenceless, despoiled of all dignity, with no hope save in the quiet of the tomb, these men found in the Kingdom of the Christ everything which a cruel world denied them. Great must have been their joy on hearing that Truth set them free, and that the only bondage is that of sin. "Whosoever is vanquished," Peter told

[1] 1 Peter iii. 8.
[2] Tatian, *Adversus Græcos*, 33; Minucius Felix, *Octavius*, 16; Origen, *Contra Celsum*, 50.

them, " becometh the slave of him who hath vanquished him." [1] Who were more completely vanquished than their masters, enslaved by a multitude of evil passions? Seeing how heavy were the chains which bound them to earth, the bondsman felt his own grow lighter. The lash and the tortures seemed less grievous to him now that he knew that his soul could not be hurt by such indignities, and that suffering did but ennoble it. This was the lesson of Peter's teaching. " Servants, be subject to your masters with all manner of respect, not only to such as are good and gentle, but also to those who are harsh and unreasonable; for it is a great grace to endure, with the wish to please God, those sorrows which they make us suffer unjustly. What is there to glory in, if, being buffeted for evil-doing, you endure it? But if, doing well, you suffer and endure, this is thankworthy before God. To this you have been called, because the Christ also hath suffered for us, leaving an example that you should follow in His footsteps. . . . By His bruises and His wounds you have been healed." [2] And not only healed, but regenerated and re-instated in a dignity so lofty that never any slave could have dreamed of such a transformation. In Rome, the contrast was more striking because the servile law was so ferocious there. It was to these " despairing ones," [3] regarded as mere animals, treated as bodies bereft of souls, to whom Peter addressed those astounding words: " You are a chosen race, a royal priesthood, a holy nation, a people God hath made His own that you may declare the greatness of Him Who hath called you out of darkness into His marvellous light." [4]

It is easy to understand the surprise and emotion of these poor unfortunates, and the eagerness with which they thronged about the Apostle. And though Peter did not speak to them then in such sublime terms,— for these words were uttered in his later years,— still it was the self-same doctrine set forth in more familiar language,

[1] 2 Peter ii. 19.
[2] 1 Peter ii. 18-24.
[3] Pliny, *Historia Naturalis*, xviii. 7.
[4] 1 Peter ii. 9.

offering them the same promises, which were at once realized in fact; for as soon as a little knot of believers could form a Church in Rome, the slaves were allowed the same rights therein, the same privileges, and the same honors that were given to their masters. Made their equals by baptism, and their brethren in Jesus Christ, they took part together in the ceremonies of worship, listened with them to the preaching of the Word, and were present together at the Holy Mysteries. In the most august of all, the Eucharist, the one same Bread of Life brought freemen and slaves together about a common table. The feeling of charity which swayed all hearts at these sacred banquets was so sweet to their souls that the name "Love, Agapë,"[1] was given them, and the respectful embrace which marked its close is spoken of in Saint Peter's letters[2] as "the kiss of love."

The slave took part in all these rites; he whom Pagan Rome adjudged unworthy of any religion, thrusting him away from the altars where his master sacrificed,[3] this outcast saw with wonder that he was admitted to the sacredest rites of the Christians' worship. His gratitude responded instantly to such kindnesses; and the feeling was lasting, because he found within the Church, besides this religious equality, a company of brethren who did not ignore him after the Holy Sacrifice was ended, but comforted him whenever the yoke of his taskmaster pressed heavily upon him, tendering him a helping hand till the day when freedom or death released his toil-worn spirit. But, in truth, the liberty so dearly desired by the servile class did not mean immediate rescue from their miserable condition. The freedman came forth from slavery penniless, without credit or influence, and accordingly his first steps in his new surroundings were beset with difficulties. The

---

[1] Kraus, *Real Encyclopädie der christlichen Alterthümer:* AGAPEN.
[2] Ἀσπάσασθε ἀλλήλους ἐν φιλήματι ἀγάπης (1 Peter v. 14).
[3] Cato *De Re Rustica*, 143; Minucius Felix, *Octavius*, 24; Cicero, *Oratio de Haruspicum Responsis*, 11, 12. "Slaves have no religion at all, or none save that of foreigners" (Tacitus, *Annales*, xiv. 44).

Church was the only organization to lend him a helping hand, at this juncture. Many came to the fold, accordingly, with the certainty of finding there a haven of rest, protection from the stormy times in which they lived, and, most of all, assurance of eternal good things to be gained from their society.

The same causes which attracted the slaves and freedmen to Christianity, operated quite as powerfully with the common people, the servants and shopkeepers. This poor but active class of citizens was making every effort to keep themselves alive as a body distinct from the slave population, which had wellnigh monopolized every sort of industry.[1] To these busy folks some sort of union and mutual aid were an urgent necessity; and yet what means were to be adopted at an epoch when their rulers and statesmen were devising every means of suppressing such associations?[2] In the small number of societies spared by Augustus there was not room enough for the multitude of free workmen.[3] Their only expedient was to become affiliated with some one of the foreign *Colleges,*— that of the Jews being particularly popular, because it enjoyed such notable privileges. For this reason a considerable number of the poorer class, urged on by poverty and loneliness, sought a refuge in the Synagogue, and found there some alleviation of their miseries. But we know how very suspicious the Rabbis were of Pagan proselytes;[4] they always doubted the

---

[1] For an account of the development of private industry in the first century and the multitude of professions in vogue then, see Friedlænder, *Mœurs romaines au temps d'Auguste,* t. iii.: *Supplément,* pp. 64-72.

[2] The senatus-consultus and imperial decrees, which are so sweeping in their proscriptions of illegal "Colleges," ordained very terrible punishments against them; for the guilty members, who were likened to the desecrators of temples, might be thrown to the wild beasts, beheaded, or burned alive. *Dig.* xlvii. 22, 2.

[3] The Corporations, founded in such numbers under the Republic, had become, in Cæsar's time, hotbeds of sedition, and almost all were suppressed by the Dictator. When renewing this proscription, Augustus tolerated only such "colleges" as were authorized by a senatus-consultus. Dion, xxviii. 13; Suetonius, *Cæsar,* 42; *Octavius,* 32; Josephus, *Antiquitates,* xiv. 10, 8; *Digest,* xlviii. 4, 1.

[4] See pp. 58, 59.

sincerity of their professions, and never opened their doors to one without misgivings and fear. To the poorer classes they showed themselves more than usually frigid and distant, for, anxious as they were to reserve all almsgifts for their needy brethren, they were loath to succor men who were neither of their blood nor faith. Furthermore, their dread of offending the Roman politicians by adding to their numbers, compelled the Jews to limit their activity to the "ghettos." Accordingly, when the rumor went abroad that new Synagogues were being founded wherein a more generous charity obtained, the poorer people hastened to join them; and, indeed, these were, as they soon discovered, their own possessions, now thrown open to receive them,—the Kingdom promised to the persecuted, to them who suffer and weep.

In every meeting-place of their confraternities, as well as in the small shopkeepers' quarters, the crowds of bystanders offered Peter frequent opportunities of conversing with strangers and communicating the Glad Tidings. He met with all the warmer welcome because he had but recently come from Judea. We have seen how the Israelites gathered together in certain parts of the Capital. Soon a little populace of Easterners grew up about them,— Syrians, Egyptians, and natives of far-off Asia. Some had been brought to Rome as captives, and managed to win their freedom later on; others had come of their own choice, wishing to enjoy the attractions of this Babylon of the West. Among these people of the same race, many traditions and longings were common to all, but one above all others filled their hearts with tremendous expectations. "Throughout the whole East," says Suetonius, "there was a long cherished and firm belief that about this date the empire of the world would devolve upon a man born in Judea."[1] Peter came from that land, and he proclaimed the advent of a Saviour. There was therefore a double reason why his preaching should be favorably received.

[1] Suetonius, *Vespasianus*, iv.; Tacitus, *Historiæ*, v. 13.

Howbeit these poor foreigners were not the only ones willing to give him a hearing; for the oracles of their Sibyls and the soothsayers of Chaldea had awakened similar longings among the Pagans of the West. More than one Roman listened with all his soul for the first tidings of salvation. Their women-folk cherished this feeling still deeper down in their heart of hearts. Involved as much as the men in the universal corruption, but more apt than they to feel shame for their sins, they longed to wash away the guilty stains. And so for many a long day their eyes had searched the Eastern horizon for some presages of Redemption. The worship of the Egyptian Isis was the first to promise them entire purification, and they had hastened to embrace the opportunities it held forth. No ablution, no penitential rite seemed too severe. Juvenal tells us how they were wont to break the ice in order to plunge thrice every morning in the Tiber, thereafter dragging themselves across the Field of Mars on their trembling knees all stained with blood. "If the white Io so ordains, she will travel to the very ends of Egypt; she will bring back with her water drawn from the neighborhood of Meroë, and therewith sprinkle the temple of Isis, which stands hard by the ancient sheepfold of Romulus."[1] In these bands of penitents were numbered women of all ranks, ladies of high social standing, as well as the freedwomen who led immoral lives. Tibullus depicts his Delia as a scrupulous observer of the rites of Isis. She performs the prescribed ablutions, attires herself in linen, and shakes the cithern while she prays.[2] But even more numerous than these followers of Isis, as we have seen,[3] were the proselytes of the Jewish religion; for the Mosaical system had one great attraction for them in that it treated women with such respect.

Such being the dispositions of a great number of Pagan women, it is easy for us to understand the motives which prompted so many eagerly to throng the

[1] Juvenal, vi 511   [2] Tibullus, i. 3, 23–32.
[3] Chapter xiv p. 260.

early Church, despite the mockery and remonstrances of the philosophers. They listened to the Christians' Message as soon as it reached their ears, simply because it actually gave them what Egypt and Judea had promised in vain, while it added new and unhoped-for good things. Not content with recognizing woman as the companion of man,[1] the new Faith made her his equal. On the one hand it declared that marriage is a holy act, and, on the other, it exalted maidenhood and virginity, yet with a never-failing compassion for the sin-stained, suffering soul. "Many sins are forgiven her because she hath loved much."[2] The woman hearkening to those words knew that there could be no mistake,— she recognized the voice of her Saviour and believed in Him.

The first Christians of Rome belonged for the most part to the lower classes. Nevertheless, it was not long before certain patrician ladies joined company with them. A short time after Peter's arrival there, a matron of the highest rank, Pomponia Græcina by name, suddenly quitted the world of fashion and pleasure, and, clothing herself in sad-colored garments, withdrew into the seclusion of her palace. It was just about the year 43 that she began to lead this sort of life. Julia, the daughter of Drusus, had been put to death recently, the victim of certain intrigues of Messalina.[3] At first it was supposed that Pomponia was in mourning for her friend; but years passed, and brought about no change in her conduct. Still she abstained from worldly pleasures, still she wore the same severely simple costume. "She lived a long time," says Tacitus, "and always in this sad state; . . . for forty years she never wore any but mourning robes." Such a singular sort of existence finally excited suspicion. Pomponia was accused of being addicted to foreign superstitions, and brought before her husband to be tried. The latter was the Consul

---

[1] Gen. ii. 18.   [2] Luke vii. 47.
[3] Dion Cassius, lx. 18; Tacitus, *Annales*, xiii. 32, 43; xiv. 63; Suetonius, *Claudius*, 29.

Plautius, one of the conquerors of Brittany. The case was investigated at a family council, according to ancient usage, and he formally declared his wife innocent. Thereafter no one could criticise her for the austerity of her life, and her constancy " turned to her glory. "[1] What was this new life? What worship was concealed under this penitential garb? And what was Pomponia Græcina? The answer is that, according to all appearances, she was a servant of the Lord Christ. It is true Tacitus does not say so distinctly; but all he recounts of her gives us the idea of a Christian rather than a Jewish proselyte, and the expression, " foreign superstitions," generally used to designate our Faith, supports this supposition. Recent discoveries have brought to light further proofs in confirmation, by establishing the fact that one of the first Christian cemeteries, the Crypt of Lucina, was the property of Pomponia Græcina.[2] That in the year 43, thirteen years after the Saviour's death, a woman belonging to the Roman aristocracy should have been numbered among the faithful,

[1] Tacitus, *Annales*, xiii. 32.
[2] This conclusion is the fruit of observations quite as ingenious as they are delicate. The first token which wakened Sig. de Rossi's attention was a discovery, in the Crypt of Lucina, of certain Pagan epitaphs containing the names of the *Pomponii Attici* and *Bassi*. These sepulchral tablets, having fallen into the subterranean galleries owing to the working of the soil over where they stood, had furnished the material for several Christian tombs. The learned archæologist was struck with the coincidence, suggesting, as it did, the idea that the unknown person to whom this land once belonged might really be none other than the *Pomponia Græcina* spoken of by Tacitus. According to a common custom, she might have assumed the title of Lucina (The Enlightened), in memory of her spiritual illumination by baptism (De Rossi, *Roma Sotterranea*, t. i. p. 319). In 1864 this was simply hazarded as a conjecture, since it had no more positive proof to support it than the presence in this crypt of some Pagan inscriptions belonging to the *Gens Pomponia*. Three years later the hypothesis became almost a certainty, for in the same spot De Rossi deciphered a Christian epitaph bearing the name of a certain *Pomponius Græcinus*. It would be wellnigh impossible to deny that this man must have been a descendant of Pomponia, like her won over to the Faith; and consequently nothing could be more natural than the supposition that this matron was the Christian lady who bequeathed her own mystical title of Lucina to the burial-grounds of her ancestors (De Rossi, *Roma Sotterranea*, t. ii. pp. 282, 263; Allard, *Rome souterraine*, pp. 164-168; Northcote and Brownlow, *Roma Sotterranea* (1879), vol. i. pp. 81, 82, 277-281).

is a fact all the more noteworthy because the upper classes, the statesmen and men of letters, evinced nothing but contempt for the Faith in Christ until a very much later date.

We possess no other evidence of personages of illustrious or noble rank having belonged to the number of the first Christians of Rome. All that the pious credulity of the following ages could do was to seize at the name of Pudens,[1] in one of Saint Paul's epistles, and connect it with that of the Consul spoken of by Martial in many of his epigrams.[2] Little by little the popular stories grew into the primitive legend, as we read it. In the sixth century it was asserted that Peter, after converting the Senator Pudens, lodged in his house, and there assembled his faithful flock for the celebration of the Holy Mysteries.[3] The dwelling of this patrician, situated on the Viminal, thus became the first sanctuary at Rome. This tradition, of which there is no trace in the first centuries of the Church, cannot be considered as having sufficient authority to warrant us in accepting it. The only fact related which has any semblance of likelihood is that Peter, during his first sojourn in the city, lived in the region of the Viminal. Vague as this conclusion may seem, it is worthy of respectful consideration, and, indeed, when taken in connection with other proofs collected by modern archæologists, it will even enable us to point out the several parts of Rome where the Apostle dwelt, and consequently help us to follow the course of his labors.

During the first days after his arrival, Peter took lodgings in one of the little by-streets in which the Jews of Trastevere and Porta Capena were crowded together. There he must have received a warm welcome from the few brethren of his own faith, for the name of Jesus had preceded the Gospel in the Capital of the

---

[1] 2 Tim. iv. 21.
[2] Martial, i. 32; iv. 29; v. 48; vi. 58; vii. 11, 97; viii. 60; xi. 53.
[3] *Martyrologium Romanum, Baronii notationibus illustratum*, 16 maii; Fiorentini, *Vestustius Occidentalis Ecclesiæ Martyrologium*, p. 697.

world. Among the strangers present in Jerusalem at the time of the descent of the Holy Ghost, and who received baptism, the Acts mention certain citizens of Rome.[1] On their return, these converts could not possibly either forget, or fail to speak of, all that they had heard; and every year their testimony was confirmed by the pilgrims who went up to celebrate the Passover. Doubtless, the leading men and the doctors bestowed little attention upon a doctrine which did not emanate from any illustrious scribe; but among the lower classes there was much talk of the Christ and His Kingdom. Accordingly, the Apostle chose this poorer quarter for the field of his first ministry, remaining among them until the Synagogue took alarm and compelled him to exercise his zeal elsewhere.[2]

The violence displayed by a number of the Jews in rejecting the faith is witnessed to by Saint Paul in his letter to the Church of Rome. "Because of their unbelief," he says, "the natural branches were broken off from the wild olive."[3] The figure used by the Apostle infers that there had been a dissension in the Roman colony. Though peaceable and charitable to one another in the ordinary course of life, yet when they felt their faith was in danger, the sons of Israel displayed a terrible fanaticism; passions burned high; from disputes they speedily came to loud outcries and bloody strifes. From all that we know, it appears that his abode in the Jewish quarter soon became unsafe for Peter, who was marked out as the head of the schismatics. Accordingly, he became the leader of an exodus whereof certain local traditions remain, making it possible to follow its course step by step.

The first locality where he made his abode is now marked on the Aventine by the church of Saint Prisca. In the fifteenth century the following inscription still stood over the door of this sanctuary: "Here stands the house of Aquila and Prisca, the charitable virgin.

[1] Acts ii. 10.   [2] Rom. xi. 1–18.
[3] Rom xi. 20: Τῇ ἀπιστίᾳ ἐξεκλάσθησαν.

... Here, Peter, thou didst give the Word Divine to be their food; many a time and oft thou didst sacrifice unto the Lord on this very spot."[1]

Living on the Aventine[2] these two faithful followers were separated by a considerable distance from the quarters peopled by Israelites. Their dwelling was a hospitable one, their hearts so filled with generosity that they gladly endangered their property and their lives to serve those they loved.[3] They were worthy of offering an asylum to Peter when he quitted his fellow-countrymen to carry the Gospel through the length and breadth of Pagan Rome.[4]

If the church of Saint Prisca on the Aventine marks the first step taken by Peter outside the limits of the Roman "ghettos," that of Saint Pudentia on the Viminal records his second resting-place. Continuing to move still farther from the lower quarters, the Apostle found his way into regions inhabited by the patricians;

[1] Hæc domus est Aquilæ, seu Priscæ, virginis almæ,
Quos . . ., Paule, tuo ore vehis Domino.
Hic Petre divini tribuebas fercula verbi,
Sæpius hocce loco sacrificans Domino.
De Rossi, *Bullettino*, 1867, May and June: S. PETER'S CHAIR, § vi.

[2] We know Aquila and Prisca (or Priscilla) from the Acts (xviii. 2, 25, 26) and S. Paul's Epistles (Rom. xvi. 3, 4; 2 Tim. iv. 19). After being driven from Rome by the edict of Claudius, which expelled both Jews and Christians, they returned together and maintained a church in their dwelling, which, in the Middle Ages, bore the name of Aquila and Prisca, and after the fourth century was generally designated under this abridged form, — "Title of Saint Prisca."

[3] 1 Rom. xvi. 3, 4.

[4] Through their intervention, apparently, the Apostle was introduced into the noble family of Pudens. In fact, the apocryphal, but very ancient, letters of Pastor and Timotheus tell us that Pudens had a kinswoman named Priscilla, the same who gave her name to the catacombs in the Via Salaria where the bodies of Pudens and his two daughters Pudentia and Praxedes have been discovered. This hypogeum also contains sepulchres bearing the names of Aquila and Prisca. De Rossi identifies these two personages with the Saints whose house is venerated on the Aventine, and the antiquity of the Catacomb of Priscilla makes this identification very plausible. But how was it that two Jews came to be interred in a burial-place belonging to members of the Roman nobility? Very likely, as the freedmen of Pudens. Slaves often took the names of the masters who restored them their liberty; thus Prisca the Jewess might have taken that of the matron Priscilla, and obtained a burial-place for herself and her family in the Christian cemetery owned by her patrons. De Rossi, *Bullettino*, 1867, May and June: S. PETER'S CHAIR, § vi.

for Pudens' residence stood in a very aristocratic centre, the so-called " Vicus Patricius. " That Peter did really make his home the foremost sanctuary at Rome, is, as we have said, an opinion for which there is slender evidence. However, the traditions which tell of the Apostle's doings in this part of the town show that at least he dwelt thereabouts, and that he even succeeded, through the medium of Jewish freedmen, in introducing Christianity into several noble families, notably that of Pudens.[1]

The last trace left us of Peter's first stay at Rome during the reign of Claudius is the ancient catacomb called the Ostrian Cemetery, lying between the Via Salaria and the Via Nomentana. The names given to this necropolis in the inscriptions and martyrologies afford some glimpses into the ministry of the Apostle thereabouts. Not only do they designate it as " the Great Cemetery," the oldest of all, and the one where they venerated " the first Chair occupied by Peter," but they often call it " the Cemetery of the waters wherein Peter baptized." [2] Evidently the throngs of catechumens were become so numerous that after a few years the Apostle was obliged to go outside of Rome, in search

---

[1] Apparently it was the memory of their intimate relations which gave rise to the belief that the throne of Peter preserved at the Vatican was a gift from this patrician. At first sight, the exterior of the precious relic seems to justify this belief. In fact, as it has been remarked elsewhere, the ivories which cover it are similar to those that adorned curule chairs; the carver's work is not unworthy of the artists contemporaneous with the first Cæsars; furthermore, the use of chairs carried by bearers was introduced during Claudius' reign, and the Vatican Chair is constructed precisely after this fashion. These indications, collected by Cardinal Wiseman, seemed at first to warrant the opinion that S. Peter received his pontifical throne from Pudens. But these illusions vanished the moment that De Rossi, on examining the monument more closely, announced the existence of a primitive chair still visible beneath the ivory and ornaments added by later ages. The real Episcopal Seat was but a poor chair of common wood: to regard it as the curule chair of a great personage of Rome was no longer possible. De Rossi, *Bullettino*, 1867, for May and June; S. PETER'S CHAIR, § iii., iv. et v.

[2] De Rossi, *Roma sotterranea*, i. p. 207; *Bullettino*, 1867, *maggio e giugno*, *Del luogo appellato ad Capream presso la via Nomentana*, Roma, 1884, pp. 7-10.

of pools larger than those he had been using at first within the city limits. These he found near the home of Pudens and the existing basilica of Saint Agnes. There some rich Pagan, a convert to the Faith of Christ, owned one of those family tombs so common then,— a vast enclosure, including gardens and parks. The domain sloped down to a low basin, formerly the bottom of a marsh which had been drained, but still collected sufficient rain-water for the immersion of the neophytes. In the sixth century, the watercourses and the little ponds[1] were still to be seen, to which the people gave the name of the " Goat's Marsh," " *ad Capream.*"[2]

But it was not only the convenient neighborhood of these waters which attracted the Apostle to the Ostrian Cemetery; for no other part of the town could have offered equal security to the new Faith. There Peter resided at the very gates of the Pretorian Camp, far from the Jews, whose menaces were no longer to be

---

[1] This fact is attested by the author of the *Gesta Liberii*, an apocryphal work of the sixth century. Constant, *Epist. Rom. Pontif.*, p. lxxxvi. App. col. 87 et seq. De Rossi, *Del luogo appellato ad Capream*, p. 12.

[2] " In via Nomentana ad Caprea in cœmeterio majore, natalis sancti Emerentiani." *Martyrologium Hieronymianum*, xvi. kal. Octobris; Fiorentini (*Martyr. Vetust. Occid.* pp. 836, 837) is at fault in adopting the reading *ad Capua;* all the manuscripts consulted by De Rossi have *ad Caprea* or *ad Capria.* The locality known by this name is renowned in Latin literature. " It is a locality," says Ovid, "which men of old used to call the Goat Marsh. One day, as Romulus was giving forth laws to his people, the sun of a sudden disappeared, and fast-flying clouds veiled the heavens; rain fell in torrents, thunders crashed, lightnings rent the air, and all men fled; nevertheless, Romulus ascended into the heavens, borne by the chariot of his father" (*Fastorum*, ii. 409 et seq.). Where are we to locate this celebrated marsh? Livy seems to place it in the Field of Mars: " Quum . . . concionem in *campo* ad capræ paludem haberet." (*Historiæ*, i. 16); but a contemporary of Augustus, Verrius Flaccus, speaks more precisely of the fields which surround it: " Cupruli (Capralis) appellatur *ager*, qui vulgo ad capræ paludes dici solet." (Festus, ed. Müller, p. 65. This author is merely giving an abridgment of Flaccus' work). Hence this spot is to be looked for outside the city; and as it is hardly likely that Rome should have had two so-called Goat Marshes, we need not hesitate about identifying this one, renowned as Romulus' death-place, as the same marshy cemetery of that name pointed out by the martyrologies and Christian inscriptions near the Via Nomentana. On the spot where the founder of Pagan Rome disappeared, Peter brought to life a new and Christian Rome.

feared. These advantages first forced him to seek out this city of the dead and finally kept him there, " where he baptized." As proof of this we have the Apostolic Chair placed on this spot, and there visited and venerated by all antiquity.

Thus, of the Apostle's first stay at Rome, we have only discovered these few, half-effaced vestiges. The doings of his ministry are still more vaguely recorded, for one single tradition is all that has come down to us,— that of the strife between Peter and Simon the Magician. The impostor, terrified, but not converted, by the disciples of the Lord,[1] fled from Judea to Rome.[2] In that city he again performed his marvellous feats with such success that he was regarded as a divine personage, and had a statue made of himself, which was adored by his disciples.[3] "The arrival of Peter," says Eusebius, " sufficed to ruin his great renown."[4]

This fact we believe to be historical, but the legends have added to it various circumstances which have little appearance of likelihood. This among others,— that the Samaritan was lifted high in air in the presence of Nero and his whole court; but at the Apostle's prayer he was abandoned to the mercy of the devils who were supporting him, and falling to the earth, was dashed to pieces. The prodigies with which this story is filled are too suspicious to warrant us in accepting it; but if Simon's defeat was not accompanied by such wonders, it was none the less sudden and complete. Eusebius gives us a very fair notion of what happened. The excitement caused by the impostor suddenly died out. His power was paralyzed, and he relapsed into the obscurity to which so many religious and philosophical sects have been doomed. To bring about this reverse of popularity, Peter had no need of appealing to a crucial trial before the Emperor and the assembled people. The grace of Jesus was on his side, and the devils,

[1] Acts viii. 18-24.
[2] See chapter v.
[3] See Appendix V.
[4] Eusebius, *Historia Ecclesiastica*, ii. 15.

fearing him as much as they did his Master, fled before him here in Rome as formerly in Galilee; with them vanished the last hope of their wicked agent. But it was through humility that Peter won his triumphs; obscure and alone, he began his preaching and the foundation of the Church of Rome.

CHAPTER XIX.

THE LEGAL STATUS OF THE CHRISTIANS.

WE have been watching the birth of the Church in Rome, poor as it was obscure in its origin, but, thanks to this same lowly estate, at first escaping the notice of the masters of the Empire. Yet we must not suppose that they feared these rulers, nor that, after the manner of some of our secret societies, they sought safety by enveloping their doings in mystery. On the contrary, until Nero's reign, the Church was free to grow and expand openly, by virtue of that tolerant spirit in which Rome treated all kinds of worship; and I know no better way of showing its liberality than by calling to mind the series of events which illustrate their conduct towards religious bodies.

"Our fathers," Sallust declares, "were the most religious of mankind."[1] The Romans still deserved this high encomium, not only because their faith continued strong, but also on account of their respect for everything religious. They had conquered the world without ever violating the divinities of the vanquished. The first care of their generals when besieging a city was to invoke its tutelary gods in a prayer remarkable for its reverent feeling.

"I pray and beseech thee, I ask of thee this favor, O thou great god who hast taken this town under thy protection, do thou desert these houses, temples, and sacred places, depart far from them; inspire this people and this city with fear, terror, and obliviousness. Abandon it, and come to Rome

[1] "Majores nostri religiosissimi mortales" (Sallust, *Catilina*, 12).

to dwell with me and mine. . . . If thou hearest my prayer, I pledge an oath that I will raise altars to thee, and celebrate games in thine honor."[1]

Nor were these vain promises. At the sacking of Veii the temples were, as usual, left untouched, while young men, chosen with care from the whole army, diligently purified themselves; then, robed in white, entered as suppliants into the sanctuary of the goddess.

"Juno," they cried, "wilt thou go to Rome?"

A shout from the spectators was their answer. They had seen the statue bow its head in token of assent. She was brought to the Aventine, where Camillus forthwith consecrated the edifice promised to her before the siege.[2] Instead of transferring the divinity after this fashion, they sometimes left a certain number of families in the depopulated towns, in order to do honor to its gods; but this measure was very rarely necessary.

Ordinarily, Rome tried to assimilate her conquests with her own body politic, and with this idea she wisely refrained from any innovations. Accordingly, so far from seeking to impose her own beliefs upon the beaten, she treated those of the vanquished with the greatest respect, often going so far as to adopt them. In Gaul, Apollo and Sirona,[3] Rosmerta and Mercury,[4] were venerated on the same altars. When the religious systems were too different to admit of such a confusion of rites and homage, the Romans took part in the religious ceremonies of the countries where they chanced to be. In Greece they asked to be initiated into the mysteries of Eleusis,[5] in Asia into those of Samothrace. On the banks of the Nile they pledged their vows to the divinities of Egypt.[6] The more credulous went, like Apuleius,

---

[1] Macrobius, *Saturnaliorum*, lib. iii. cap. ix. Macrobius had read these formulas in a treatise on *Rerum Conditarum*, by Sammonicus Serenus, who asserted that he had copied them from a very ancient work written by a certain Furius.

[2] Livy, *Historiæ*, v. 22.   [3] Orelli, 2407.
[4] Id., 5909.   [5] Lobeck, *Aglaoph.* p. 37.
[6] Friedländer, *Mœurs romaines*, t. ii. p. 447, and the Supplement to Book Second in vol. iv. p. 50; Letronne, *Inscript. de l'Égypte*, t. i. p. 241.

from sanctuary to sanctuary in order not to neglect any source of favor and protection.[1]

Nor was it only in the provinces that Rome displayed this tolerant spirit. Within her own walls she allowed even to the most singular sects a liberty which was almost unrestricted. All foreigners attracted thither were given full permission to bring their gods with them, and to honor them after their own fashion. Consequently, they soon had temples of their own, with befitting ceremonies, which, begun inside the sanctuary, presently appeared outside the edifice. Long processions were to be seen filing along the streets. Here the devotees of Isis, clad in fine linen, with shaven heads, bearing her statues aloft in solemn state;[2] elsewhere, the priests of Cybele and Bellona went through their bloody scourgings in the presence of a curious but respectful public.[3]

Such scenes as these stirred the souls of a people eager for evidences of real piety, and they abandoned the cold practices of their national worship, turning with hope to these devotions of the Orient. Particularly in the more populous quarters the crowds of worshippers increased daily, and threatened the very existence of the gods of Rome. A serious danger this; but moved more by religious scruples than by prudence, the politicians avoided using any vigorous measures against it. Leaving unnoticed the ancient edict which forbade the consecration of any divinity without the approbation of the Senate,[4] they were content with merely conferring upon a college of priests, called the Quindecemvirs, the right to supervise foreign forms of worship and nominate their ministers.[5] By this means they established some authority over them, while in many cases they made them adopt the Roman rubric. The formularies for public prayers, their ceremonies, and their demon-

[1] Apuleius, *Florida*, i. 1.
[2] Marquardt, *Römische Staatsverwaltung*, B. i. S. 79, 80.
[3] Id., S. 74, 334, 353–358. [4] Tertullian, *Apolog.* v.
[5] Marquardt, *Römische Staatsverwaltung*, B. iii. S. 368, 381; *Inscript. Reg. Neapol.* 2558.

strations of joy or sorrow were regulated beforehand and watchfully ordered in the execution.[1]

But these precautions were not always sufficient to prevent abuses; and however much the Romans might shrink from striking a blow at anything religious, it often became necessary under the Republic to display great severity. One hundred and eighty-seven years before our era, the Consul Postumius denounced the *Bacchanalia*, imported from Greece, branding it as such a farrago of crimes and obscenities that the Senate felt moved to order the arrest of all persons compromised by these guilty rites.[2] Seven thousand were apprehended, and, as always in Rome, justice was executed after a pitiless fashion. Half of the male offenders fell under the axe, while the women, after being tried by their kinsfolk, were put to death within their own houses. Despite the vigorous spirit displayed by the Senate in this occurrence, usually it was as timorous about using force as before. Instead of a rigorous interdiction, the laws merely forbade the celebration of the feasts of Bacchus by more than five persons, and without the authorization of the Prætor. Indeed, while exhorting the Conscript Fathers to act with all sternness, Postumius had justified their moderation in advance. "Even at such times," he said, "when religion serves as a cloak for crime, we greatly dread lest in punishing the guilty we should ourselves commit some impiety."[3]

Such scruples were still more manifest in the measures taken against the worship of Isis. The Egyptian

---

[1] Orelli, 2314, 2315; Cicero, *De Legibus*, ii. 15.

[2] After being initiated into these Mysteries before reaching their twentieth year, the members held the dogma that there is no line of demarcation between good and evil in men's actions; consequently any crime is lawful. In their meetings, which took place five times a month, they indulged among themselves in the most monstrous excesses. "From this unclean sink," says Livy, "issued forth false witnesses, forged signatures, counterfeit wills, calumnious attacks, murder, and poisoning. Such as refused to undergo initiation, or rather, recoiled from its infamy, were precipitated by an apparatus into gloomy caverns. Savage howls, with the uproar of drums and cymbals, smothered the cries of the victims who were either slaughtered or dishonored" (Livy, xxxix. 8, 18).

[3] Livy, xxxix. 16.

priests were emboldened to erect a statue of this divinity in the Capitol, the very abode of Jupiter. A decree of the Senate ordered them to be driven away; but we shall see what was the result of this resolution. In the year 58 before Christ, the Consuls Piso and Gabinius enforced this senatus-consultus for the first time.[1] Again in 53, Calvinius and Messala were obliged to institute a similar course of proceedings.[2] Yet three years later the sanctuary of Isis was still standing, and as no workman could be found willing to violate it, the Consul Emilius had to take the axe into his own hands, and with it break in the doors.[3]

This stubborn superstition of the populace was as favorable as was the hesitancy of the patricians to the maintenance of foreign rites in perfect liberty. In the disorderly scenes of the Republic's last hours, this tolerance went to such lengths that the Triumvirs themselves, in their eagerness for popularity, dedicated an altar to Isis and Serapis.[4] This was so scandalous an act of complaisance that Augustus hastened to repudiate any responsibility for it, by returning to the traditions of the olden days of Rome. With all respect for the religions of the various peoples who made up his Empire, he countenanced and even favored them so long as they remained within their own territories; but in Rome he treated them with suspicion, keeping watch on their actions, and interdicting any out-of-door ceremonies, while on one occasion he went so far as to destroy several temples.[5] Tiberius and Claudius followed the same policy. Thus, then, under the first of the Cæsars, legislation on religious affairs was notable for two features,— perfect freedom granted the provinces to practise their peculiar cults; at Rome, a similar liberty accorded to foreigners, provided that they caused no disturbances and did not endeavor to

[1] Tertullian, *Apolog.* vi.; *Ad Nation.* i. 10; Arnobius, ii. 73.
[2] Pauly, *Real Encyclopädie;* Isis, t. iv. p. 290.
[3] Valerius Maximus, i. 3, 3. [4] Dion Cassius, xl. 47.
[5] Suetonius, *Augustus*, 93; Dion Cassius, liv. 6.

make proselytes. The minds of the politicians were pre-occupied by the desire of keeping order rather than of defending the ancient gods. What they feared most of all was " lest the introduction of new divinities should give rise to secret meetings, with their passwords and conspiracies,— dangerous things for the one-man power."[1] Accordingly, every time that the Emperors attacked a system of worship, the end in view was not so much to harry the religion itself, as it was to prevent the assembling of men, to which it offered dangerous facilities. They did not demand that the members should abjure their faith, but simply forbade them to meet together to profess it; and in case of obstinate resistance they were content with banishing the offenders.

But so far as these associations were concerned, the magistrates were already armed with legal weapons, notably the Senate's decree against the Bacchanals, whose main features were as follows: A clause obliging them to obtain a license from the city Prætor and the Senate; another limiting the membership; finally, a prohibition of anything like a common treasury, or the establishment of a permanent priesthood.[2] Augustus took advantage of this legislation to suppress those societies whose turbulent spirit disquieted him, and to interdict the creation of any new " Colleges."[3] His immediate successors were no less severe in their policy towards such confraternities. Consequently, as the Cæsars were strongly opposed to these associations, the Christians could not think of such a thing as trying to form themselves into " Religious Colleges," as very many foreigners had been wont to do under the Republic. And, furthermore, what was the use of soliciting this right, one only to be obtained with great difficulty, when they were assured of living in security so long as they were not distinguished from the larger body of Israelites? When examining the condition of the latter

[1] Dion Cassius, lii. 36.
[2] Livy, xxxix. 8–18; *Corpus Inscriptionum Latinarum*, i. pp. 43, 44.
[3] Suetonius, *Augustus*, 32.

THE LEGAL STATUS OF THE CHRISTIANS. 357

under the Empire, we have seen how Christianity grew up everywhere under the shadow of the Synagogue. As the first disciples at Rome, like those of Jerusalem, were Jews by birth, they continued for some time to be confounded with their brethren who clung to the ancient Law, up to the day when the open hostility of the latter rendered a separation inevitable. This division, however, did not prevent the Christians from keeping up the major part of their former practices. Aside from certain peculiar rites, the churches which met in the dwellings of Prisca and other baptized Israelites were not very different in outward aspects from the strict Mosaical synagogues. Owing to this fact, they enjoyed the legal prerogatives of their nation, and shared its fortunes.[1] Those of Hebrew origin were not the only ones to profit by these privileges; for Pagans who frequented the synagogues were likewise participants. Accordingly, the Christian Churches of Rome, so long as Jews were in the majority, offered to neophytes of Gentile birth the same sureties possessed by the sanctuaries of Israel.

This toleration was shown to gatherings composed almost entirely of Pagan converts. In fact, whatever the disagreements between the Church and the Syna-

---

[1] When Claudius, wearied with the tumults which followed the progress of Christianity in the Roman ghettos, decided to restore the peace of the city at any cost, he found no better means of accomplishing his object than by banishing all Israel, Jews and Christians alike (Suetonius, *Claudius*, 25). In other parts of the Empire, the magistrates followed his example, refusing to discriminate between the disciples of Moses and those of the Christ. Gallio, Proconsul of Achaia, answers the Jews who drag S. Paul before his judgment-seat: "If this were a question of any injustice or some evil deed, I should consider myself obliged to hear you patiently: but if it has to do with doctrinal contentions, — an interpretation of words or of your law, — do you settle your differences as you deem fit, I will not make myself your judge" (Acts xviii. 14, 15). In Palestine, Lysias, Felix, and Festus all act in like manner (Acts xxiii. 29; xxiv. 22–25; xxv. 18–21). Everywhere where S. Paul does suffer maltreatment, — at Antioch in Pisidia, Iconium, Philippi, Thessalonica, Berea, and Ephesus, — his persecutors are municipal authorities (Acts xiii. 50; xiv. 5; xvi. 20–23; xvii. 6, 13; xix. 23–40). Rome never interferes; her officers only take cognizance of the senatus-consultus and decrees which allow the Jews entire freedom in religious matters.

gogue, the magistrates of Rome had seen for themselves that one was the offspring of the other; and in order not to have to proceed against the former as a foreign system of worship, they continued to treat them as two branches from the same parent trunk. It is true that any such confusion as this,— which was a sore trial to the Jews, — only existed as a legal fiction kept up by the Roman authorities. The common people, indeed, had no difficulty in distinguishing the disciples, whom they called "Christians"[1] (a term of contempt), and whose worship they held to be an "execrable superstition."[2] So when Nero cast about for some one to accuse of the burning of Rome, he had only to lay hands upon this "great multitude"[3] spoken of by Tacitus, hated by the populace, and disowned by the Jews. The Church, suddenly deprived of the guarantees which had favored her growth, was for some years[4] thereafter at the mercy of violent enemies. But the tortures devised for her children were so odious that the universal hatred soon turned to compassion. "Men took pity on them, because they were sacrificed, not for the general good, but to gratify the cruelty of one man."[5] This new reversal of popular feeling had its effect on the magistrates, who by degrees returned to their former tolerant mode of treatment.

Two facts support this hypothesis, and make us believe that the milder political measures of Roman statemanship again came in force after the death of Nero. According to the account of Sulpicius Severus, when Titus was besieging Jerusalem (70), he agreed with his staff-officers that the Temple should be razed to the ground, "in order to destroy at one and the same time

[1] "Quos per flagitia invisos, vulgus Christianos adpellabat" (Tacitus, *Annales*, xv. 44).
[2] "Exitiabilis superstitio" (Id.).
[3] "Igitur primo conrepti, qui fatebantur, deinde, indicio eorum, multitudo ingens, haud perinde in crimine incendii, quam odio humani generis, convicti sunt" (Id.).
[4] From 64 to the death of Nero, June 11, 68.
[5] "Quanquam adversus sontes et novissima exempla meritos, miseratio oriebatur, tanquam non utilitate publica, sed in sævitiam unius, absumerentur" (Tacitus, *Annales*, xv. 44).

the Jews' religion with that of the Christians, since both, though opposed to each other, have a common source."[1] Twenty years later, Domitian, to replenish his empty treasury, forced the Christians to pay the same tax which, since the year 70, had been forthcoming from every Israelite community.[2] The imperial decree designates the faithful by these words, "those who live after the manner of the Jews,"[3] — thus giving us to understand that they enjoyed the privileges granted to Israel, and that it was on these grounds that they were compelled to fulfil the same duties. So then it seems to be an established fact that in the first century the Christians had but one safeguard, politically speaking, though it was a solid one, — to wit, the tolerant spirit of the magistrates, who persisted in regarding them as merely a sect of Israelites.

The early conversion of certain patricians, while fostering these liberal notions among statesmen, also helped to shield the Church from the popular malevolence. In the residences of these great personages, almost as vast as a city district,[4] hundreds of clients entered every morning to salute their lord.[5] So numerous were the visitors that a slave, called the Nomenclator,[6] was appointed to announce them, and oftentimes it happened that his trained memory failing him, he would

---

[1] "Fertur Titus adhibito consilio prius deliberasse . . . at contra alii et Titus ipse evertendum templum in primis censebant, quo plenius Judæorum et Christianorum religio tolleretur; quippe has religiones, licet contrarias sibi, iisdem auctoribus profectas: Christianos ex Judæis extitisse; radice sublata, stirpem facile perituram" (Sulpicius Severus, *Chron.* ii. 30). Here this author is reproducing a passage from Tacitus, otherwise lost to us.

[2] Josephus, *Bellum Judaicum*, vii. 6.

[3] "Præter cæteros Judaicus fiscus acerbissime actus est; ad quem deferebantur qui vel improfessi Judaicam viverent vitam, vel, dissimulata origine, imposita genti tributa non pependissent" (Suetonius, *Domit.* 12).

[4] "Domos in urbium modum exædificatas" (Sallust, *Catilina*, 12).

Urbis opus domus una fuit: spatiumque tenebat
Quo brevius muris oppida multa tenent.
OVID, *Fastor.*, vi. 641, 642.

[5] Marquardt, *Handbuch der Römischen Alterthümer*; DAS PRIVAT LEBEN, t. i. pp. 200-208.

[6] Pauly, *Real Encyclopädie*: NOMENCLATOR.

give them fictitious names.[1] At meal-times there was the same throng; for the rich gloried in displaying generous hospitality, and often their dining-halls contained as many as thirty tables sumptuously decked and served.[2] It is easy to fancy what opportunities these crowds must have given the Christians. The common people, accustomed to seeing a multitude daily besieging the gates of the patricians, would be unable to distinguish the companies of disciples who came thither to meet in the houses of their wealthy brethren.

Still more available as meeting-places were the burial domains which the noble families possessed round about Rome. These funereal regions enclosed, besides the tombs, very many edifices, — lodges for the keepers,[3] large halls for festivals and sacrifices,[4] cellars, wells,[5] and long galleries; farther away were gardens, shady avenues, with orchards and vineyards.[6] They visited these places of sepulture, not only on the feast-days of the dead,[7] but on oft-recurring anniversaries; for few rich persons died without leaving instructions in their wills that on stated days libations and offerings should be made about their tombs. The distributions of food and money promised to every one who attended the ceremonies, insured a large crowd on each occasion.[8] Consequently, no one

[1] Seneca, *De Benef.* i. 3; Macrobius, *Saturn.* ii. 4.
[2] Plutarch, *Quæst. Conviv.* v. 5, 9.
[3] "Ceterum erit mihi curæ, ut testamento caveam, ne mortuus injuriam accipiam; præponam enim unum ex libertis sepulcro meo custodiæ causa" (Petronius, *Satyr.* 71; Orelli, 4366, 4367, 4353, 4368, 4369, 4371).
[4] Orelli, 4433; Marini, *Atti e monumenti de' fratelli Arvali*, t. ii. p. 616.
[5] Wilmanns, *Exempla Inscriptionum Latinarum:* "Huic monumento cedet hortus in quo tricliæ, viniola, puteum, ædiculæ . . . " (240). "Taberna cum ædificio et cisterna . . . " (Marini, *Atti*, t. i. p. 12).
[6] "Hortus cinctus maceria" (Orelli, 4373); "Agellus" (Id., 4561); "Hortos cum ædificio huic sepulturæ junctos vivos donavit, ut ex redditu eorum largius rosæ et escæ patrono suo et quandoque sibi ponerentur" (Id., 4418). "Omne genus etiam pomorum volo sint circa cineres meos et vinearum largiter" (Petronius, *Satyr.* 71).
> Hoc nemus æterno cinerum sacravit honori
> Fœnius et culti jugera pulchra soli.
> MARTIAL, i. 116.

[7] For these festivals of the dead, see chapter xvii.
[8] Cf. Paul Allard, *Histoire des Persécutions pendant la première moitié du trosième siècle*, Appendix A.

would be surprised to see Christians flocking to the burial-grounds of friendly patricians. Indeed, all kinds of religious worship were treated with more respect there than elsewhere; for tombs were declared by law to be sacred and inviolable, and easily escaped the prescriptions of hostile religious edicts.[1] For a long time Jews, Syrians, worshippers of Isis or of Mithra had also owned cemeteries, and therein sacrificed as they pleased. In this great diversity of rites, and all the questions as to personal property, what could the pontiffs charged with the general supervision do, except close their eyes until such time as abuses occurred, forcing them to interfere?

Nevertheless, valuable as these franchises must have been, a necessity more urgent than mere freedom of worship soon forced the Church to frequent these regions of the dead: this was her anxiety to inter with decency those of her members who slept in the faith. To bring any Gentiles into the Jewish cemeteries was no longer possible after the rupture with the Synagogue; to deposit them in a *columbarium*,[2] crowded with urns which were covered with idolatrous emblems, could not be done without irreverence, for the body of a Christian, consecrated by baptism and united by the Holy Eucharist to the Blood of his God, was regarded as a hallowed relic. Furthermore, it was an irrefragable custom in the East, not only to refrain from undue haste, but still more to delay as long as possible the dissolution of mortal remains. This cherished tradition of the Jews was in accordance with Christian principles, and the Church, on coming in contact with Roman customs, continued to give her dead all the honors of burial. So it came about that these cemeteries were established,[3] — verita-

---

[1] Paul Allard, *Hist. des Persecutions*, Appendix B.
[2] This was the name the Romans gave the sepulchres erected for the reception of the members of a whole family or fraternity. They were called a "Columbarium," or dovecote, on account of the niches, shaped like pigeons' nests, wherein the burial-urns were deposited.
[3] Originally " cemetery, cæmeterium ": κοιμητήριον, sleeping-place, from κοιμάω, to slumber.

ble "resting-places," where the brethren slept side by side, waiting for the last great wakening.

Although entire liberty was granted them to own private burial-places,[1] brotherly love generally made them desire to be united in death as they had been in life. From the outset, it would seem that certain wealthy citizens of Rome received their poorer brethren in their funeral domains. The Ostrian Cemetery, where, as we have seen, stood the first chair of Peter's Episcopate, belonged to some rich neophyte. That of Lucina was set apart from the burial-ground of the Pomponia Family. The Catacomb of Priscilla was within property belonging to the Senator Pudens. On the Via Ardeatina, a daughter of the Flavians, named Domitilla, was soon to consecrate to Christ the cemetery which still bears her name, where, too, she welcomed the slave Ampliatus, apparently the one mentioned by Saint Paul,[2] and Petronilla, a descendant of T. Flavius Petro, also of the Flavian stock.[3]

Without fixing upon the precise date when these little cities of the dead passed into the hands of the Church, archeologists hold it as a settled fact that even in the first century they were used for Christian gatherings. We need only wander through one of them to understand how easy it was for the disciples to find a safe refuge therein. Pagan observers could discover nothing unusual in them, nothing to distinguish them from the mausoleums which the noble Romans were erecting on all sides. Later on, to gain ampler room, the catacombs were extended underground; but at the outset, the sepulchral edifice rose above the surface. The monument of Lucina stands beside the Appian Way; Domitilla's is on the Via Ardeatina. In the latter the inscription over the door indicated the name of the owner, and the

---

[1] "We have withdrawn apart," says a Christian couple in their epitaph; "we have set up this sarcophagus in our own gardens." Gruter, 1059, 6.

[2] Rom. xvi. 8.

[3] Paul Allard, *Rome souterraine*, p. 54; supplement, pp. 605–612; also the *Cubiculum d'Ampliatus* in his *Lettres chrétiennes*, t. iv. p. 416.

THE LEGAL STATUS OF THE CHRISTIANS. 363

vestibule stood open to the gaze of passers-by. Any one curious enough to penetrate within the sacred precincts would find nothing there to excite his surprise. On the arches the same paintings as in Pagan sepulchres,— scenes from the vintage, the trailing vines delicately sketched, while here and there bright birds and spirits flit about. These frescos rival those at Pompeii in grace. Christian artists had not created anything original as yet, but merely reproduced the arabesques with which the patrician residences were decorated; only they banished everything that was idolatrous or immoral. Nor was there anything about the epitaphs on these earliest tombs which differed essentially from the profane inscriptions. The lapidary style and all the formulas compatible with Christian doctrines are still in use. Much of the ornamentation is still the same as in Pagan times,— palms, crowns, footprints, and figures of animals. The visitor must needs be a keen observer to detect in the aspirations for " peace, refreshment, the Vision of God," indications of a New Faith.[1]

So, too, with the Christian Ritual: although borrowed from the Synagogue, it resembled the usual rites of funeral festivals in so many particulars that at first no one noticed any striking divergences. The Eucharistic Banquet was the soul of the new Worship; now just such repasts, eaten in common, played a considerable part in the anniversary feasts celebrated by the Pagans.[2] The important position assigned to these ceremonies, and the festival halls requisite for them, made it possible for the Church to construct large meeting places in every necropolis. These became the first sanctuaries, wherein they took care to introduce as few innovations as possible. One instance will suffice to show how far this prudence was carried. The mortuary monuments usually exhibited a picture of the banquets

---

[1] Martigny, *Dictionnaire des antiquités chrétiennes:* INSCRIPTIONS.
[2] One of these "Funeral Colleges" that were allowed to multiply unhindered in the second century, adopted the following title, which betrays the main object of its meetings: "Society of men who dine together." "Convictorum qui uno epulo vesci solent" (Orelli, 4073).

celebrated on the birthdays of the donors, and these feasts were also designated by some such formulary as this:—

"The VIII. before the Ides of March: birthday of Cœsennus . . . father.

"The XIII. before the Kalends of September: birthday of Cœsennus Silvanus, brother.

"The XIX. before the Kalends of January: birthday of Cœsennus Rufus, patron of the municipium."[1]

These time-hallowed terms in no wise offended the New Faith, and the Church accordingly adopted them in making the calendar of her feasts.[2] The sole change was that, to the disciples, "birthday" (*natalis dies*) no longer meant the anniversary of one's birth, but that of one's death, inasmuch as with the Christian's last breath on earth his true life begins in Eternity and in the bosom of his God.

So, then, whether preserving the outward aspects of Judaism, or whether casting them aside, the Church found her safety assured in either case here in Rome. Up to the year 64 she profited by this state of affairs, free to expand unhindered, and partaking of the protection granted to all subjects of the Empire. A precious safeguard this, which Heaven had provided to shield this cradle of the New Faith from the Jews, bent upon exterminating it. At this date they were her only enemies, and for a quarter of a century she knew hardly any others; and yet she had everything to dread from these fraternal strifes. Twice since the Saviour's death the Jews of Jerusalem had succeeded in obtaining the right to pronounce sentence of death. They had made use of it to slay Stephen and James,[3] while they "compelled the disciples, by means of tortures and executions, to blaspheme the Christ."[4] If they had been but once permitted to give free rein to their fanatic hatred, they

---

[1] "VIII. Id. Mar. natali Cæsenni . . . patris.
XIII. k. sept. na[t. Cæse]nni Silvani fratris.
XIX. k. Jan. n[at. Cæs]enni Rufi patr[oni] muni[cipii]."
WILMANNS, *Exempla Inscriptionum*, 319.

[2] Our Martyrologies still preserve these Roman formulas.
[3] Acts vii. 56-58; xii. 1, 2. [4] Acts xxvi. 11.

would have crushed the lowly edifice erected in honor of the Saviour; but the iron hand of Rome held them in check, and allowed nothing more serious than passing outbursts of frenzy. Here we see outbreaks of the mob promptly repressed, elsewhere, infrequent abuses of authority on the part of provincial magistrates. Taking everything into consideration, we may conclude that during the whole of the first century the Church was protected oftener than she was disturbed by the Roman authorities.

She merited this kindly treatment, not only because of her anxiety to avoid anything which might shock the Pagans, but still more for her ready obedience to decrees of the State. The Rationalist critics endeavor to represent our fathers in the Faith as a constant menace to the institutions of Rome, a dangerous faction in open revolt against religious order. Hence, they conclude that the magistrates must be excused for visiting the rebels with those atrocious punishments common at that date, and that the best and wisest of sovereigns were right in letting justice take its course. The best answer to these novel views is the spectacle presented during the first thirty years, when Rome watched Christianity growing up within her walls, without evidencing the slightest alarm; still further, we have the teaching imbibed by the disciples of that day. Never was respect for the law preached with greater insistence, together with perfect submission to legitimate rulers. Just at this date Saint Paul wrote to the Christians of Rome, " Let every soul be subject to the higher powers; for there is no power which cometh not from God, and He it is Who hath established all those that exist. Therefore he that resisteth the powers, resisteth the ordinance of God. . . . The prince is an instrument of God to execute his vengeance on him who doeth evil. Wherefore we must be subject not only out of fear of punishment, but for conscience' sake. Therefore, also, you pay tribute to princes, because they are the ministers of God. " [1] It is true that Christians used very different language later on. When Nero was suspected of burning Rome,

[1] Rom. xiii. 1-6.

he threw the odium upon the new sect, and to prove to the people that the Christians were really guilty, devised all manner of horrible tortures for them. It was natural that a cry of horror should escape the lips of virgins delivered over to unspeakable indignities,[1] and from that throng of martyrs steeped in resin and set aflame like living torches.[2] They could no longer regard Rome as other than " the great Babylon, the Mother of prostitutes, and the abominations of the earth,— the Woman drunk with the blood of the Saints and of the Martyrs of Jesus."[3] To them it seemed that Cæsar was the Beast having seven heads and ten horns,— a scarlet Beast, covered over with names of blasphemy.[4] In his Apocalypse Saint John has voiced these lamentations which, one and all, bewail the past and foretell a future reparation; but he never incites the surviving victims to revolt. It is for God to avenge His elect, for them to suffer patiently, evermore repeating the Christian's words of mourning, " Blessed are the dead who die in the Lord; from henceforth now, saith the Spirit, that they may rest from their labors, for their works do follow them."[5]

Clearer still rang forth the words of Peter. The Head of the Twelve survived the first persecution. Bitter and severe as that time of trial was to him, it brought about no change in his teaching. What Saint Paul had written ten years before, this the Apostle repeated once more, then, as ever, giving an immutable form to the doctrines of Christianity. " Be ye subject for the love of God to all established governments, whether to the King, as being above all, or to Governors sent by him for the punishment of evil-doers and for the praise of the good. . . . Fear God; honor the King."[6] Yet this King was Nero, who had been torturing the Christians, and was about to crucify Peter.

[1] Αἰκίσματα δεινὰ καὶ ἀνόσια παθοῦσαι (S. Clement, *I. ad Corinthios*, vi.).
[2] Tacitus, *Annales*, xv. 44. [3] Apoc. xvii. 5, 6.
[4] Apoc. xvii. 3. [5] Apoc. xiv. 13.
[6] 1 Peter ii. 13–17.

CHAPTER XX.

THE GOSPEL OF SAINT MARK.

WE know very little as to the form in which Saint Peter clothed his preaching at Rome; but the substance of it is better known; for, according to the testimony of all ancient writers, we possess it to-day as Saint Mark compiled and preserved it in the Second Gospel. In the capital of the world Peter continued the work he and his brethren had begun in Judea. He set forth the Life and teachings of the Master, and every day and in much the same terms he repeated a sort of historical catechism to the neophytes who surrounded him. A contemporary of the oldest of the Apostles, John the Priest,[1] tells us that this spoken Gospel was almost immediately put in writing.

"Mark," he says, "who became interpreter to Peter, put together very exactly, but without any precise order, all that he recalled of the words and actions of the Christ. For he had never heard, nor had he accompanied the Lord; but later on, as I have said, he followed Peter, who arranged his instructions according to the needs of his audience, and not as if he wanted to construct a methodical collection of the discourses of the Lord. Mark is not to be blamed for having written only a small number of details, just as he remembered them; for he had only

---

[1] This personage was one of the "Elders" who while living with the last of the Apostles, gathered together their traditions. All that we know of him is that he resided at Ephesus, in the company of S. John the Apostle, his master, whose name he bore (Papias, in Eusebius, *Historia Ecclesiastica*, iii. 39; *Constitutiones Apostolicæ*, vii. 46). In the third century their tombs were still shown in that city (Dionysius of Alexandria, in Eusebius, *Historia Ecclesiastica*, vii. 25).

one object in view, — not to omit anything he had heard, and not to allow anything untrue to creep into his narrative."[1]

Though rather confusing on the whole, this bit of evidence nevertheless furnishes us with a few invaluable details as to the preaching of Saint Peter. The title of Interpreter given Mark leads us to infer that the Apostle did not speak Greek well enough to be easily understood. The Evangelist therefore stood beside him, and repeated the discourses of the Galilean fisherman in the popular tongue. This sort of sermon was really a recital "of the words and actions of the Christ,"[2] but "without any set order;"[3] for Peter thought only of instructing his hearers, and adduced events and parables "according to the needs of his subject-matter."[4] He was to proclaim Jesus to the world; and to that end any one of the striking features of His Life answered his purpose; he had no idea of attempting the work of an historian, still less of constructing a moral treatise out of the doctrines of the Saviour. He did not try "to make a synopsis of His discourses,"[5] as the writer of the Fourth Gospel was afterwards to do: "his only end in view was to be careful neither to omit nor to alter anything whatever."[6]

If we are to accept this tradition, Mark, it seems, had a very small part in the compilation of the work which bears his name. Yet we find the same idea repeated in the following centuries. Saint Justin calls the Second Gospel "the Memoirs, the Recollections of Peter;"[7] Saint Irenæus asserts again that "Mark did no more

---

[1] This testimony of John the Priest has been handed down to us by Papias, Bishop of Hierapolis. Eusebius, *Historia Ecclesiastica*, iii. 39, 15.
[2] Τὰ ὑπὸ τοῦ Χριστοῦ ἢ λεχθέντα ἢ πραχθέντα.
[3] Οὐ μέντοι τάξει.
[4] Πρὸς τὰς χρείας ἐποιεῖτο τὰς διδασκαλίας.
[5] Οὐκ ὥσπερ σύνταξιν τῶν κυριακῶν ποιούμενος λόγων (λογίων).
[6] ... Ἑνὸς ἐποιήσατο πρόνοιαν, τοῦ μηδὲν ὧν ἤκουσε παραλιπεῖν.
[7] Ἀπομνημονεύματα τοῦ Πέτρου (S. Justin, *Dialog.* cvi.). Eusebius makes use of this expression twice. Πάντα γὰρ τὰ παρὰ Μάρκῳ τοῦ Πέτρου διαλέξεων εἶναι λέγεται ἀπομνημονεύματα (*Demonstr. Evangel.* iii. 5). Τούτου (Πέτρου) Μάρκος γνώριμος καὶ φοιτητὴς γεγονώς, ἀπομνημονεῦσαι λέγεται τὰς τοῦ Πέτρου περὶ τῶν πράξεων τοῦ Ἰησοῦ διαλέξεις. (*Id.*)

than set down in writing just what the Apostle taught;"[1] Origen says that "he composed it under the supervision of Peter."[2] At the same period Clement of Alexandria heard "from his elders of the preceding generation" a similar tradition. "'So this is the way,' said these venerable witnesses, 'that Mark went about the writing of his Gospel. Peter had preached the word of God publicly in Rome, and, under the inspiration of the Holy Ghost, had announced the Glad Tidings. Many of his hearers besought Mark, who had been in Peter's company for now a long time and had a lively remembrance of his words, to write down the discourses of the Apostle. Accordingly, Mark composed his Gospel and gave it to all who asked for it: and when Peter was apprised thereof, he neither forbade nor encouraged him."[3]

Any such indifference on the part of the Apostle in regard to the inspired pages did not seem at all shocking to the contemporaries of Clement of Alexandria. It caused more surprise in succeeding centuries, and doubtless that was the reason why they modified the tradition, giving it the meaning which Eusebius has handed down to posterity in his account. "Those who listened to Peter were not content with hearing his doctrine as it fell from his lips, they earnestly begged Mark to give it to them in written form, and allowed him no rest until he consented to compose his Gospel. Enlightened by the Holy Ghost, Peter was well aware of what he was doing; the ardent zeal of these people filled him with exceeding joy, and he authorized the work to be used for reading

---

[1] S. Irenæus, *Contra Hæreses*, iii. 1, 1.
[2] Ὡς Πέτρος ὑφηγήσατο αὐτῷ. Origen, quoted by Eusebius (*Historia Ecclesiastica*, vi. 25).
[3] Clement of Alexandria, quoted by Eusebius (*Historia Ecclesiastica*, vi. 14). The same Father, in his *Adumbratio ad I Ep. Petri* (*Patrologie grecque*, t. ix. p. 732), records this tradition, at the same time adding a curious matter of detail: "Marcus, Petri sectator, palam prædicante Petro Evangelium Romæ coram quibusdam Cæsarensis equitibus et multa Christi testimonia proferente, penitus ab eis ut possent quæ dicebantur memoriæ commendare, scripsit ex his quæ Petro dicta sunt, Evangelium quod secundum Marcum vocitatur." The presence among his hearers of certain knights of Cæsar's household is especially worthy of note.

in the churches. This is the report left us by Clement in the sixth book of his Institutions."[1] The Alexandrian Doctor had said nothing of the sort, as we have just seen, and the actual evidence of Clement is that Saint Peter did not concern himself at all in the matter of Saint Mark's Gospel. "He had not commanded him to write it," says Rufinus in his translation of this passage; "but the work once completed, he did not interdict it."[2]

The conduct of the Apostle is to be explained in the light of the command given both to him and to the Twelve, — to wit, that they were to preach the Gospel, not write it.[3] Peter saw clearly that his unhampered and impetuous manner of preaching had already penetrated everywhere, under the fostering aid of the Spirit, adapting itself to time, place, and the peculiar characters of his hearers, and ever increasing in power and clearness. To embody it in a written book would be tantamount to giving it an invariable form, robbing it of that glowing enthusiasm which day by day inspired the messengers of the Good News with renewed fervour. He knew well that some part of the Christian doctrines would come, after a time and by degrees, to be set down in written documents; but he knew, too, that the entire Deposit of Faith could not be contained in fixed and rigid language; he saw that the Apostolic word would always continue to be an unfailing source of Truth, ever living and ever fruitful, embodied in the teaching of his successors. On their lips it was to pass down from age to age, illuminating and explaining the written revelation, penetrating farther than revelation, and freed from all slavery to the letter which killeth. Apparently this was the reason why Peter allowed Mark to write the reminiscences of all he heard from him "without either hindering or encouraging him."

But the Christians of Rome recognized the teaching of their Pastor as contained in the Second Gospel, and like them we need but re-read this book if we wish to listen to the very language of the Apostle and be present at the

---

[1] Eusebius, *Historia Ecclesiastica*, ii. 15.
[2] Id., vi. 14.   [3] Mark xvi. 15.

instructions he gave in the great Capital. If the form is Mark's, the matter came from Peter, — not merely the principal ideas, but the minor details in the events related and the peculiarities of expression as well. Indeed, nothing hinders us from supposing that the Evangelist limited his share of the labor to a careful selection of those words in the Greek language which would best convey the exact meaning of his teacher.[1]

Composed in this manner, the Life of the Saviour differs sensibly from the one Saint Matthew had written previously for the Hebrews of Jerusalem. Certainly, the general lines are, broadly speaking, the same; sometimes, indeed, they are set forth in precisely similar terms;[2] but outside the points where the two sacred authors meet and agree perfectly, the teaching of the Prince of the Apostles displays, first of all, his own character, cleancut, exact, and of a practical rather than a speculative turn; but, what is most interesting, it tells us of his personal relations with Jesus.

The priceless advantage possessed by Peter was that he had been in the Saviour's company from His Baptism to the Ascension,[3] and that he was one of the three disciples whom Jesus kept by Him always, in Tabor as in Gethsemani.[4] He had been an eye-witness of all he relates; the minuteness of his narrative is enough to prove that he was an attentive observer. Before him, the First Evangelist had told the story of the calling of the four disciples on the shores of Lake Genesareth;[5] but Saint Matthew does not speak as one who was present, as we perceive at once when reading the account in Saint

---

[1] We are warranted in inferring this from the emphasis which John the Priest lays on his words to Papias, reiterating that "Mark, Peter's interpreter, wrote down *exactly* . . . *all whatsoever he recalled* of the words or deeds of the Christ; that he wrote them . . . *just as he recalled them*, . . . and that he had no anxiety save to *omit nothing of that which he had heard*." Eusebius, *Historia Ecclesiastica*, iii. 39.

[2] What has been said above (chap. xii. pp. 206–216) of the oral Gospel as delivered by the Twelve sufficiently explains these similarities.

[3] "Oportet . . . incipiens a baptismate Joannis usque in diem qua assumptus est . . . testem resurrectionis fieri" (Acts i. 21, 22).

[4] Mark v. 37; ix. 1; xiv. 33.   [5] Matt. iv. 18–22.

Mark:[1] thus Peter recalls the fact that the boat belonging to the sons of Zebedee lay near the one in which he himself was fishing[2] when the Saviour called him; and that Zebedee was not left alone upon the departure of his sons, but that his hired servants remained with him. Everywhere there is the same exactness; the other Evangelists remark that certain men carried the paralytic of Capharnaüm;[3] but Peter had counted them, and tells us they were four in number.[4] He had noticed that there was but one loaf of bread to be found in their little vessel.[5] He knew all about Jaïrus' daughter, and remarks that she was twelve years old; in the chamber whither he accompanied Jesus, he describes her as not simply rising at the Master's bidding, but "running back and forth" with all the natural petulancy of a hungry child.[6] The dearest and liveliest remembrances are of Jesus Himself; His looks, gestures, attitudes, all live again here. How often and often he represents Him as bending his gaze upon the crowds which encircle Him, or with a glance sounding the depths of their hearts;[7] here we see Him embracing the little ones,[8] and again walking before the terrified Twelve![9] Peter has heard his sighs,[10] and repeats His very words, as they still ring in his ears: "*Talitha cumi! Eppheta! Eloi, Eloi, lamma sabachtani!*"[11]

It is partly owing to the fact that these impressions were so deeply graven in his memory that the narrative in the second Gospel possesses such a vivid and original character. And yet we can note everywhere the character of Simon, for the Galilean fisherman appears side by side with the Apostle: always the man of the people, the illiterate seaman, neither caring for elegant expressions, nor attempting anything more than the most vigorous

---

[1] Mark i. 16-20.
[2] "Jesus had taken but a few steps," he says (προβὰς ὀλίγον), "when he caught sight of James the son of Zebedee, with John, his brother."
[3] Matt. ix. 2; Luke v. 18, 19.   [4] Mark ii. 3.   [5] Mark viii 14.
[6] Mark v. 35-43.   [7] Mark iii. 5, 34; v. 32; vi. 6; x. 21, 23; xi. 11.
[8] Mark ix. 36; x. 16.   [9] Mark x. 32.   [10] Mark vii. 34; viii. 12.
[11] Mark v. 41; vii. 34; xv. 34.

expression of his thoughts. The appropriate word, however rude it might sound, was used without hesitation. Thus he depicts for us the scene when the kinsfolk of the Saviour seized him by force, and treated him as a "madman;"[1] so, too, he says the Pharisees accused our Lord of being possessed "by an unclean spirit."[2] He calls Jesus "the carpenter;"[3] describes him at Nazareth in the family-circle "of brothers and sisters;"[4] at eventide, after long hours of preaching, he tells how He went on board tired out, stained with sweat and dust, "just as He was;"[5] at Gethsemani he says that He was "in a state of stupor."[6] Nowhere do the other Synoptic Writers bring out the details in such bold relief. They do, indeed, paint the possessed creature at Gergesa in sufficiently sombre colors; but the salient feature is found in Saint Mark: "night and day he wandered among the tombs and the mountains, crying out and cutting himself with stones."[7] It is the same, too, in the case of the possessed boy, healed after the Transfiguration. In Saints Matthew and Luke the scene is sketched with a light hand; Saint Mark lingers over it until it is a living picture, — the poor victim writhing at Jesus' feet, foam flying from his lips, while he grinds his teeth; the father in tears; the devil driven from the child, uttering a shriek and dashing him to the ground: "He is dead!"[8] the bystanders exclaim. Peter had heard these words, and he describes what he has seen. And, furthermore, how many minor incidents he gives us which are peculiar to his Gospel! The name of Alpheus,[9] father of Levi the publican; those of Bartimeus[10] and Boanerges, the title given to the sons of Zebedee,[11] — all these we owe to him; from him we learn that Simon the Cyrenean had two sons called Alexander and Rufus;[12] and that the poor suppliant, vaguely designated by Saint Matthew as a Cha-

[1] Mark iii. 21.   [2] Mark iii. 30.
[3] Mark vi. 3.   [4] Mark vi. 3.   [5] Mark iv. 35, 36.
[6] Ἤρξατο ἐκθαμβεῖσθαι. Mark xiv. 33.   [7] Mark v. 5.
[8] Mark ix. 14–27; Cf. Matt. xvii. 14–21; Luke ix. 37–43.
[9] Mark ii. 14.   [10] Mark x. 46.   [11] Mark iii. 17.
[12] Mark xv. 21.

naanitish woman, spoke the Greek tongue, and came from the Phœnician provinces of Syria.[1]

In view of these many individualities of style in the second Gospel, it is hard to explain the verdict of Saint Augustine: "Mark appears to be the abbreviator of Matthew."[2] The truth is that, though the Good News as taken down from the lips of Saint Peter by his interpreter contains fewer facts than are found in the other Synoptical Writers, it gives us, on the other hand, a more circumstantial series of narratives. Far from being a faded copy, the picture left us by Saint Mark seems, on the contrary, fresher and more original than that of any of the other four inspired Witnesses.

It differs from Saint Matthew notably in the absence of long discourses. Not a trace remains of the Sermon on the Mount; the instructions to the Apostles are reduced to a few lines;[3] only four Parables are reported, and in concise terms.[4] The Master's example, His deeds, and especially His Miracles, in Peter's eyes, seemed the preaching best fitted to touch the souls of men, and thus harmonized perfectly with his end in view. Saint Matthew had shown the Jews how in the Christ was realized all that had been foretold of the Messiah; Saint Luke, later on, was to proclaim Him to the Gentiles as the Saviour of the World; but the title given to the Gospel of Peter indicates a very different design: "The beginning of the Gospel of Jesus Christ, the Son of God."[5] Son of God! in the very same terms the Apostle had proclaimed the Divinity of his Master at Cæsarea Philippi.[6] This his solemn Confession always remains his controlling

---

[1] Mark vii. 26.
[2] "Pedissequus et breviator ejus videtur" (S. Augustin, *De Consensu Evangel.*, i. 4).
[3] Mark vi. 8-11.
[4] The Parable of the sower (iv. 3-8), the mustard-seed (iv. 31, 32), the murderous husbandmen (xii. 1-9), and finally that of the seed which grows up unperceived, which this Gospel is the only one to recount (iv. 26-29).
[5] Mark i. 1.
[6] Mark viii. 29. The Sinaïtic MS. (א) and the Codex Regius Parisiensis (L) contain the words ὁ υἱὸς τοῦ Θεοῦ, as we have it in the Vulgate. Cf. Matt. xvi. 6; Luke ix. 20; John vi. 70.

thought; it impels him to remind Cornelius that Jesus is "the Lord of all; . . . that God hath anointed Him with the Holy Spirit;"[1] and throughout the Second Gospel it is the central point toward which all his teaching tends. In the very first lines, Jesus, descending to the waters of Jordan, is called the Son of God;[2] in the desert He manifests Himself as sovereign Lord, dominating the wild beasts and served by Angel ministers.[3] Then begins a long series of Miracles, wherein we are shown the almighty powers of the Christ: nature and mankind alike yield to His orders; the demons fall down before Him, crying out, "Thou art the Son of God;"[4] His death is followed by such prodigious happenings, His last sigh is so triumphant, that the Centurion exclaims, "Surely this man was the Son of God!"[5] So then on this fundamental point, the testimony of Peter at Rome is precisely what it had been at Jerusalem, — the preaching of the Saviour's Divinity. The Apostle, on leaving the Supper Room, concluded his first discourse thus: "Let all the House of Israel know most certainly that God hath made Him Lord and Christ, — this same Jesus Whom you have crucified."[6] The last words of the Second Gospel repeat the same thought: "So then the Lord was lifted up on high into Heaven, and sitteth on the right hand of God."[7]

Moreover, the God Whom Peter announced to Rome revealed Himself to the Apostle in increasing splendor from Pentecost morning to the hour of his death. He Whom the first Christians of Jerusalem worshipped was still the Jehovah of the old Covenant, a God belonging peculiarly to Israel, a jealous God Who had declared by the mouth of Moses, "The Eternal shall raise up from among your brethren a Prophet like unto me; Him you shall hearken to in all that He may say unto you, and it shall come to pass that every soul which will not hear that Prophet shall be destroyed from among the people."[8] But at Joppa the Heavenly mandate had decreed that he was to

[1] Acts x. 34–42. [2] Mark i. 9, 11. [3] Mark i. 13.
[4] Mark iii. 11, 12. [5] Mark xv. 39. [6] Acts ii. 36. [7] Mark xvi. 19.
[8] S. Peter's second discourse. Acts iii. 22.

publish the Glad Tidings to all men, laying aside, little
by little, every peculiar feature of Judaism.[1] The Second
Gospel testifies to the fidelity with which Peter obeyed.
Therein we find no traces of the spirit which had inspired
Saint Matthew in writing his book for the Hebrews.
The genealogical tables of the Jews are omitted, the Saviour's childhood is passed over in silence ; Peter leaves
it to his fellow-countrymen to meditate upon those early
years when as yet the Christ did not differ in outward
appearances from other sons of Israel: but among the
Gentiles he begins his narrative with the opening of His
Public Ministry. Saint Matthew is never tired of reminding his hearers how at every step the Prophecies
were fulfilled in Jesus ; only once does Saint Peter cite
the Old Testament on his own account.[2] He never manifests any such anxiety, as the First Evangelist displays,
to prove that the words of Jesus are in accordance with
all his hearers have heard from the Ancients ; he never
so much as mentions the name of the Law ; instead of
the Rabbinical terms current in the church of Jerusalem, he makes use of expressions which would convey
a clearer meaning to the Gentiles, — thus, the " Kingdom
of Heaven " becomes " the Kingdom of God." He goes
even further when he boldly avows that the truth as set
forth by Jesus is "a new teaching ;"[3] he condemns the
practices which the Synagogue imposed upon the people
with such rigorous penalties, — " all those things, observed out of custom, such as the washing of cups, pots,
brazen vessels, and beds."[4] He looks upon all this as a
mere mask for hypocrisy, and reminds us that the Master
had uttered against them that anathema from Isaiah :
" This people honoreth Me with their lips, but their

---

[1] Acts x. 13.
[2] This citation, placed at the beginning of the Gospel, was taken from two of the Prophets, Malachy (iii. 1) and Isaiah (xl. 3). Another quotation is found in the Vulgate (xv. 28), " Et cum iniquis reputatus est." But modern editors, not finding these words in the oldest manuscripts (A, B, C, D, X, ℵ), question their authenticity. The other texts are quotations as made by the Saviour in the very words which S. Mark records as His.
[3] Mark i. 27. [4] Mark vii. 4.

heart is far from Me ; in vain do they honor Me, teaching for their doctrines the commandments of men."[1]

Before Peter began to preach to the Romans, had he already given this purely Christian coloring to his teaching ? In the earlier days, had his sermons been divested of the Judaic terms of expression, with the other manners and reminiscences of Jewry which impregnate the Gospel of Saint Matthew ? There is every reason to believe the contrary, for although the Vision at Joppa had shown the Apostle how the Mosaical worship was to fade away before the bright sunlight of the Gospel, yet at the same time the inspiration of the Holy Spirit kept him from dazzling his brethren of Israel with the noontide brilliancy of Faith. In the synagogues which he visited on his way from Judea to Rome, his language was accommodated to the weakness of his hearers ; again, during the first days after his arrival, in the "ghettos" of Trastevere and Porta Capena, he refrained in like manner from offending his fellow-countrymen's prejudices. The Good News, as we read it in Saint Mark's version, could not have been preached until a later date, when, after the Synagogue had finally rejected the Christians, the latter possessed sanctuaries of their own, where the Pagans foregathered with them. The omission of any reference to the Law, and the absence of all subserviency to the prejudices of Israel, are not the only signs which point to this conclusion. There are numerous tokens besides these, all going to prove that the Christians evangelized by Peter were strangers to the Mosaical system ; thus we find the customs and rites of Israel explained,[2] Hebrew words are translated,[3] while the value of Jewish money is given in Roman coin.[4] Few of his hearers could ever have seen Judea, for he sees fit to inform them that the Jordan is a river, and that the Mount of Olives rises opposite the Temple.[5]

[1] Mark vii. 7.
[2] Mark ii. 18; vii. 1–4; xi. 13; xii. 18; xiv. 12; xv. 6.
[3] Mark iii. 17; v. 41 ; vii. 11, 34; x. 46; xiv. 36; xv. 34.
[4] Mark xii. 42.   [5] Mark i. 5; xiii. 3.

Taken together, these details leave no question as to the fact that the Gospel of Saint Mark was intended for Gentile readers, and, according to all appearances, for those living in the Capital.[1] Indeed, no style of preaching could be better adapted to this virile race, of whom Livy has said, "To do and to endure manfully, — that is the whole Roman."[2] Men of action, as was Peter himself, like him paying more heed to deeds than to words, these Romans found a doctrine suited to their needs in Peter's preaching of the Glad Tidings, — facts, not long speeches. We have remarked above that these facts are for the most part Miracles. Now, no incitement to faith was more eagerly looked for by the Pagan society of Rome. The belief in dreams, presages, and astrology was general; the laws condemned magicians and astrologers to the flames and wild beasts, — but all in vain; the people still trembled before them. The most serious thinkers — Livy and Tacitus among them — fill their histories with accounts of prodigies. Pliny the Elder, who did not believe in the gods, accepted many stories of marvellous happenings as really unquestionable.[3] To the minds of men so hungry for the supernatural, Peter's words were doubly welcome; for he did not tell them of gross impostures, but of the very handiwork of God, — divine deeds, whereof all Judea was the living witness.

However, as to the mere fact that this Gospel, with its many indications of Roman influence, was actually written at Rome, there is nowadays no difference of opinion; the only point at issue concerns its date. To defer its compilation as late as the year 120, as critics of the extreme school contend, would seem impossible in the light of modern investigations.[4] Even the Rationalists acknowledge that these pages were finished "before all

---

[1] The frequent use of Latinisms in the Second Gospel supports this opinion: Κεντυρίων, xv. 39, 44, 45; Κοδράντης, xii. 42; Σπεκουλάτωρ, vi. 27; Ξέστης, vii. 4, 8, etc.
[2] Livy, *Historiæ*, ii. 12.
[3] Friedländer, *Mœurs romaines*, t. iv. p, 209 et seq.
[4] Davidson, *Introduction to the Study of the New Testament*, vol. ii. p. 111.

the eye-witnesses of the Life of Jesus were dead."[1] Naturally they would like to choose some one of the years which followed the destruction of Jerusalem,[2] but their only motive is that they find this catastrophe predicted in Saint Mark. Instead of this gratuitous hypothesis, no one will be surprised if I prefer the opinion handed down on the authority of Eusebius, and with the learned historian hold that the Second Gospel was compiled during the reign of Claudius.[3] This date was given by him, not for fanciful reasons, but in accordance with evidence so trustworthy that succeeding centuries have accepted it without questioning.[4] Furthermore, it is confirmed by the eagerness shown by the Romans when urging Mark to take down the Apostle's words. And certainly it could only have been at the beginning of his preaching that this abstract of Peter's sermons, as arranged by his disciple, would have possessed that attraction of novelty which the Fathers say it had.[5] Finally, the traditions which give us an account of Mark's apostleship at Alexandria, would also lead us to infer that he wrote in the time of Claudius; for it is during his reign that they tell of Mark's arrival in Egypt, adding that he brought with him the Good News, composed by him only a short time before that event.[6]

[1] Renan, *Les Évangiles*, p. 125.
[2] The concessions which the Rationalistic school makes on this point are of considerable importance, for if S. Mark's Gospel was written about 70, that is, not over forty years after the death of the Saviour, we have in our hands the evidence of a contemporary.
[3] Eusebius, *Historia Ecclesiastica*, ii. 15.
[4] Theophylactus, *Proœmium in Matth.*; Euthymius Zigabenus, *Patrologie grecque*, t. cxxix. p. 116; the concluding glosses of MSS. G and K. As to the passage from S. Irenæus (*Adversus Hæreses*, iii. 1) which seems to contradict all the ancient authorities, and apparently defers the publication of the Second Gospel till after the death of S. Peter, see the Appendix (III.).
[5] Note the testimony of Papias and Clement of Alexandria, referred to in the course of this chapter.
[6] It is quite the fashion of late to contest this fact on the pretext that there is no mention made of it earlier than the fourth century. Certainly, Eusebius is the first historian to speak of it; but he had before him the episcopal lists collected by Hegesippus from the principal Churches; the latter had examined his authorities on the spot, and has compiled as com-

The last-mentioned fact merits particular attention on our part, because it completes the evidence which goes to show the supremacy of Peter over the new-born Church: it proves, in fact, that from the first his preaching found its way into the three great Metropolises of Christianity,— Antioch, Rome, and Alexandria. If we are to believe Saint Epiphanius,[1] it was the Prince of the Apostles himself who sent Mark to preach the Gospel in Egypt; Eusebius and Saint Jerome, however, make no mention of this.[2] And yet, whatever may have been the origin of this mission, Mark carried thither no other faith but that which he had received from Peter. Accordingly, we know that the three watch-fires which were soon to illuminate the world with the light of the Gospel, had all been kindled by the same breath, — the word and authority of that Apostle to whom Jesus once said, "I have prayed for thee that thy faith fail not. . . . Do thou confirm thy brethren."[3]

plete a catalogue of the pastors of Alexandria as of Rome, Antioch, and Jerusalem. He names the series of Alexandrian Bishops, in unbroken succession, from his own times back to the first century, down to Cerdon, Avilius, and Annianus, the successor of Mark Evangelist (Eusebius, *Historia Ecclesiastica*, ii. 24; iii. 14, 21). So then he did not accept untrustworthy traditions, but relied upon the truth of ascertained documentary evidence, when he ascribed the foundation of the Church of Alexandria to S. Peter's Interpreter. Furthermore, it is quite impossible to suppose that Egypt was inaccessible to Christianity at a time when the Gospel was spreading over the whole Roman world. The Glad Tidings, as we know, was transmitted so easily, thanks to the mutual relations subsisting between the scattered Jews of the Dispersion; and we know also what numbers the children of Israel could boast of along the banks of the Nile.

[1] S. Epiphanius, li. 6.
[2] S. Jerome, *Interpretatio Chronicœ Eusebii*, A. D. 45. "Marcus Evangelista, interpres Petri, Ægypto et Alexandriæ Christum annuntiat" (*Patrologie latine*, t. xxvii. p. 579). This year 45 is only an approximate date. Eutychius, Patriarch of Alexandria, mentions the ninth of Claudius (*Patrologie grecque*, t. cxi. p. 903). Apparently this was the local tradition, and certainly it is likelier than any other, for this was the very year, according to Orosius, in which the Jews were driven from the Capital of the Empire. As this expulsion compelled Peter and Mark to quit Rome, the event must also have impelled the latter to leave his Gospel in writing for the benefit of those baptized Pagans who were not affected by the edict of Claudius, while he himself set forth for Egypt to carry thither the Faith.
[3] Luke xxii. 32.

Albeit united by the ties of a common origin, the Christian peoples of the three great Sees followed each their own line of action. Alexandria pressed forward in the paths of noble speculation ; with them Plato became a Christian, but he continued to reign supreme. Antioch was less given to theorizing: there Aristotle held sway ; mysticism and allegory they abandoned to the Alexandrians, in order to devote themselves to the study of the literal meaning of Holy Writ. As for Rome, whether Christian or Pagan, she remained true to her native genius, — always a government, not a school. With little taste for anything that smacked of novelty, her first care was to strengthen the bonds of unity, and thereafter act as judge ; as in the domain of politics, so too in the realms of Faith, it was her destiny to be Queen of the world : *populum late regem*.[1] Hereafter when we shall come to study these mother Churches engaged in very various spheres of action, it will be fitting to bear in mind that as sisters they were nourished with the same milk of Truth, and that all three, from their earliest hours, received the words of Jesus from the Gospel of Saint Peter.

[1] Vergil, *Æneid*, i. 25.

EPILOGUE.

In the latter half of this work Rome has absorbed all our attention. Not that the Church founded in that city had already attained the important position which it held later on, — to all appearances, indeed, it was still one of the most unassuming among the Christian communities, — but Peter was there, and by virtue of that fact she was destined to become the centre of that New Kingdom, whose rule was to extend over the whole world. And therefore, to show that, from the beginning, the seat of infallible authority was established there where we still revere its utterances, was a point which involved such weighty consequences that we have been forced to study its surroundings with more than usual care.

Nor was it less important to determine how far the Head of the Twelve had succeeded in fostering the Church of Rome, before the period when Saint Paul came to support the Apostle's teaching by his own revelations from God. Hazardous as this attempt to study the progress of the Faith may seem, surely no one can accuse us of indulging in arbitrary *dicta* when we hold that the Gospel of Saint Mark contained the generally accepted doctrine of the Roman Church up to the day when Saint Paul began his mission work there. This line of demarcation between the work of Peter and that of Paul will make us realize all the better how wonderfully the Apostle of the Gentiles enlarged the scope of Christian Theology.

Another advantage we have reaped from this historical study has been that we can now judge better of the moral state of the world which the Evangelists endeavored to reform. And Rome must give us a better idea of this than any other place on earth; for men flocked thither from all parts, while the tombs, votive tablets, and inscriptions, furnished the scholar by this city in such abundance, give us a very fair insight into the minds, not only of the citizens, but of the foreign element as well. All these witnesses, as we have seen, testify that, despite the unparalleled decadence in manners, their religious spirit was never more alert, — the need of a Saviour never more keenly felt. It is necessary to grasp this distinction in order to get a clear idea of the struggles which fill the history of Saint Paul's Apostolate. With this in mind, we shall comprehend something of the part which the Church has to play in the restoration of the Pagan world; and, further, the resources which, by God's providence, she made use of to consummate her triumph.

The principal instrument put in her hands was the Roman Empire. After centuries of wars, revolutions, and internal strifes, the sovereign nation suddenly ceased to display any interest in battles. Well satisfied at having put the known world under their yoke, the Romans were ready to exchange all their liberties for a quiet life, and yielded submissively to the will of Augustus. The very name of Rome, which for so many years had been symbolical of bloody conquests, now became a pledge of peace. From the Atlantic to the Indies, from the heart of Africa to the shores of Great Britain, there were no rumors of war; even the brigands had ceased their depredations, and pirates were no longer seen upon the high seas. In this profound quiet the " Roman Peace "[1] became world-famous. The Jewish Philo and the Greek Philosopher Epictetus speak of it with as much enthusiasm as do the Romans by birth.[2] Aristides, a rhetorician of Smyrna, when lauding the sovereigns of the Empire, tells us how under their rule the harbors are filled with vessels, the mountain passes are as safe as the city streets, the country is happy

---

[1] "Immensa romanæ pacis majestas" (Pliny, *Historia Naturalis*, xxvii. 1).
[2] Philo, *Legatio ad Caium*, 21, 22, 39, 40; Epictetus, *Dissert*. iii. 13, 9; Pliny, *Historia Naturalis*, xiv. 2; xxvii. 2, etc.

and prosperous, all fears have vanished, while the streams and straits are opened to commerce.[1]

Even those whom Rome persecuted, felt an attraction to her. Implacable as he was in scourging the vices of the Empire, Tertullian delights to expatiate on its benefits. "The world is better known every day," he says, "better cultivated and richer. New routes are opened to commerce. Deserts are transformed into fruitful domains. Seed is sown where heretofore nothing but barren rocks met the traveller's eye. Marshes are drained, and the flocks no longer fear wild beasts. No island now excites terror, no rock affrights us; but everywhere we find houses, peoples, and cities, — everywhere human life."[2]

This calm was certainly most favorable to the preaching of the Gospel; the minds of men, freed from temporal anxieties, found leisure hours when they could listen and ponder on the words of salvation. The very fulness of present joys left their hearts still unsatisfied, while it awakened vague desires for less fleeting goods. And this expectant feeling spread from nation to nation. All barriers between them being swept away, Rome's voice was heard from one end of the world to the other. Thus the Christian's words uttered there, re-echoed through the whole earth. Nor were the Apostles of the Christ oblivious of the fact that they owed these advantages to the Romans. "It is due to them," says Saint Irenæus, "that we can traverse any highway with impunity, while ships bear us whither we are pleased to go."[3]

Day after day, in fact, armed bands of legionaries extended the network of roads which united the provinces of the Empire. These stupendous highways have been diligently investigated by modern savants; it would be difficult to conceive a system of communication on more majestic or bolder lines. They span the marshes of wild northern regions and traverse the sandy wastes, of the desert, pushing their way to the far-off Eastern frontiers, into solitary reaches nowadays abandoned to nomad tribes.

[1] Aristides, *Encomium Romæ*. [2] Tertullian, *De Anima*, xxx.
[3] S. Irenæus, iv. 30, 3

Modern armies have followed the ancient routes from the Mediterranean coasts to the oases of Sahara. Besides a secure passage, these roads assured the travellers' safe repose during the night; the itineraries of antiquity indicate the numberless way-stations, with the distances which separated them.[1] At no time in the history of the world was intercourse between various nations easier or more agreeable.[2]

With the extension of these ties, different peoples, isolated hitherto, became so closely united as to make one body politic; commercial and social relations expanded; a common language, Greek, was spoken throughout the Empire; the peculiar constitutions of each State gradually shaped themselves in conformity with that of the Capital; the national religions, while remaining free and distinct, had one point in common, — the cultus of Rome and Cæsar, or at least sacrifices offered in their behalf. Philosophy performed its part in bringing about a union of minds by summing up the dictates of reason in a few concise rules concerning the duty of man. These moral ideas, first enunciated in the form of maxims, passed from the precincts of the schools into the Theatre, the orator's discourses, and the poet's verse. Granted that only the thinking part of the community grasped their true meaning, still the multitude kept repeating these wise saws, and, as they grew more familiar with the turns of thought, managed to get some glimpses of true wisdom. In this way the Stoics fostered sentiments of humanity and the brotherhood of mankind; thus they popularized their dream of a City which should embrace the whole world, governed by one only Law, eternal, immutable, and the same to all men alike. True, these splendid aspirations were never to be realized as they conceived them, for the world was sunk too low to be restored by any theories; nevertheless, they did this great

---

[1] Vicarello's *Itinerary* (Henzen, ANTIQUITÉS DE VICARELLO in the *Rheinisches Museum*, 1853); *Itinerarium Antonini Augusti et Hierosolymitanum*, ed. Parthey and Pinder.
[2] Friedländer *Mœurs romaines*, t. ii. 1. vii. : LES VOYAGES.

good, that they made men sensible of the wretchedness of the struggle for life about them, and of their own inability to rise above it.

To souls prepared for its coming by these means, Christianity stood revealed as a present Saviour. Its universal mission, while placing it at once on a higher plane than any of the religions which divided the world, made their exclusive and unsatisfying character all the more manifest. From the very fact that it was a "worship of the spirit,"[1] it far excelled their materialistic beliefs, and ruined their ascendency; but at the same time, with its powers of revivifying what was barren in itself, the New Faith retained all their outward practices which could be made to express its own sublime beliefs.[2] In like manner, the Church appropriated for her use the administrative methods of Pagan Rome, adopted its public and private customs, and willingly accepted society as she found it, if only she might accomplish its regeneration. A faith which realized to the full so many aspirations must have been gladly welcomed by the minds of men weary of doubting and vain expectations.

But it was principally because it spoke to their hearts that the Heavenly Message triumphed. The wretched and unfortunate, so numerous at that time, were hungering for some consolation. The Christian life had everything to attract them: it realized the philosophers' Vision of a City wherein reigned a charity which was boundless, knowing no respect of persons, filled with peace born of an equal share in all privileges and duties; with one stroke it swept away those odious prejudices which made for the debasement of the slave and womankind. Instead of the

---

[1] John iv. 24.
[2] In chapter xix. p. 363, it has been shown by means of several examples, how the Church brought about these transformations. Perfect independence was preserved throughout, despite all that was borrowed from local sources; for though it seemed fitting to adopt the customs and formularies prevalent in Rome, on the other hand, the name used to designate the democratic Assemblies of Greece was taken to denominate the meetings of Christian believers, — ἐκκλησία· *Ecclesia*. From the Hellenic confraternities they took the titles of the new Hierarchy also, ἐπίσκοπος, κλῆρος. . . See Wescher, *Revue archéologique*, avril, 1866.

timid essays of statesmen who hardly ventured to lessen a few of their hardships, the New Faith spread forth that great charter of emancipation : " There is no longer either Jew or Gentile, there is neither slave nor free, nor male nor female. You are all one in Christ Jesus." [1] Assured of recovering their dignity and self-respect in this new Kingdom, the humble folk, who are God's little ones, thronged the Church, and, once within the fold, labored to extend His rule. Their zeal found greater facilities for obtaining a hearing in those times, because, in point of culture and intelligence, the difference between the common people and the upper classes was not so marked as it is to-day. Furthermore, in the masses of the working-people there were many men noted for their qualities, some national, others gained in the pursuit of letters, — Greek freedmen, of as keen intelligence as their brethren of Attica or Ionia; Orientals, too, who were in nowise inferior to them in everything which demanded subtle genius. Despite their ragged garb, these strangers showed the fruits of thoughtful habits, and a language ever ready, eloquent, and instinct with charm : no wonder, then, that Rome listened to them.

These were some of the natural causes which favored the foundation of Christianity. We must not imagine, however, that they operated constantly, nor that they exercised the same influence over all. The arch-enemy now marshalling his forces against them was too strong to be vanquished by a series of unvarying victories ; at the slightest sign of weakening, he recovered his former domains. The hands which were raised in prayer to their Redeemer were the hands of poor captives powerless to break their heavy chains. Soon the pall of darkness would overshadow them once more and blind their hearts. All that remained to them was the light Saint John speaks of, — a Light glimmering amid the shades of night, shadows so murky that the daylight is no longer to be seen.[2] That was the condition in which the great majority of Pagans

---

[1] Gal. iii. 28.   [2] John i. 5.

were languishing at this time. To arouse and save them, the feeble resources we have been describing were not enough; such means are not in proportion with a restoration so far-reaching and entire. Herein God reveals His workings, and His handiwork appears all the mightier, when, taking the events which seconded the diffusion of the Gospel, we contrast with them the obstacles which the Apostles had to overcome.

On every hand, indeed, hatred and insurmountable feuds impeded their work. Man's reason, while attracted, on one hand, by the lofty tone of Christian dogma, on the other was repelled by what seemed incomprehensible. Many points of morality offended their pride and the promptings of human nature,—forgiveness of injuries, love of one's enemies, humiliation and poverty pronounced blessed: this was "the Cross of Jesus, a scandal to the Jews, and to the Gentiles sheer folly."[1] The austere worship of the one and only God, Who manifests Himself only to man's heart, shocked men from childhood familiar with the fables of Olympus and the pomp of Pagan rites. Christianity, with no altars crimsoned with the blood of sacrifices, and with no images of the Divinity, seemed to them like a religion fit only for atheists. Many even regarded it as a seditious system of worship; for instead of accommodating its practices to the Roman ceremonial, like the rites of all the conquered peoples, it declared that the Christian religion was the only true and acceptable service of God. The Jews, who made the same pretensions, consented at least to immolate victims for the well-being of Cæsar; yet these Christians offered him nothing but their prayers! Grievances of this kind, exaggerated by perfidious foes, raised such barriers about the Church that in the second century the scholars of Rome continued to confound the doctrines of Christ with the obscene Mysteries of the East. In a sarcastic epigram, Celsus gives us the common opinion of his times: "While all other religions summon those whose consciences are pure to take part in their ceremonies, the Christians

[1] 1 Cor. i. 23.

promise the Kingdom of God to sinners, fools, and those who are accursed of the gods."[1]

Even more to be dreaded than such offences against reason, were other teachings which were repugnant to their tastes. Paganism had so far penetrated every feature of social life that the disciple must needs break with all his old customs if he would not do violence to his Faith. The games, the theatres, circuses, baths, and banquets were all noxious to his sight and his soul; the public functions, even the slightest intercourse with society, constrained him to take part in idolatrous acts incompatible with his new beliefs; at Rome especially, where every legal act was consecrated by a religious rite, to live in the Christ was indeed to die to the world.[2] Assuredly, those who made this sacrifice found ample recompense in a brotherly union so comforting that even the Gentiles were moved at beholding it. But this very union, which attracted the poorer folk, was a subject for the scornful criticism of the great. Their pride revolted at the thought of treating as brethren vile laborers, slaves, and poor women, who made up the great mass of the faithful. Like the rich young man in the Gospel, they withdrew in sadness because they had "great possessions."[3] These feelings of disdain for Christianity were those generally found among the Pagans; then, at rare intervals, came days when the anguish of doubt, the repulsiveness of sin, remorse and fear of a world to come, seized upon their souls and impelled them to flee for refuge to the Church.

We shall see the history of the infant Church developing amid these alternations of shadow and sunshine, — of resistance and yielding to the promptings of Grace. Saint Paul's ministry, especially, will illustrate these changes, as they follow one another in swift succession; at his first appearance the Apostle is welcomed with transports of joy, — on the morrow he is repulsed and execrated. From those earliest times, Jesus stands forth

[1] Origen, *Adversus Celsum*, iii. 59.   [2] Philip. i. 21 ; Col. iii. 3.
[3] Mark x. 22.

revealed to the world, as in our own day, even as He shall be unto the end of time, "a Sign of contradiction," clear and evident enough to attract the souls of men and to make faith reasonable, yet so veiled in mystery to mortal eyes that haughty minds mistake His meaning. "Lo, this Child is set for the fall and for the resurrection of many, . . . and for a Sign which shall be contradicted."[1]

[1] Luke ii. 34.

APPENDIX.

I.

THE CHRONOLOGY OF THE FIRST YEARS OF THE CHURCH.

THE only certain date, in the history of the first twenty years of the Church, is that of Agrippa's death, which Josephus sets down in the third year of the reign of Claudius (44 A. D.).[1] For the rest of this period the chronological order can be determined only approximately, with the exceptions of Saint Paul's conversion and the Council of Jerusalem, their dates being fixed by certain facts in profane history with which these two events have certain obvious connections.

Indeed, both the conversion of Paul and the martyrdom of Saint Stephen, which preceded it by a few months, took place under peculiar circumstances. The holy Deacon is tried according to the ancient Rules and before a Jewish tribunal; he suffers the penalty decreed by the Law[2] without any efforts being made, as in the trial of Jesus, to obtain the ratification of the Procurator. After this opening act in the persecution that followed, Saul receives unlimited powers from the Sanhedrin to imprison, torture, and put to death all followers of the Christ; in a word, the Roman authority, hitherto all-powerful, appears suddenly to have relaxed its hold. There is only one known fact which can explain this sudden change, — the death of Tiberius, which occurred on the 16th of March, A. D. 37. Caligula, adopting a policy the opposite of that pursued by his predecessor, allowed the various peoples of the East to regain their autonomy; thus it came about that during the first

[1] Josephus, *Antiquitates*, xix. 8, 2.   [2] Deut. xiii. 6-10

two years of this Prince's reign, the Roman rule seems annulled in Palestine. Consequently, this is the interval to which we must set down the martyrdom of Stephen and the conversion of Saint Paul, — that is to say, about the year 37.

Other circumstances, no less exceptional, lead us to decide for 52 as the date of the Council of Jerusalem. A tradition, traced back to the first Fathers and repeated by a long line of witnesses,[1] informs us that Saint Peter arrived in Rome during the reign of Claudius, and according to the best evidences did not return to Jerusalem until that Emperor expelled the Jews and Christians from the Capital of the world. Wieseler has demonstrated that this edict was promulgated in the month of January, 52.[2] So, then, it was not until some time during this year that Peter appeared again in Jerusalem, and that Paul repaired thither to bring before the Apostolic Council certain weighty questions which were dividing the Church of Antioch.

It only remains to be seen whether the two dates we have just determined — 37 for Paul's conversion, 52 for the first Council — harmonize with what we learn from the Acts and the letters of Saint Paul concerning the various journeys which that Apostle made to Jerusalem. The Acts mention three missions, — the first after the conversion of Saul,[3] the second before the great famine,[4] the third on the occasion of the Council of Jerusalem.[5] In the Epistle to the Galatians the Apostle speaks of only two visits to the Holy City, — one three years after his conversion,[6] which all scholars not biassed by rationalistic prejudices identify with the first journey recounted by Saint Luke; the other fourteen years later, which evidently coincides with the third mentioned in the Acts.[7] To obtain this number from 37 and 52, we must bear in mind that the Jews were accustomed to count the unfinished and incomplete year as if it was a full twelvemonth. According to this method of computation, the first journey, which he made three years after his conversion, took place in 39, and the fourteen years which elapsed between this first visit and the third are the years from 39 to 52.

[1] See Appendix IV. [2] *Chronologie des apostolischen Zeitalters*, p. 127.
[3] Acts ix. 26. [4] Acts xi. 30. [5] Acts xv. 2.
[6] Gal i. 18. [7] Gal. ii. 1.

APPENDIX. 393

II.

DATE OF THE MARTYRDOM OF SAINT JAMES THE GREATER AND THE IMPRISONMENT OF SAINT PETER.

FROM the historian Josephus,[1] we learn that Agrippa ended his life at Cæsarea in the year 44 of our era. As the Acts recount his death immediately after the persecution of the Church, some scholars infer that the two events occurred in the same epoch. This conclusion does not flow necessarily from the sacred text,[2] for although Saint Luke did not usually invert the order of events, yet he often neglects to mention any fixed date, and connects incidents separated by a considerable interval, with the sole end in view of showing that one was the consequence of the other. This is the case with the passage we are considering. The narrator, regarding the disease which preyed upon Agrippa as the just punishment for his crimes, appends the account of this awful sequel to the tyrant's persecutions in order to make their relation more apparent, but without intending to have us understand that the Prince died immediately after Peter's miraculous release from prison. Indeed, there is nothing to indicate this in the text of the Acts, where we read simply, "And he went down from Judea to Cæsarea;"[3] or, in other words, on leaving Jerusalem, Herod, as Josephus relates, visited various cities of Judea, — Beyrouth, Tiberias,[4] — arriving finally at Cæsarea, where he died. Between his decease and the persecution we must suppose that several years elapsed, and we have only to study Josephus' account of Agrippa's reign to admit that the hypothesis is a very plausible one which puts the imprisonment of Saint Peter in the Passover-tide of 42, and the death of the King some time in the beginning of 44.[5]

[1] Josephus, *Antiquitates*, xix. 8, 2.
[2] Eusebius, it is true, says that Herod's death followed immediately upon the martyrdom of S. James and the deliverance of Peter (*Historia Ecclesiastica*, ii. 10) ; but he relies solely upon the authority of the Acts, which he interprets as it ordinarily is understood.
[3] Acts xii. 19.   [4] Josephus, *Antiquitates*, xix. 7 and 8.
[5] Here I have merely adopted and summarized the scholarly dissertation by Father de Smedt (*Dissertationes selectæ in primam ætatem historiæ ecclesiasticæ*, dissert. i. : DE ROMANO S. PETRI EPISCOPATU).

The Jewish historian describes this Prince as solely occupied, from the day of his arrival at Jerusalem (41), in winning the good-will of his subjects. Now, Agrippa knew that the Jews hated the Christians, and that the surest way of making himself popular was to persecute the disciples of Jesus. How can any one suppose that he would have waited until 44 — until the last days of his reign — to make use of this weapon? Agrippa assumed the sovereign power about the middle of 41; there is every reason to believe that it was during the following Pasch — that of 42 — that this Prince put Saint James to death and cast Saint Peter into prison.

The close of Josephus' account confirms this hypothesis, and also enforces the conclusion that the persecution in which Saint James was martyred did not take place at the Passover of 44, since Agrippa was dead before that date. The great historian of the Jews, after making us acquainted with the incidents worthy of note during the King's stay at Beyrouth and Tiberias, continues in these words: "Agrippa had just completed the third year of his reign over all Judea when he made his entry into Cæsarea." Thereupon he tells of the festivals held in that city, in the midst of which the King died, and ends his narrative thus: "So, then, Agrippa reigned seven years, four under Caius, and three under Claudius."

These two passages seem to be contradictory, one speaking of four years, the other of only three, during which Agrippa governed his Empire, which Claudius had just restored, or, as it was called, "all Judea." To reconcile his statements, we must suppose that the King had indeed entered upon the fourth year of his reign under Claudius when he arrived at Cæsarea, but that he lived so few days thereafter that Josephus, in his general computation, makes no reckoning of it. If we look farther, and try to determine the exact date in this lesser half of the fourth year, we find that the games in honor of Claudius were celebrated twice a year, — the 24th of January, to commemorate his coming to the throne, and the 6th of August, in honor of his birthday. The latter date cannot be the one referred to, for seven months is too considerable a lapse of time to be passed over by the historian when giving the full duration of Agrippa's reign. Accordingly, the only plausible conclusion from these facts is the one proposed at first; namely, that this Prince died during the festivals in honor of Claudius' accession, toward the end of January, 44.

It follows that the facts related in the twelfth chapter of the Acts — the martyrdom of Saint James and Saint Peter's imprisonment — did not occur during the Paschal-tide of that year (44), but during one of the preceding, either 42 or 43. It would seem natural to select 42, not only for the reason given above, that Agrippa certainly did not defer his persecution of the Christians until the close of his reign, but also because the last-mentioned date accords with three important traditions, — one [1] which tells us that the Apostles dispersed twelve years after their Master's death, — that is, in 42; while another says it was during the second year of Claudius (42) that Saint Peter went to Rome and there founded the Apostolic See;[2] finally, a third asserts that Peter's Pontificate at Rome lasted twenty-five years (4?–67).[3]

III.

THE TESTIMONY OF SAINT IRENÆUS AS TO THE DATE OF THE COMPOSITION OF SAINT MATTHEW'S GOSPEL.

THE traditions, with one accord, attribute the composition of the First Gospel to the time when the Apostles quitted Jerusalem. One witness alone dissents from this unanimous testimony: this is Saint Irenæus, who seems to adopt a later date, — the year 62. In the text of this Father, as it is usually punctuated and understood, we read these words: "Matthew wrote his Gospel for the Hebrews and in their tongue, while Peter and Paul were evangelizing

---

[1] Apollonius (sec. iii.), quoted by Eusebius (*Historia Ecclesiastica*, v. 18): "Tanquam ex veterum traditione refert Dominum Apostolis suis precepisse ne intra duodecim annos Hierosolymis excederent." We find this tradition again in Clement of Alexandria (*Stromata*, vi. 5).

[2] S. Jerome, *De Viris Illustribus*, i. "Simon Petrus, secundo Claudii anno . . . Romam pergit, ibique viginti annis cathedram sacerdotalem tenuit."

[3] Liberian Catalogue, " Petrus ann. xxv. mens. uno d. viii." Duchesne, *Liber Pontificalis*.

Rome and founding the Church in that city. After their departure [from this world], Mark, Peter's disciple and interpreter, left us in writing all that Peter had proclaimed; and Luke, who had accompanied Paul, gathered together in his book the Gospel preached by the latter." [1]

Taken in this sense, the passage gives rise to serious difficulties. Not only does the author disagree with all the other Fathers as to the date of Saint Matthew's writing, he even leads us to infer that Saints Peter and Paul came to Rome together, which, as we shall see, is contradicted by the whole mass of Tradition. Furthermore, he refers the composition of the Third Gospel to a date much too late (after the death of the two Apostles in 67); for all critics concede that Saint Luke wrote his Gospel before the Acts. Now, the latter work was completed, at the latest, in 64, before Saint Paul was released from prison, since the closing lines of this book which mention the confinement of the Apostle, do not speak of its end. It is a wise rule of criticism that when a single isolated text contradicts the whole body of traditions on any point, we should either accept it with great reservations, or look about for some more satisfactory interpretation of the text itself. Adopting the latter course, Father Patrizi [2] calls our attention to the fact that the vague expression ἔξοδον, "departure," may refer either to the death of the Apostles or to their leaving Rome. Again, the punctuation remains a very uncertain question, as always in the case of ancient writers, and these words, "*when Peter and Paul were evangelizing Rome,*" need not be referred to the foregoing sentence, where the writer is speaking of Saint Matthew's Gospel, but to the following phrase, which sets forth the origin of the Gospels of Saints Mark and Luke. This slight change will suffice to make the testimony of Saint Irenæus coincide with all the other traditions: [3] "Matthew wrote his Gospel for the Hebrews and

---

[1] Eusebius, *Historia Ecclesiastica*, v. 8.
[2] Patrizi, *De Evangeliis*, i.
[3] The text of S. Irenæus is given above, with the punctuation adopted by Father Patrizi: "Matthæus in Hebræis ipsorum lingua scripturam edidit Evangelii. Cum Petrus et Paulus Romæ evangelizarent et fundarent ecclesiam, post vero horum exitum, Marcus, discipulus et interpres Petri, et ipse, quæ a Paulo annuntiabantur, per scripta nobis tradidit, et Lucas autem sectator Pauli, quod ab illo prædicabatur, evangelium in libro condidit."

in their tongue. Mark and Luke composed theirs during the time when Peter and Paul were preaching in Rome; later on, however, when both these Apostles had left the city."

All we know about the missionary labors of these two Apostles, their sojourn in and departure from Rome, would compel us to separate the facts grouped together here in one sentence, and refer them to different dates; for so much seems to be quite incontestable, — to wit, that Saint Peter appeared in Rome a long time before Saint Paul's arrival there, and that he left the Capital several times. His first visit was as early as 42, as we shall see shortly; but as, according to the testimony of the Acts, he was present at the First Council of Jerusalem, about 52, we are warranted in concluding that he had quitted Rome at some earlier date, — probably when Claudius banished all Jews from Rome (in the ninth year of his reign, according to Orosius, — 49 A. D.).[1] Consequently, we must believe that this is the period to which Saint Irenæus assigns the composition of Saint Mark's Gospel.

Saint Paul, on the contrary, did not go to Rome until some time in 62. After remaining there for two years as a prisoner, he left in 64. His departure determined Saint Luke to give the Christians of Rome the Gospel which he had compiled from the preaching of the great Doctor of the Gentiles, — probably composed at Cæsarea during the imprisonment of Saint Paul.[2]

Any one can see at a glance the new meaning this commentary gives to Saint Irenæus' words, and what we must conclude from them as to the date of each Gospel. The first was composed for use among the Hebrews of Jerusalem, — consequently, before Saint Matthew left the Holy City; the second was edited by Saint Mark, after Peter, with all his fellow-countrymen, was expelled from Rome by Claudius, in or about 52; Saint Luke published the third when Paul on getting out of prison, left the Imperial Capital, in 64. It seems almost beyond question that Eusebius understood the text of Saint Irenæus in this sense, for in

---

[1] Orosius, *Histor.* 7, 6. In 52, according to Wieseler's reckoning. See above, p. 392.
[2] The Acts, as we have seen, were finished in 64, and S. Luke wrote his Gospel at an earlier date.

the very book in which he quotes this passage,[1] he states expressly that Saint Matthew[2] wrote his work before leaving Jerusalem, while Saint Mark wrote at a later date, during Claudius' reign.[3] In the following century Saint Jerome, who studied all the traditions attentively, and notably those he found in Saint Irenæus, — Saint Jerome makes use of almost the same words as Eusebius: "Matthew, also called Levi, was the first to write the Gospel of the Christ in Judea for those of the Circumcision who were believers, and he composed it in the Hebrew tongue."[4] This imposing body of witnesses not only demonstrates the force of this conclusion, it also confirms and explains the testimony of tradition.

Accordingly, we may feel justified in drawing the following conclusions. Those critics who defer the date of the composition of the First Gospel as late as 70, can find no text, nor any tradition in the writings of antiquity, to justify their hypothesis. On the contrary, all down the ages we hear the fact asserted and reiterated that Saint Matthew was the first of all the Evangelists to set down the Good News in writing; and this he did in the Hebrew language, for the Jews of Palestine, before he quitted his native land. Now, we have seen that the Apostles abandoned Jerusalem and went forth to evangelize the world, twelve years after the Ascension; so then we must conclude that the First Gospel was composed at this juncture. I should be far from contending that this date is beyond all question, but I do believe that it is better founded than any other, because it rests, not on any gratuitous conjectures, but on facts attested by the five first centuries of Christianity.

IV.

SAINT PETER AT ROME.

WHICHEVER opinion the reader adopts touching the period when Saint Peter first appeared in Rome, the actual fact of his having resided there is hardly ever disputed nowa-

---

[1] Eusebius, *Historia Ecclesiastica*, v. 8.
[2] Id., iii. 24. [3] Id., ii. 14, 15.
[4] S. Jerome, *De Viris Illustribus*, 3.

days;[1] for although no contemporary writer makes any express allusion to that event, we have a series of witnesses in testimony of it, from the third century back to Apostolic times, together casting a continuous light on this turning-point of history.[2]

One hundred and fifty years after the death of Saint Peter, we find his martyrdom at Rome spoken of everywhere in the Church as one of the most assured events, well known to all. Caius, who wrote his work in that city during the pontificate of Zephyrinus (202-219), describes the tomb of the Apostle at the Vatican;[3] and no other city has ever laid claim to possessing his remains. Tertullian, about the same time, reminds the African Church that Peter established his pontifical seat in Rome, that he there endured the same tortures which his Lord had suffered, and that he baptized in the Tiber, as John had done in the Jordan.[4] Twenty-five years later, Saint Dionysius of Corinth testifies to the same facts in Greece;[5] Clement and his disciple Origen relate these events in Alexandria.[6] The East abounds with similar traditions. If we pass over into Gaul, we find Saint Irenæus writing his treatise against heresies, in which he twice alludes to the fact that Peter and Paul founded the Roman Church.[7] Now, the Bishop of Lyons had known many contemporaries of the Apostle in Asia; he was a disciple of Saint Polycarp, who, in turn, had listened to the teachings of Saint John the Evangelist; through these men we have a continuous record of the first century of the Church. Their testimony, even if unsupported, would make us certain of the fact which we are

---

[1] "I regard the tradition of Peter's sojourn at Rome as very probable; but I believe his stay was of short duration, and that Peter suffered martyrdom a little while after his arrival in the Eternal City" (Renan, *L'Antechrist*, p. 556).
[2] See Father de Smedt's DE ROMANO S. PETRI EPISCOPATU, in his *Dissertationes Selectæ*, pp. 1-48.
[3] Eusebius, *Historia Ecclesiastica*, ii. 25; *Patrologie grecque*, t. xx. p. 207.
[4] Tertullian, *De Præscript*. 36; *Scorpiac*. 15; *De Baptismo*, 4; *Patrologie latine*, t. ii. pp. 49, 151; t. i. p. 1203.
[5] S. Dionysius, quoted by Eusebius (*Historia Ecclesiastica*, ii. 25; *Patrologie grecque*, t. xx. p. 210).
[6] Clement and Origen, quoted by Eusebius (*Historia Ecclesiastica*, vi. 14; iii. 1.: *Patrologie grecque*, t. xx. pp. 551, 214).
[7] S. Irenæus, *Adversus Hæreses*, iii. 1: *Patrologie grecque*, t. vii. pp. 844, 848.

considering; but we have other witnesses, less explicit certainly, yet sufficiently clear when studied in the light of later traditions.

Forty years after Saint Peter's death (107), Saint Ignatius, then brought to Rome to die in the amphitheatre, wrote the Christians of the Capital: "I beseech you not to display, for my sake, a kindness which is out of place; let me be the prey of their wild beasts. . . . I do not command you, like Peter and Paul: they were Apostles, I am only a condemned man."[1] These words are easily understood if we admit that the two Apostles governed the Roman Church; they are quite unintelligible if we dispute it. We again encounter the same belief toward the end of Domitian's reign (96); Saint Clement of Rome, speaking of the Christians immolated by Nero after the burning of the city, reckons Saints Peter and Paul in the number. "They have been great ensamples in our midst,"[2] he adds; thereby showing that they suffered death in the presence of their Roman foes and followers.

This Epistle of Saint Clement is the first Christian document, outside of the inspired books, which has come down to us.[3] The latter make no explicit mention of Saint Peter's sojourn at Rome. The first Epistle written by the Prince of the Apostles does, however, contain one indication which has attracted the attention of historians. His letter is dated from Babylon. This word is not used to designate the city of that name in Mesopotamia, for it seems hardly likely that the Apostle could have journeyed so far as those distant regions; here Babylon is only the symbolic name for Rome, now become in Jewish eyes the centre of a universal impiety, just as the Capital of Assyria had been to their fathers.[4] The children of Israel were always fond of

---

[1] S. Ignatius, *Ep. ad Romanos*, iv.: *Patrologie grecque*, t. v. p. 690.

[2] S. Clement, *Ep. i. ad Corinthios*, 5, 6: *Patrologie grecque*, t. i. p. 218.

[3] The Epistle of S. Barnabas is not, of course, the work of the Apostle whose name it bears, and does not seem to have been composed earlier than the opening years of the second century; Mgr. Hefélé thinks it was written between 107 and 120; Funk, on the other hand, dates its composition in the last years of the first century (*Opera Patrum Apostolicorum*, t. i.; *Prolegomena*, v.).

[4] M. Renan does not suggest a doubt as to the signification of the word "Babylon" in this Epistle. "The Church of Rome is here designated by the words, 'the elect which are in Babylon.' . . . In order to baffle the suspicions of the police, Peter thought best to use the name of the olden

such mystical appellations: thus, in the Book of Esther, Aman is called "the Amalekite, and the son of Agag;"[1] the Samaritans and other Gentiles are spoken of as Cutheans;[2] Edom and Nineveh also serve as injurious epithets whereby to designate the Roman Empire. The Christians acted in like manner: in the Apocalypse, as well as in the Sibylline Books, Babylon always is meant to signify Rome.[3] No one in that day could misunderstand the allusion. Furthermore, they knew well what were the reasons which compelled them to use such secrecy,—the dangers threatening the Church, now on the eve of Nero's persecution; the surveillance exercised over all leaders of their community by the Imperial power; finally, the necessity of keeping Peter's residence a secret, especially in case his letter should be intercepted. The veil was so transparent to all believers that the Fathers never dreamed of interpreting it in any other light. Taken together with posterior testimony, and explained and confirmed by it, this evidence, standing at the end of his Epistle, leaves no room for doubt that Peter was in Rome once, at least to die there.

Is it possible to bring forward arguments of equal value to prove that the Apostle not only visited that city, but that he was its first pastor? Saint Ignatius of Antioch implies as much, as we have just seen; and after him it is vouched for by all ancient writers, with not a single authority to gainsay the universal tradition. However, we have no documents to establish the fact of Peter's Pontificate as old as the one referred to above, since Saint Irenæus is the first to plainly attribute the foundation of the Roman Church to the Chief of the Apostles.[4] This Doctor of the

Capital of Asiatic impiety to designate Rome,—a name whose symbolical import could not be mistaken by any one" (Renan, *L'Antechrist*, p. 122). If we are to believe the Copts, the Apostle referred to Old Cairo, where in his time there was a small town called Babylon by the Assyrian colonists who founded it (Strabo, xvii. 1). This tradition, although adopted by several modern critics, is not generally accepted as credible.

[1] Esther iii. 1, 10; viii. 3, 5.
[2] Josephus, *Antiquitates*, ix. 14, 3, and the *Talmud, passim*.
[3] Apoc. xiv. 8; xvi. 19, xviii. 5, 9, 18; xviii. 2; *Oracula Sibyll.* v. 143, 159.
[4] S. Irenæus, *Adversus Hæreses*, iii. 1, 3. From this period documentary evidence is to be had in abundance. Tertullian, the author of the poem against Marcion, Caïus, S. Cyprian, Firmilian of Cæsarea, and indeed all writers of the third century, speak in the same terms as S. Irenæus.

Church, writing more than a century after Saint Peter's death, does not impress us with the same confidence as would a contemporary of like character. His testimony, nevertheless, cannot be set aside as devoid of authority; for the anxiety shown by the great Bishop of Lyons to treasure up the lessons of his elders, as also his youth spent in the company of Saint Polycarp, ought to be sufficient to gain him a respectful hearing as an echo of the Apostolic times. And especially so far as concerns the Pontificate of Saint Peter, his teachings are of exceptional importance, since, before betaking himself to Gaul, he had resided for some time in Rome, and had studied its traditions; "in order to confound the heretics, he found no mightier argument to bring forth against them than the faith of that Church, wherein the succession of pastors from Peter's time was manifest and acknowledged by all." [1]

Twenty-five years before Saint Irenæus, a converted Jew named Hegesippus had visited the Churches of the East and West, testified to the agreement of their doctrine with that of Jesus Christ, and investigated especially into the series of pastors by whose ministrations they had each received the teachings of the Apostles. On coming to the Capital of the Empire, he collected facts giving him the succession of Pontiffs down to Saint Anicetus (156).[2] These notes of Hegesippus were under Eusebius' eyes, who made great use of them, and, it would seem, extracted therefrom the list inserted in his history. Now, this is what we find in his relation: "Linus was the first to become Bishop of the Roman Church after Peter; Clement was the third." [3]

---

[1] "Maximæ et antiquissimæ et omnibus cognitæ, a gloriosissimis duobus Apostolis Petro et Paulo Romæ fundatæ et constitutæ Ecclesiæ, eam quam habet ab Apostolis traditionem, et annuntiatam hominibus fidem, per successiones episcoporum pervenientem usque ad nos indicantes, confundimus omnes" (S. Irenæus, *Adversus Hæreses*, iii. 3).

[2] Διαδοχὴν ἐποιήσαμεν μέχρις Ἀνικήτου. Hegesippus, quoted by Eusebius (*Historia Ecclesiastica*, iv. 22: *Patrologie grecque*, t. xx. p. 377). The word διαδοχή is used here to signify the series of Roman Bishops as far as Anicetus; for, immediately thereafter, Hegesippus employs the same expression when stating that Soter replaced Anicetus: Παρὰ Ἀνικήτου διαδέχεται Σωτήρ, and he adds that, so far as concerned the succession of Bishops in each city (ἐν ἑκάστῃ διαδοχῇ καὶ ἐν ἑκάστῃ πόλει), everything was ordered in accordance with the proclamations of the Law, the Prophets, and the Lord.

[3] Eusebius, *Historia Ecclesiastica*, iii. 4: *Patrologie grecque*, t. xx p. 221.

Saint Irenæus could not have been acquainted with Hegesippus' book,[1] for he never quotes it, nor does he invoke his authority against the heretics. Hence, these are two independent depositions which go far to confirm one another.

A third proof is found in a chronicle of the Popes compiled about 350 and called the Catalogue of Liberius, because that is the name of the last Pontiff given in it. Mommsen[2] has established the fact that up to 223 this series of the successors of Peter is a reproduction of the annals which Saint Hippolytus composed at Rome in the beginning of the third century, wherein was made mention "of the names of the Bishops of Rome and the duration of their pontificates." Not content with merely copying these authentic lists, the author of the Liberian Catalogue wished to do more, even going so far as to settle the precise months and days, and decide under what Emperors and Consuls each Pope lived. In this mass of details, he committed numerous errors; but these additions, for which he alone is responsible, do not deprive the primitive documents of their intrinsic value. In the chronicle of the names of Sovereign Pontiffs with the years of their Episcopates, we have the testimony of Saint Hippolytus himself. Now, this witness wrote in Rome, and had the official catalogues to refer to, the same which Hegesippus and Saint Irenæus speak of before him; from them he transcribed the list as it stands in his chronicle. At the head we read the name of Peter.

These evidences, each confirming the other, are sufficient to establish the fact of the foundation of the Roman Church by the Chief of the Apostles. Furthermore, there is no tradition which contradicts it; no Christian community has ever claimed him as its first pastor: Antioch alone, on this point always in accord with Rome, glories in having pos-

---

[1] Hegesippus published his work during the Pontificate of Eleutherius (175-189). Now, at this time S. Irenæus had already left Rome, for we find that in 177 he had been named as the coadjutor and future successor of S. Pothinus at Lyons; in all likelihood he had already resided in that city for some years.

[2] Consult Mommsen (*Ueber den Chronographen vom Jahre* 354, p. 634); De Rossi (*Roma Sotterranea*, t. ii. p. 111), and especially M. l'Abbé Duchesne (Introduction to the *Liber Pontificalis*, § i. 4; § ii. pp. 7 and 8). The text of the Liberian Catalogue is published with admirable fidelity at the head of this scholarly work.

sessed Peter's episcopal chair for seven years;[1] and notwithstanding she never considered the great Apostle as, properly speaking, Bishop of Antioch, for Eusebius, who had before him, as we have said, the catalogues of the Eastern Churches collected by Hegesippus, — Eusebius names Saint Evodius as first Pontiff of Antioch, and Saint Ignatius as the second.[2]

So general a belief overawed even the heretics. The Ebionite and Gnostic apocryphas,[3] which invented a thousand fables concerning Saint Peter, never located his Episcopal See anywhere else but at Rome. How would they dare to do so, indeed, face to face with the monuments of that city, the Apostle's tomb on the Vatican, the cemetery "where Peter baptized," and especially the Episcopal Chair, that symbol of his pontificate? In Signor de Rossi's judgment, the last-named relic has so many marks of authenticity that he gives it a place among the witnesses from whose testimony it has been demonstrated that Saint Peter founded the Roman Church.[4] The time-hallowed chair is well known to all readers; nevertheless, certain points in its history are so important to the understanding of the question before us that it will not be a digression to freshen our memory of them.

Though generally enclosed in its throne of gilded bronze, which stands at the end of the apse of Saint Peter's, this chair, in 1867, was exhibited to assembled multitudes. Underneath the ivories and the plates of acacia wood which cover it, it was possible to distinguish all that was left of the ancient seat, — four legs, connected by their cross-pieces, and two uprights for the back. These pieces, of a yellowish oak, coarsely fashioned, are worm-eaten with old

---

[1] Tillemont, *Mémoires*, t. i. p. 167: S. PIERRE, art. xxviii.
[2] Eusebius, *Historia Ecclesiastica: Patrologie grecque*, t. xx. p. 255.
[3] The principal examples of these apocryphas are the *Gospel* and the *Acts of Peter*, the *Preaching of Peter*, and several writings wrongly attributed to S. Clement, — the *Recognitions*, *Homilies*, and *Apostolic Constitutions*.
[4] Here I simply reproduce, in brief, a dissertation which the illustrious archæologist published in the *Bullettino* for May and June, 1867. His series of ingenious deductions should not be passed over in silence by any one treating this subject, although they may not seem to establish with absolute certainty the particular point De Rossi has in view. The passages cited do indeed prove that Rome was the seat of Peter's Pontificate, but they do not demonstrate with equal clearness that the chair mentioned by his witnesses was the material seat which was used by the Apostle.

age and worn by the handling of pilgrims. This shabby and almost shapeless object is in harmony with the simplicity of the Apostles and the primitive Church. The rings set in the wood are just large enough to admit the poles, by which it was converted into a *sella gestatoria*. It is impossible to decide whether these accessories existed from the beginning, or were added when the custom was established of enthroning the new Popes on this chair. This much at least Commendatore de Rossi regards as certain, — that at the end of the sixth century Ennodius of Pavia saw it in the baptistery of Saint Peter's Church, just as it has come down to us; the name he gives it is sufficient proof of this, for he speaks of it as "the gestatorial chair of the Apostolical Confession." "Thereon," he says, "the Pontiff was wont to sit when he conferred on the neophytes who came forth from the baptismal waters, another heavenly gift, — the grace of Confirmation."[1]

A century and a half earlier the same custom existed, and the fonts of the Vatican already contained Saint Peter's Episcopal throne; for proof of this we have the inscription engraved by Saint Damasus on the pediment of this monument. "The one and only Chair of Peter, one only and true baptism!"[2] — a thought which we find reproduced and explained in the epitaph of his successor, Soricius : "As Sovereign Pontiff he was worthy to take his seat in the sacred fonts."[3] To prove that here the allusion is to the material seat of the Apostle, Signor de Rossi cites a passage from Saint Optatus of Miletus; writing against the Donatists about the year 372, this author in his controversy with the Bishop argued that the Romans rejoiced in the possession of an unbroken series of legitimate pastors who had one and all been installed on the papal throne. "If you ask Macrobius what position he occupies here, can he make answer, 'The Chair of Peter'? I know not whether he ever beheld that Chair with his own eyes; but certainly he never approached it, for he is a schismatic."[4]

[1] "Ecce nunc ad gestatoriam sellam apostolicæ confessionis uda mittunt limina candidatos; et uberibus, gaudio exactore, fletibus collata Dei beneficio dona geminantur" (Ennodius, *Apolog. pro Synod.*).
[2] "Una Petri sedes, unum verumque lavacrum" (Gruter, *Inscript.*, p. 1163, 10).
[3] "Fonte sacro magnus meruit sedere sacerdos" (Gruter, *Inscript.*, p. 1171, 6). [4] S. Optatus, *Ad Parmeniam*, lib. ii. 4.

The baptistery, wherein these witnesses of the fourth century assert that the illustrious relic was preserved, had just been erected by Saint Damasus. Where had it been kept up to that time? Perhaps in the basilica built by Constantine, or in the crypt of Saint Peter's tomb. No one can tell; but certainly its shrine was in Rome, and there the Christians venerated it "as Saint Peter's own Chair, whereon he himself was wont to sit, and from which he ordained that Linus should be the first to take this seat after him."[1] This is the language of the author of a poem against Marcion, written at the beginning of the third century. Tertullian testifies to the same effect. "Travel through the Apostolic Churches, and you will behold in them the very seats once occupied by the Apostles, each in its proper place. If you live near Italy, you have Rome."[2] Consequently, this city had preserved the Episcopal throne of Saint Peter up to that time, as Jerusalem had that of Saint James, and Alexandria Saint Mark's. Now, Tertullian lived in Rome toward the close of the second century, and among the oldest of the faithful, whom he met there, were many who had known the later contemporaries of the Apostles. This unbroken series of witnesses, to Signor de Rossi's mind, establishes the authenticity of the chair at the Vatican, and, accordingly, he contends that it is a tangible, visible sign of Saint Peter's Pontificate at Rome.

Whatever opinion we may hold as to the value of this last proof, reading over the foregoing pages we shall find that two facts stand out so plainly that no unbiassed mind will think of disputing them, — first, that the Chief of the Twelve came to Rome, and that he died there as Bishop of the Mother Church. Can we go further and fix the year when he first appeared in the city of the Cæsars? On this point such documents as we possess, are neither so harmonious nor so clear, while those which exactly determine the date are too recent to be accepted as reliable. However, the tradition which states that Saint Peter arrived at Rome in the year 42 is handed down to us by

---

[1] Hac cathedra, Petrus qua sederat ipse, locatum
Maxima Roma Linum primum considere jussit.
Carmina adv. Marcionem, l. iii. c. ix.: *Patrologie latine*, t. ii. p. 1077.

[2] Tertullian, *De Præscriptionibus*, xxxvi.

trustworthy authorities, who are generally very exact; and furthermore it accords so well with what we know of the first years of the Church that we need not hesitate about adopting it.

The first historian to mention it is Eusebius, in his Chronicle, written about 310.[1] In the following century we find his testimony repeated by Orosius[2] and Saint Jerome.[3] "Simon Peter," says the latter, "came to Rome to combat the teaching of Simon the Magician, in the second year of Claudius, and he there occupied the sacerdotal chair during twenty-five years, until the last year of Nero." The Catalogue of Liberius gives the same duration for the Apostle's Pontificate;[4] yet, on this point, it did no more than reproduce the Chronicle of Saint Hippolytus, — as we have seen already. At the end of the second century, therefore, it was an accepted tradition that Peter's Episcopate lasted twenty-five years, and consequently that he established his seat at Rome at an early date, — or about 42, — if we adopt the common opinion, according to which he was martyred in 67.

The principal difficulty rises from a passage in Lactantius (sixth century), which recounts that Peter came to Rome during Nero's reign.[5] Hence, it is inferred that even in the time of Eusebius the traditions were contradictory and, for that reason alone, untrustworthy. This conclusion strikes us as too sweeping, for Lactantius, when mentioning the Apostle as being at Rome about 64, does not deny that he had been there at some previous time. All that he has in mind is to give an account of the miserable deaths of the persecutors of the Church. The first of these was Nero; our author begins with him, and incidentally reminds his readers that Saint Peter evangelized the Capital of the Empire during the reign of this Prince. May we not conclude from this that in the fourth century the Roman people treasured the memory of a twofold visit from Saint Peter, one being his sojourn during Claudius' reign mentioned by Eusebius, Saint Jerome, and Orosius; the other during

[1] Eusebius, *Patrologie grecque*, t. xix. p. 539.
[2] Orosius, *Hist.* vii. 6: *Patrologie latine*, t. xxxi. p. 1072.
[3] S. Jerome, *De Viris Illustribus*, 1: *Patrologie latine*, t. xxxiii. p. 607.
[4] *Liber Pontificalis*, ed. Duchesne, t. i. p. 2.
[5] **Lactantius,** *De Mortibus Persecutorum*, 2: *Patrologie latine*, t. vii. p. 50.

Nero's, as related by Lactantius? This hypothesis furnishes a reasonable explanation of a peculiar contradiction which we come upon two centuries later. In the Catalogue of Felix IV.,[1] an abridgment of the primitive compilation in the *Liber Pontificalis* (sixth century), we read that Saint Peter visited Rome in the time of Nero, and then, immediately after this, that he was Bishop of that city for twenty-five years. Apparently without perceiving it himself, the author of this Catalogue has here joined together, and thereby acquaints us with, the traditions of two successive visits of the Apostle.

These evidences, to which no valid objection has been raised, are sufficient to make it, if not certain, at least very probable, that Peter visited Rome during the reign of Claudius.[2] Commendatore de Rossi believes that we possess a complete confirmation of this fact in the monuments of Christian antiquity. Although his deductions, under their present form, still seem to lack that something which would make them positively convincing, we cannot pass over them here without serious consideration; for it needs only some new discovery to strengthen the weak points in his argument, and we all know that the hypotheses of the illustrious archæologist have almost always had the good fortune of being verified promptly.

De Rossi finds his first traces of the two successive sojourns of the Apostle at Rome, in the liturgical remains; to his thinking, the feasts celebrated on the eighteenth of January and the twenty-second of February in honor of the Chair of Saint Peter, referred to two different Episcopal seats, — one venerated at the Vatican, the other at the Ostrian Cemetery, near the waters where Peter baptized at the time of his first visit. This incident in the Apostle's career, De Rossi brings forward in a clearer light by adducing certain curious references on an old papyrus, and some vials of oils preserved at Monza.[3] We owe these relics to John the Abbot, who visited Rome under Gregory the

[1] *Liber Pontificalis*, ed. Duchesne, t. i. p. 50.
[2] "Petrum 25 annos Romanam cathedram tenuisse diserte testantur auctor primæ partis *Catalogi Liberiani*, Eusebius, Hieronymus, Orosius, et alii, nullo antiquo auctore vel monumento directe aut indirecte contradicente. Hanc sententiam igitur ut longe probabiliorem tenendam esse censemus" (De Smedt, *Dissertationes Selectæ*, diss. i. cap. ii. art. iv. 18).
[3] See the *Bullettino* for May and June, 1867.

Great, and brought back to Queen Theodolinda a few vials of oil taken from the most celebrated churches. On each of them the pilgrim made a note of the spot whence he procured them, and, setting down these inscriptions on a papyrus as he journeyed through the city, he thus arranged a topographical list, which might serve as an itinerary for a visitor to the Holy City.

After collecting his oil from the sanctuary " of the Chair which Peter occupied *for the first time,*" he visits the holy places along the new Salarian Road, from there crosses the Tiber, and arrives at the Vatican, where, near the Tomb of Saint Peter, as De Rossi has proved, stood a second Pontifical seat, distinct from the one which the Abbot John saw on the other side of the stream. Not far from the Via Salaria, the savants of our times have discovered the most ancient catacomb in Rome, the Ostrian Cemetery, "where Peter baptized." Here, then, as it would certainly seem, the pilgrim from Lombardy venerated the first Chair of which he speaks, more ancient than that at the Vatican; for on the Papyrus of Monza, as well as in the Martyrologies and Calendars of the period, it is called " the first whereon Peter was seated."

The cultus of these relics gave rise to the two feasts celebrated in our Liturgy, on the eighteenth of January and the twenty-second of February. The first was instituted in honor of the Chair at the Ostrian Cemetery; to this the most ancient Martyrologies bear witness by marking this as the day " Of the Dedication of Saint Peter's Chair, whereon for the first time he took his seat at Rome."[1] This, as we see, is the same formula as that which John the Abbot transcribed on the *ampulla* and the papyrus of Monza; it seems most likely that he found this inscription in the oratory which he visited. As to the feast of February twenty-second, our liturgical books give it this title, " Saint Peter's Chair at Antioch." But De Rossi has proved that the words "at Antioch" were added by a clerk of the Church of Auxerre, who, in the seventh century, attempted to correct and harmonize the ancient catalogues of the martyrs. Finding two feasts of Saint Peter's Chair, the

---

[1] " Dedicatio cathedræ S. Petri Apostoli, qua primum Romæ sedit" (*Martyrologium Hieronymianum*). " Cathedra S. Petri qua primum Romæ sedit " (*Parvum Romanum Martyrologium*).

first referring to the Apostle's sojourn at Rome, the second without any specific reference, he fancied that the latter was meant to recall Saint Peter's Episcopate at Antioch, and his erroneous conjecture little by little obtained universal credence, especially as the compilation made by the clerk of Auxerre was the principal source of our existing martyrologies. To convince oneself of his mistake it will suffice to examine the calendars and liturgical books anterior to the seventh century.[1] Nowhere is the name of Antioch connected with the chair commemorated on the twenty-second of February. Furthermore, the feast of this day was considered too solemn then for us to believe now that it merely recalled an event of secondary importance in the life of the Apostle. As late as the sixteenth century it continued to be one of the principal solemnities in the papal city; in the time of Saint Leo it was celebrated at the Vatican by a great concourse of bishops; more than any other, this was the Day of the Apostle, "Dies Apostoli."[2] The prayers proper to this anniversary, particularly those in the ancient Gallican Liturgy, clearly indicate its object; all recall that Profession of Faith made by Peter at Cæsarea-Philippi, and the promises which were its recompense, — the Apostle made chief over his brethren, and thus becoming the immovable foundation of the Church.[3] Hence it was to celebrate this great event in the Gospel history, together with the Primacy of Peter, that they observed this day; in the other Feast, as a visible symbol of the Sovereign Pontificate, the Chair of the Vatican, the one which the Apostle had occupied toward the close of his life, which

---

[1] In the *Depositio Martyrum* (a Roman Calendar of the fourth century), which forms part of the Philocalian collection, we read these words alone: viii. kal. mart. *natale Petri de catedra* (Duchesne, *Liber Pontificalis*, p. 11). Almost all the manuscripts in S. Gregory's Sacramentary have xiii. kal. mart. *cathedra sancti Petri*. The *Codex Ratoldi* (980) is the only one to add *in Antiochia* (see *Patrologie latine*, t. lxxviii. pp. 50, 302, 588). According to John the Deacon's statement (*Vita Gregorii*, ii. 17), S. Gregory's Sacramentary is merely the work of S. Gelasius (492–496), revised and abridged.

[2] De Rossi, *Bullettino*, for May and June, 1867.

[3] Mabillon, *De Liturgia Gallicana*, p. 226. "Deus qui hodierna die beatum Petrum post te dedisti caput Ecclesiæ, cum te ille vere confessus sit et a te digne prælatus sit. . . ." In the beginning of the Gallican Mass, this feast is called: "Beatissimi Petri sollemnissimus dies, quem ipsa divinitas consecravit delegando cœlorum claves." Mabillon, *Mus. Ital.* t. i. p. 297.

was preserved beside his tomb and on which his successors had been enthroned, was venerated by the Church.

However ingenious these conclusions may seem, they do not make it absolutely certain that Rome possessed two Chairs once used by Peter, for the one which the Abbot John venerated at the Ostrian Cemetery might have been transferred to the Vatican at a later date; and the texts cited to prove that in the latter locality there had always been a Pontifical throne, are not explicit enough to remove all doubts on the question. The only definite conclusion to be drawn from these archæological researches, is that Rome ever cherished the memory of the Apostle's first visit, and connected it in some way with the Ostrian Cemetery. To determine the epoch in which he arrived at the Capital, we have only two pieces of documentary evidence, strictly speaking, — the Liberian Catalogue, and the chronology generally received in the Church from the beginning of the third century.

V.

SIMON THE MAGICIAN.

THE details invented to embellish the meeting of Saint Peter and Simon the Magician at Rome, are enough to arouse suspicions in any judicious mind. Two points in particular are open to criticism, — the public contention between the Apostle and the Magician, wherein the latter succumbed; and the statue erected on the island in the Tiber, between the two bridges, bearing on it this inscription: SIMONI DEO SANCTO, "To Simon, the holy God." [1]

Eusebius has a brief allusion to the first of these facts. After recording that the impostor astounded Rome by his marvellous performances, he merely adds: "The arrival of Peter sufficed to extinguish his great renown." [2] If the historian alludes to the second overthrow of the Samaritan in these terms, without mentioning the circumstances, we may conclude that he regarded the traditions current in his own times [3] as devoid of foundation. He had encountered

[1] Eusebius, *Historia Ecclesiastica*, ii. 13. [2] Id., ii. 15.
[3] The Abbé Duchesne has written a dissertation on Simon the Magician, which forms the eighth chapter of his signed pamphlets; his lumi-

them in as great numbers in the East as in the West, for Simon had become the central figure for the legendary lore of that period. In the beginning of the third century, the Essenian Ebionites of Syria[1] had woven lengthy romances anent the strifes between Saint Peter and the Magician. Two of these works have come down to us, — the Recognitions and Homilies, falsely attributed to Saint Clement. They make Saint Peter the hero of adventures which are as absurd as they are fictitious, — relating how he travelled over the whole Syrian coast, from Cæsarea to Antioch, everywhere gaining new triumphs over Simon. Eusebius was too conscientious to draw his facts from such sources. In the West he found another series of legends from those which were common in Syria. Here the scene of his victory is Rome, and the time that of Nero, in whose presence Saints Peter and Paul together strive against the Magician. As his last resort, Simon promises, in proof of his divinity, to ascend into the air; but no sooner does he begin his flight than he falls to the ground and is dashed to pieces.[2] This Western legend gained currency about the same time that the Ebionites of Syria were inventing their fabulous tales; for we find it circulated far and wide during the fourth century. In Africa it was known to Arnobius (305);[3] the legates of Pope Liberius speak of it in their letter to Eusebius of Vercellæ (355);[4] and Saint Cyril of Jerusalem also alludes to it (347).[5] In earlier times, however, a very different account of the Magician's death prevailed. The author of the *Philosophumena*, who wrote about the year 225, does not mention any attempt at an

nous critical genius has shed invaluable light on this subject. We have done little more above than follow in his footsteps.

[1] For an account of these sectaries, see article headed ELKESAÏTES in Smith's *Dictionary of Christian Biography*.

[2] The *Apocryphal Acts of Peter and Paul* is the principal work from which this legend is taken (*Acta Apostolorum Apocrypha*, by Tischendorf); but it had been known for two centuries, since various authors of the fourth century allude to it. "Baronius (68, § 14) accepts the story of Simon as we read it in Dion Chrysostom (*Orat.* xxi. 9); to wit, that for some time Nero maintained at his court a man who had pledged himself to fly through the air. Suetonius (*Nero*, xii.) also relates that once, at the games, a man endeavored to fly in Nero's presence, but that at the first attempt he fell to the earth, and his blood spurted up even to the pavilion whence this Prince was observing the performance" (Tillemout, *Mémoires*, S. PIERRE, art. xxxiv.).   [3] *Patrologie latine*, t. v. p. 828.

[4] *Id.*, t. xiii. p. 765.   [5] S. Cyril of Jerusalem, *Catech.* vi. 14, 15.

ascension. He represents Simon as seated on a plane-tree and disputing with his opponents. To bring the contest to a triumphant close, the Magician offers to submit to being buried alive, affirming that he will arise on the third day, as the Christ had risen; he was buried, but never came forth from his voluntary tomb.[1] These divergences in the stories, in which the scene, the incidents, and the personages vary according to the fancy of the narrator, were enough to excite distrust in a writer like Eusebius. The only point which seemed to him worthy of credence was that, in the time of Claudius, Peter encountered Simon again at Rome, and again covered the impostor with confusion as he had done in Samaria. So far history; the rest belongs to legendary lore.

Most modern critics also relegate to the realm of fable the story of the statue set up in the *Isola Tiberiana* "to Simon the Holy God." Eusebius, it is true, quotes two of the first Fathers, Saint Justin and Saint Irenæus,[2] as his authority for this fact. But his first witness, whose critical powers are often at fault,[3] has probably fallen into an error here. On the island of the Tiber, "Semo Sancus," an ancient Sabine divinity, received special honors, and in the sixteenth century the pediment of a statue was discovered there, bearing the words: SEMONI SANCO DEO FIDIO SACRUM.[4] This inscription may explain Saint Justin's

---

[1] *Patrologie grecque*, t. xvi. p. 3326.

[2] Tertullian likewise mentions this fact; but here, as in many other circumstances, he is merely copying SS. Justin and Irenæus; it all comes down, therefore, as M. Duchesne has demonstrated, to the single testimony of S. Justin.

[3] In his first Apology (*Patrologie grecque*, t. vi. p. 376), he does not hesitate to call Ptolemy Philadelphus a contemporary of Herod.

[4] For an account of Semo Sancus and the statues of that deity, with their inscriptions which have been discovered, consult an article by Professor Visconti in the *Studi e Documenti di Storia e Diritto* (anno ii. fascicoli 3° e 4°, p. 105). The inscription, found in the fourteenth century in the island of the Tiber, ran,—

SEMONI
SANCO
DEO · FIDIO
SACRUM
SEX · POMPEIUS · SP · F
COL · MUSSIANUS
QUINQUENNALIS
DECUR
BIDENTALIS
DONUM · DEDIT

Corp. Inscript. Lat. vi. 576.

mistake. As for Saint Irenæus, he does no more than repeat, not without some hesitancy, the testimony of this Father; for although he had resided at Rome,[1] he had never seen the image of Simon, and is content to remark that "It is said that he was honored with a statue."[2] Thus there are weighty reasons for doubting the fact that the Magician ever had an image erected in his honour on the *Isola Tiberiana*, a sanctuary of the most ancient divinities. Nevertheless, we may willingly concede that Saint Justin was deceived merely as to the spot where this statue stood, and that elsewhere in the city Simon was the recipient of similar honors, for in an apology addressed to the Emperors and the Roman Senate, Saint Justin would not have lightly adduced a fact which could have been so easily refuted.

Nor should we forget that at this time Rome had a mania for statues. They erected them by hundreds, not only to the gods and the Cæsars, but to persons of far less importance, such as artists, orators, or athletes of any renown.[3] In this way clients paid honor to their patrons. Regulus, the rival of Pliny the Younger, after covering his gardens across the Tiber with long colonnades, lined the river-side with images of himself.[4] The porches of public buildings, the ancient Forum, the approaches to the Capitol, were encumbered with them to such an extent that Augustus was obliged to transport a goodly number of these marbles to the Campus Martius.[5] During Claudius' reign, finding that the artistic invasion was continuing, it became necessary to restrict the liberty then allowed to every private individual of decreeing such public honors to himself. Thereafter the authorization of the Senate had to be procured.[6] But there could have been no difficulty about obtaining it for such a noted character as Simon, and nothing is more likely than that his disciples should have solicited the permission; for we know that it was the general custom to erect statues to the arch-impostor, and to adore him as a divine being.

[1] About fifteen years after the date of S. Justin's writing.
[2] "Statua honoratus esse *dicitur*, propter magicam" (S. Irenæus, *Adversus Hæreses*, i. 23, 1: *Patrologie, grecque*, t. vii. p. 671).
[3] See Friedländer's *Mœurs romaines*, t. iii. pp. 250–273.
[4] Pliny, *Epist.* iv. 2, 5.
[5] Suetonius, *Caligula*, xxxiv.
[6] Dion Cassius, lx. 25.

APPENDIX. 415

Usually he was represented with the features of Jupiter;[1] at Rome, however, this likeness would have been impossible, for the God who was enthroned at the Capitol admitted none as his equal. His followers must needs select some other image, — probably that of *Semo Sancus*, the ancient Sabine divinity, analogous to the Roman Jupiter.[2] The statues of the Sabine god were numerous in Rome; often their inscription bore but the two words, SEMO SANCUS.[3] Saint Justin, knowing that they had given the Magician the exterior marks of this divinity, might easily have been mistaken as to the locality where the statue was placed, without any unfortunate consequences arising from his error in the estimation of his contemporaries, and without affecting the trustworthiness of the facts he was relating.[4]

[1] S. Irenæus, *Contra Hæreses*, i. 23, 5: *Patrologie grecque*, t. vii. p. 673.
[2] His name, Semo Sancus, which signifies God of the heavens, is connected with the celestial Jupiter, "Diespiter, diei pater," father of the day, the enemy of darkness, error, and falsehood, and the avenger of treachery. Hence the two names that usually follow *Semo Sancus* in the inscriptions, *Deus Fidius*, the god of fidelity, the faithful Jupiter, according to the translation of Dionysius of Halicarnassus: 'Εν ἱερῷ Διὸς Πιστίου, ὃν 'Ρωμαῖοι Σάγκτον καλοῦσιν (iv. 58). See Pauly, *Real Encyclopädie*, SANCUS, t. vi. p. 740.
[3] Orelli-Henzen, 6999.
[4] M. Studemund has discovered a very ancient manuscript of the Acts of Peter and Paul, wherein there is mention of the statue erected to Simon. De Rossi hopes to obtain from it a confirmation of the fact related by S. Justin (*Bullettino*, 1882, pp. 107, 108). It is scarcely possible to adopt any opinion in the premises before the publication of the document in question, which M. Studemund delays longer than any one could have foreseen.

INDEX.

ABANA, 117.
ABYSSINIA, 92; Church of, 97.
ACTS (Authenticity of the), viii–xvi.
ADIABENË, 185.
AFRICA, when evangelized, 97.
AGRIPPA (Herod), Letter to Caligula, 44; in Rome, 136; made King, 137; intercedes for Jews, 147; persecutes Christians, 172; Jewish policy, 173; religious zeal, 174; beheads James, 176; imprisons Peter, 177; royal progress, 181; his death, 183; chronology of his reign, 393.
ALABARCHS, 44.
ALEXANDER the Great. His treatment of Jewish subjects, 43; character, 328.
ALEXANDER (Tiberius), Procurator of Judea, 172.
ALEXANDRIA. Treatment of its Jewish citizens, 42; religious tendencies, 54; persecutions of Jews, 139; contrasted with Rome, 268; its Christian Schools, 381.
AMASEA (Church of), founded by Saint Peter, 247.
AMBROSE (Saint), on the Creed, 233.
AMMON, 47.
ANANIAS and Saphira, 29–33.
ANANIAS, Jewish trader of Adiabenë, 185.
ANANIAS of Damascus, 120.
ANDREW (Saint), 203.
ANGEL of the Lord, 73; appears to Cornelius, 148; to Peter, 179; to Agrippa, 183; "Angel of the Congregation," 190.
ANGELS (Guardian), believed in by Primitive Church, 187.
ANIANUS (Bishop), successor of Mark the Evangelist, 180.
ANNAS, regarded as real High Priest, 23.
ANTIOCH, chap. ix.; pp. 157 et seq.; its Christian Schools, 380.

ANTIOCHUS EPIPHANES, 160; rebukes people of Antioch, 162; reparations to Jews, 164.
ANTIOCHUS the Great, 43.
ANTIPAS (Herod), 137.
APOSTLES, see the TWELVE.
APOSTLESHIP, 197.
APULEIUS, chap. xv. *passim*.
AQUILA, 346.
AQUILEIA, 75.
ARAMÆAN, Paul's mother-tongue, 109.
ARCHONTES, 44, 270.
ARETAS, King of Petra, 114.
ARISTOBULUS of Alexandria, 55.
ARISTOTLE, taught at Antioch, 387.
ART of Rome, 282.
ASP (URŒUS), 91.
ASSYRIAN Empire and its treatment of Jews, 41.
ATHENODORUS of Tarsus, 102.
AUGURIES, 280.
AUGUSTINE (Saint), on the Creed, chap. xiii. *passim*.
AUGUSTUS, treatment of Jews, 46, 253; superstitions, 80; on the Law, 261; synagogue named after him, 262; why worshipped, 285.
AVENTINE (Mount), 345.
AZOTUS, 97.

BÀB BOLOS (Saint Paul's Gate), 167.
BABYLON, Jewish population, 41; mystical name for Rome, 291, 400.
BACCHANALS, 354.
BARNABAS (Pseudo-Epistle of), 400.
BARNABAS (Saint), 28; welcomes Paul, 132; envoy to Antioch, 166; seeks Paul, 167.
BARSABAS, 5.
BARTHOLOMEW (Saint), 204.
BEAUTIFUL Gate, 20.
BEIT-DJIBRIN, 93.
BEÎT EL-MA, site of Daphnë, 163.
BEYROUTH, 182.
BEZETHA, 173.

418 INDEX.

BLASTUS, Agrippa's Chamberlain, 183.
BLOOD, regarded as of mystic power, 287.
BOSTRA, 123.
BREAKING of the Bread, 18; and see EUCHARIST.

CÆSAR, his policy for the Jews, 45; mourned by Jews, 253; why worshipped, 286.
CÆSAREA, built by Herod, 98; home of Cornelius, 148; visited by Agrippa, 182.
CAÏPHAS, High Priest, 23.
CALF of Gold, worshipped by Israel, 72.
CALIGULA, his policy, 114; friendship for Agrippa, 136; madness, 138; persecution of Jews, 139; his death, 142.
CALLINICUS, 160.
CALLISTUS (Nicephorus), his description of Saint Paul, 127.
CAMPUS MARTIUS, Jews' trading-place, 265; Synagogue of the Campenses, 267.
CANDACES, Queens of Ethiopia, 91.
CAPENA Gate, 344.
CARMEL, 143.
CELSUS, on the Christians, 388.
CEMETERIES, of the Jews, 265; Romans, 324; the Ostrian Cemetery, 347; privileges, 367.
CHAIR of Saint Peter, 347, 404, 409.
CHARON (Statue of), at Antioch, 162.
CHRISM, 85.
CHRISTIANS, origin of name, 168; popular significance, 169; among Romans, 358.
CHRONOLOGY of the Early Church, App. I., 391.
CICERO and Roman Jews, 252, 257.
CILICIA, 104.
CIRCUMCISION of Proselytes, 53.
CLAUDIUS, accession to the throne, 173; banishes Jews and Christians, 357.
CLEMENT (Saint), 400.
CLEMENTINE (Pseudo-) writings, 87.
CLIENTSHIP, at Rome, 307, 359.
COHORTS of Roman army, 147.
COLLEGES of Rome, suppressed by Cæsars, 253, 268, 339, 356.
CONFIRMATION, administered by Peter, 85.
CORNELIUS, the Centurion, 147-154.
COUNCIL of Jerusalem, 392.
CREED (Apostles'), 232 et seq.
CYPRUS, 165.

CYRENE, 165.
CYRUS, 40.

DAPHNE, worshipped at Antioch, 163.
DAMASCUS, its government, 114; site described, 116; house whence Paul escaped, 130.
DAVID, prophecy of Christ, 12.
DEACONS (Order of), its institution, 60; duties, 199.
DECAPITATION, introduced by Agrippa, 176.
DESCENT of the Holy Spirit, 8-27; at Samaria, 85; on Gentiles at Cæsarea, 154; gifts accompanying it, 202; gradual illumination, 227.
DISPERSION (Jews of the), 39 et seq.
DIVORCE under Roman laws, 304.
DOCTORS of the Church, 202.
DOLABELLA (Consul), 46.
DORCAS, 144.
DOSITHEUS, 81.

EDUCATION, in Tarsus, 103; in Rome, 301.
EGYPT, Jewish colonies, 42.
ELAMITES, 44.
ELDERS of the Church, 190, 200.
ELEAZAR (Rabbi), 48.
ELIAS, 123.
ELIONAS, the High Priest, 174.
ELISEUS, entombed with John Baptist, 79.
ENEAS, 143.
EPICURUS, 317.
EPIPHANIA of Antioch, 160.
EPISCOPACY, its primitive powers, 199; founded by Apostles, 201.
EPITAPHS of Roman matrons, 300.
ESSENES, 15.
ETHIOPIA, 90.
ETHNARCHS, 44.
EUCHARIST, dispensed by Deacons, 61; treated of by Evangelists, 215; at Rome, 338, 363.
EUNUCH of the Candace, 93; regarded by Jewish laws, 94; his conversion and return home, 97.
EUPHRATES, 80.
EUSEBIUS, 369.
EVANGELISTS, their duties, 202; manner of preaching, 210.
EXEMPTIONS of the Jews, 45.

FADUS (Cuspius), Procurator of Judea, 172; Jewish policy, 184.
FALÂSHAS, 92.
FAMILY life in Rome, chap. xvi. passim.

INDEX.   419

FAMINE, prophesied by Agabus, 172; its severity, 184.
FORTUNE-HUNTERS in the Augustan age, 310.
FREEDMEN, their synagogue in Jerusalem, 64; their numbers at Rome, 252, 358.

GAMALIEL, defends Apostles, 34; regard for proselytes, 53; his school, 106; Seven Rules, 110.
GAZA, 93.
GAZITH (Hall of), Sanhedrin's meeting-place, 67.
GENARCHS, 44.
GENIUS of Rome, 286.
GENTILES admitted after Peter's Vision, 151; at Antioch, 165; in Saint Matthew, 220.
GEORGE (Saint), of Damascus, 130.
GETHSEMANI, 74.
GHETTO, described, 254; a field for Christian labor, 56.
GLADIATORS, 313.
GNOSTICISM, its germs in Simon's doctrine, 90.
GOSPELS (Synoptic), oral form, 208-213; theories of their origin, 214; Gospel of the Nazarenes, 225; Saint Mark's 213 and chap. xx.; Saint Matthew's, 216.
GRÆCINA (Pomponia), same personage as Lucina, 342.
GREEK, spoken by Stephen, 70.

HAGADA, 209.
HALAKA, 208.
HEBREWS, use of the name in New Testament, 38.
HEGESIPPUS (Chronicle of), 402.
HELEN, disciple of Dositheus, 82; and of Simon Magus, 89.
HELEN, Queen of Adiabenë, 185.
HELLENISTS, as used in New Testament, 38; in Stephen's time, 58; new views of this class, 63; preached to by Paul, 133.
HERODIAS, 137.
HIERARCHY of early Church, 60, 189, 203.
HIGH PRIESTS, their power at Rome, 46; under Agrippa, 174; their depravity, 175.
HILLEL, Gamaliel's grandfather, 34; high regard for proselytes, 53.
HIPPOLYTUS (Saint), 403.
HORACE, on Jews and their proselytes, 256, 261.

IGNATIUS (Saint), of Antioch, 170, 400; his version of the Creed, 242.
IMMORTALITY of the soul, 322.
INCARNATION (The), central point of Apostles' preaching, 210.
INDICITAMENTA of the Romans, 276, 285.
IRENÆUS (Saint), on the Creed, 242; on Saint Matthew, 395.
ISIS (worship of), 284, 287, 341; tolerated at Rome, 355.
IZATES, King of Adiabenë, 185.

JAFFA (see Joppa).
JAMES (Brother of the Lord), receives Paul, 132; Bishop of Jerusalem, 192.
JAMES (Son of Zebedee), martyrdom, 176; its date, 393.
JERUSALEM, its customs and people, 16; disciples' daily life there, 224.
JESUS, prayer in His Name, 5, 26; appears to Stephen, 74; as preached by Apostles, 277; in the Gospels, 215.
JEWS, daily life, 16; political influence and colonies, 42; in Parthian and Roman empires, 43; exemptions, 44; commercial power, 47; gatherings, 51; schools, 105; heroism, 139; of Antioch, 163; methods of teaching, 206; of Rome, 249.
JOHN THE BAPTIST, his tomb, 79.
JOHN THE EVANGELIST, is arrested, 24; goes to Samaria, 84.
JOHN THE PRIEST on Saint Mark's Gospel, 368.
JONAS, prefigures Resurrection, 147.
JONATHAN, High Priest, 174.
JOPPA, Tabitha's home, 144; described, 146.
JOSEPHUS on the Law, 56.
JUDAIZERS, xii, 155.
JUDAS' fall predicted, 4.
JUDAS of Galilee, 35.
JUDE (Saint), 204.
JUPITER, 274.
JUS TRIUM PUERORUM, 297.
JUVENAL, on the Jews, 260; on Roman life, chap. xvi. passim.

KANTHERA (SIMEON), 174.
KAPHAR GAMALA, 75.
KEDRON, 74.
KEFAR-BARKAÏ, 174.

LACTANTIUS, 407.
LAME man healed by Peter, 21.

LAODICEA, 159.
LAW of Jehovah, its attractions for Romans, 260; observed by proselytes, 271; contrasted with Roman customs, 279.
LEVITES, converted to Christianity, 67.
LIBERIAN CATALOGUE, 403.
LINUS, 407.
LUCIAN the Priest, on the finding of Saint Stephen's body, 74.
LUKE, his work, viii; his name, ix.
LYDDA, 143.

MAGICIANS, of Rome, 378.
MALALA, 167.
MARK (Saint), same as John Mark, 180; his Gospel, 213 and chap. xx.
MARRIAGE, under Roman Law, 293.
MARTIAL, on Roman Jews, 256.
MARYLLUS, Pilate's successor, 137.
MATHIAS (Saint), his election, 4; his life, 205.
MATHIAS, the High Priest, 174.
MATTHEW (Saint), his life, 205; his Gospel, 216.
MEDES, 44.
MEROË, 91; commerce, 93.
METILIUS, Jewish proselyte, 52.
MISCHNA, 105.
MOLOCH, 72.
MONZA (Papyrus of), 408.
MOSES, 71.
MUSONIUS Rufus, 332.

NAPATA, 91.
NAZARITES, consecrated by Agrippa, 173.
NICANOR, the Deacon, 60.
NINEVEH (Jews of), 41.

ORACLES, 217.
ORACULA SIBYLLINA, 56.
ORONTES, 159.
ORPHEUS, 55.
OSTRIAN CEMETERY, 409.

PANTHEISM, the foundation of Zeno's system, 319.
PAPIAS on Saint Mark's Gospel, 217.
PARTHIAN Empire and its Jewish colonies, 43.
PASTOR and Timotheus (Apocryphal Letters of), 346.
PASTORS of the Synagogues, 270.
PAUL (Saint), his mission contrasted with Peter's, vi; one of Stephen's judges, 69; his conversion due to Stephen's prayer, 75; date of his birth, 100; Saul, 101; his family, 106; at Gamaliel's School, 107; zeal against Christians, 113; commission to Damascus, 114; struck down at the gates, 119; baptism, 122; long retreat in Arabia, 123; revelations, 124; bodily afflictions, 126; returns to Damascus, 129; flees to Jerusalem, 131; vision in the Temple, 133; wanderings, 134; Greek culture, 136; found in Tarsus, 166; glories in his Apostleship, 197; Letter to the Romans, 271.
PEACE of the Church, 142; of Rome, 383.
PENTECOST, 6.
PERSECUTIONS, by the Sanhedrin, 65; under Agrippa, 172; its close, 184; their effects on the Church, 389.
PERSEUS, on Roman Jews, 255, 261.
PERSIANS and Jewish colonists, 42.
PETER (Saint), in the Acts, i; discourse in the Supper Room, 2, 12; heals a cripple, 21; healed before Sanhedrin, 24; his miracles, 32; in Samaria, 84; meets Simon Magus, 85; receives Paul, 131; Angel of the Synagogue, 132; mission-journey to Joppa, 143; his Vision, 149; Cæsarea, 152; at Jerusalem, 155; at Antioch, 157, 164; imprisoned by Agrippa, 177; miraculous release, 179; headship over Apostles, 188, 198; legendary history, 208; his *witness*, 211; his preaching embodied in Mark's Gospel, 213; progress of his genius, 228; mission-journeys, 246; Peter's wife, 248; at Rome, 271, chap. xviii.; his Gospel that of Saint Mark, chap. xx.; dates of his visits to Rome, App. IV.; his death, 412.
PETRONIUS, Prefect of Syria, 141.
PHARISAIC Observances, 259.
PHARISEES, 220.
PHARPAR (River), 117.
PHILIP (Saint), the Apostle, 204.
PHILIP (Saint), the Deacon, his election, 60; mission to Samaria, 83; meets Eunuch, 94; in Azotus, 97; Cæsarea, 99; possibility of his having preached before Cornelius, 148.
PHILO, 139.
PHILOSOPHERS, of Tarsus, 103; of Rome, chap. xvii.
PHILOSOPHUMENA, 89.
PILATE, 66.
PLATO and the Stoics, chap. xvii. *passim*; taught at Alexandria, 381.

INDEX. 421

PLINY the Younger, 299.
PLUTARCH, on Roman Jews, 257.
POLYCARP, 207.
PORCH (School of the), chap. xvii.
PORTA CAPENA, 264.
PREACHING in the primitive Church, 210.
PRIESTS, 199.
PRISCA, 345.
PROCHORUS, 60.
PROLETARIAT of Rome, 306.
PROPHECY, its significance, 171; Agabus, 172; its functions, 202; in Saint Matthew's Gospel, 219.
PROSELYTES (Jewish), 52; "of the Gate," and "of Justice," 54; at Rome, 261, 270, 339, chap. xviii. *passim*.
PTOLEMIES and their Jewish subjects, 43.
PUDENS, 344.
PUDENTIA (Saint), 346.

RABBAN, 106.
RABBIS and proselytes, 53; their method of teaching, 110.
RABII (Rabbi), 48.
RENAN on Saint Luke, vi, ix; on Saint Matthew, 220.
RENUNCIATION of property, 15, 27.
REPHAN, 72, note 6.
RESURRECTION of the dead, 20.
RHODA, Saint Mark's maid-servant, 180.
ROME, foundation of Church there, vi; its Creed, 237; Peter's advent, 249; Jews of Rome, 255; Pagan cultus, chap. xv.; "Roman Peace," 383; Roman roads, 385; growth of the Church, chap. xviii.; its ritual, 363.
RUFINUS on the Creed, 232.

SADDUCEES, hostility to the Apostles, 20; influence with the Pharisees, 24.
SAMARIA, 78; its reception of Simon Magus, 89.
SAPHIRA, 30.
SARDANAPALUS, tutelary deity of Tarsus, 104.
SATIRISTS, on Roman Jews, 257.
SAUL, see Paul.
SEBASTE, 79.
SELEUCUS NICATOR and the Jews, 43; founder of Antioch, 159.
SEMO SANCUS and Simon Magus, 413.
SENECA, on Jews of Rome, 257; and Saint Paul, 314, chap. xvii.
SENNACHERIB, 42.

SHARON, 98, 143.
SIBYLS, 55.
SIDON, 183.
SILPIUS (Mount), 160.
SIMON MAGUS, early life, 81; conversion, 84; character and teaching, 87; at Rome, 349; statue in Rome, App. V.
SIMON (Saint), the Zealot, 204.
SIMON the Tanner, 145.
SIMONY, 85.
SINAÏ, Saul's retreat there, 123.
SINGON, 167.
SINOPE (Church of), founded by Saint Peter, 257.
SLAVERY, number of Jewish slaves in Rome, 251; effects on Roman social life, 306; mitigated by Stoics, 329; position of slaves in the Church, 336.
SLEEP, a figure of death, 75.
SOCIETY (Pagan), chap. xvi.
SODALITIES of Rome, 268.
SON of God, 374.
STEPHEN (Saint), the Deacon, election, 60; origin, 63; preaching, 65; before the Sanhedrin, 69; scene of his martyrdom, 74; death, 75; burial, 76.
STOICS, of Tarsus, 103, 135; of Rome, chap. xvii.
STYLITES, 170.
SUBURA, peopled by Jews, 264; its Synagogue, 267.
SUPPER ROOM (Cœnaculum), 2.
SYMBOL, meaning of term, 233.
SYNAGOGUES, of Jerusalem, 17; numbers and wealth, 49; in Rome, 266, 270.

TABITHA, 144.
TACITUS, on the persecution of Jews, 254; on Roman Jews, 257; on Roman life, chap. xvi. *passim*.
TANNERS, despised by Pharisees, 145.
TARSUS, Paul's birthplace, 102; schools, 105; Paul's return thither, 134.
TENT-MAKING, Paul's trade, 106.
THEATRE of Rome, 281; its effect on women, 302.
THEUDAS, or Theodas, 35.
THOMAS (Saint), Apostle, 205.
TIBERIUS, 66; his superstitions, 80, persecutions of Jews, 254.
TRADITION, 231.
TRASTEVERE, 263, 344.
TYRE, visited by Paul, 134; its trade with Judea, 183.

TWELVE (The), mystical significance of the number, 2; their arrest and trial, 33; bade to stay in Jerusalem, 77; how regarded by Primitive Church, 189, 272; dispersed, 191; prerogatives, 197; growth of their genius, 231.

VATICAN, peopled by Jews, 263.
VERGIL, 260.
VIMINAL, 344.

VITELLIUS, Legate to Syria, 66; leaves Jerusalem, 67; against Aretas, 115.

WHIPPING of the Synagogue, 36.
WIDOWS, their position in the Church, 59.
WOMEN of Rome, 297, 342.

YOUNG MEN (νεώτεροι), an Order in the Primitive Hierarchy, 30.

ZENO, doctrines taught at Tarsus, 135; at Rome, chap. xvii. *passim*.

A SELECTED LIST

FROM THE CATALOGUE OF

LONGMANS, GREEN, & CO.
15 EAST SIXTEENTH STREET, NEW YORK.

Newman.—Works by JOHN HENRY, CARDINAL NEWMAN.

PAROCHIAL AND PLAIN SERMONS. Edited by REV. W. J. COPELAND, B.D., late Rector of Farnham, Essex. 8 vols. Sold separately. Crown 8vo. Each, $1.75

CONTENTS OF VOL. I.: Holiness necessary for Future Blessedness—The Immortality of the Soul—Knowledge of God's Will without Obedience—Secret Faults—Self-Denial the Test of Religious Earnestness—The Spiritual Mind—Sins of Ignorance and Weakness—God's Commandments not Grievous—The Religious Use of Excited Feelings—Profession without Practice—Profession without Hypocrisy—Profession without Ostentation—Promising without Doing—Religious Emotion—Religious Faith Rational—The Christian Mysteries—The Self-Wise Inquirer—Obedience the Remedy for Religious Perplexity—Times of Private Prayer—Forms of Private Prayer—The Resurrection of the Body—Witnesses of the Resurrection—Christian Reverence—The Religion of the Day—Scripture a Record of Human Sorrow—Christian Manhood.

CONTENTS OF VOL. II.: The World's Benefactors—Faith without Sight—The Incarnation—Martyrdom—Love of Relations and Friends—The Mind of Little Children—Ceremonies of the Church—The Glory of the Christian Church—St. Paul's Conversion viewed in Reference to his Office—Secrecy and Suddenness of Divine Visitations—Divine Decrees—The Reverence Due to the Blessed Virgin Mary—Christ, a Quickening Spirit—Saving Knowledge—Self-Contemplation—Religious Cowardice—The Gospel Witnesses—Mysteries in Religion—The Indwelling Spirit—The Kingdom of the Saints—The Gospel, a Trust Committee to us—Tolerance of Religious Error—Rebuking Sin—The Christian Ministry—Human Responsibility—Guilelessness—The Danger of Riches—The Powers of Nature—The Danger of Accomplishments—Christian Zeal—Use of Saints' Days.

CONTENTS OF VOL. III.: Abraham and Lot—Wilfulness of Israel in Rejecting Samuel—Saul—Early Years of David—Jeroboam—Faith and Obedience—Christian Repentance—Contracted Views in Religion—A particular Providence as revealed in the Gospel—Tears of Christ at the Grave of Lazarus—Bodily Suffering—The Humiliation of the Eternal Son—Jewish Zeal a Pattern to Christians—Submission to Church Authority—Contest between Truth and Falsehood in the Church—The Church Visible and Invisible—The Visible Church an Encouragement to Faith—The Gift of the Spirit—Regenerating Baptism—Infant Baptism—The Daily Service—The Good Part of Mary—Religious Worship a Remedy for Excitements—Intercession—The Intermediate State.

A SELECTED LIST OF WORKS

Newman.—WORKS BY CARDINAL NEWMAN.—*Continued.*

PAROCHIAL AND PLAIN SERMONS.—*Continued.*

CONTENTS OF VOL. IV. : The Strictness of the Law of Christ—Obedience without Love, as instanced in the Character of Balaam—Moral Consequences of Single Sins—Acceptance of Religious Privileges Compulsory—Reliance on Religious Observances—The Individuality of the Soul—Chastisement amid Mercy—Peace and Joy amid Chastisement—The State of Grace—The Visible Church for the Sake of the Elect—The Communion of Saints—The Church a Home for the Lonely—The Invisible World—The Greatness and Littleness of Human Life—Moral Effects of Communion with God—Christ Hidden from the World—Christ Manifested in Remembrance—The Gainsaying of Korah—The Mysteriousness of our Present Being—The Ventures of Faith—Faith and Love—Watching—Keeping Fast and Festival.

CONTENTS OF VOL. V. : Worship, a Preparation for Christ's Coming—Reverence, a Belief in God's Presence—Unreal Words—Shrinking from Christ's Coming—Equanimity—Remembrance of Past Mercies—The Mystery of Godliness—The State of Innocence—Christian Sympathy—Righteousness not of us, but in us—The Law of the Spirit—The New Works of the Gospel—The State of Salvation—Transgressions and Infirmities—Sins of Infirmity—Sincerity and Hypocrisy—The Testimony of Conscience—Many called, Few chosen—Present Blessings—Endurance, the Christian's Portion—Affliction, a School of Comfort—The Thought of God, the Stay of the Soul—Love, the One Thing Needful—The Power of the Will.

CONTENTS OF VOL. VI.: Fasting, a Source of Trial—Life, the Season of Repentance—Apostolic Abstinence, a Pattern for Christians—Christ's Privations, a Meditation for Christians—Christ the Son of God made Man—The Incarnate Son, a Sufferer and Sacrifice—The Cross of Christ the Measure of the World—Difficulty of realizing Sacred Privileges—The Gospel Sign Addressed to Faith—The Spiritual Presence of Christ in the Church—The Eucharistic Presence—Faith the Title for Justification—Judaism of the Present Day—The Fellowship of the Apostles—Rising with Christ—Warfare the Condition of Victory—Waiting for Christ—Subjection of the Reason and Feelings to the Revealed Word—The Gospel Palaces—The Visible Temple—Offerings for the Sanctuary—The Weapons of Saints—Faith Without Demonstration—The Mystery of the Holy Trinity—Peace in Believing.

CONTENTS OF VOL. VII.: The Lapse of Time—Religion, a Weariness to the Natural Man—The World our Enemy—The Praise of Men—Temporal Advantages—The Season of Epiphany—The Duty of Self-denial—The Yoke of Christ—Moses the Type of Christ—The Crucifixion—Attendance on Holy Communion—The Gospel Feast—Love of Religion, a new Nature—Religion pleasant to the Religious—Mental Prayer—Infant Baptism—The Unity of the Church—Steadfastness in the Old Paths.

CONTENTS OF VOL. VIII. : Reverence in Worship—Divine Calls—The Trial of Saul—The Call of David—Curiosity, a Temptation to Sin—Miracles no Remedy for Unbelief—Josiah, a Pattern for the Ignorant—Inward Witness to the Truth of the Gospel—Jeremiah, a Lesson for the Disappointed - Endurance of the World's Censure—Doing Glory to God in Pursuits of the World—Vanity of Human Glory—Truth hidden when not sought after—Obedience to God the Way to Faith in Christ—Sudden Conversions—The Shepherd of our Souls—Religious Joy—Ignorance of Evil.

SERMONS BEARING UPON SUBJECTS OF THE DAY.

Edited by the REV. W. J. COPELAND, B.D., late Rector of Farnham, Essex. Crown 8vo. $1.75

CONTENTS : The Work of the Christian—Saintliness not Forfeited by the Penitent—Our Lord's Last Supper and His First—Dangers to the Penitent—The Three Offices of Christ—Faith and Experience—Faith unto the World—The Church and the World—Indulgence in Religious Privileges—Connection between Personal and Public Improvement—Christian Nobleness—Joshua a Type of Christ and His Followers—Elisha a Type of Christ and His Followers—The Christian Church a Continuation of the Jewish—The Principles of Continuity between the Jewish and Christian Churches—The Christian Church an Imperial Power—Sanctity the Token of the Christian Empire—Condition of the Members of the Christian Empire—The Apostolic Christian—Wisdom and Innocence—Invisible Presence of Christ—Outward and Inward Notes of the Church—Grounds for Steadfastness in our Religious Profession—Elijah the Prophet of the Latter Days—Feasting in Captivity—The Parting of Friends.

Newman.—WORKS BY CARDINAL NEWMAN.—*Continued.*

SERMONS PREACHED ON VARIOUS OCCASIONS.
Crown 8vo. $2.00

CONTENTS : Intellect the Instrument of Religious Training—The Religion of the Pharisee and the Religion of Mankind—Waiting for Christ—The Secret Power of Divine Grace—Dispositions for Faith—Omnipotence in Bonds—St. Paul's Characteristic Gift—St. Paul's Gift of Sympathy—Christ upon the Waters—The Second Spring—Order, the Witness and Instrument of Unity—The Mission of St. Philip Neri—The Tree beside the Waters—In the World, but not of the World—The Pope and the Revolution.

FIFTEEN SERMONS PREACHED BEFORE THE UNIVERSITY OF OXFORD, between A.D. 1826 and 1843. New Edition.
Crown 8vo. $1.75

CONTENTS : The Philosophical Temper, first enjoined by the Gospel—The Influence of Natural and Revealed Religion respectively—Evangelical Sanctity the Perfection of Natural Virtue—The Usurpations of Reason—Personal Influence, the Means of Propagating the Truth—On Justice as a Principle of Divine Governance—Contest between Faith and Sight—Human Responsibility, as independent of Circumstances—Wilfulness, the Sin of Saul—Faith and Reason, contrasted as Habits of Mind—The Nature of Faith in Relation to Reason—Love the Safeguard of Faith against Superstition—Implicit and Explicit Reason—Wisdom, as contrasted with Faith and with Bigotry—The Theory of Developments in Religious Doctrine.

DISCOURSES ADDRESSED TO MIXED CONGREGATIONS. Crown 8vo. $2.00

CONTENTS : The Salvation of the Hearer the Motive of the Preacher—Neglect of Divine Calls and Warnings—Men not Angels—The Priests of the Gospel—Purity and Love—Saintliness the Standard of Christian Principle—God's Will the End of Life—Perseverance in Grace—Nature and Grace—Illuminating Grace—Faith and Private Judgment—Faith and Doubt—Prospects of the Catholic Missioner—Mysteries of Nature and of Grace—The Mystery of Divine Condescension—The Infinitude of Divine Attributes—Mental Sufferings of Our Lord in His Passion—The Glories of Mary for the Sake of Her Son—On the Fitness of the Glories of Mary.

SELECTION, ADAPTED TO THE SEASON OF THE ECCLESIASTICAL YEAR, from the "Parochial and Plain Sermons."
Edited by the REV. W. J. COPELAND, B.D. Crown 8vo. $1.75

CONTENTS : *Advent:* Self-Denial the Test of Religious Earnestness—Divine Calls—The Ventures of Faith—Watching. *Christmas Day:* Religious Joy. *New Year's Sunday:* The Lapse of Time. *Epiphany:* Remembrance of Past Mercies—Equanimity—The Immortality of the Soul—Christian Manhood—Sincerity and Hypocrisy—Christian Sympathy. *Septuagesima:* Present Blessings. *Sexagesima:* Endurance, the Christian's Portion. *Quinquagesima:* Love, the One Thing Needful. *Lent:* The Individuality of the Soul—Life the Season of Repentance—Bodily Suffering—Tears of Christ at the Grave of Lazarus—Christ's Privations, a Meditation for Christians—The Cross of Christ the Measure of the World. *Good Friday:* The Crucifixion. *Easter Day:* Keeping Fast and Festival. *Easter Tide:* Witnesses of the Resurrection—A Particular Providence as Revealed in the Gospel—Christ Manifested in Remembrance—The Invisible World—Waiting for Christ. *Ascension:* Warfare the Condition of Victory. *Sunday after Ascension:* Rising with Christ. *Whitsun Day:* The Weapons of Saints. *Trinity Sunday:* The Mysteriousness of Our Present Being. *Sundays after Trinity:* Holiness Necessary for Future Blessedness—The Religious Use of Excited Feelings—The Self-Wise Inquirer—Scripture a Record of Human Sorrow—The Danger of Riches—Obedience without Love, as instanced in the Character of Balaam—Moral Consequences of Single Sins—The Greatness and Littleness of Human Life—Moral Effects of Communion with God—The Thought of God the Stay of the Soul—The Power of the Will—The Gospel Palaces—Religion a Weariness to the Natural Man—The World our Enemy—The Praise of Men—Religion Pleasant to the Religious—Mental Prayer—Curiosity a Temptation to Sin—Miracles no Remedy for Unbelief—Jeremiah, a Lesson for the Disappointed—The Shepherd of our Souls—Doing Glory to God in Pursuits of the World.

Newman.—WORKS BY CARDINAL NEWMAN.—*Continued.*

LECTURES ON THE DOCTRINE OF JUSTIFICATION.
Fourth Edition. Crown 8vo. $1.75

CONTENTS : Faith considered as the Instrumental Cause of Justification—Love considered as the Formal Cause of Justification—Primary Sense of the term "Justification"—Secondary Senses of the term "Justification"—Misuse of the term "Just" or "Righteous"—The Gift of Righteousness—The Characteristics of the Gift of Righteousness—Righteousness viewed as a Gift and as a Quality—Righteousness the Fruit of our Lord's Resurrection—The Office of Justifying Faith—The Nature of Justifying Faith—Faith viewed relatively to Rites and Works—On preaching the Gospel—Appendix.

ON THE DEVELOPMENT OF CHRISTIAN DOCTRINE.
Crown 8vo. $2.00

ON THE IDEA OF A UNIVERSITY. Crown 8vo. $2.50

AN ESSAY IN AID OF A GRAMMAR OF ASSENT.
Crown 8vo. $2.50

TWO ESSAYS ON MIRACLES. 1. Of Scripture. 2. Of Ecclesiastical History. Crown 8vo. $2.00

DISCUSSIONS AND ARGUMENTS. Crown 8vo. $2.00

1. How to accomplish it. 2. The Antichrist of the Fathers. 3. Scripture and the Creed. 4. Tamworth Reading-room. 5. Who's to Blame? 6. An Argument for Christianity.

ESSAYS, CRITICAL AND HISTORICAL. 2 vols. Crown 8vo. $4.00

1. Poetry. 2. Rationalism. 3. Apostolical Tradition. 4. De la Mennais. 5. Palmer on Faith and Unity. 6. St. Ignatius. 7. Prospects of the Anglican Church. 8. The Anglo-American Church. 9. Countess of Huntingdon. 10. Catholicity of the Anglican Church. 11. The Antichrist of Protestants. 12. Wilman's Christianity. 13. Reformation of the XI. Century. 14. Private Judgment. 15. Davison. 16. Keble.

HISTORICAL SKETCHES. 3 vols. Crown 8vo. Each $2.00

1. The Turks. 2. Cicero. 3. Apollonius. 4. Primitive Christianity. 5. Church of the Fathers. 6. St. Chrysostom. 7. Theodoret. 8. St. Benedict. 9. Benedictine Schools. 10. Universities. 11. Northmen and Normans. 12. Mediæval Oxford. 13. Convocation of Canterbury.

THE ARIANS OF THE FOURTH CENTURY. Crown 8vo. $2.00

SELECT TREATISES OF ST. ATHANASIUS IN CONTROVERSY WITH THE ARIANS. Freely translated. 2 vols. Crown 8vo. $5.00

IN THEOLOGICAL LITERATURE. 5

Newman.—WORKS BY CARDINAL NEWMAN.—*Continued.*

THEOLOGICAL TRACTS. 1. Dissertatiunculæ. 2. On the Text of the Seven Epistles of St. Ignatius. 3. Doctrinal Causes of Arianism. 4. Apollinarianism. 5. St. Cyril's Formula. 6. Ordo de Tempore. 7. Douay Version of Scriptures. Crown 8vo. $3.00

THE VIA MEDIA OF THE ANGLICAN CHURCH. 2 vols. With Notes. Crown 8vo.
Vol. I. Prophetical Office of the Church. $2.00
Vol. II. Occasional Letters and Tracts. 2.00

CERTAIN DIFFICULTIES FELT BY ANGLICANS IN CATHOLIC TEACHING CONSIDERED. 2 vols.
Vol. I. Turler Lectures. Crown 8vo $2.50
Vol. II. Letters to Dr. Pusey concerning the Blessed Virgin, and to the Duke of Norfolk in Defence of the Pope and Council. Crown 8vo. $2.00

PRESENT POSITION OF CATHOLICS IN ENGLAND.
Crown 8vo. $2.50

APOLOGIA PRO VITA SUA. Crown 8vo. 2.00

VERSES ON VARIOUS OCCASIONS. Crown 8vo. 2.00
*** To be had also in half calf, gilt top. 3.50

LOSS AND GAIN. The Story of a Convert. Crown 8vo. $2.00

CALLISTA. A Tale of the Third Century. Crown 8vo. 2.00

THE DREAM OF GERONTIUS. 16mo, sewed. 0.20
Cloth, 0.35
German Calf, gilt edges. 1.50

*** Messrs. LONGMANS, GREEN, & CO. beg to say that they have always on hand sets of CARDINAL NEWMAN'S works in *fine bindings*, suitable for presentation or for private libraries. Prices upon application to booksellers.

Newman.—WORKS BY CARDINAL NEWMAN. — Cheap Editions (*Silver Library*).

Parochial and Plain Sermons. 8 vols. Each, $1.25
Fifteen Sermons preached before the University of Oxford, 1.25
Sermons bearing on Subjects of the Day, 1.25
Discourses addressed to Mixed Congregations, 1.25
Selection, from the Parochial and Plain Sermons, 1.25
On the Development of Christian Doctrine, 1.25
On the Idea of a University, 1.25

Newman.—WORKS BY CARDINAL NEWMAN.—*Continued.*
Cheap Editions (*Silver Library*).—*Continued.*

An Essay in Aid of a Grammar of Assent,	$1.25
Biblical and Ecclesiastical Miracles,	1.25
Discussions and Arguments on Various Subjects,	1.25
Essays, Critical and Historical. 2 vols.,	2.50
Historical Sketches. 3 vols. Each,	1.25
The Arians of the Fourth Century,	1.15
The Via Media of the Anglican Church. 2 vols. Each,	1.25
Difficulties felt by Anglicans considered. 2 vols. Each,	1.25
Present Position of Catholics,	1.25
Apologia pro Vitâ Sua,	1.25
Verses on Various Occasions,	1.25
Loss or Gain,	1.25
Callista,	1.25

Newman.—THE LETTERS AND CORRESPONDENCE OF JOHN HENRY NEWMAN during His Life in the English Church. With a brief Autobiographical Memoir. Arranged and edited, at Cardinal Newman's request, by MISS ANNE MOZLEY, Editor of the "Letters of the Rev. J. B. Mozley, D.D., Regius Professor of Divinity in the University of Oxford." With Index and two Portraits. 2 vols. Crown 8vo. $4.00
Half calf, $7.50

Fouard.—THE CHRIST, THE SON OF GOD. A Life of Our Lord and Saviour Jesus Christ. By the ABBÉ CONSTANT FOUARD, Honorary Cathedral Canon, Professor of the Faculty of Theology at Rouen, etc., etc. Translated from the Fifth Edition with the Author's Sanction. By GEORGE F. X. GRIFFITH. With an Introduction by Cardinal Manning. THIRD EDITION. With 3 maps. 2 volumes. Small 8vo, gilt top. $4.00
Half morocco. 7.50

Fouard.—SAINT PETER AND THE FIRST YEARS OF CHRISTIANITY. By the ABBÉ CONSTANT FOUARD. Translated by GEORGE F. X. GRIFFITH. [In the Press.

The success of Mr. Griffith's translation of the Abbé Fouard's "Life of Jesus," in this country, has encouraged the translator to undertake another volume of the author's series on the Origins of the Church. "St. Peter and the First Years of Christianity" is in the printer's hands, and will be published shortly.

IN THEOLOGICAL LITERATURE. 7

Lyons. — CHRISTIANITY AND INFALLIBILITY—Both or Neither. By the REV. DANIEL LYONS. 12mo. Cloth. $1.25

"His method is thoroughly popular, and while he has admirably succeeded in avoiding that didactic and argumentative style which is apt to repel the ordinary reader of our day, he nevertheless leaves the distinct impression that his reasoning is based on sound logic, and strengthened by such authorities as would command the attention of every theological student.

The work is full of erudition, as is shown by the numerous notes indicating a wide range of pertinent and careful reading. . . . The book is a solid and timely contribution to the theological literature of the day."—*American Ecclesiastical Review.*

Clarke.—A PILGRIMAGE TO THE HOLY COAT OF TREVES. With an Account of its History and Authenticity. By RICHARD F. CLARKE, S.J. With illustrations. Crown 8vo. $1.50

Christian Biographies.—HENRI DOMINIQUE LACORDAIRE. A Biographical Sketch. By H. L. SIDNEY LEAR. With Frontispiece. Crown 8vo. $1.25

A CHRISTIAN PAINTER OF THE NINETEENTH CENTURY; being the Life of Hippolyte Flandrin. By H. L. SIDNEY LEAR. Crown 8vo. $1.25

BOSSUET AND HIS CONTEMPORARIES. By H. L. SIDNEY LEAR. Crown 8vo. $1.25

FÉNÉLON, ARCHBISHOP OF CAMBRAI. A Biographical Sketch. By H. L. SIDNEY LEAR. Crown 8vo. $1.25

A DOMINICAN ARTIST. A Sketch of the Life of the Rev. Père Besson, of the Order of St. Dominic. By H. L. SIDNEY LEAR. Crown 8vo. $1.25

THE LIFE OF MADAME LOUISE DE FRANCE, Daughter of Louis XV., also known as the Mother Thérèse de S. Augustin. By H. S. SIDNEY LEAR. Crown 8vo. $1.25

THE REVIVAL OF PRIESTLY LIFE IN THE SEVENTEENTH CENTURY IN FRANCE. Charles de Condren—S. Philip Neri and Cardinal de Berulle—S. Vincent de Paul—S. Sulpice and Jean Jacques Olier. By H. L. SIDNEY LEAR. New Edition. Crown 8vo. $1.25

LIFE OF S. FRANCIS DE SALES, Bishop and Prince of Geneva. By H. L. SIDNEY LEAR. New Edition. Crown 8vo. $1.25

HENRI PERREYVE. By A. GRATRY, PRÊTRE DE L'ORATOIRE, Professeur de Morale Evangélique à la Sorbonne, et Membre de l'Académie Française. Translated, by special permission, by H. L. SIDNEY LEAR. With portrait. Crown 8vo. $1.25

WORKS IN THEOLOGICAL LITERATURE.

Fenelon.—SPIRITUAL LETTERS TO MEN. By ARCHBISHOP FÉNÉLON. Translated by H. L. SIDNEY LEAR, author of "Life of Fénélon," "Life of S. Francis de Sales," etc., etc. 16mo. (*Devotional Works.*) $1.00
Crown 8vo. 2.00

SPIRITUAL LETTERS TO WOMEN. By ARCHBISHOP FÉNÉLON. Translated by H. L. SIDNEY LEAR, author of "Life of Fénélon," "Life of S. Francis de Sales," etc., etc. 16mo. (*Devotional Works.*) $1.co
Crown 8vo. 2.00

Drane.—THE HISTORY OF ST. DOMINIC, FOUNDER OF THE FRIAR PREACHERS. By AUGUSTA THEODORA DRANE, Author of "*The History of St. Catherine of Siena and her Companions.*" With 32 Illustrations. 8vo. $5.00

Lavigerie.—CARDINAL LAVIGERIE AND THE AFRICAN SLAVE TRADE. Edited by RICHARD F. CLARKE, S.J., Trinity College, Oxford. 8vo. $4.50

Jameson.—Works by MRS. JAMESON :
SACRED AND LEGENDARY ART. With 19 Etchings and 197 Woodcuts. 2 vols. Cloth, gilt top. $8.00

LEGENDS OF THE MADONNA : The Virgin Mary as Represented in Sacred and Legendary Art. With 27 Etchings and 165 Woodcuts. 1 vol. Cloth, gilt top. $4.00

LEGENDS OF THE MONASTIC ORDERS. With 11 Etchings and 88 Woodcuts. 1 vol. Cloth, gilt top. $4.00

HISTORY OF THE SAVIOUR, His Types and Precursors. Completed by LADY EASTLAKE. With 13 Etchings and 281 Woodcuts. 2 vols. Cloth, gilt top. $8.00

—— The set, complete (6 vols.). Cloth, gilt top. 24 00

Northcote and Brownlow.— ROMA SOTTERANEA ; or, An Account of the Roman Catacombs, especially of the Cemetery of St. Callixtus. Compiled from the Works of Commendatore de Rossi, with the Consent of the Author. By the REV. J. SPENCER NORTHCOTE, D.D., Canon of Birmingham, and the REV. W. R. BROWNLOW, M.A., Canon of Plymouth. New Edition, Re-written and Enlarged. With Woodcuts and Plates in Chromo-lithography.

Part I. History. 8vo. $8.50
Part II. Christian Art. 8vo. 8.50
Part III. Epitaphs of the Catacombs. 8vo. 3.50
Three Volumes in Two. 20.00

www.ingramcontent.com/pod-product-compliance
Lightning Source LLC
Chambersburg PA
CBHW032002300426
44117CB00008B/863